CLUBMEN

History of the Working Men's
Club and Institute Union

By the same author

The First Century
Seventeen Rock Music Biographies
Living Cities
Caitlin: Life with Dylan Thomas (with Caitlin Thomas)

George Tremlett

CLUBMEN

History of the Working Men's Club and Institute Union

Secker & Warburg
London

First published in England 1987 by
Martin Secker & Warburg Limited
54 Poland Street, London W1V 3DF

Copyright © The Working Men's Club and Institute Union 1987

British Library CIP data to follow

Tremlett, George
  Clubmen: The History of the Working
  Men's Club & Institute Union. – Rev. ed.
  1. Working Men's Club & Institute Union
  – History
  I, Title II. Tremlett, George
  367′.942   HS2515.G72L6

ISBN 0-436-52704-9

Typeset in 11pt Baskerville
Printed by Richard Clay Ltd, Bungay, Suffolk

CONTENTS

ILLUSTRATIONS

Preface by Lord Brooks of Tremorfa

George Tremlett has achieved what I thought would have been impossible. Following his 'First Century' history of the Working Men's Club and Institute Union, he has now written this monumental work on 125 years of the C.I.U. and, as the author himself says, he has taken the opportunity to write in greater detail how this great working-class institution was born and how it developed into the great organization we know today.

This work is not simply a history of the C.I.U. Its fascination for me is that it is also a social history which will compare with many other more formal works on the development of working people and the institutions created by them. Compelling also are the portraits of many of the individuals who have shaped the history of a unique organization not found in any other part of the world.

I was particularly interested in the account of the setting up of the All-Party Parliamentary Group which was formed in December, 1983. Set up as a result of the initiative of C.I.U. President Derek Dormer, the Group has grown into the largest active All-Party Group in Parliament. For too long, legislation affecting Clubs has been passed without the Club Movement being consulted. The Parliamentary Group has acted on a number of occasions to influence Ministers on matters of vital concern to Non-Profit-Making Members' Clubs.

I hope that this book will be read by all those Club members concerned with the well-being of the Club Movement. They will be well rewarded – it is, after all, their story.

Author's Preface

Only rarely can an author return to a subject after a gap of twenty-five years. I have found it a strangely satisfying experience, the more so because in writing this history of the Working Men's Club and Institute Union I have been given the opportunity to think again about ideas first formed as a very young man.

The invitation to write *The First Century* came almost by accident. The late Pat Ansell, then Warwickshire member on the Union National Executive, was a good friend when I was beginning my career as a writer; he looked like my grandfather, proposed me for membership of the Stoke Aldermoor Social Club, and introduced me to many Coventry clubmen. One day Pat told me that the Union was looking for someone to compile its history for publication in its centenary year. He introduced me to the then President, Edward McEnery; the General Secretary, Frank Castle; the Assistant General Secretary, John Holmes, and clubmen like Ernest Connelly and a young man by the name of Derek Dormer, in whose career Pat was also taking an almost fatherly interest. From those introductions came that invitation.

Looking back now I can see that *The First Century* contained some young men's faults. I was too keen to summarize events in a few crisp words, and would sometimes fall for the dazzling phrase rather than take the extra time one needs to prepare a careful judgement. It was my first book, and though still proud of it I have much enjoyed going back over the ground again, deleting some comments, adding others, carefully revising and expanding the early chapters to tell in more detail how a group of young aristocrats and middle-class liberals created a working-class institution, largely at their own expense, and then readily faded away into history when they sensed that the Union was ready to become wholly democratic. This episode sheds unusual light on the social attitudes of Victorian England. These revisions include many quotations from the Rev. Henry Solly's memoirs, *These Eighty Years*, published in 1893. These two volumes are now scarce. The Union does not possess a complete set, and I have advertised in the book trade press without finding one. I have also quoted from Solly's book *Working Men's Clubs*, originally published in 1867, and then revised in 1904 by B. T. Hall, who remains the key figure in the Union's history. I have quoted from his book *Our Fifty Years* (1912) and the later version *Our Sixty Years* (1922), and also from the records of the Fabian Society, of which he was an early member.

Having substantially rewritten that first section, I felt that a proper balance had been established with the middle section of the book, which I wrote with the help of Tom Nicoll, who had undertaken much of the original research for *The First Century*. Tom had served the Union since 1909, and had known many of its leading personalities – men like Hobson, Argyle and Dent, who themselves formed the vital link with the pioneers, the Rev. Henry Solly and his opponents, Pratt, Tayler and Paterson. Tom had been personal clerk to B. T. Hall and Assistant General Secretary under both Bob Chapman and Frank Castle, and so his guidance was invaluable. I shall always remember Tom; he was a lovely man, facially similar to Clem Attlee, short, clipped and carefully spoken, weighing his words as he puffed away at his pipe. In this book, I have preserved the material that was written with his help largely in its original form, with two exceptions: the chapters dealing with the formation of the branches (Chapter Eight) and the opening of the convalescent homes (Chapter Nine) have been expanded to include much more of B. T. Hall's own writing on these two important phases in the Union's history. This seemed the right thing to do; these were his great achievements, and I thought it better to use his own words, wherever possible.

In the chapters dealing with more recent years I have been greatly helped by Derek Dormer, who is now the Union's President and the only member of the National Executive who was 'in post' when *The First Century* was written; by Frank Morris, who was General Secretary from 1973 to 1982, and by Jack Johnson, the present General Secretary, who has been kindness itself and has given me a valuable insight on the clubs of the North, which he knows well from his days as Durham Branch Secretary. The Union's Head Office staff, notably Peter Ford, Kevin Smyth and Peter Miller, have all been unfailingly courteous in the face of many requests for further information.

This has not been an easy book to write. I have been conscious always that my subject is the Union and not the individual clubs or the local traditions that exist within the branches, and which could form the subject of a quite separate study. With nearly four thousand member clubs and twenty-nine branches, one could never write a history that embraced each one, and yet each forms part of the whole, and the Union belongs to them all. My difficulty arose in trying to trace the origins of particular events within a time sequence; it meant zigzagging backwards and forwards, covering events that were unfolding in parallel. Hopefully, this is a problem that the reader seldom notices; the author always does.

The other problem is a happy one. The Union is an unusual institution in several respects. It avoids party politics or religious debate, and is devoted to one main objective – the well-being of the working man. Inevitably the ideas that unite the Union are far greater than those which divide it, with the result that clubmen tend to be kinder and more generous people than those one meets in some spheres of life. This may sound strange to those who do not know the Working Men's Club and Institute Union, and who therefore do not realize that it is possible for a great national institution to reach its 125th anniversary without being bedevilled by factional disputes and personal bitterness. But I do believe this to be true, and possibly the reason why so many fine men have contributed so much of their lives to its work. It is an honour to have known so many of them, but my work would have been easier had they been less modest.

George Tremlett
Laugharne
January 1987

I

The history of the Working Men's Club and Institute Union runs parallel with that of the trade unions and the great social reforms of the late nineteenth century. Unions were formed to protect men at work and to improve their wages and working conditions. Reformers strove to limit the exploitation of women and children in the mines, mills and factories of industrial Britain, to bring proper sanitation and better health to our towns and cities, and to give every child an education. At school we are taught all about these social changes, and yet, somehow, working men's clubs are seldom seen as part of this pattern; they barely get a mention in the history books, and it is only in very recent years that our Union has had its own All-Party Parliamentary Committee.

Could the explanation be that leisure has always been taken less seriously than work? That historians and the State are less concerned with the way men lead their private lives? The question deserves a passing thought for it was the clubs and institutes that gave working men somewhere to meet and relax once their day's work was done; somewhere to develop hobbies and skills, from gardening to snooker, from darts to the breeding of racing pigeons; a place where they could perhaps, by taking part in the management of their clubs, make a real contribution to the communities in which they lived.

In more recent years, with the demise of the music hall, the closure of many cinemas and the decline of religion, clubs have become an even more central part of many communities. In the depressed regions of Britain, where work is hard to find and family life endangered, a thriving working men's club is more than just somewhere to go for a quiet pint of beer. It's the only form of live entertainment left. The concert held on a Friday or Saturday night may be the only chance an unemployed man gets to take his wife out for an evening, and in time of real disaster, like the long miners' strike of 1984/85, the working men's club comes into its own as somewhere to relax with friends or (as did happen) to offer family support through soup kitchens and supplies of food to the needy.

Now, in the 125th anniversary year of the union, we can see that working men's clubs are an essential part of the life of the nation, and that many small towns would be, quite literally, lost without them.

How did it all begin? To understand the social forces that produced our great movement we have to go back over two hundred years.

Prior to 1750, Britain was an agricultural nation with the bulk of its population living in villages and small towns. Over the previous centuries, kings had come and gone; wars had been fought across Europe; a civil war had been waged at home; settlements had been established in many parts of the 'New World', with Britain a maritime power. And yet, for all that, little had altered for the great mass of the people. This was a nation that lived off the land, and whose life patterns followed the seasons.

By 1750, the total population of England, Scotland and Wales had reached approximately 6,500,000, which, by comparison, is the present-day population of Greater London. And then, in the mid-eighteenth century, the inventions of Newcomen, Boulton and Watt revolutionized manufacturing processes and were followed by the growth of industrial towns. Medical knowledge was improving. The introduction of root crops, especially turnips, meant that cattle could be fed through the winter, making it possible to maintain supplies of fresh meat and milk all the year round. People became healthier; the birth rate increased; the death rate dropped, and in the early nineteenth century the population rapidly grew:

Year	Population of England and Wales	Percentage increase over the decade
1801	8,893,000	—
1811	10,164,000	14.00
1821	12,000,000	18.10
1831	13,897,000	15.80
1841	15,914,000	14.30
1851	17,928,000	12.70

These population trends reflected a total change in the nature of our society, in the way people worked and spent their lives, and in the pattern in which their homes were distributed across the nation. Many small towns like Bradninch or Crediton in Devon, which had been prosperous since mediaeval times, now declined in importance while, in other areas, small villages like Wolverhampton, Llanelli or Merthyr Tydfil became large towns. Over the next fifty years, the population nearly doubled again: by the time the Census was conducted in 1901 the number of people living in Britain's towns and cities had grown to 25,000,000, which was nearly four times the rural population. In a time-span of little more than a century, our population had grown nearly four-fold. We had become an industrial nation, with the great mass of the people, if not actually working in factories, then dependent upon them, as the railways linked the centres of production, and made it possible for raw materials and finished goods to be transported from one part of the country to another and then, through our ports, to every part of the world.

The harnessing of steam power, the invention of spinning and weaving techniques, the widespread use of heavy machinery, the growth of the canals and then the railways, brought demands for more steel and more coal, and then, in turn, led to the invention of electricity and more industrial innovations. These changes happened with such speed that they outstripped the capacity of the State to protect the weak. The existing framework of law was in-adequate to shield them against exploitation; there was no system of taxation to ensure that the wealth so newly created was fairly distributed, with the result that relatively few prospered while millions sank into a new and terrible poverty. Those who did well were the manufacturers and traders, who produced and sold these new industrial goods, and the professional men – managers, account-ants, lawyers and bankers – who serviced their companies. This was a new class in society: the middle class, the white-collar ex-ecutives, who had more bargaining power and demanded better homes for themselves, better opportunities for their children.

At the very bottom of the social pile were the new unskilled working class. Only a generation before, their families had been part of that rural Britain that had remained unchanged for cen-turies. Now, they dug the coal, made the steel, drove the trains, pulled the levers and pressed the buttons that ran industrial Britain. They had migrated to the towns and cities in search of higher wages and, so they thought, a higher standard of living, but in this new, harsh, industrial society, there was always someone who could take their place, or would do their job for a lower wage, or work longer hours. The early industrialists were able to offer higher wages than the squires, but they did not offer the same security. Vast estates of terraced cottages were built around the mills and factories, and, often lacking in sanitation, degenerated into the slums that are still being cleared in some parts of the country by local councils. Where-as country people had been able to work long hours on the land without any ill effects, the new industrial working class had to work just as long under primitive factory conditions, exposed to heat, fumes, injurious chemicals, and machinery that was often dangerous. While Britain had been an agricultural community, it was quite usual for women and children to do light work on the land; such work may have been healthy, if arduous. But for the wives and children now working side by side in the factories with the new industrial workers conditions were appalling.

This was almost a form of slavery; this new working class had little time left at the end of a working day for any life of its own, and within that working day was exposed to a constant risk of industrial injury, or even death (we hear so little now of the great mining disasters that were such a feature of those times). The result of such indignity was that men banded together in brotherhood to protect themselves. The Combination Act of 1799 had forbidden them to form trade unions, so they had to do so in secrecy. Twenty-five years later this Act was repealed, and the underground trade unions came out into the open to campaign for the Factory Acts, for increased wages, for laws making it illegal for children to be employed in mines and factories, for proper holidays and a more reasonable working day.

What is more, the social traditions of country life had not survived in the towns and cities; there was no maypole or village green, country market or rural pub, where men could meet at the end of a day. Instead, the towns and cities spawned a new horror of their own – the vast Victorian gin palaces that soaked up men's wages, drove them into drunkenness and destroyed their families. One does not have to be a supporter of the Temperance movement to realize that this, too, was a social evil that had to be fought with the same vigour that reformers were applying to conditions in the mines and factories.

> Hideous slums, some of them acres wide, some no more than crannies of obscure misery, make up a substantial part of the metropolis. Because they are so densely occupied they are profitable, and seldom cleared away except to make way for new thoroughfares and frontages. In big, once handsome houses, thirty or more people of all ages may inhabit a single room, squatting, sleeping, copulating on the straw-filled billets or mounds of verminous rags that are the only furniture. There are cellar-homes, dark, foetid and damp with sewage, where women keep watch for the rats that gnaw their infants' faces and fingers . . .
>
> *The Victorian Underworld,*
> by Kellow Chesney (1970)

And so it was elsewhere. The new working class had never been

told that there were good things in life; they only saw the bad.
There was nowhere for them to meet in their spare time, to talk, to
relax, and to develop their ideas; all they could do was drink in
those gin palaces, and multiply.

It was in this social atmosphere that our movement began.

Although there were many in the upper classes who had no social
conscience, there were also others who saw that men were not
destined to live like this. It was the age of Gladstone's Liberalism
and the Noncomformist conscience, when earnest social pioneers met
in chapels and meeting halls and laid down the foundations of the
Labour movement. Some were driven by a desire to save souls;
others saw that man could only advance if he were to benefit from
the increased time he had for leisure. Such a man was our founder,
the Rev. Henry Solly.

It was the energy and enthusiasm of this Unitarian minister that
established the Working Men's Club and Institute Union, but the
initial work had been done before Solly started campaigning. Lord
Brougham, who was to become the Union's first President, had
already lent his support to the Mechanics' Institutes. Originated by
Dr Birkbeck, their aim was to teach working men the principles of
their particular trades, and their function was purely educational.
Consequently, 'reading rooms' were opened up and down the
country, which meant that working men had somewhere to pass
their leisure hours reading either newspapers or books – both of
which were too expensive to be bought by the working class of the
nineteenth century.

'Next,' wrote Solly later, in his own book *Working Men's Social
Clubs and Educational Institutes* (1867), 'came the formation of the
Mutual Improvement Societies, which met chiefly in school rooms
and aimed at classes, discussions, and especially at the preparation
of short papers on interesting and improving topics. There was often
a good deal of sociable spirit in these little organizations, but they
were often short-lived.' Solly himself had formed a reading room
while engaged as a Unitarian minister in Yeovil in 1842. In that
same year, a People's College had been formed in Sheffield by the
Rev. R. L. Bayly, and then in 1849 the Rev. F. R. Robertson,
incumbent of Holy Trinity Church, Brighton, had established the
Brighton Working Men's Institute.

'The large-hearted, Christian sympathies of that gentleman, and
his striking eloquence, procured a considerable amount of attention
to his enterprise,' wrote Solly, noting that soon thereafter a similar
Institute was formed in South Shields, and that he himself then
helped to establish another in Cheltenham while engaged there as

a minister between 1847 and 1851. In Yorkshire, Lancashire and South Staffordshire, it was night schools that were established with the similar objective of teaching mechanics 'the correct knowledge and principles of their own trades'. However, none of these ventures were very successful and it is to Solly's everlasting credit that he could see why. He recognized that 'the first want of working men after their long day's toil' was somewhere to chat with one another, to be with friends, in a relaxed and happy atmosphere, with or without refreshments. Solly wrote: 'All efforts, as far as we are aware, to benefit working men, not aiming directly at their moral, religious, or pecuniary welfare, previous to 1852, appear to have ignored this their primary and simplest, but most urgent want. Hence their very limited success . . .'

But even Solly could not see that beer was the key. Another twelve years were to pass before he was able to bring himself to accept that working men liked to relax with a pint or two of beer at the end of the day, but he was still far ahead of his contemporaries in recognizing that a much more relaxed, informal atmosphere was what these institutes needed if they were to attract a regular attendance. The Colonnade Working Men's Club, which was opened in 1852, was much more successful when it offered refreshments as well as newspapers and books. In 1855, a Mr Horlock Bastard of Charlton Marshall, near Blandford, Dorset, founded a similar club without having heard of the Colonnade. And when the idea was tried again on an estate in Hertfordshire, it was so successful that the village pub was forced to close. Similar village clubs were soon founded at Littlemore and Iffley and later at Kingham, Chipping Norton and Adderbury, all of them in Oxfordshire.

A similar development, which was praised by Solly, was the establishment of the London Working Men's College by the Rev. F. D. Maurice in 1854. This institution owed more to the ideals of Robert Owen, the Co-operative movement and the early Christian Socialists, and, although not a club as we know it, the College was trying to meet the needs of the industrial working class. Even more significant was a club started in Salford by the Rev. E. Boteler Chalmer in 1858. Here, the main aim was the provision of premises where working men could meet socially; this time, refreshments were provided and the Salford venture was outstandingly successful. Two years later, in 1860, the Westminster Working Men's Club was opened in Duck Lane, Westminster, in the heart of London, by Miss Adeline Cooper, and then in 1861 a Mrs Bayly opened the Notting Hill Workmen's Hall in the Kensington Potteries. Both women believed that the wives and children of working men were being degraded by the amount of time and money their menfolk spent in public houses. Their achievement was soon noticed by Solly, who had begun to understand that 'by far the larger number of men who frequent the public house go there for the company rather than for the drink'. In these new establishments, as well as books and newspapers, games like chess, draughts and dominoes were available, and in some, even beer. This set the Rev. Henry Solly thinking. Here, perhaps, was the answer to the question that troubled him: why had so many other ventures failed? At first, he could not comtemplate the thought of alcohol on the premises, but he was much impressed by a pamphlet written by a young curate in Manchester, the Rev. W. T. Marriott (who was later called to the bar, entered Parliament and became Judge Advocate General). Marriott had helped to form a club at Hulme, similar to the one already established in nearby Salford, and he argued that working men needed clubs where they could meet their fellows every bit as much as the upper classes, who already had their own clubs in London and in all the main provincial cities.

It was to be a year or two yet before the formation of the Working Men's Club and Institute Union, but the Rev. Henry Solly could see that the basic idea was good and in 1861 he campaigned with the Rev. David Thomas of Brixton to raise what was then the enormous sum of £3,000,000 to establish a society that would build a nation-wide chain of working men's clubs. What they envisaged initially was a limited liability company with a share capital of £3,000,000, and presumably borrowing powers, that would *build* clubs *for* the working classes, more or less as a trading venture. Their first appeals for money were not successful, and again it is to Henry Solly's credit that he realized they had to change their minds and make the proposed company philanthropic rather than commercial. The Rev. David Thomas agreed with the change, and they were able to persuade the Lord Chancellor, Lord Brougham, to preside at their inaugural meeting, which was held at the Law Amendment Society's Rooms in Waterloo Place on 14 June 1862. It was at this meeting that THE WORKING MEN'S CLUB AND INSTITUTE UNION was formed, after speeches by John Bainbridge, an upholsterer, and Mr Bebbington, a costermonger who had become secretary of the Westminster Working Men's Club. The minutes were taken by Mr E. Clarke, later to become one of the country's most distinguished barristers as Sir Edward Clarke KC. Mr W. M. Neill of Liverpool made an initial donation of £100, and Lord Brougham £20, on the spot. A Council was elected there and then, and

for the first few months the Rev. J. H. Rylance and the Rev.
Henry Solly acted jointly as honorary secretaries.

And then, only a few months after the inaugural meeting, Solly
resigned his pulpit at the English Presbyterian Chapel in Lancaster
to become the first full-time paid Secretary of the Union.

2

Henry Solly was a hard-working idealist of a rather familiar type. As a Unitarian minister from a strongly Puritan family background, he possessed that sense of religious belief that knows no alternative. Reading his memoirs, *These Eighty Years* (1893), one senses the grief felt at some points in his life when other people did not always see the world as he saw it. A man of initiative, certainly, but with many faults: a tendency to curry favour with the rich and powerful; a habit of name-dropping; a prickly sense of his own importance, and yet still possessing that driving zeal which all organizations need in their early years. B. T. Hall, one of the Union's greatest pioneers, described this quality as 'a scorching enthusiasm', a phrase that implies much more than it says.

In appearance, Solly was somewhat Pickwickian. 'Short, rather portly, but erect and square-shouldered with a full grey beard and perfectly bald on top of his head,' was how his grandson Joseph Wickstead described him in a memoir published after his death.

When I was researching *The First Century* back in 1960/61, one of the points that troubled me was that Solly's personality did not emerge more clearly. It was easy to see from the books and papers that had survived that Solly was fond of his own authority; when voted out as the Union's General Secretary, in circumstances which caused him much distress, he founded a rival organization with Lord Lyttelton as its president, and attracted to it many of the Union's earliest supporters. It was also clear that Solly, though a clergyman, was not inclined to sacrifice; he was constantly asking for a higher salary, even though the Union's finances were far from sound, and when a damaging split came in 1867 it was because his Executive Council felt that it would be a financial saving to dispense with Solly's services.

This brief account of Solly's life was published in a journal called *The Inquirer*, shortly after he had died on 27 February 1903, approaching his ninetieth birthday:

He was born in London, and through his father and mother inherited the blood of famous Puritans, including the Hollis family,
to which Harvard owes so much, and the Neals, celebrated in and
celebrators of Puritan history. The Sollys themselves, as he was fond
of declaring, traced back their ancestry to Kentish yeomen far in the
Middle Ages; their kith and kin are numerous among our congrega-
tions to-day. His father was a man who, in spite of a catastrophe in
the 'crisis' of 1837, worthily maintained the commercial traditions of
the family, and to the rest of his many business engagements added the
first chairmanship of the London and Birmingham Railway Company,
which afterwards developed into the London and North Western, and
the chairmanship of the first company that sent steamships across the
Atlantic.

Henry spent his early days in old London city, and in the neighbourhood of Walthamstow, where his grandfather with others had
erected a meeting-house about 1730. The Rev. Eliezer Cogan, preacher
at this meeting-house, and of high reputation as a Greek scholar, was
his first schoolmaster; and his elder brothers were schoolmates with
Benjamin Disraeli at Mr Cogan's school. Later he studied at another
school well known among Unitarians – Dr Morell's, at Hove, Brighton.
In 1829 he entered the new University of London, i.e. University College, Gower Street, and continued his classical and mathematical studies
with considerable success. His father's intention, however, was to make
a business-man of him, and, to his intense disappointment, he had to
leave college and enter 'the counting-house' in a leading shipbroker's
establishment. For some years the struggle between natural inclination
and obedience to parental purposes went on. He worked assiduously at
the business by day, and got all the culture he could by night; fretted at
his destiny, wrote tragedy, broke down in health, fell in love, and, above
all, became (he says) ever more 'conscious of intolerable disorder all
around me, and an overpowering desire to right all the wrongs in the
universe'. For a brief period he was engaged in a private scientific
laboratory, which might have proved a gold-mine, but did not. Then
he was tried as a banker in sundry branch establishments in the country
round London, his mind all the while gravitating more steadily towards
the life of ameliorative labour which was to bring blessings to many,
and to himself something like fame.

It was in 1840 that, on the advice of the Rev. Robert Aspland, he
determined, after a brief period of study with the Rev. Benjamin
Mardon, of the General Baptist Academy, to take at least temporary
charge of the Yeovil congregation. This led to his entering the regular
ministry, and the following succession of pastorates fell to his share –
Yeovil (1840–42), Tavistock (1842–44), Shepton Mallet (1844–47),
Cheltenham (1847–51), Carter-lane, London – now Unity, Islington
(1852-57), Lancaster (1858-62).

Mr Solly took a distinct line in theology, and to the last he had a
mediating word to offer both to Trinitarians and Unitarians. He was a

keen disputant, and did not take his ministerial responsibilities lightly. But it is evident that the chief motive power in all his work was love for the common people. This it was that led him while but new to the ministry at Yeovil to begin a long course of publications with a discourse on *What Says Christianity to the Present Distress?* He flung himself into all sorts of 'dangerous' agitations, and soon had to quit his first pulpit in consequence ... in everything he undertook Mr Solly was greatly in earnest. He was, if any man, *tenax propositi*, and he spared neither pains nor words to convince his antagonist. Yet there was a kindly humour as well as sincerity about him that secured the genuine homage of juniors often apt to be impatient of 'old men eloquent' ...

It was through his experiences as a minister that Henry Solly saw the need for working men's clubs and it was through the establishment of the Union that he achieved a lasting reputation, although all his life he seems to have been a driven man, disturbed by the poverty of working people in Victorian England, anxious to improve their conditions, always trying to convince others, whether from the pulpit, through his work for the Union, or by his writings.

In a sense, Henry Solly was a man of his time. This was the period in England's history when many social pioneers emerged; it was the time when the trade-union movement was laying down its roots; when there were demands that every man should have the vote, and Parliament was beginning to approve the legislation that improved the lot of the industrial working class, partly through a growing sense of social conscience, and partly through a realization that unless *something* was done Britain might also be affected by the revolutionary fervour sweeping across Europe. Solly was an early supporter of the Chartist movement, whose pioneers also came from a Puritan background, and this was reflected in his writing. Besides his religious works, such as *The Great Atonement* (1847), *Lectures on the Development of Religious Life in the Modern Christian Church* (1849) and *The Doctrine of the Atonement* (1861), Solly also wrote poetry and plays, a biography of the Chartist James Woodford (1881) and *Rehousing of the Industrial Classes* (1884), all of which gives an indication of the breadth of mind that he brought to his work for the Union.

While a minister at Yeovil, Solly married and it was while he was still living in that town that he and his wife witnessed the growth of several early working-class movements. The Chartists were active in that part of Somerset, and one of the more advanced mutual improvement societies was also formed in Yeovil. Indeed, Solly became far more closely identified with the working-class movements of the town than was generally wise for a clergyman,

which was why he had to move to Tavistock. He undoubtedly
sympathized with the aims of the Chartists, who were seeking to
establish democracy within Britain – the universal vote by secret
ballot, and the principles of Parliamentary democracy as we know
them today. But at the same time he also saw that the working men
of Britain needed something more: places where they could meet
socially, and it was thus that he envisaged the working men's clubs,
although at the time he did not see them as places where men
would *drink*.

One has to remember that at this stage in his life our pioneer was an
ardent teetotaller, and it is one of the richer ironies of the Union's
history that our founder's principal objective was, as he put it in
These Eighty Years, ' . . . the social and moral elevation of the hard-
working industrial classes . . . of helping them to throw off the
wretched and degrading bondage to the public-house. . . .'

By the time he moved to Lancaster in 1858, Solly had already
spent several years supporting calls for the establishment of working
men's colleges, clubs and institutes. He had given evidence to royal
commissions, and had travelled around the country, addressing religious and temperance congresses, trade unions and friendly
societies. It was this energy that gave the Union its early momentum, though being of a somewhat quarrelsome nature Henry
Solly also had other reasons for leaving the ministry and taking up
his post as the Union's first General Secretary. Once again he had
fallen out with his fellow Unitarians, just as he was later to have
disputes within the Union. In his early days as a minister Solly
had been forced to leave Yeovil for what we would today call left-
wing activities, and then in 1861 he caused an even wider upset by
challenging some of the Unitarians' fundamental beliefs in his book
The Doctrine of the Atonement. Solly felt compelled to leave his ministry
in Lancaster, and it is clear from his memoirs that he had 'lost
some support on account of being regarded as a heretic'. Although
there were ministerial vacancies in Nottingham and Bristol, Solly
was not invited to apply for either of them and he was probably
quite relieved when offered employment with the Union, because
he was never a wealthy man and needed to work for a living. He
was paid £200 per annum.

Solly set about the business of raising money and inviting peers
and parliamentarians and wealthy social reformers to become the
Union's first Vice-Presidents (in the expectation that they would
all come up with substantial donations), and established the
Union's first offices at 150 The Strand, in the heart of London,
where he swiftly installed an iron bedstead in a rear room so that

he could work late at his desk. His first step was to draw up a prospectus or manifesto, outlining the Union's aims:

This union is formed for the purpose of helping Working Men to establish Clubs or Institutes where they can meet for conversation, business, and mental improvement, with the means of recreation and refreshment, free from intoxicating drinks; these Clubs, at the same time, constituting Societies for mutual helpfulness in various ways.

It will be the aim of the Council of the Union to assist in extending or improving existing Associations which have in view objects of a kindred nature with the above, as well as to promote the establishment of Clubs or Institutes where no such Associations may now be found. In order to consolidate and strengthen the action and mutual fellowship of these various Associations, Clubs, or Institutes, the Council will invite them to become Registered Members of the Union. (In reference to the use of intoxicating drinks on the premises, the Council are strongly of the opinion that their introduction would be dangerous to the interests of these Societies, and earnestly recommend their exclusion. They make this recommendation simply on prudential grounds, the reasonableness of which, it is believed, the Working Classes will be the first to acknowledge. *) The Council also recommend that at least one-half of the managing body should be bona-fide Working Men.

The Council propose to carry out the objects of the Union:

1. By correspondence with the Officers of existing Associations throughout the kingdom.

2. By personal visits, by their own Officers and by honorary deputations, to such places as may seem to require to be visited. At these visits conferences will be held with the Working Classes, and with others in the locality who may be interested in the object.

3. By the dissemination of tracts, or special papers, on subjects lying within the sphere of the Society's operations.

4. By supplying instructions for the guidance of persons who may wish to establish Clubs or Institutes; together with rules to define their objects, and to regulate their proceedings.

5. By grants or loans of Books for Club Libraries, Apparatus, Diagrams, etc., to Societies in membership with the Union, in cases where local circumstances may seem to call for such aid.

6. By grants of money in special cases, by way of loan or otherwise, towards the building, enlarging, or altering Club Houses, or procuring recreation grounds, for Societies in the Union.

As soon as a sufficient number of Clubs shall have joined the Union within a given district, the Council will combine them in local organisations, under specified conditions. Half-yearly, or sometimes quarterly, meetings of Delegates from the various Clubs will be held in each dis-

* The sentences shown in brackets were introduced in later modifications of the prospectus; they were added, in 1864, to copies of the original document.

trict, for the consideration of matters of local interest, and for the discussion of social questions; while an annual conference of District Representatives will be held at various large towns in succession, to consider matters of a more general character.

The council will be glad to receive communications addressed to their Secretary, from persons desirous of promoting these objects either in their own locality or generally. Information and assistance will be gladly given and received.

Donations and subscriptions for the Union will be thankfully received by the Secretary, or they can be paid at the London and Westminster Bank (St James's Square, S.W.), or any of its Branches.

An Annual Subscription of not less than £1, or a Donation of not less than £10, constitutes the contributor a member of the Union.

Notwithstanding all the efforts made to improve the character and condition of the Working Classes in this country, intemperance, ignorance, improvidence, and religious indifference still abound among them to a deplorable extent. One main reason of the want of more complete success is probably to be found in the incompleteness of the measures adopted. Vast good, for instance, has been accomplished by the Temperance Reform, but it often fails to retain those whom it has reclaimed from intemperance, in not supplying something to occupy the leisure hours formerly spent at the public-house. Mechanics' Institutes, also, with efforts of a kindred character, have done a great work; but they, too, generally fail in not providing *recreation* and *amusement*. Their aims have been too high for the great majority of Working Men; hence, while they have attracted and benefited many, the inducements held out have failed to withdraw the multitude from habits and indulgences which all alike deplore. As a result, we find such Institutions now generally given up to the trading and middle classes. Working Men's Colleges, admirable as they are, require some such intermediate step between them and the public-house as the Societies above described.

Recreation must go hand in hand with Education and Temperance if we would have real and permanent improvement; while efforts should be specially made to awaken or cherish a brotherly spirit of mutual helpfulness among men themselves, as well as between them and the classes socially above then. The best hope of success is in thus binding people together for worthy ends in a true brotherhood, so that each may be led to give as well as to receive, striving to contribute to the common good. Higher results will follow as these preparatory measures are successful; and when the temptations to debasing indulgence are removed the way is open for good influences of every kind.

The aim of the Union in all cases would be to help Working Men to help themselves, rather than to establish or manage Institutions for them – this being as essential for the moral usefulness as for the permanent success of our endeavours. Local and Working Class efforts may frequently be fostered and developed by external help with the happiest result, when the establishment of entirely new institutions, managed by the higher classes in the neighbourhood or by a central Society, would be viewed with jealousy or indifference. The very first step towards forming a Club or Institute would be to interest the Working Men of the district in the undertaking, and to make them feel that, when once started, its management and success must depend mainly on themselves.

The next point in forming these Societies would be to procure suitable premises for the accommodation of the members, containing rooms to be used for conversation, refreshments, recreation, etc., and others for classes, reading, lectures, and music. A library of entertaining and instructive books, scientific apparatus, diagrams, etc., a supply of newspapers, and some works of art, should be aimed at. The services of efficient teachers, paid and unpaid, should be procured; Discussion Classes, to awaken thought and a desire for knowledge, should be established; readings from amusing and eloquent writers, interspersed with music and recitations, should be given periodically; and, generally, any similar measures adopted for effecting the objects in view. Women should have the privilege, on a small payment, of taking books out of the library, and of admission to the lectures and concerts of the Institute; also to classes, when efficient female superintendence could be procured. The very valuable influence of educated women has of late years shown itself in various schemes to improve the condition of the Labouring Classes. A much wider field for this influence may be afforded by Societies such as those now advocated.

The Club Rooms in every locality will form the strongest counteraction to the allurements of the Public House. The desire for social enjoyment and the love of excitement are the impulses that habitually drive the Working Classes to visit the Beer Shop. These instincts also form a great temptation of reclaimed drunkards. They remain as strong as ever in their nature after they have become abstainers, and the Public House stands before them as the most available means for their gratification. Music, also, which ought to purify and refine, is now extensively employed as a temptation to drinking and other vices. Until there shall be established in every locality an institution that shall meet these instincts with superior attractions, but without temptations to evil, it is unreasonable to expect a great diminution in the drinking customs of the working population. This want the proposed Clubs will supply. Here the Working Man will obtain, at a charge within his reach, social intercourse and healthy mental excitement – the refreshment he requires or the improvement he seeks.

The extent to which Working Men suffer from their dependence upon the Public House merely *for business purposes* is also an immense evil, and one that is still inadequately appreciated. (See Mr Tidd Pratt's last Report where he remarks, 'The holding of these Societies at a Public House is also another ground of their failure ... in the course of last year the Registrar found that in Herefordshire, since 1793, the number of Societies enrolled and certified were 136; of this number 123 were held at Public Houses and 13 at schools or private rooms. Of those held at Public Houses no less than 42 had broken up, but of those held at schools or private rooms only one had been dissolved.' Even where no drinking is allowed during business hours a considerable sum is often spent afterwards, especially by the younger men.) Gradually, however, the proposed Clubs and Institutes will become the Houses of Call for men in search of work and will be the centres of various Working Men's Societies, such as Friendly Societies, Freehold and Building Associations, Co-operative Societies, Circulating Libraries for the district, Temperance Societies, and of any similar agencies calculated to improve the condition of the Working Classes.

These are no mere visionary ideas. They have been already reduced to practice with most beneficial results in Westminster, Notting Hill, Clare Market, Brighton, Norwood, Manchester, Shrewsbury, Leeds, Farringdon, Liverpool, Carlisle, Southampton, Scarborough, and many other places. THE WORKING MEN'S CLUB AND INSTITUTE UNION aims at multiplying such results by *stimulating and assisting local effort.*

The time is evidently ripe for this movement. In all directions earnest and benevolent people are groping after the means of making isolated efforts for elevating the Working Classes above debasing vice and ignorance; but these efforts often need judicious guidance or timely support, and would be greatly assisted by united counsels and organised power. Our hard-working brethren can seldom find time to initiate, or can rarely obtain adequate support among their own class for local enterprises of this nature. Those best acquainted with them, however, know that they thankfully welcome such help as it is now proposed to afford.

In conclusion, it will be seen that, while the Working Men's Club and Institute Union may be useful with the smallest, it will be able to make efficient application of the largest means that may be placed at its disposal – beginning with selected localities, and widening its sphere of action in proportion to the public support it may receive. The council earnestly solicit the assistance, personal and pecuniary, of all who approve their objects; and, sincerely praying that the Divine blessing may rest upon this undertaking, they commend it to the support of all who desire the true welfare of the Working Classes of this country.

It all seems so very strange, reading that manifesto now, 125 years later: so patronizing, almost magisterial in style, with the prime aim always the promotion of temperance – but these *were* the motives that led to the foundation of the Union. The first clubs became members with that same objective, and Henry Solly's first successes came when he followed the advice of Hugh Owen, a member of the Executive Council, and mailed that manifesto to every temperance society in Britain. 'The advice was excellent, born of much experience in the Temperance movement, and I acted on it at once,' wrote Solly in *These Eighty Years*. 'The result was remarkable, and the ball then set rolling, though intermittent in its progress, has never stopped since.'

The first club to be established as a direct result of Solly's work for the Union was the Faringdon Working Men's Club and Institute, formed as a result of a public meeting held in Faringdon, a small town on the Berkshire/Wiltshire downs, and addressed by Solly and a member of the Executive Council, the Rev. J. H. Rylance. In all the advance publicity, the chairman had been advertised as Tom Hughes, QC, MP, and Solly drily commented in his memoirs, '. . . he was prevented from coming, [but] his name on the bills helped to draw a good attendance'. At Solly's initiative, the committee was recruited from among the audience, and the men, all total abstainers, held their first meeting that very same night. Soon thereafter, a similar meeting arranged in Lincoln, addressed by Solly and a very young Edward Clarke (who was later to become one of Britain's most distinguished lawyers), led to the formation of a second club, and then others were formed in Southampton and Leeds.

Solly undoubtedly worked hard to achieve these swift results, often sleeping at the office and distributing vast quantities of literature; he sent out 25,000 leaflets in the first year alone, and maintained a constant supply of long and very wordy letters to every newspaper and magazine that he could find. In the first year, he addressed over forty meetings, and nearly three times as many the second year. He seems to have been tireless, and a very clever money-raiser, always asking for donations and recruiting distinguished patrons for the Union. Lord Brougham, the Lord Chancellor, became our first President, and in that first year we had thirty-three vice-presidents, including six peers, three members of the House of Commons, the Deans of Carlisle, Chichester and Ely, eight other clergymen, and the Recorders of London, Birmingham and Oxford. As B. T. Hall commented later, 'the new movement did not want for great and good Godfathers'. These were the first officers of the Union:

President
The Rt Hon. Lord Brougham

Vice-Presidents

The Rt Hon Earl Spencer	T. Rathbone, JP (of Liverpool)
The Rt Hon. Earl Fortescue	Rev. Canon Robinson, MA
The Rt Hon. Earl of Ducie	A. J. Scott, MA
The Rt Hon. Lord Lyttelton	J. Abel Smith

The Rt Hon. Lord Calthorpe
Viscount Raynham, MP
The Very Rev. Dean of Carlisle
The Very Rev. Dean of Chichester
The Very Rev. Dean of Ely
Sir William Beckett
Hon. and Rev. W. H. Lyttelton, MA
S. Bowley (of Gloucester)
Rev. W. Brock (of London)
J. I. Briscoe, MP
F. Crossley, MP
Rev. H. Gibson, MA
Russell Gurney, QC, Recorder of
    London

Rev. Dr Guthrie
Rev. Newman Hall, Ll.B.
G. W. Hastings
J. Heywood, FRS
M. Davenport Hill, Recorder of
    Birmingham
T. Hughes, BA
The Rev. Canon Jenkyn, MA
A. H. Layard, MP, DCL
Sgt Manning, Recorder of Oxford
W. M. Neill (of Manchester)
J. S. Pakington
Rev. W. Morley Punshon, MA

Council

John Bainbridge
Captain Bayly
Mrs Bayly
John Bebbington
Rev. J. Baldwin Brown, BA
Miss Janet Chambers
Edward G. Clarke
Miss Adeline Cooper
Miss Isa Craig
Rev. A. J. D'Orsey, BD
Mrs William Fison

W. E. Franks
R. B. Litchfield, BA
G. Lushington, MA
Mrs (Sergeant) Manning
Hugh Owen
Rev. J. H. Rylance
Russell Scott
T. Shorter (sec. Working Men's College)
Miss Anna Swanwick
Rev. D. Thomas, DD
Miss E. Twining

Solly even asked Gladstone to become a Vice-President, and would probably have succeeded had Gladstone not had so many other interests, for the great Liberal statesman replied: 'I am really sorry, but you know when a pint pot is full all that you pour in only runs over.' However, Gladstone did donate £10 to the Union's funds, as did Joseph Chamberlain, who impressed Solly as 'a young gentleman of clever and resolute aspect'. Of Britain's twenty-two dukes, Solly persuaded ten to contribute donations to the Union's funds, notably the Duke of Bedford, who made three donations, each of £100. The Prince of Wales, later to become King Edward VII, gave donations of twenty guineas in 1865 and 1866. So much did Solly convince those he met of the virtues of his cause, that when the Postmaster-General, Henry Fawcett, introduced Solly to his wife, he did so with the words: 'This is Henry Solly, my dear, who believes that Heaven consists of working men's clubs.' This may have been facetious (and it certainly suggests that Solly could sometimes try a little *too* hard), but he had all the drive of the true believer. His success in persuading the most unlikely people to contribute donations shows that he was able to convince them that here was an idea which deserved to flourish. In the first twelve months, the Union received £614 in donations and only £102 in subscriptions; in the second year, £405 from donations and £208 from subscriptions, and in the third no less than £1,125 from donations and subscriptions totalling £317.

Solly did as much as any man could in those early days, but could hardly have done it all on his own – and yet, sadly, there are no papers surviving in the Union's records to tell us who else made a vital contribution in those formative years. We know that John Bainbridge spoke at the inaugural meeting; that the Rev. David Thomas had tried to help Solly in his earlier venture to raise £3,000,000; that Rylance was for a short time joint honorary secretary; that Babington was secretary of the club at Duck Lane, Westminster, which Miss Cooper had helped to form; and that the club at Notting Hill was founded on the initiative of Miss Craig. In *These Eighty Years*, Solly himself acknowledged:

> Among the most efficient workers on the Council in those early days, besides Mr Hugh Owen and Mr Rylance, were Miss Adeline Cooper, Miss Anna Swanwick, Mr James Heywood MP, Mr E. Clarke, my old friend and invaluable counsellor, Mr Bainbridge, Mr Bebbington, and especially Mr Russell Scott, the wise, wealthy, and philanthropic friend to whom Miss Carpenter and her noble Reformatory for Girls, at Red Lodge, Bristol, and for boys at Kingswood, owed so much. Mr Scott gave me peculiarly valuable help in the (to me) most difficult business of keeping accounts, as well as in the general administration of the Society and its work . . . not long after we had put up a brass plate by our street door, a gentleman called at the office and announced himself as the author of an able pamphlet on working men's clubs, which gave an interesting account of the partially successful endeavours he and a few other gentlemen had been making in one of the Manchester suburbs to establish a club there. His name was W. T. Marriott (later Sir W. T. Marriott MP, Judge Advocate), and I was very glad to make his acquaintance as one who had been in the field before our Society was formed, and to secure his help in our movement, as a member of the council . . .

But even if the role each played individually is obscure, we know that collectively they achieved a great deal, for at the end of the first year Solly was able to report that the Union had been instrumental in forming thirteen clubs; that thirteen others had joined the Union; that ten were in the process of formation under the Union's guidance, and that another seventeen had received advice or assistance from the Council.

These were the clubs that were established as a direct result of Solly's work in that first year:

> Wandsworth Working Men's Club
> Kentish Town, Camden Town and South Hampstead Working
>   Men's Club
> Bradford Working Men's Institute
> West Bromwich Working Men's Club
> Wednesbury Working Men's Club
> Scarborough Working Men's Club
> Soho Working Men's Club
> Faringdon Working Men's Club
> Chichester Working Men's Club
> Halifax Working Men's Institute
> Alton Working Men's Hall
> Bethnal Green Working Men's Club
> Holloway Working Men's Club

These were the clubs, previously in existence, which became members of the Union during the first year:

> St Mathias Salford Working Men's Club
> Colonnade (London) Working Men's Club
> Ramsgate Working Men's Club
> Brighton Working Men's Club
> West Cliff (Brighton) Working Men's Club
> South Shields Working Men's Club
> Sedgely Workmen's Hall
> Bridport Working Men's Mutual Improvement Association
> Southampton Workmen's Hall
> Hounslow Working Men's Club
> Cheshunt Working Men's Institute
> Kingham Reading and Recreation Club
> Devonport Working Men's Association

The following clubs were described as 'being formed under the impulse and advice of the Union', but were not yet affiliated:

Pimlico	Birmingham	Lincoln
Forest Hill	Bristol	Kingston
Somers Town	Wolverhampton	Walworth
	St Pancras	

These were the clubs or institutes, which had already been formed before the Union came into being, and were receiving advice or assistance:

Chipping Norton	Ledbury	St George's Mission
Clapton	Liverpool	Sunderland
Devonport	Mansfield	Belgrave (Tunbridge Wells)
Gravesend	Peckham	Wakefield
Hereford	Rotherham	Walthamstow
Laurencekirk	South Shoebury	

At first sight, that first annual report makes impressive reading, but the Union was far from being firmly established. There were many setbacks to come. Indeed, it is difficult for us now to establish the true strength of the Union in Solly's first years because it was not until Mr J. J. Dent became secretary in 1886 that complete records were kept of the Union's business. Correct assessments are made doubly difficult by the fact that nearly all these clubs were to disappear, but for the Walthamstow Working Men's Club and the Southampton No. 1 Club. But one thing we do know: Solly was determined to keep the clubs teetotal. That was probably why they failed, for the emphasis of the Union's leadership in those early years was not upon helping the members achieve what they wanted, but upon deciding what was good for them. Skittles was the chief recreation, and even smoking was heartily discouraged. A Mr Westlake, vice-president of a club in Southampton, wrote of beer, 'it is a mistake to suppose that a working man wishes this', and of smoking, 'Is it needful to allow smoking? Yes, if you mean to pick up the lowest class.'

Of the fifty-five clubs established during the second year, only one – at Hoddlesdon – was to develop into the sort of club we know today. There was still a club at Hoddlesdon, Lancashire, until shortly before the Union celebrated its centenary in 1962.

In 1864 the Council began to work on its first major project: drawing up a system of internal government suitable for working men's clubs. In this, they were helped by the then Home Secretary, Sir George Grey, who extended the provisions of the Friendly Societies Act to cover working men's clubs – even today, most clubs make an annual return to the Chief Registrar of Friendly Societies. This procedure was established on a sound footing by the Act of 1875, which defined working men's clubs as 'institutions for social intercourse, mental and moral improvement and rational recreation'. In this year, it was also decided to appoint an assistant secretary (at half Solly's wages), and a resolution was passed expressing the view that an extra £500 income was needed annually. In commenting on the assistant secretary's income, it is interesting to note that though £200 a year was a considerable sum in those years (it was a good wage for a working man even in the years immediately before the Second World War), it was not enough for Solly, who was beginning to grow discontented, as we all do at times, about his pay. The Council agreed that his salary was 'very inadequate to the amount of time and labour he gives to the Union', but noted when declining his request for more that they had 'been guided, not by the real value of the Secretary's services, but by the funds at their disposal'. It is interesting, too, to note that in that year, 1864, the Union had an income of £695 – but only £14 6s (£14.30 in today's decimal currency) was accounted for by the affiliation fees of member clubs. Solly was earning his salary by encouraging donations!

In that second annual report, it was noted that several clubs were on the verge of extinction, owing to 'the absence of resident gentry', but that hardly seems the explanation. Almost certainly, the real cause was the Union's initial reluctance to allow beer to be sold on club premises, and it seems significant that in the third year, 1865, when Lord Brougham was still President, a special meeting of the Council was called to discuss this vexed question. The decision was made: there would no longer be any restriction on the sale of beer in member clubs, although a rider was added (perhaps to mollify Henry Solly) that its exclusion was still to be recommended on 'prudential grounds'. This must have been a major crisis of conscience for Solly, whose pioneering zeal had been fired by his belief in total abstinence from the demon drink, and who had persuaded the Temperance movement to help him in the formation of the first clubs. In *These Eighty Years*, he refers to the issue as 'the great controversy in our Club world', and adds:

It was only with the greatest reluctance that I contemplated even the possibility of its being either right or wise for members of clubs to be able to get the drinks there which had wrought them so much mischief in the public-house, and for several years I combated with all my power the arguments of those who contended for the opposite course. But when I found at last by sad experience that the men whom we specially wanted to attract from the public-house would not come to clubs where they could get only the drinks which they did *not* want; that scarcely any club we could hear of was self-supporting, and had to be shut up when the gentry became tired of paying the annual deficit; that nearly all the clubs we had started had, in consequence, to be closed after two or three years' existence; that even if men joined a club where no alcoholic drinks were to be had, they continued to go to the pub. for a glass, and there met old companions and frequently remained, and lastly, and chiefly, that they almost passionately declared, *and proved*, that 'if the pressure of the landlord were taken off and the salt kept out of the beer', they should not themselves be tempted to take too much, and would not allow of excess on the part of others – I gave way. Even

Mr Raper, the indefatigable organizing secretary of the United Kingdom Alliance, when he heard all the arguments, *pro* and *con*, at a conference I held in Sheffield, after a Social Science Congress, publicly admitted that if men would drink intoxicating liquors they had better do so in a club, where there was no compulsion to drink at all, than at a public-house.

While I was still undecided in the matter, a large boot and shoe manufacturer at Leicester, Mr Walker, who was sincerely anxious to benefit the workmen in the town, invited me to come and help establish a club there. The meeting, as usual, was enthusiastically in favour of it, and a really good start was made. But in spite of my arguments and warnings, Mr Walker soon sent me word that the members had quite determined that they 'must have the beer'. I answered that I was very sorry, but of course, as I had always said, it was a question which should be decided *by* the members, not *for* them, and that I should watch the experiment with great interest. At the end of a year Mr Walker invited me down again to meet the members and hear what they had to say about it. It was a well-attended and very well-conducted gathering. One man after another got up and stated simply and straight-forwardly his conviction that the cause of Temperance as distinguished from Total Abstinence had been greatly promoted by members being able to get their pint or their glass at the club, instead of having to get it at their old haunts. One man in particular I remember – a thoughtful man, with a will of his own – telling us that before he joined the club he regularly got fuddled every Saturday night, but that since he became a member he had never once been intoxicated the whole year through – adding, however, very emphatically, that if he couldn't have got a glass of ale there he should never have become a member. In fact, they all sang the same song – they didn't want more, but they wouldn't take less, and there had not been a single case of intemperance in the club. As Mr Walker drove me home by starlight, I confessed that I found the ground considerably cut from under me. . . . Of course, I would much rather have found them willing to give up the use of intoxicating drinks altogether, whether at the public-house or the club; but until they saw the wisdom and advantage in every point of doing so, I was finally and entirely convinced that by far the lesser evil of the two was the one the men of Leicester had chosen. And what was specially interesting to discover was the extent to which men, when they had got a club of their own, and felt responsible for its good name, were jealous of its credit and honour, and carefully guarded against any excess on their own part or that of their fellow members.

3

In the same year in which the Union made its crucial decision to allow the sale of beer in clubs, Solly was awarded a higher salary. By all accounts, he had earned it. The man never stopped working, and would happily stretch out on that bed at the Union's office rather than lose time walking home to Primrose Hill. No doubt he was driven by a religious zeal and a desire to save souls, for his own writings are peppered with anecdotes about working men being saved from drunkenness so that they may live in 'comfortable, happy, Christian homes'. He was always busily arranging public meetings with distinguished speakers so that the Union could receive their endorsement, and after hearing the then Bishop of London (Dr Tait) commending the Union at one such meeting Solly wrote in his memoirs, *These Eighty Years*, '. . . all our hearts were gladdened, and the Council went on its way rejoicing. And we printed all these facts in "Occasional Papers", and sent them flying through the country, and into rich men's and titled men's homes, and money flowed in, and great men were added to our list of vice-presidents, and large numbers of working men and their wives blessed the day when they joined a club.'

This is hardly the way a working-class organization would be launched in these more egalitarian times, and one cannot but smile at Solly's innocent enthusiasm. Note that word 'flying'. Its use changes the whole spirit of his sentence and one can almost visualize this busy little man, labouring away at his desk for over twelve hours a day (which he thought was the very minimum he should spend at his work), compiling all those letters and pamphlets that really were 'flying' into the homes of the great and the good.

This was not the way the trade unions started; theirs was a long hard struggle to defend their members against victimization, and to ensure safer conditions at work and a fair return for their labour; a noble battle in which women and children would often willingly endure great hardship so that their menfolk could strike for a principle. Solly was doing something quite different; he never took to the barricades; he was making an almost genteel approach to the better natures of what we would today call the Establishment, a ruling aristocracy that had slowly come to realize that something had gone terribly wrong in the way the State was ordered. Listen to Solly's own description of what he was doing to recruit their support:

... the way to get money and influential support, for any undertaking deserving them, is first to do good work, *and then* to let all the world know you have done and are doing it. The council agreed that we should have a grand conversazione some evening in suitable rooms during the London season, and I got Lord Brougham, Lord Lyttelton, and (through the latter) the Dean of Chichester to put their names on a handsome card requesting, on behalf of the Working Men's Club and Institute Union, the honour of So-and-So's company on such an evening. The 'rank and fashion' of the West End and upper middle class, with a contingent of representative artizans (leading London Trade Unionists), responded to the invitation. Lord Brougham unfortunately could not leave Cannes in time for the eventful evening, but sent a very cordially written welcome, while Lord Lyttelton and the dignified Dean did the honours of receiving our guests with exemplary fortitude and fidelity for at least an hour. For a brief interval, indeed, the Dean lost sight of his aristocratic companion, and some majestic member of the Council or other vice-president did duty for him, and was supposed by some to be a lord. Very soon, however, the real nobleman, who had come first in ordinary morning dress, reappeared in proper costume. No doubt he had been thinking at first he was coming to an ordinary public meeting; but when he saw the elegantly attired ladies and faultlessly costumed gentlemen filing into the spacious hall in evening dress, he was struck with remorse, fled swiftly home and back again with a light heart. Tea, coffee, and other innocent refreshments were served in one of the side-rooms, and when the guests had done talking, they listened to the beautiful part-singing of the Working Men's College choir, which Mr R. B. Litchfield (barrister), their gifted teacher, had most kindly brought to promote our good cause. ... Lord Lyttelton mounted the platform, took the chair, and opened the proceedings, calling on me to expound the aims and principles, the claims and prospects of our movement. This I did with a will, but it was almost impossible for me, I fear, with such a topic, such an audience before me, and the memories of twenty years behind me, to cut my remarks as short as perhaps I should have done. ... The Dean of Chichester also spoke well ... a mysterious and important personage standing near the platform was pointed out to me as actually being Mr George Augustus Sala himself. One serious defect only was noted in our proceedings, and that arose from our guileless innocence in conducting such functions – we ought to have distributed attractive-looking slips among the company inviting them to give subscriptions or donations to our funds. 'Ah,' said one of our friends (more knowing than the rest), with a sigh, 'there might have been a lot of money got out of that assemblage!' as he saw them silently departing . . . the affair, indeed, cost us a good round sum, but it paid well – not merely in lifting our organisation to the rank of a national movement by fixing all eyes upon it, thus revealing its real and great importance, but also in bringing us, for a time at least, abundant pecuniary resources by subsequent contributions . . .

What could be more innocent? All that courting of the rich and the powerful, with no doubt months spent drawing up the invitation list, printing literature, distributing invitations, organizing refreshments and entertainment. All that delight as 'elegantly attired ladies' and 'faultlessly costumed gentleman' nibbled their way through 'innocent refreshments'. Perhaps Solly was so overwhelmed by it all that he clean forgot to hand round the hat!

And what must those trade unionists have been thinking about it all? We know that they included George Odger (Secretary of the London Trades Council), William Allan (Secretary of the Amalgamated Engineers), Robert Applegarth (Secretary of the Amalgamated Carpenters), W. R. Cremer (of the General Carpenters) and Daniel Guile (Secretary of the Ironfounders). These were men with solid working-class credentials. How did they react to this strange 'assemblage'? We have a clue in Solly's admission that they had been 'excited by the remarks of one of our speakers' and that they 'scented danger of registers for "blacklegs" being opened at our clubs, and of wages being thus lowered through non-union workmen'. Solly went on to record, 'Most of our Council were quite enough in touch with the working classes to be aware that, though this danger was infinitesimal, the danger of rendering the Trades Unions hostile to our movement, if this mistake were not at once corrected, was very great indeed. Accordingly we invited the London Trades Council to come to our offices for mutual explanations . . .'

These recollections, again taken from Solly's *These Eighty Years*, are the only record we have of what must have been an important phase in the Union's history. It is clear from B. T. Hall's book *Our Fifty Years* that there was a growing feeling among members of the Union's Council that Solly had to get results. All this campaigning had to produce real benefits for the Union. Hall noted that Solly 'continues his fertile output of leaflets and pamphlets, discussing and meeting difficulties, always cheerful, never doubting', but there is an undercurrent; a feeling, perhaps, that the General Secretary for all his many talents may be scattering his energies too widely.

We can only suppose. No minute books survive from those early years. None of our other pioneers left memoirs of the Union's beginnings. There are no albums of press cuttings, or files of pamphlets and early correspondence, to be consulted in the archives at Club Union House. Many of the papers that I was able to refer to when compiling *The First Century* twenty-five years ago were lost in the fire at Club Union House on 20 June 1978. The personal collection of papers gathered by former Assistant General Secretary, Tom Nicoll, which I also studied in 1961/62, appears to have been lost. (Tom was such a modest man that he probably never thought of leaving his papers to the Union in his Will.) While researching this book, I have, however, been able to refer to one volume of Solly's memoirs, which was not available to me last time, although extensive advertising has failed to find a copy of the second. It is from *These Eighty Years* that one finds the first clues to the way in which the Union changed into a genuinely working-class movement.

One of the first is in the reaction of Solly and the Union Council to the fears expressed by those trade unionists attending that rather grand conversazione at the Hanover Square Rooms, which clearly set alarm bells ringing. Solly records that Mr T. Hughes, MP, an early friend of the Union who was also trusted by the trade unionists, attended the meeting that was called at our offices to speak on behalf of the Club and Institute Union.

> Before an hour had passed the Trade Unionist leaders were perfectly satisfied, and we all parted excellent friends, for we were able to show them that nothing was further from our intentions, as a society, than to exercise the slightest interference with the rate of wages, or, indeed, with any economic questions – least of all to promote a reduction in wages – while we explained that each club 'stood on its own bottom', and that the Club Union neither had, nor desired to have, any power to dictate or control their action. But the difficult problem adverted to previously became more pressing every month. It came specially and prominently before us in the new club at Scarborough. The members naturally wished to govern it themselves, and the gentry who had started it and found the money wished to do the same. So they formed two committees, one chosen by these gentlemen, the other by the working men, and of course the plan worked as badly as possible . . .

Again, one senses the strains that were beginning to develop within the Union, but Solly was not the man to see problems ahead; he tended to gloss over the fact that many of the clubs that were opened soon closed (noting once again that this was due to 'the absence of resident gentry'), and in that second year, when the Council was anxious about the Union's finances and passed a resolution saying that further income of £500 a year must be found, Solly had failed to see this as another warning sign, and continued to press for a higher salary for himself. It must have been an expensive business, trying to keep up with all those dukes, peers and ladies in fine attire. The Dukes of Argyll and Devonshire had now joined the list of vice-presidents, along with James Vaughan, the Bow Street magistrate, but the union's accounts continued to tell a dismal tale; very little was being raised through affiliation fees, because few clubs were surviving.

Solly himself was as busy as ever, rushing around the country, addressing over a hundred meetings in a year, and announcing to the the Council that 41 new clubs had been formed, bringing the total formed by the Union to 116 in its first two·and a half years. Solly rarely dwelled on the numbers that were closing as he drummed up more and more donations from the House of Lords. It was in this third year, 1865, the year that beer was allowed in member clubs, that an appeal was launched to raise funds to establish a Central Hall for the Union, together with offices and a club. Again, Solly's hand can be seen, touching his forelock; the appeal was arranged rather in the pattern of that grand conversazione. Eight 'social meetings' were arranged at the Exeter Hall, London, presided over in turn by the Duke of Argyll, Lord Brougham, the Earl of Shrewsbury, the Earl of Lichfield, J. Abel Smith, MP, and the Duke of Devonshire, with Tom Hughes, MP, Lord Lyttelton, Frederick Denison Maurice and Wilfrid Lawson, MP, adding further encouragement. Among the donors were John Ruskin, Gladstone and the Earl of Rosebery. The device was financially successful. During this same year, the Union started its own monthly magazine, forerunner of the *Club and Institute Journal* (not one copy of that first magazine has survived), and the annual report also states that Solly's salary had at last been increased – the Council 'did rejoice that an increase of income this year has now enabled them to compensate him more fairly than in the first two years'. (The emphasis on the word 'rejoice' may have been Solly's, but again the accounts told a different story; income from affiliation fees was still falling, nearly halved in the third year from £14 6s to £7 4s.)

In that third year two new names appeared in the annual report; names of men who were to figure prominently in the Union's history, as it slowly turned into a very different organization to that originally envisaged by Henry Solly – Stephen Seaward Tayler, who became a subscriber, and Hodgson Pratt, who joined the Council in 1865. Both seem to have joined the Union at Solly's suggestion.

All through those early years, as well as organizing these grand London social gatherings, Solly was also touring the country, visiting the lords in their stately homes, believing as he always did that the success of a club depended upon the support of the gentry, and if not them, then the clergy. These passages from *These Eighty Years* illustrate his approach very clearly, and also show us how he was able, sometimes, to gain very valuable recruits:

> One of the early meetings for forming clubs in London was held somewhere in Lambeth or Southwark, being called by the excellent incumbent of a parish bordering on the river. A club was started, but we were not then sufficiently in possession of means and plans for attracting London working men, nor were we always able to secure the adoption of such plans as we did know to be essential to success. One considerable and lasting benefit (felt by the movement generally and the Club Union to this day) came from that attempt, for it attracted the notice of that true friend of clubs and working men, Mr Stephen S. Tayler, now Chairman of the Council of the Society. He not only took part, I think, in forming the club just mentioned, but got up another close to Stamford Street and came on the Council. . . .

– sometimes to help establish new clubs:

> I pass on to mention the origin of one of the best London clubs – one of the few that was so well taken up by men who could give it permanence that it has lasted and flourished to this day – viz., the St James and Soho Club and Institute. Our work in the Soho district began with a deputation of four or five working men waiting on the Council early in 1863 (in consequence of an article in *The Builder*) to ask our help in establishing a club in that neighbourhood, and describing so graphically what working men in London suffer from having no place to go to of an evening but the street-corner or the public-house, that Mr Russell Scott guaranteed the rent of a house in Crown Street, Soho, and gave £10 towards the necessary alterations, fittings and furniture. The Council took up the matter warmly. Mr Rylance and I used to plod to and fro on many a dark and rainy night, and for a time considerable work was done . . . early in 1864 another attempt was made to form a good London club by holding a public meeting in some hall near Covent Garden (I think), presided over by Sir John V. Shelley, MP for Westminster. This meeting was remembered specially by the fact of a working man getting up in the body of the hall and saying, 'Mr Chairman, a good deal has been said about workmen getting shorter hours of work and more leisure. Well, all I can say is that when men left work at six o'clock on Saturday afternoon I used to meet them drunk between eight and ten, and now that they leave work at four, I meet them drunk between six and eight. That's all the difference I can see.' Of course we assured him that the clubs we wanted to start were the very things to cure that evil . . .

– and then sometimes, when a club like the one just mentioned ran into difficulties, to intervene when it seemed as though the club was about to collapse:

> . . . when all appeared in vain, and the landlord was about to put in the brokers, I got Mr Henry Hoare, jun., the banker, who was Treasurer to the Union, to accompany me one night to the club, when we found the few men who still stuck to the sinking ship (among them was Mr Watts, still a member) sitting without a fire and almost in despair. We 'cheered and chafed them'. I gave them five shillings to get some coals. Mr Hoare lent them £5 to pay the landlord, and when shortly afterwards comparatively excellent premises were found in Rose Street, Soho, he most kindly guaranteed the rent. Ever since, under the title of the St James and Soho, this club has had a very useful and prosperous existence, especially since its removal to Gerrard Street, Soho, where again Mr Hoare gave it large and invaluable pecuniary help, until, under the exceedingly able and businesslike management of its late hon. sec., Mr Fishbourne, it became independent, I believe, of all outside assistance, and has been, as I said, one of the most successful and best-managed clubs in London . . .

One begins to understand his real sense of commitment, reading these memoirs, but at the same time one also realizes that this was another age, when attitudes were different, and social pioneers like the Rev. Henry Solly had to tread cautiously, taking care to solicit the support of those who sat in Parliament or occupied other positions of importance. Just once or twice, a feeling of doubt enters his narrative:

> We ought to have worked the East End or South London more; but in those days the ladies and gentlemen who were anxious to promote the movement naturally wanted to see the progress of the work for which they subscribed their money, and the 'slums' were regarded somewhat with fear, as well as disgust, by even the most philanthropic of the upper classes; while we were continually being disappointed, and even tripped up, by the indifference, or – though not often – the unfair dealing of men who should have been the best and chief supporters of the movement. We had, however, the privilege of bringing some effectual help to a useful and unpretending institution somewhere between Shoreditch and Spitalfields, called the Bedford Institute, by holding a good meeting in a schoolroom hard by, to introduce into it more of the club element. Sir Thomas Fowell Buxton presided . . . shortly afterwards I spent a pleasant breakfast hour with Sir Thomas and Lady Buxton (who had attended the meeting) at their house in Mayfair, when I told him of my correspondence with his father, many years before, re the noble effort that true philanthropist had made to check the abominable slave trade on the West Coast of Africa. . . .

There we have, in a few short sentences, the conflicts that lay at the heart of the Union in its early days. Men like Sir Thomas Buxton, no doubt totally sincere in their motives, would leave their homes in the most luxurious parts of London to spend an hour or two in the East End, encouraging working men at a public meeting to form a committee with a view to opening a club for themselves. After nearly every meeting, such a committee appears to have been formed – and when the 'gentry' offered some financial support, premises were often found, frequently with the help of a well-intentioned local clergyman, of whatever denomination. At Wisbech, the Working Men's Club and Institute was established through the work of the Society of Friends; there were other clubs established with the support of prominent Jews and Roman Catholics, but it was to be some years yet before the Union acquired a genuinely working-class character, although the 1870s were to see the emergence of another strong element within the Union, the Progressive or Radical clubs which were much more closely linked to the Labour movement.

In those early years, the impetus was so very different and appears to have come largely from Solly himself, who must have been trying to create a very different body from the Union that eventually emerged. As ever, his enthusiasm knew no bounds. In the fourth year of the Union's history, 1866, he travelled the length and breadth of the nation, addressing another 118 meetings, and reported to the Council that the then magnificent sum of £300 had been raised through a public dinner presided over by the Duke of Argyll. The Prince of Wales gave a donation to the Union of £21. Some worthwhile innovations were being tried; the first branches of the Union appear to have been formed in London and also covering Lancashire and Cheshire, and the first Union tournament was organized, for chess-players. A new journal was started, with the unlikely title, *Gossip, Chat and Song*. Solly himself now had a new title, Organizing Director, with a Miss Horsburgh taking over the role of Secretary. But all was not well, as B. T. Hall clearly realized when compiling *Our Fifty Years*, having access then to Union archives that have not survived; he noted drily that in that fourth year the income from affiliation fees had fallen yet again, this time to £4 15s, and although more distinguished figures had joined the list of Vice-Presidents – the Earl of Shaftesbury, Samuel Morley and Frederick Denison Maurice – Hall notes that at the annual general meeting, a bricklayer, George Howell, had commented upon 'the patronizing spirit which was too much shown towards the working classes'. Those underlying tensions were clearly still there.

None of these contradictions seem to have been very apparent to the Rev. Henry Solly, who continued to enjoy his travels. During those first four years, Lord Brougham continued to be the Union's President and, as he journeyed across the land, Solly would call at the homes of the Vice-Presidents. This quotation from *These Eighty Years* gives us yet another insight into Solly's character during that period:

> Nearly at the end of my holiday I received an invitation from Lord Lyttelton to go to Hagley Hall on a certain day, when the Earl of Dudley was to bring his beautiful bride thither to be welcomed in due form and state . . . I reached the baronial residence in much better time for dinner than on my previous visit. Its owner was reclining on a bench at the top of the flight of steps leading up to the front door, and hailed me from afar as I came up the drive. We had a lot of interesting talk on that bench, and I was afterwards introduced to his eldest son, renowned then in the cricket world as the best amateur batsman in England. The earl, who was as pleasant and free from starch as possible, enlivened the dinner with amusing talk and anecdotes, while the countess, shining resplendent in the magnificent diamonds presented by her lord, certainly looked very lovely . . . the next morning Lord Lyttelton, as Lord-Lieutenant of the county, had to don his uniform and ride off to a grand review of the Worcestershire Yeomanry; and I could not easily forget the curiously comical impatience and disgust with which he (of all men the most anti-conventional enemy of forms and ceremonies) at first resisted, then sadly submitted to, Lord Dudley's endeavours to adjust his sword-belt and other trappings in a rather more correct and dignified state than that in which it had pleased the noble owner thereof to make his appearance in the hall before mounting his charger and sallying forth to the fray. . . .

An almost comic picture sometimes appears within the pages of *These Eighty Years*, without the author being aware of the humour, and yet at the same time he was certainly laying down the Union's foundations, with that constant round of public meetings, and even a three-day conference on the opening of Working Men's Clubs and Institutes. 'By securing the presence of more or less eminent men, especially of members of the House of Peers, we obtained capital reports in the daily newspapers, and sent the main features of the movement and recommendations of our plans into many hundred thousand homes of rich and poor in England, as well as over half the world,' he wrote.

As the Union entered its fifth year, 1867, those underlying contradictions began to assert themselves. Subscriptions and donations from the rich and powerful were starting to fall, and the Union did not have the strength to withstand such a drop in income; its leadership had yet to realize that the strength of a movement like ours has to be in the support of its members, *not* in the charity shown by others. In this fifth year, the income received from affiliation fees fell to £1 17s 6d, and, belatedly, the Council decided to 'direct attention more to the strengthening of existing clubs than the formation of new ones'. Almost without Solly being aware of it, the Union was starting to change. This becomes clear from B. T. Hall's analysis:

> The Council must have felt its efforts too far flung and the need for concentration. The increasingly diffuse character of the reports warrants this. Probably it was here when the trouble began with Henry Solly. Nothing was too diffuse for *him*. Diffusion and not concentration was his forte. The whole planet was not too wide for his abounding enthusiasm and passion. He joyfully records that opening of a club at Hobart, and has heard of another in Sydney. But others wish to harvest and think the seed time should await for a while its proper season. . . .

As the year passes, different characters emerge within the Union. Hodgson Pratt makes a donation of £10 to encourage public lectures within clubs; the London Branch holds a dinner and sports at the Crystal Palace, and organizes an excursion to Paris for its members to see the Great Exhibition. The London Trades Council is invited to tea. B. T. Hall notes:

> Names, to be well known and honoured later, begin to appear. The Trade Unionists evince some interest, but are shy and suspicious. Robert Applegarth (secretary, Carpenters and Joiners) is, as usual, hearty and downright in support. But W. R. Cremer is coy; and Coulson, Allan, and other members of the Junta are at best negatively neutral . . .

The plans for the Union to have its own headquarters are taking shape. The new Central Building is expected to cost £12,000, and Solly suggests that he should devote himself to this as 'salaried Principal', but he resumes the Secretaryship when Miss Horsburgh retires, and there are clear signs of serious differences within the Union's Council, for Solly has given up the post within a few months.

In the meantime, however, the Duke of Bedford has responded to the appeal for donations towards the cost of the new Central Building with a gift of £100 and the Dukes of Devonshire and Buccleuch have each given £50. Another £25 has been contributed by the Prince of Wales, later King Edward VII, and the banker Henry Hoare has donated £100. The new Vice-Presidents include

Earl Derby, Sir Stafford Northcote, MP, later to become Chancellor
of the Exchequer and important friend to the Union, and Earl
Chelmsford, the Lord Chancellor.

On the surface, all was well; but within the Council, division.
Two of Solly's recruits, Thomas Paterson, who was by trade a
cabinet maker and had been secretary of an early co-operative
society, and Hodgson Pratt, who had held high office in the Indian
Civil Service, had joined forces, almost certainly with the support
of Stephen Seaward Tayler. B. T. Hall records:

> It is an ungracious and unpleasing task, even in the interest of historic
> accuracy, to probe too deeply for explanations. Certain it is that Solly
> was opposed in Council by Paterson and Pratt, and that these latter
> dominated. There is nothing dishonourable to any of the parties, who
> differed as to the lines on which the Union should proceed. Solly was all
> for propaganda – at times. At others he was all for the Central Hall;
> where with himself as Principal he dreamt of a range of usefulness and
> activity of a kind, but far beyond, that subsequently achieved by
> Toynbee Hall. Nothing here to shame his record.
>
> But Paterson and Pratt were of another type. They believed that the
> organization should for a while rest content with its position, and de-
> velop itself from within. It was taking too much in its baby hands. It
> relied as much as ever on subscribers and well-wishers, whilst it should
> begin to awaken sentiments of self-reliance and self-support. It may be
> supposed that both views were expressed with all the force in which
> Pioneers and Propagandists excel. Perhaps there was a feeling that the
> principles and accepted practice of office routine should sway a Secre-
> tary more than they could an eager and passionate soul – a preacher,
> not an administrator – like our founder. There was friction, and in the
> end the resignation was accepted by the Council . . .

That was as far as B. T. Hall went in his own book, *Our Fifty
Years*, and it was as much as I knew when writing *The First Century*.
As mentioned before, there are no early archives to tell us what
really happened – but fresh light is shown on this important
moment in the Union's history by that lately-discovered volume,
These Eighty Years. Thomas Paterson was another of those early
stalwarts recruited by the Rev. Henry Solly, who had organized an
evening meeting at which a Mr I. M. Ludlow had delivered an
address entitled 'Can Arbitration Be Successfully Used In Disputes
Between Employers and Workmen?' (which just shows how deadly
sober they all were in the early days of the Union). Lord Lichfield
had presided, and drew Solly's attention to a contribution made
from the audience by Paterson,

> who, as he said, had just made some very clever remarks on the question

before us. I spoke to this man after the meeting, and invited him to come on the Council, where for several years he was known to us as Thomas Paterson, and took an active part in its deliberations and management. He was a man of considerable mental power and original faculty, with an ardent desire to be of use in the world, and with a certain amount of 'vaulting ambition', but quite free from mercenary motives. . . .

The crunch came in the early summer of 1867, after Paterson had formed a group within the Council with Hodgson Pratt, probably Stephen Seaward Tayler, and others. Whether they were meeting privately or not, or whether this was just a coming-together of like minds, no one now knows, but the immediate source of their anxiety was the state of the Union's finances, and the way in which Solly was doing his job. This becomes clear from Solly's reminiscences in *These Eighty Years*:

> Several members of the Council, and especially a clever artizan, wished to save the expenses of a salaried secretary, and thus to make a larger sum available for assisting working men in establishing clubs. Others no doubt thought, quite honestly, that the Society could be better managed under their own immediate direction than under mine; and yet others were troubled at the idea of my giving up the travelling propagandist work, and taking to the administration of the Central Hall and Club instead. Thus there came to be on the Council a relatively strong party that desired to see my services dispensed with.
>
> As I look back upon all the sufferings, regrets, and heartburnings that are associated with one of the most painful experiences of my life, it is a source of satisfaction and thankfulness to me to remember that when these views were communicated to me by the treasurer, my first thought was one of geniune satisfaction that the Society had grown strong enough to be able to dispense with my services, while my second was one of regret that, not having a private fortune, I was obliged to earn my own living and contribute to that of my family, and was unable to serve the Society without taking pecuniary compensation. The majority of the Council, however, took the view that it was essential to the welfare of the Society that I should remain in office, and a decisive vote settled the matter for a time. Those who desired my resignation did not acquiesce in this decision. Alas! it is seldom indeed that such a question can be fought out on the lines of principle and policy unaffected by personal considerations. The persistency with which a section of the Council seemed bent on securing my resignation, however honourable the motives that inspired it in the main, allied itself with personal dislike and hostility towards myself in the case of one or two persons, who, as I discovered to my great distress, were taking indirect means to discredit my work, if they could not discredit my character; and the embittered feeling that this introduced into the situation, perhaps, re-acted upon me, and made me consult what I felt to be my own dignity, even at the

risk of injury to the Society. It was under these feelings that, when things were made increasingly painful to me, I tendered my resignation at a meeting of the Council, from which many of the most influential members, and many who deeply regretted my action, were absent. My resignation was accepted by a narrow majority.

To me personally the severance of this tie was a blow of almost crushing severity. Apart form the sad and sordid associations which made the whole matter so painful, it seemed as though my life were broken in two, and that the work to which I had consecrated it, as the most effectual way open to me for exercising the Christian ministry, and helping to establish the kingdom of God on earth, was suddenly wrenched from my hands. But this would have mattered little to any one except myself; and I trust I should soon have risen above any feeling of personal disappointment had the step taken proved to be for the good of the cause. From the first it was my wish that nothing should be wanting on my side that could secure this result. At the urgent request of Lord Lichfield, Mr Hugh Owen, and several of the oldest and best friends of the cause, who had voted in the minority (Lord Lyttelton unfortunately being then in New Zealand), I accepted a seat on the Council, hoping that my experience and influence might be, as I was assured they would be, of service to the honorary secretaries (Messrs Hodgson Pratt, Thomas Paterson and the Hon. Auberon Herbert), who were now to be responsible for the working of the Society. But the results of this disruption cannot, I think, be said to have secured the aims or fulfilled the hopes of those who caused it. As regards the pecuniary saving, the income of the society fell away so seriously, .and the management of its finances and its work was such, that for many years afterwards it was in a chronic state of debt – never, in fact, was free from that condition, until, at length, Lord Rosebery generously paid off all its liabilities. . . .

Quite clearly, there was the mother-and-father of a row within the Union – the kind of dispute that could so easily have killed it stone dead. The plans to build the new Central Hall came to a temporary halt, and Solly suggests that there was a further crisis when money he had salted away over the years was 'frittered away in small loans to clubs, which were not repaid', with another £150 being allegedly embezzled by the then Assistant Secretary. He himself was deeply hurt, and tried later to establish a rival organization to the Union, The Social Working Men's Club Association, taking with him some of the Union's members.

This is, perhaps, the opportune moment to acknowledge the Union's debt to Henry Solly; most organizations need someone like Henry Solly in their early years, an enthusiast who refuses to be put off by all the obstacles that block other people's way. Solly was certainly one of that kind, but he also had what is often their failing:

he was always pursuing new objectives without making sure that those already begun had been accomplished. And when a new idea came into his head, like that dream of becoming Principal of the proposed Central Hall, he could become obsessive. His friend and constant supporter, Lord Lyttelton, who was given to writing odd rhymes about his friends, pictured Solly's thoughts thus:

> When I wake, when I sleep, when I stand, when I fall,
> I can think of nothing but that Central Hall,
> In my cups, on my back, on my knees, in my tub,
> My thoughts still keep running on that Central Club.
> While eating, while drinking, through teas and through coffees
> I'm all of a bubble for that Central Office.
> Most easy, most modest, most fair within bounds
> Is the trifle I ask for, but twelve thousand pounds,
> Most airy, most lofty, most spacious, most jolly,
> Shall be our new house, or my name is not Solly.

There is a rather acid touch of humour in these lines; Solly's enthusiasm was very praiseworthy, but there comes a time in the early history of most voluntary organizations when successes so far gained have to be consolidated, and a firm financial and administrative base secured. And this was where Paterson and Pratt were making the better argument. It was Paterson who had made the running in his criticisms of Solly within the Union Council, with the support of Pratt, who was later to become the Union's President for seventeen years. Both practical men, they were agreed that Solly was inclined towards rather wild spending, which they considered inconsistent with the proper aims of an organization that was as yet by no means self-sufficient and had to rely upon donations.

Solly, who was more of a preacher than an administrator, had the last explanatory word on the dispute at the annual meeting in 1867 when he took his seat on the Council. He said it was undesirable to trouble a wider audience with personal matters, and, therefore, 'he should not say more than that there existed so considerable a divergence of opinion between himself and some members of the Council that further co-operation was impossible'.

4

The whole history of the voluntary movement is littered with personal feuds, splits and schisms that frequently wreck the organizations concerned, or lead to separate associations being formed, with each then weakening the other. That great dispute within the Council could have been one of those, for the Union was not then a democratic organization in the firm control of its membership, and the departure of the Rev. Henry Solly could have meant a sudden, disastrous change of direction. Luckily, that did not happen.

For some time, Solly remained on the Council himself and, although he went off to form his Social Working Men's Club Association in the years that followed, taking Lord Lyttelton and other members of what B. T. Hall dubbed that 'glittering train' with him, Solly still retained close links with the movement. Throughout his life, he seems to have been driven by a genuine, religiously driven desire to uplift the working man. He regularly attended Bible classes for working men, continued lecturing, and then, at the suggestion of Hodgson Patt, rented some premises in Newman Street, off Oxford Street, and opened a club himself, called The House-Painters and Decorators' Club and Institute, which later changed its name to The London Artizans Club and Institute. The leading Victorian writer and politician, Samuel Morley, gave him £100 for this venture; Sir John Lubbock gave £50, and many of his old friends from within the Union lent their support. In *These Eighty Years*, Solly recalled:

> Lord Lyttelton, the Rev. J. Baldwin Brown, Mr Bebbington, and other of my old colleagues, with several influential new ones, worked with me on the provisional committee, and materially helped in giving us a good start. The members insisted on my being president of the club, though I advised their electing one of themselves; and for a considerable time the club had a prosperous career. Of course it was decided by the members that they must have the same facilities for getting there the refreshment which gentlemen could get at their Westminster clubs, and to which they had become accustomed; and although there was a

little mischief from intemperance at first, I was very thankful to see how sternly the great bulk of the members set their faces against anything like excess. One of them said to me one night, 'Look at the difference between this place and a public-house. So-and-so (mentioning an active member) was drunk here a few days ago, and last night he came into the club looking as ashamed of himself as could be. If he had got drunk at a pub, he would have been rather proud of it – have come up to the bar next night, called for a glass of "dog's nose", tossed it off, and been as jolly as you please!'

It was after retiring from the secretaryship of the Union that Solly wrote his book, *Social Working Men's Clubs and Institutes*, which was published through the Union's office, then still at 150 Strand, so it is clear that some kind of a relationship continued between Solly and the Union, although it must have been strained, for he recalls one occasion in his memoirs when two members of the Council attended one of his lectures, 'standing inside the room during the evening, making uncomplimentary remarks, and jeering at the whole proceedings'.

The Union was now being run by three honorary secretaries – Thomas Paterson, Hodgson Pratt and another volunteer willing to work without salary, Auberon Herbert. They were a powerful combination, but all three had many other outside interests and none could devote all his energies to the job. Paterson had to work for a living, Pratt spent his winters abroad, and Herbert had other commitments. But they knew what the Union needed, and their first report was frank enough:

> The work of this Society may be described as two-fold; first, that of aiding the establishment of Workmen's Clubs and Institutes where they do not exist at present; and secondly, that of strengthening and developing them when established.
> The Council feel strongly impressed that the second of these two objects is quite as important as the first. It cannot be said that the movement has taken firm root in this country . . . working men have yet to be convinced of its importance . . .

There was much truth in that perception. At the time when the triumvirate wrested control of the Union away from Solly, there were known to be somewhere between 280 and 300 working men's clubs in Britain. Hardly any of them paid affiliation fees to the Union. We have already noted that in Solly's last year the income from affiliation fees had fallen to £1 17s 6d. In the next year, this income was to fall even further, to just 17s 6d, before the Council came to realize that the strength of the Union must lie in its membership.

Of those clubs known to the Union in June 1867, only five were to survive – the Walthamstow Working Men's Club, which is the oldest in the Union; the Coventry Working Men's Club, which claims to be the oldest working men's club in the country (but was late joining the Union); the Southampton No.1; the Newcastle-on-Tyne, and the Northampton St Giles.

The failure of so many of these early clubs may have been largely due to the lack of democracy, to the *presence* and not the absence of local gentry, but B. T. Hall in *Our Fifty Years* comments:

> The Reports of these years are too uncertain in their statistical method to enable any tables of value to be set out concerning them. They were valuable in that they produced a band of sympathisers and a rich crop of experience. They taught, if not what *would* ensure the success of a workmen's club, very emphatic lessons as to what would not. There was yet much to learn in this direction. The reasons given for the demise of clubs are good enough. But the catalogue is not complete. Those which the Reports record are:
>
> 1. Absence of Beer
> 2. Presence of Youths
> 3. Absence of Resident Gentry
> 4. 'Too positive presence of the Parson's hand'
> 5. 'Gentlemen who guaranteed became tired of cost, disheartened from expecting completely successful results prematurely'
> 6. The 'present political agitation'
> 7. The present strained relations between master and man [It was the period leading up to the Broadhead activities in Sheffield, and Trade Unionists and Trade Unionism were suspect].
> 8. In the Metropolis – the number of rival attractions
>
> As we know now, failure lay principally in the fact that clubs were not spontaneously originated and democratically controlled ... the workers in those days were but little capable of the thought of, or the power to originate and manage clubs, until inspired and taught by others. For those it could not have been a grateful task, and that many retired hurt is not surprising ...

Solly himself was both the propeller and the brake on the new movement; he got it going, but his objects were typically those of a Victorian minister. His reluctance to countenance the sale of beer, and his diatribes against smoking, show how great was the gulf between Solly and those working men whom he did so much to help in the days when education was not open to all and when, as a result, they had few examples to guide them towards better ways of spending leisure hours. And yet it remains to Solly's credit that he was not greatly discouraged by the poor initial response. In that last report he commented:

The Council ... are aware that in every important and widely extended movement there must be a large number of failures – especially during its early stages. The Co-operative Movement, which is now taking such deep hold on the working class, thirty years ago appeared to be a total failure, and died down to the roots. But these pioneer efforts were far from lost. Thoughtful men here and there were thoroughly imbued with the idea, and it again sprung into vigorous life; while its present leaders have learned much from the mistakes and discouragements of their predecessors.

Future leaders of the Club and Institute Union learned much from the mistakes, or over-enthusiasm, of Henry Solly, and much more emphasis is given to this period in the Union's history in this book than in *The First Century* because it becomes clearer, from reading *These Eighty Years* and from John Taylor's study, *From Self-Help to Glamour: The Working Men's Club 1860–1972* (published in the History Workshop series of pamphlets, 1972), that Solly continued to exercise influence within the Union long after that ruction in 1867. In January 1873, we find him back in office as Organizing Secretary, with his old friend Lord Lyttelton as President, again appealing to the aristocracy for support. In 1876, when the Dean of Westminster, the famous Dean Stanley, became an active President of the Union for five years, we find Solly once more a member of the Union's Council, although he continued to fall out with his colleagues from time to time, and even managed to run into trouble at the Artizans Institute, which he had largely built himself as a model club for London's painters and decorators, who sometimes shocked him with their ingratitude – one of them appears to have switched the lights off during a recitation of Byron's poem, 'Darkness'! Solly, who could never be sure whether even this was a joke, was still trying to improve the lives of others, organizing lectures on ancient Egypt or Shakespeare's *King John*, and even helping to stage a production of *The Merchant of Venice*. All the world had to revolve round his enthusiasm – and he was much put out when club members objected to his sleeping on the premises! After all, he had built the club, hadn't he? It was *his* club, wasn't it?

The one debt that the Union undoubtedly has to Solly is that he retained the interest of the rich and powerful at a time when their support was essential, for they continued to send in donations while the Union was at last endeavouring to build up grass-roots support. This link with their lordships was to continue through the 1870s and into the 1880s, until in 1886 the Union became a much more representative body. Throughout the intervening years the Union's

Annual Reports retained a distinctly aristocratic flavour. Take this list of office-holders from the Annual Report of 1875:

President
The Earl of Rosebery

Vice-Presidents

The Duke of Abercorn	The Earl of Ducie
The Duke of Argyll	The Earl Fortescue
The Duke of Devonshire	The Earl of Lichfield
The Duke of Westminster	The Earl of Shaftesbury
The Marquis of Lorne, KT, MP	The Earl of Shrewsbury and Talbot
The Earl of Caernarvon	The Earl Spencer, KG
The Earl of Derby	The Earl Russell, KG

Council

The Bishop of Carlisle	W. T. M'Cullaugh Torrens, MP
The Bishop of London	Sir J. P. Kay-Shuttleworth, Bart
The Bishop of Winchester	Sir John Lubbock, Bart, MP
Lord Aberdare	Sir Titus Salt, Bart
Lord Chelmsford	The Dean of Chichester
Lord Ebury	The Dean of Westminster
Lord Overstone	Hon. and Rev. W. H. Lyttelton
Lord Stratford de Redcliffe	Hon. G. E. Brodrick
Lord Hampton	Hon. Auberon Herbert
Lord Henry Lennox, MP	Hon. C. G. Lyttelton
Lord Frederick Cavendish, MP	Ernest Nel, MP
Lord Elcho, MP	Rev. William Arthur
Rt Hon. Acton S. Ayrton	Edmund Backhouse, MP
Rt Hon. Sir R. P. Collier	Samuel Bowley
Rt Hon. Russell Gurney, MP	W. W. Bramston Beach
(Recorder of London)	Thomas Brassey, MP
Rt Hon. Sir Fitzroy Kelly	Rev. J. Baldwin Brown
Rt Hon. Austen H. Layard	Rev. H. G. De Bunsen
Rt Hon. Sir Stafford Northcote,	John Crossley, MP
MP	Henry Edwards, MP
Rt Hon. James Stansfeld, MP	Roger Eykyn
Rt Hon. W. F. Cowper Temple,	Julian Goldsmid, MP
MP	Rev. Newman Hall
Sir Robert Anstruther, Bart, MP	G. W. Hastings
Sir Antonio Brady	James Heywood
Sir Charles Dilke, Bart, MP	Thomas Hughes, QC
Sir Harcourt Johnstone, Bart, MP	Prof. T. H. Huxley
Sir Henry Cole	Ralph Ward Jackson
William M. Neill	Rev. Canon Jenkins
Hugh Owen	Col. G. H. Kennard
Hon. John S. Pakington	Rupert Kettle, JP
Robert Rawlinson, CB	William Longman

Sir Charles Reed, MP
Henry Richards, MP
Samuel Morley, MP
E. Vansittart Neale
Frank Mowatt
A. J. Mundella, MP
Miss Anna Swanwick

William McArthur, MP
Evan Matthew Richards
Rev. Canon Robinson
W. H. Smith, MP
John Storrar
P. A. Taylor, MP
Forbes Watson

In each year, there would be one or two changes; the following year, 1876, the Archbishop of Canterbury and Lords Harris and Mount-Temple joined the list of Vice Presidents, and we can see from the list of other officers that although the nature of the Council was slowly changing, the Union remained a very different body to the one we know today:

Chairman of Council
Hodgson Pratt

Vice-Chairmen of Council

Lord Frederick Cavendish, MP
Sir Harcourt Johnstone, MP

Rev. M. S. A. Walrond
Stephen Seaward Tayler

Council

John Babbs (Kennington)
Berry, B. (Stratford)
Blatchley, E. R.
Buckmaster, J. C.
Cubbon, A. (Warwick St., SE)
Fishbourne, T. (St James & Soho)
Hamilton, W. A. B.
Hardwicke, William
Heward, A.
Hill, Hamilton Hay
Holland, E. T.
Jackson, A. E.
Lawrence, Henry W.
Lamport, Charles
L'Estrange, Rev. A. G.
Lowe, J. (Boro of Hackney)
Marriott, W. Thackeray
Maurice, C. E.
Newton, Joseph

Paterson, Thomas
Paterson, Mrs
Pearson, E. S.
Plummer, John
Pratt, Hodgson
Preston, Alfred
Rowland, F. A. A.
Savage, G. F.
Slack, H. J.
Solly, Rev. Henry
Tayler, Stephen Seaward
Thick, Frank E.
Verney, Frederick W.
Walker, David
Walrond, Rev. M. S. A.
Waterman, Orlando
Watson, James
Webber, Rev. Thornhill
Whitlock, J.
Wilson, J. F.

Treasurer
Hamilton N. Hoare

Eventually, all this was to change as the Union became a body controlled by its member clubs; but that was still a long way off.

Throughout the first twenty-four years of its life, those distinguished
names appeared on the Union's stationery and no doubt symbolized
Solly's initial aims, but with his first removal as Secretary the
emphasis of the Union's *direction* did start to change.

In 1868, Herbert, Paterson and Pratt were able to report to the
Annual Meeting that they were bringing the Union's administration under control; the income from affiliation fees had sunk to
the all-time low of 17s 6d, and the income from donations and
subscriptions had fallen to £480, but salaries had been cut back to
£280 as well, and a Circulating Library had been established; clubs
were being visited, and – for the first time – member clubs were
also beginning to admit visitors, the beginnings of the 'Affiliation'
principle. At last, we are beginning to get firm figures in the Annual
Report: eleven clubs have joined the Union during the year,
bringing the total to a firm seventy-two, and although annual
membership income has yet to be established, the new clubs are
paying 2s 6d on registration (which makes one wonder how only
17s 6d was raised!).

By the following year, 1869, the changes are becoming more apparent; the Report for that year shows that during the twelve
months fifty-six more clubs have affiliated to the Union, and that
fifty-three of them have actually paid their 2s 6d fee, bringing in
affiliation income of £6 7s 6d. Solly is still working for the Union
intermittently, and we learn that Pratt, Herbert and Paterson are
also visiting clubs in different towns, and that the Circulating
Library has established such a good name for itself that Queen
Victoria herself has donated several autographed copies of her
Life in the Highlands and *The Early Years of the Prince Consort*. Financially, it is clear from the Report that all is far from well; the
Council has had to borrow £25 from the Central Hall Fund and
has lost £130 when the Union's Collector, Connelly Peyton,
issued himself with a duplicate receipt book, and began embezz-
ling Union funds; lawyer's fees have added another £26 to the
loss.

Over the next four years, 1870–74, the character of the Union
began to take more definite form in the firm hands of Hodgson
Pratt, who was clearly the most committed member of the triumvirate. He was strongly supported by Auberon Herbert, who
resigned the joint-secretaryship in the first year to become
Chairman of the Council, but Thomas Paterson was limited in the
hours that he could spend working unpaid in the Union offices
because he still had to work every day at his trade as a cabinet-
maker, and during this period also took on family responsibilities

when he married Miss Emma Smith, who had been employed in the offices as an assistant between 1869 and 1872.

It is clear now that it was Hodgson Pratt who held the Union together during this difficult phase, when many members had gone off to join Solly in his rival organization (only to come back again when he did), when the Union was teetering on the brink financially, and did not have the resources to employ extra staff even if the Council had wanted to. Hodgson Pratt had been a career civil servant, posted out to India, where he became Under-Secretary for the Government of Bengal. In those days, one year's work in India counted for two years' work at home in pension terms, which meant that Hodgson Pratt was able to retire from the Indian Civil Service at the age of thirty-eight, and so had the time and the independence to devote himself to the Union. Like Solly and Stephen Seaward Tayler, Pratt was a Unitarian and, despite his background, he was also a political radical. The ideals that lay behind the formation of the Union clearly touched a chord, for he was to devote much of his life to its work, labouring away unpaid as Honorary Secretary, paying his own expenses when he travelled around the country, visiting clubs and lecturing (which he did extensively during this period; it was reported in 1870 that he travelled to Sheffield, Leeds and Gainsborough, visited thirty clubs in London and delivered eleven lectures, and in 1873 that he attended forty-one meetings, presented thirteen lectures, and visited twenty-one clubs).

B. T. Hall used to tell a story about the impression that Pratt made at many of the clubs he visited: Hall once called at the Great Wigston Club in Wigston Magna, Leicestershire, and was greeted by the president, the late J. Abbott, who died in 1921.

'How long have you been president?' asked Hall.

And the answer was, 'Ever since Mr Pratt came down and spoke in the schoolrooms and started our club.'

'How long ago was that?'

'Twenty-two years ago,' came the reply.

As Hall said, Abbott 'spoke as though it were firmly fixed in his mind that no club could start without Mr Pratt'.

And it was certainly true that during Hodgson Pratt's long association with the Union, as Honorary Secretary, as Editor of the *Journal* (which he helped to revive), and then as President for seventeen years, from 1885 to 1902, the Union membership grew dramatically as it changed from being the rather patronizing organization that Solly had created to a fully democratic body controlled by its members. Pratt's achievement was to effect this transition painlessly and without the Union losing much of its initial momentum. Clearly his civil-service background helped; he had the political skill to move ahead gradually, drawing more and more working men into the movement without discarding its early supporters. When Miss Smith left to marry Paterson, Pratt recruited a clubman, W. Allam of the St Pancras Club, as a paid secretary to the Honorary Secretaries. Likewise, he started to encourage other clubmen to join the Union Council.

In Pratt's first years of office, the Union seemed to move from one financial crisis to another (although crisis may be too strong a word); there was constant cost-cutting at the Union's offices, and in 1873 poor Mr Allam was said to be 'terribly overworked, but there is no money to pay him more or to engage assistance'. The following year, Queen Victoria sent a donation of £50 and the Duke of Bedford contributed £100, which enabled the Union to pay Allam a little more, but it is clear from these figures that it was 'a little':

	Union income £	Salaries £
1870	530	260
1871	503	154
1872	410	134
1873	627	178
1874	443	193

Those donations from Queen Victoria and the Duke of Bedford represented over a third of the Union's income for 1874. Without them, the Union would have been in severe financial difficulties, for money was now being borrowed from the Central Hall Fund, and Hodgson Pratt was lending money to the Union as well as paying his own travelling expenses. When Lord Rosebery became President of the Union in 1875, and heard of its debts, he sent a cheque for £174 to enable the Union to straighten its affairs.

The key to stabilizing the Union's affairs lay in cementing its relationship with its members; a special sub-committee recommended an increased affiliation fee, and this was agreed in 1874, by which time the Union's Council was becoming so much more representative of the clubs. The new working-class members recruited by Hodgson Pratt all pressed for higher fees, and a provincial registration fee of 5s was set. It was also agreed that London clubs should pay an annual fee of 5s per 100 members, with an annual maximum of £1. One of the new members who had been pushing strongly for these changes was Mr Fishbourne of the St James and Soho Club, which had been making voluntary donations to the Union for the previous three years, levying a halfpenny a month from all its members. In 1874, this one club raised £7, while 5s was the highest that any other club contributed.

It was during this troubled period that another of the clubmen who had joined the Council, E. Eisenhardt of the Bedford Club, came up with the idea which was to solve all the Union's long-term financial problems; he suggested that an Associate Card should be introduced, with club members who acquired a card paying 1s annually to enable them to use it when visiting other member clubs. Lord Lyttelton, who had by then become Chairman of the Council, at once saw the merits of the proposal, and signed a circular to members of all the Union clubs recommending its adoption. A competition was then held to choose a design for the associate card, and this was won by Henry Hill of Ashton-under-Lyne, who received a prize of two guineas; his design is still in use today, and every member who renews his annual card carries it in his pocket as he enjoys the hospitality of other clubs within the Union.

As is so often the case, it was a simple idea like this that was to change the Union's finances, and also its relationship with its members. Initially, members using the associate card were not permitted to buy alcoholic drinks when visiting other clubs, but one of the Union's Vice-Chairmen, Sir Harcourt Johnstone, MP, took up the matter privately with the Chancellor of the Exchequer, Sir Stafford Northcote, MP, who had also been a great friend of the Union and became a Vice-President. Sir Stafford took the matter up personally with the Commissioners of the Inland Revenue, and then gave a personal direction that enabled holders of the associate card to buy drinks or cigarettes when visiting other clubs. This was an enormous step forward, and its significance was realized at once by the Union's officers, who sent out this private letter to the membership:

Affiliated Clubs and the Sale
of Exciseable Articles

As the members of Clubs affiliated to the Working Men's Club and Institute Union are doubtless aware, the sale of exciseable articles by a bona fide Club to its own Members is not a breach of the excise laws, because the Members are joint owners of all the property of the Club. A sale of such articles to anyone else *is* a breach of those laws, the penalty for which, however, can only be enforced by the Inland Revenue Commissioners.

When the system of Associate and Monthly Pass Cards issued by the Union – which has proved so useful in promoting mutual intercourse between affiliated clubs and their members – was established, it was felt that it would be a serious drawback to the full enjoyment of the privileges sought to be conferred by the system, if members visiting other clubs and obtaining exciseable articles were to render the Club they visited liable to prosecution by the Inland Revenue Commissioners, such risk being inevitable, inasmuch as the visiting members would have no share or ownership in the articles they purchased.

In order to remove this danger, the Commissioners were approached in 1875 with a view to ascertain whether any arrangement could be arrived at by which clubs whose bona fide was guaranteed by their affiliation to the Union (the conditions required before affiliation being similar to the points regarded by the Commissioners as indicative of bona fide) should receive immunity from prosecution, so long as the sales of exciseable articles were confined to members of other clubs affiliated to the Union.

After considerable negotiation with the Commissioners, the then Chancellor of the Exchequer, in the letter given below, conceded the necessary exemption from prosecution to clubs, which admit to honorary membership members of other bona fide clubs affiliated to the Union, and supply such honorary members with exciseable articles on the same terms as their own members.

By this arrangement, therefore, clubs affiliated to the Union can, by means of the Associate and Pass Cards, enjoy to the full, and without fear of prosecution, all privileges which were sought to be conferred when the system was inaugurated.

You will understand that this explanation is for the guidance of your-self and your committee, and is not intended for publication. The letter referred to follows:

11 Downing Street
May 1875

Dear Sir Harcourt,

With reference to the interview which I had on May 5th with the deputation introduced by you to discuss the position of Working Men's Clubs in regard to excise licences, I have communicated with the Commissioners of Inland Revenue on the subject, and I find considerable difficulty has arisen in the administration of the law relating to it. Along with many bona fide clubs which have been recently established to the great advantage of the working classes, there have also sprung up some which are only public-houses under the name of clubs. The Inland Revenue have spared no pains to distinguish between the true and the false clubs, and appear to have hitherto succeeded in drawing the line between them. But it is a difficult matter, and the Commissioners may claim the consideration of those to whom they may appear severe and exacting, as they are bound to protect the heavily licensed trader as well as the Revenue.

The points to which they particularly look as indicative of bona fides are –

1. That the liquors, etc., sold should be the property of the club

and not of any individual; that they should be supplied to members of the club only, and should be consumed on the premises.

2. That the membership should be real and not nominal; that is to say, that members must be regularly elected, and become thereby sharers in the property of the club.

There seems no reason for refusing the exemption to a club because it admits to honorary membership subscribing members of other bona fide clubs affiliated to the Working Men's Club and Institute Union, and supplies them with liquors on the same terms as its own subscribing members, and I shall be happy to give directions for the adoption of that extension of the rules applied to the clubs.

> I remain,
> Dear Sir Harcourt,
> Yours very faithfully,
> Stafford H. Northcote

This exchange of correspondence was to have the most far-reaching effects within the Union, and, happily, the original letter from Sir Stafford Northcote, written in his own hand (this was written before typewriters had come into general use), still remains in the Union archives, having even survived that disastrous fire in 1978.

Its importance lay in the fact that the associate card became a considerable personal benefit for members whose clubs joined the Union; it gave them something to join the Union *for*, because now a man could join his local club and also visit others in the same area, or even further afield if, say, his work took him to another part of the country. The card also helped to increase the income of the clubs generally, and, from the Union's point of view, there was the extra bonus that the Union now had a basic annual income through the 1s charge levied every time the card was renewed. The membership of the Union's clubs now started to grow rapidly, and so did the Union's income, with the income from associate cards soon outstripping that received in subscriptions and donations. These figures tell the story:

Year	*Number of clubs in Union*	*Income from associate cards*	*Income from subscriptions and donations*
		£	£
1875	not known	3	703
1876	not known	22	1,054
1877	not known	41	1,057
1878	not known	not known	651
1879	not known	65	885
1880	not known	118	603

Year	Number of clubs in Union	Income from associate cards £	Income from subscriptions and donations £
1881	not known	162	372
1882	not known	178	341
1883	not known	188	332
1884	not known	272	388
1885	not known	402	279
1886	not known	498	232
1887	328	606	215
1888	365	705	185
1889	328	1,064	204
1890	384	1,138	338
1891	422	1,188	216
1892	410	1,170	183
1893	421	1,182	175
1894	460	1,080	121
1895	518	1,264	80
1896	571	1,412	45
1897	627	2,314	66
1898	649	1,817	45
1899	701	1,901	44
1900	710	2,324	37
1901	751	2,264	34
1902	808	2,691	33
1903	937	3,337	24
1904	1,002	3,100	19
1905	1,041	3,086	40

5

Although Hodgson Pratt was clearly the man whose work left the most lasting imprint on the Union during the last two decades of the nineteenth century, and whose own ideas were to be so influential, it is important not to underestimate the skill with which he ensured that all those whom Solly had recruited continued to make a contribution until our fledgling had developed sufficient wing-power of its own. This was a very considerable achievement, and the mark of a man who could undoubtedly have risen to great heights in politics, commerce or the trade unions had he so chosen.

We have already seen in the last chapter how he as the Honorary Secretary had taken up much of the administrative burden, incurring his own expenses, and who can doubt that the same man ensured that his own Chairman, Lord Lyttelton, signed that crucial letter to the clubs urging their members to make use of the new system of associate cards? Who can doubt that Hodgson Pratt's hands were also there, carefully guiding the tiller, when the Vice-Chairman, Sir Harcourt Johnstone, went to see Sir Stafford Northcote, always ensuring, like the good civil servant that he had been, that his officers were properly briefed, and that he himself held back? These are the skills that we can see being employed during this crucial period in the Union's growth.

Another of his contributions, which is again less obvious, was that Hodgson Pratt, although himself a man of strong political opinions (as a life-long supporter of the Co-operative Union and the Peace movement), was careful to hold together people of all political persuasions so that the Union itself became truly non-party-political and non-sectarian. It would have been so easy for him to have done otherwise, for those were the years when the trade unions were becoming more powerful, and when many clubs had a strong political leaning, but Hodgson Pratt avoided the temptation, and under his leadership the Working Men's Club and Institute Union became the 'broad church' that it has remained ever since.

Hodgson Pratt would welcome the support of the bishops and even the Archbishop of Canterbury, and then gladly receive a donation from Charles Darwin, author of *The Origin of Species*, whose ideas were so opposed to their own. He would recognize the different contributions that could be made by Liberal or Conservative peers or Members of Parliament, and was careful to ensure that both parties were represented within the Union's leadership. Herbert Praed, who was to become Treasurer of the Union for over thirty years during the period of tremendous growth, was a Conservative Member of Parliament, a guiding spirit in the development of the National Association of Conservative Clubs, and also a banker, an ex-soldier (he had been in the King's Own Scottish Borderers), a magistrate, a Deputy Lieutenant, and a member of many distinguished London clubs like the Carlton, Arthur's, the Turf and the Beefsteak. Pratt's achievement was that he would welcome contributions from people like Praed, and others who had come into the movement at Henry Solly's suggestion, while still carefully guiding the Union towards democracy.

This ability to see the strength in opposites was clearly his own forte; during his first years as Honorary Secretary, the Rt Hon. A. J. Mundella, the Marquis of Lorne, the Duke of Westminster, the Earl of Rosebery and Dean Stanley were the Union Presidents, and one can see from the work that they did for the Union that *someone* was carefully harnessing them; that *someone* could only have been Pratt, for he was in the key position of influence, but you never see his hands move; his own contributions are always restrained, and he ensures – which again is the hallmark of a civil servant – that the President is seen to be taking the initiative. We have already noted that Lord Rosebery sent a donation of £174 to pay off the Union's debts, but how did he know that that was the sum that was needed? And how did he, a future Liberal Prime Minister, holding many public offices, know so well the direction in which the Union was moving? Just read between the lines of Rosebery's speech to our annual meeting in 1875:

> We ought all to be glad and proud of being engaged in maintaining a most important cause. We are acknowledging a most important principle.
>
> The principle upon which the Working Men's Club and Institute Union is based is that working men are to be raised by their own endeavours, and are not to be patronised, and fostered and dandled. All that is to be done for the working men is to be done by themselves. What a man does for himself is worth ten times as much as what can be done for him by anyone else.

Considering that this is my view of the utility of Working Men's Clubs, it may be asked what is the absolute utility of this Union, which is not indeed in itself a club?

This Union is a central authority which guides and supports the spontaneous endeavours of the working men living in provincial towns.

It lets fall the good seed in places where it has not hitherto fallen, and what is even of more importance than this, it embodies the entire experience of the movement from its very foundation, and is, therefore, able to give the best advice to all clubs which may need it.

The influence of this central authority is felt all over the country. Through all the ramifications of the working men's club system you will see the progress that has been made, and which sprung in the first instance from the Central Union.

I believe that there are three requisites for a thoroughly satisfactory system of working men's clubs.

The first is that each club should be altogether free from all vexatious infantile restrictions on the consumption of intoxicating drinks and all similar matters – restrictions which tend to make these institutions moral nurseries rather than clubs intended for the use of the citizens of a great empire.

Secondly, if they are to be a great success they should be self-supporting.

Thirdly, they ought to set before their members some object higher than the mere social object of getting a comfortable place in which to meet. At the same time it will be very easy to aim at too much. From time to time one reads in the papers of persons discoursing to the members of these clubs, and drawing pictures of enlightened miners returning from their underground toil to the consumption of the aesthetic tea or the discussion of the subtleties of *Hamlet* or the mysticism of Greek literature.

I think, therefore, we may put our hands to this good work with confidence and hope; but we must not indeed expect too much at present. I believe that the labour of those that would ameliorate the conditions of the working classes is slower and more imperceptible than that of the insect which raises the coral reef from the bed of the ocean.

There are many who, looking at this slow progress, may fail to see what these Institutes are likely to effect in the future. Our outward display is certainly small. Our daily expenditure is small, but the work we do is great.

I believe that if success in the past, achievement in the present, and the certainty that both will be doubled, or even quadrupled, in the not remote future can influence public favour towards our Institutions, we on this occasion shall not have appealed in vain on behalf of the Working Men's Club and Institute Union.

How true these words ring today! And how certain that the influence of Hodgson Pratt lay behind their expression! Lord

Rosebery alone would not have had that sureness of touch, for he, as President, would only have been expected in those days to make the occasional appearance on behalf of the Union, and yet very little remains in print of Hodgson Pratt's own contribution to the Union, for he was the most modest of men, always taking attention away from himself, writing discreet, succinct minutes that minimized his own contribution to any discussion. B. T. Hall wrote, in a personal memoir at the end of *Our Fifty Years*:

> Of the dry facts of Mr Pratt's life it is difficult to speak. Probably no man has left so deep a mark on national movements, and none cared less for recorded glory or for the usual means of marking public appreciation. Too tolerant and catholic in thought to accept the shibboleths of party, Mr Pratt never felt able to offer himself as a candidate for Parliament. Too diffident and careless of fame to keep even a personal record of work done, actually and often known to excise reference to himself in Journals and Reports, Mr Pratt leaves for possible biographers only a sense of a vast and superhuman activity, of a far-reaching and all-pervading effort for progress, than of small and carefully-ticketed achievements . . .

The theme of Lord Rosebery's speech at that annual meeting was further emphasized by the tone of two resolutions that were passed. The first was proposed by Lord Frederick Cavendish, the Liberal MP and Secretary of State for Ireland who was later murdered in Phoenix Park, and seconded by Sir Harcourt Johnstone (later Lord Derwent), a country squire who also made a great contribution to the Union's progress, as we have seen already, with his personal intervention with Sir Stafford Northcote. Their motion read:

> That Working Men's Clubs and Institutes are calculated not only to diminish excess in the use of intoxicating liquors, but also to promote self-culture and the growth of a healthy public spirit among the mass of the people.

This resolution was supported by Alexander Macdonald. The second was moved by Earl Fortescue and seconded by Sir Henry Cole, and read:

> That there are few social reforms of greater importance to this country than the substitutions of Clubs and Institutes for public houses as places of resort for the recreation and business of the working classes.

As B. T. Hall said of these people of such widely opposed views in *Our Fifty Years*, 'There was not then another possible institution which could have brought these men together under the presidency of Lord Rosebery, supported as they were by Hodgson Pratt, fiery Radical, and Herbert Praed MP, of the Carlton Club.'

The next ten years were to see the Union slowly transformed in the manner that Hodgson Pratt had envisaged, with his own hand clearly guiding the process, making sure that change did not come too quickly, and that the members of the Union did not take over control of its affairs until they were themselves ready to do so. The first thing to be done was to give the Union a broader constitution; this appears for the first time in that Annual Report for 1875 (see Appendix 1), and was to remain in force for over ten years (until the Special General Meeting in 1886 which was to set the seal on Pratt's transformation, turning the Union overnight into a fully democratic organization).

In the previous chaper, we saw how the introduction of associate cards gave the Union financial stability; the other important innovation lay in this new Constitution, for through it 'Representative Members' were brought on to the Council for the first time, working men chosen to represent their clubs, although (as can be seen from Appendix 1) with somewhat limited powers.

Although one can see that in the general sweep of the Union's history, this period between 1876 and 1886 was one of the most important, it is difficult now to trace *who did what* with accuracy, for the minute books do not survive, and even those Annual Reports which were referred to by B. T. Hall when writing *Our Fifty Years* told him very little about the progress that was being made. Just as Hodgson Pratt would delete references to himself from the minutes or the *Journal*, so the equally modest Thomas Paterson would ensure that there were the briefest mentions of his own work in the Annual Reports. 'All the Union workers had the same modesty,' wrote B. T. Hall, adding that in those years the Reports were 'poor and hard and stony soil out of which to dig a personal conception. Yet in them Paterson is always, year by year, speaking at conferences – he was a fine debater – addressing meetings, editing the *Journal* in Pratt's frequent absences – at work for the Union always, and this after a ten or twelve-hour day.'

And yet we know so little about Paterson the man, other than from these comments recorded by his wife, which she contributed as a preface to Paterson's only book, *New Methods of Mental Science*, which was published in 1886, three years after his death:

When the movement for establishing Workmen's Clubs and Institutes was commenced, Thomas Paterson entered into it with energy, devoting most of his leisure time to the duties of Honorary Secretary to the Club first established in Clerkenwell, and to one of the earliest distributive Co-operative Societies, connected with it. In 1866, a series of discussions upon social questions was held by the Working Men's Club and Institute Union, in Exeter Hall, and one of these, when he opened the subject of *The Dwellings of the Working Classes*, excited considerable attention, and led to his being invited to join the Council of the Union. Afterwards, he acted for some time as one of the Honorary Secretaries of the Union, and, for two or three years before his death, as a Vice-Chairman of the Council. He was thus brought into contact with Mr Hodgson Pratt, the late Lord Lyttelton, Mr Stephen Seaward Tayler, Dr W. B. Hodgson and many others well known for their untiring efforts on public work. One of these, Mr C. E. Maurice, thus wrote of him in *The Spectator*, shortly after his death: 'It was in the year 1866 that I first saw Thomas Paterson. He was then reading a paper on the question of the way in which working men could best save money, and, if I remember right, could buy their own homes. I remember my father who was with me was much impressed with Paterson's clearness of statement and with his power of passing from somewhat dry statistics to eloquent appeal. He also said that there was something in Paterson, I think both in his face and way of putting things, that reminded him of John Stuart Mill.' ... He was an intense lover of debate, and it was chiefly his remarkable skill in such contests that first brought him into active life. His speech at a Conference held in 1864 to consider *Why Working People Do Not Attend Church?* deeply interested the Chairman, Dean Stanley, who shortly afterwards invited him and a few of his friends to the Deanery to further discuss the question. One suggestion made by my husband was that visits of working people to Westminster Abbey on Saturday afternoons should be organised. The Dean readily assented, and added that he and Lady Augusta Stanley would themselves guide the parties, and give historical accounts of the Abbey and its monuments. How popular these visits have become is well known, and the present Dean, Dr Bradley, continues them. . . . My husband's evenings were frequently engrossed by meetings of the Council of the Workmen's Peace Association, the Labour Representation League, the Free Libraries' Association, and the Land Tenure Reform Association . . . I should indeed be ungrateful if I did not also record here his readiness at all times to assist in any projects for the benefit of women . . . indeed his views upon the necessity of raising the political and social position of women were so liberal and unprejudiced that they frequently drew down upon him the displeasure, and even the contempt of some of the men with whom he was publicly associated . . .

During those ten years, as Auberon Herbert became more remote, it fell to Pratt and Paterson to guide the movement; they were both Radicals, Pratt from a Unitarian background and Paterson schooled in Calvinism, and their closest ally was undoubtedly Stephen Seaward Tayler, another Unitarian, and of similar modesty, who had been secretary and president of the Southwark Working Men's Club, and served on the Union Council for thirty-five years, chairing the Executive for seventeen years and then holding office as President for another seven years. Tayler was also Treasurer and later President of the Unitarian Society, and became one of the first aldermen on the newly-created London County Council. Like Pratt, he always served the Union on an honorary basis, paying his own expenses, his own income being received through his skills as an engineer; he manufactured the steam launches that travelled up and down the river Thames. Of Tayler's contribution to the Union, B. T. Hall wrote:

> Devoid of red-hot passion, all the aspirations of democracy, of freedom, and of tolerance yet burnt in him with steady brightness – a white light – tempered by a sweet astucity which gave both force and charm to his counsels. An active and vigorous career had left him with leisure for public service, a great understanding of men and things, and a business acumen which proved of invaluable service to our movement. Full of the ideal of his fellow promoters of the Union, he never lost heart because progress was slow. Of an observant and analytical temperament, he was able to detach himself from the present, see the past clearly, and note the change. And what he thus saw gave him hope, and such cheerful optimism as put heart into the ebullient youngsters who, at each occasional check, were plunged into temporary despair ... kept them resolute when baffled, hopeful when frustrated, allayed irritation, slew animosity, and evaporated quarrels – and when one thinks how often other movements have died or suffered from the need of Stephen Tayler's qualities, then it is that one appreciates, in some shallow way, the service which he rendered ...

The developments within the Union over those ten years were to be of lasting importance; we have already seen in the table quoted at the end of the last chapter how the Union's financial fortunes were becoming more stable, and we have noted how working men were now being brought on to the Council, although its chief figures – Pratt, Paterson and Tayler – continued to work unpaid for the Union, travelling to all parts of the country at their own expense.

Pratt travelled through England and Wales, encouraging working men to form their own clubs, and in 1881 he went to Ireland and helped to form the Dublin Working Men's Club; in the north, he helped to develop relationships with the independently formed Manchester Association of Clubs, which was eventually to become integrated within the Union, receiving branch status in 1920. It was during this period, too, that the first attempt was made to open a seaside home – at Margate – though this closed after only two years with a loss of £270, and the Union became embroiled for the first time in legal disputes before the courts.

The first case fought was in 1881, when the steward of the Cyprus Club at Silvertown in the East End of London was convicted of selling intoxicants to a non-member. It was quite clear that the steward had been breaking the law, but the police also prosecuted the Trustees of the Club, who argued that they could not be held responsible if their steward disobeyed his instructions, without their knowledge. At the magistrates' court hearing, the bench accepted the police argument and convicted the Trustees, who then sought the assistance of the Union, which agreed to help the Trustees with their appeal. The appeal to the then Queen's Bench was upheld, the sentence was quashed, and the police were ordered to pay the costs of the appeal.

The second case, which was heard before the Queen's Bench in February 1882, established an important legal principle when Mr Justice Field and Lord Huddlestone reversed a decision of the London stipendiary magistrate, Mr D'Eyncourt, and resolved that the Grosvenor Club and its staff had not broken the law in supplying drinks to its members, because the transaction did not constitute a 'sale', the members being owners of both the club and its property. This case established one of the basic principles of club law.

The Union now began to attract the hostility of the Licensed Victuallers – an animosity that has continued to this day, despite the fact that most of the old free houses are not tied to the same brewers who supply clubs with beer and spirits.

Their campaign began in 1876 with what has become the Victuallers' favourite weapon, the after-dinner speech. It was a Member of Parliament, Mr A. Mills, who started the ball rolling. By 1880, the Victuallers were beginning to feel worried about the growing influence of working men's clubs (which was not surprising since the clubs were now taking some of their trade), and they petitioned Gladstone, who was then Chancellor of the Exchequer, to levy a tax on clubs. The great Liberal statesman, who had once given us a donation, replied that he would consult the Union before making a decision. Hodgson Pratt drafted the reply, and no more was heard of the suggestion.

The following year, another danger appeared: the Burnley Town Commissioners, who had promoted a Bill covering the future government of the Lancashire cotton town, included within it a clause that would give them the power to control and inspect clubs. The Union contacted its friends in Parliament, notably W. T.

Marriott, Henry Broadhurst and Thomas Burt, and the clause was withdrawn.

These moves against the Union taking place made at a time when many internal changes were being made, now that the Union's officers could see that its financial position was becoming stronger, and the administrative workload had reached the point where more paid staff would have to be recruited to assist the honorary officers.

The Union was on the move, in every sense. Even the head office moved. When a massive increase in rent was suggested in respect of 150 Strand, where the Union had been based since its formation in 1862, the Council resolved to take up less expensive premises elsewhere, leasing offices at 31 Southampton Street. Almost coincidentally, the Council seemed to realize that one era was coming to a close and another dawning. Donations and subscriptions were falling, but the Union's income from its member clubs was rising, and although there were many problems to be overcome, they were of a type familiar to those concerned with running voluntary organizations. The *Journal* lost money steadily, £392 in its first year and then £5 a week thereafter; the first seaside home was a failure, with a loss of £270, and the first assistant secretary to be appointed, a Mrs Lawrenson, was dismissed, and found to have embezzled £50. Her successor was no better; he, a young man named J. S. Howell, disappeared with £75.

But there is still a feeling of change in the air. The Union can take such problems in its stride now, and is strong enough to provide leadership for its member clubs.

A barrister, William Minet, joins the Council, and soon thereafter takes charge of the Union accounts, introducing efficient bookkeeping systems for the first time, and providing advice thereon to many member clubs; he drafts model rules for clubs' use, and prepares a pamphlet, *Clubs and How to Start and Manage Them*, providing practical guidance for members. B. T. Hall recalled that Minet 'personally instructed dozens of club secretaries in account keeping, and there must be very many well-governed and prosperous Working Men's Clubs which owe a great measure of their efficiency [to him] . . .'

And then another lawyer, T. F. Hobson, later to become a Fellow of the Society of Antiquaries, a borough councillor in Hampstead and a member of the London County Council, also volunteers to teach book-keeping to club secretaries, and to increase the educational activities of the Union. 'I value Education because it causes discontent,' he tells one Annual Meeting of the Union. 'I believe in an educated democracy, but also in the necessity of a presently discontented democracy.'

With minds like these and men like these, the Union is moving forward. Its next staff appointment proves a great success, with John James Dent becoming the first paid Secretary of the Union since Henry Solly. The Report for 1883 states that the council:

> always desirous that the Union should be associated as closely as possible with the clubs, and truly represent them, endeavoured to find a new Secretary among the officers or members of Clubs. They had much satisfaction in selecting from a large number of candidates Mr J. J. Dent, who had done good service on the committee of an important club (the Eleusis), which, although not affiliated to the Union, has played no small part in the movement. Mr Dent has been known for several years to some members of the Council as a young man of very high personal character and ability who has made disinterested efforts in the cause of progress . . .

Dent was to remain Secretary for ten years, before taking up a Government appointment as Labour Correspondent to the Board of Trade, whereupon he joined the Union Council, becoming Vice-President, and then succeeding Tayler as President in 1909.

As the membership grows, the finances are stabilized and men of high quality take up positions within the Union, that feeling of change is still in the air; the Union is taking a definite shape. Until now, the *Journal* has appeared somewhat erratically, but now the Executive resolves that it shall be published regularly every month, with a permanent editor instead of volunteers. Mark Judge is appointed to the task.

Likewise, the Circulating Library is now an established part of the Union's work, with boxes of books being distributed regularly to clubs, and donations being received for the maintenance of the Library from the Duke of Devonshire and Lord Rothschild. The Gilchrist Trustees send £20 for the purchase of scientific books; Sir Thomas Brassey donates 500 copies of *Work and Wages*, and Lord Rosebery, 200 copies of Albert Smith's *Tour Round the World*. By 1882, the Library is self-financing, and Mr E. S. Pearson is appointed the Union's first Honorary Librarian.

In similar vein, the Union also promotes competitions in Essay Writing, either upon given subjects or in the examination of a selected book. Lord Francis Hervey donates special prizes in this subject, with Hatcham Liberal Club often the winners. In other clubs, there are lectures by distinguished figures in the Church, the Sciences and Literature, such as Dean Stanley, Professor Huxley and Anthony Trollope. B. T. Hall noted:

The form of education which combines with social gatherings was also at full tide. The Duke of Westminster is host for a large party of club men and their wives at Cleveden, Lord John Russell the same at Pembroke Park (a visit highly prized this – to see and speak to the great little man face to face), Dean Stanley invites to a great soiree, and every year to chats and social meetings at the Deanery, the Duke of Westminster also invites to a soiree at Grosvenor House, and in 1883 Lord and Lady Brassey receive a party of a thousand at South Kensington Museum . . .

In athletics, too, the Union is encouraging its membership. Warren Hastings Sands establishes rifle shooting contests, for which Lord Brabazon gives a shield, and Lord Elcho helps to purchase a massive silver trophy. Sir Thomas Brassey donates £25 to a special fund for the promotion of athletics; the Duke of Abercorn presents a swimming trophy.

These years, too, saw continued support from Queen Victoria, the Prince of Wales, the Duke of Cambridge, Lord Rosebery, the Duke of Westminster, Samuel Morley, Sir Anthony Cleasby, Sir Frances Hopwood and the Duke of Devonshire, but that feeling for change was still there, not very far below the surface, as the Union approached its twenty-first birthday. The Annual Report for 1883 had a distinctly prophetic ring:

This organisation has been in existence for 21 years, and may fairly claim to have left its mark upon the history of social progress in England. It has created a new class of institutions, which have more or less directly, through its agency, been established in all parts of the kingdom, and have become increasingly popular with the working classes. These clubs must exercise a large influence in shaping the habits, tastes, and ideas of their members and of the people generally . . . the social and political problems with which the growing Democracy will have to deal are serious. To prepare for their solution we must not depend upon the 'chapter of accidents', but upon enlightened and systematic efforts. These clubs may become in time schools where half-a-million adults learn how best to take part in the great evolution which the next generation or two will witness . . . with the progress of time must come many changes in the little body of men who have done this work from the beginning; but such service will always be needed while human society is constituted as at present. There is no true civilisation, no true and lasting prosperity, unless the condition of the mass of the people steadily improves, not only in material comfort or in security from destitution, but in all that makes life valuable – an opportunity for enjoying the highest kinds of happiness of which God, regardless of class divisions, has made all men capable.

There is no true civilisation where the principle expressed by the words, 'All for each, and each for all', is not that which rules the spirit of the majority. . . .

6

As the Union moved towards democracy, and the great break with its past, one senses, reading B. T. Hall's account of that period, an old regime preparing to hand over the reins with no great reluctance, perhaps realizing that they had all been involved in something more than the development of the Working Men's Club and Institute Union; that they had all taken part in that peaceful process by which Britain somehow managed to progress from the chaos of the Industrial Revolution to the more ordered society that we have today.

Nobody planned it that way. No one political party charted the course of change. Quite often, a Conservative Government would introduce changes that a Liberal predecessor had failed to achieve, and vice versa.

And the process hardly seemed 'peaceful' at the time, with the earliest trade-union pioneers being transported to Australia, and some even facing execution. There were far more serious industrial riots in the last century than we have known in this. The Army and the police were frequently in violent conflict with strikers, notably in the London docks and the coalfields of South Wales, and there were some activists who thought a revolution was just round the corner. Instead, Britain adapted as Parliament responded to this period of vigorous political debate and the growing calls for constitutional change. Acts of social reform quickly followed each other through the House of Commons, to be met by louder calls for further advances and a wider democracy.

This extension of politics, party politics, into every corner of the nation's life was, naturally enough, reflected within the Working Men's Club and Institute Union, even though Solly and then later Hodgson Pratt had both discouraged anything that smacked of political division. As early as 1865, Solly had argued:

It is a universally-recognised and most important principle that this Union, all Working Men's Clubs, and the whole movement generally, must not only be rigidly kept free from religious or political bias, but must scrupulously avoid becoming in any shape or way, organisations for promoting political or theological purposes. . . .

And then, in 1876, Pratt had written in the *Workmen's Club Journal* (forerunner of the present *Journal* – see p. 131):

Political questions which involve the *personal* merits of individuals and mere party squabbles should be avoided . . . we must learn to consider great public questions apart from names and war cries, apart from predilections against this or that man . . .

But this was a tide they could not stop, as we learn from the researches of Stan Shipley, author of *Club Life and Socialism in Mid-Victorian London* (published by the Journeyman Press and the London History Workshop Centre, 1983), and John Taylor, who wrote *From Self-Help to Glamour: The Working Man's Club 1860–1972* (History Workshop, 1972). They both had access to early socialist archives containing early Club and Institute Union papers that are not in the Union's own records, and I have referred to both their pamphlets in writing this chapter. Their researches do explain part of the background to the sudden upheavals within the Union in a way that even B. T. Hall could not, for by the time he came to compile *Our Forty Years* in 1912 the Union's minute books had disappeared.

There were many Radical clubs in London, particularly in the East End, and B. T. Hall noted that there were, at different times, calls for an East End Radical Union of clubs, and then for a Radical Union for the whole of London, which would have been party-political in a way that even the Conservative clubs were not.

One of the most strongly political clubs was the Borough of Hackney Club, whose premises were often used for party gatherings. In the *Workmen's Club Journal* for 2 September 1876, there was a report of one meeting at the club called 'to protest against the action of Her Majesty's Government with regard to the atrocious barbarities of the Turks in Bulgaria'. Speakers at the meeting included Thomas Mottershead of the Labour Representation League, who was also Secretary of the London Patriotic Club, and a Mr Giles, who 'in the course of his speech read Victor Hugo's thrilling appeal to Europe'. When the members of the Borough of Hackney Club visited the Walthamstow Club in February 1877, the *Workmen's Club Journal* reported that they

 . . . marched into Walthamstow with their brass band and gigantic banners flying, on which were inscriptions expressing the advanced political opinions known to distinguish the men of Hackney . . . it was a sight to see the 350 members gallantly plunging through the mud and mire everywhere prevalent at this season, but nowhere so prominent as in the roads near Markhouse Common . . .

This is all put into a wider context by Stan Shipley in *Club Life and Socialism in Mid-Victorian London*:

> . . . what one finds in the London of the 1870s is a small but influential group of working men, holding strategic positions in the life of the Clubs and the West End trade societies, promoting one another as speakers, joining together in the debate of social issues, and banding together on political issues as they arose. One finds these men playing a proselytising role in any number of metropolitan organisations, acting under a variety of different titles. Their fraternal base was the Manhood Suffrage League, where most of them can be found at one time or another in the years from 1875 to 1881. But they were ready and anxious to urge their views anywhere. Some of these men had arrived at a self-consciously socialist position well before 1881 . . . the Manhood Suffrage League was an intellectual meeting place for boot and shoe makers, tailors and cabinet makers, and all sorts of artizans . . .

All this political activity was to lead in time to the formation of the Social Democratic Federation, through which H. M. Hyndman and Karl Marx exercised their influence on the early Labour movement; to the birth of the Fabian Society, which brought Sidney and Beatrice Webb and George Bernard Shaw to positions of public influence; and, later still, to the coming-together of many different societies in various parts of the country to form the Independent Labour Party. At the time of which we are writing, however, all these movements were fragmented; there was the whiff of political change in the air, without it having as yet taken its later form.

The Working Men's Club and Institute Union itself was in the curious position of still *appearing* to be the kind of organization that Solly had envisaged, while its leadership was slowly changing with the times.

Hodgson Pratt, who had gently steered the Union forward, resigned as Chairman of the Council in 1884 on the grounds of ill-health (he had to have an operation for removal of cataract), although he went on to become President of the Union from 1885 to 1902. In his last Annual Report as Chairman, Pratt predicted that the Union would become self-governing within four years, but *from the outside* the Union still seemed unchanged. That same Annual Report for 1884 stated that Sir Thomas Brassey was the President, and there was the usual formidable list of Vice-Presidents:

Archbishop of Canterbury
Duke of Argyll
Duke of Devonshire
Duke of Westminster
Earl of Derby
Earl Fortescue
Earl Wemyss
Bishop of Carlisle
Bishop of London
Viscount Cranbrook
Lord Ebury
Lord Harris
Lord Lyttelton
Lord Mount Temple
Sir Stafford Northcote, MP
Sir Charles Dilke, MP
James Stansfeld, MP
W. H. Smith, MP
A. J. Mundella, MP
Acton S. Ayrton, MP

Dean of Westminster
Sir John Lubbock
Hon. G. C. Brodrick
Miss Anna Swanwick
Matthew Arnold
Samuel Bowly
Rev. H. G. De Bunsen
Thomas Burt, MP
Frederic Harrison
J. R. Holland, MP
Thomas Hughes, QC
Col. E. H. Kennard, MP
F. D. Mocatta
W. Neill
George Palmer, MP
Hodgson Pratt
P. A. Taylor, MP
W. T. M'Cullagh Torrens, MP
Professor Tyndall, FRS
Forbes Watson, MP

All these distinguished figures were ex-officio members of the Union Council, although they were not expected to attend its meetings. The Council also included thirty-six subscribers, elected by the members, plus a further ten nominated by those London clubs that were paying not less than 5s a year to the Union. B. T. Hall commented:

Five of these Councillors formed a quorum, evidence that of the 46 members few attend, and that the meetings of the Council are small. Unhappily the minutes of the Council between 1863 and 1883 have been lost. How or when no-one living appears to be able to say. The loss is a considerable one, and must prevent the telling of a full story. The clubs hold monthly delegate meetings, at the Union office, at which scarcely any provincial and not more than half the London clubs were represented, to advise the Council, but beyond nominating the members of the Council (increased from seven to ten in 1883) had no power . . . it is easy to see that the members of the inferior body would itch and that some conflict between the lower and upper chambers was inevitable.

The Union, if it were neither wealthy nor powerful or coherent, was an established organisation. It did what it could in the matter of physical and mental culture amongst its clubs and their members.

It organised Conferences on 'Book-keeping', 'Registration Under the Friendly Societies Acts' etc. Its Circulating Library was appreciated and made full use of from the first. It held Examinations in History (the first prize in 1884 being won by W. Johnson of Bedworth, now MP for that district), and in Essay Writing. It held Debates for prizes, organised Saturday Afternoon Visits and Excursions, and provided Lectures. In Games and Athletics, there were Contests in Rifle Shooting (this must always have been a sore thing with Hodgson Pratt), Drilling, Swimming, Rowing, Cricket, Billiards, Whist and Chess. An Annual Sports Meeting was also held. The President (Sir Thomas Brassey) has an annual soiree. In 1883 it is held at South Kensington, and Lord Rosebery is present and makes a short speech. This occasion was favoured also with the presence of the Maori King and his Prime Minister. There is also an Annual Outing; in this year to Normanhurst, Sir Thomas Brassey's seat, at which Lord Houghton (once Monckton Milnes, poet and politician), and M. Waddington, the French Ambassador, addressed the assembled clubmen and their wives. The President pays £150 towards the cost of this outing. . . .

It all seemed so staid and conventional, so ordered, and, dare one say it, so *middle-class*. Whatever descriptive phrase one uses, it is clear that this was not a conventional *working*-class organization. And it certainly did not reflect the Radical and Liberal clubs that were being formed all over the country; indeed, there was hardly any real contact with clubs outside London, other than through the introduction of the associate cards. District unions had been formed in Kent, Manchester, Worcestershire, Suffok and Hampshire, but they had not been incorporated within the Union as a whole. And even as late as 1883, only 106 clubs responded to the annual request for particulars of their organization.

An analysis of those returns shows that the average membership was 164, and most of them seemed to be institutes rather than clubs – 83 per cent of the clubs had libraries, and 40 per cent of them arranged lectures for members. In a third of these clubs, there were provident societies of different kinds: penny banks; clothing, money, goose, boot, blanket, loan, coal and sick clubs; friendly, temperance and building societies – all the different kinds of savings clubs that helped working men to put money aside for future needs.

By the 1880s the Working Men's Club and Institute Union had become a solid, respectable institution. It brought together clubs *for* the working classes, rather than *of* the working classes – and therein lay the demand for change. There are no surviving records to tell us who voiced these demands, although it is clear enough from the history of the period where they were coming from, and it is clear, too, that the demands became so constant that the Council reached the conclusion in 1883 that a Conference ought to be held to discuss the matter. Earlier that year, the *Journal* had been revived after a five-year absence and in the issue preceding the conference the following comment appeared in an editorial:

> The question as to the representation of the clubs is a serious one. There seems to be a feeling, which we must all admit is well founded, that the clubs have not sufficient voice in the management of the Union's affairs. Certainly the number of representative members on the Council – ten – does seem very small in proportion to the maximum number of which the Council may consist. It certainly seems but right that the clubs should elect a larger number of members as representatives to the Council . . .

The Conference was held on 10 November 1883 in the hall of the St James and Soho Club at 39 Gerrard Street, London W1. One of the two new 'Honorary Secretaries', Warren Hastings Sands,* took the chair, which seems to have been a strange arrangement, for Stephen Seaward Tayler, who had succeeded Hodgson Pratt as Chairman of the Council, was present at the meeting, and participated in the discussion.

The meeting seems to have begun with one delegate, Mr Fletcher Pape from the Commonwealth Club, reading a discussion paper suggesting 'federalization'. He thought that 'the Clubs of each district should group themselves together and elect delegates to a district delegate meeting, and from these district meetings the central body should be formed.'

This proposal clearly touched a chord because Mark Judge, a member of the Council who had been partly responsible for reviving the *Journal*, went on to move a formal resolution:

> That the time has now arrived for making the Club and Institute Union in fact what it has hitherto been only in name, i.e. a Union of Clubs and Institutes, and that a committee be appointed to draw up and report upon a scheme to an adjourned meeting of this conference. The new Rules not to be exclusive on social, political or religious grounds.

It was B. T. Hall's view that the last sentence in that motion probably reflected 'the seething tumult of violent political and religious differences which in those years bubbled into every phase of social life', and it certainly seems to be a form of words chosen to satisfy those members of the Council who might have thought the

---

* Ever since the removal of Solly in 1867, the Union had elected 'Honorary Secretaries' whose purpose was 'to lighten the labours of the Chairman of the Council'. Initially, there were three Honorary Secretaries; now there were two – plus a full-time paid Secretary in J. J. Dent.

motion a little threatening. In the discussions that followed, speaker after speaker talked of the principle of 'patronage' being wrong, and at one point Stephen Seaward Tayler dwelled on the difficulty of devising a constitution that would allow for full representation of the clubs outside London. (There were only two provincial clubs represented at the Conference – Arnold in Nottinghamshire and Kidderminster.) When the resolution was put to the meeting, it was passed. A committee was then formed to draw up a new constitution. It comprised sixteen members with the two Honorary Secretaries, Warren Hastings Sands and T. A. Nash, and the full-time Secretary, Dent.

As is so often the case in situations like these, the call for change went far beyond the initial proposal – or the compromise suggested by the Council. In another editorial in the *Journal*, for 18 January 1884, it was admitted that 'when the Conference was first proposed, there was no idea that it would result in such great changes as now seem likely to take place . . .'

Some years were to pass before the Union found itself with a settled constitution; flaws were found in each new arrangement; the demands for even greater democracy grew, and all this was no doubt accompanied by fairly strong argument and counter-argument. First, the Council came up with their own report – only to find that the membership preferred a minority report proposed by Fletcher Pape and Mark Judge. This was duly ratified by a Special General Meeting in 1884, and then another Special General Meeting was held two years later. Eventually, it was decided that it would be better to adopt a totally different constitution altogether, registering the Union as a 'Society' under the Industrial and Provident Societies Act.

In 1884, the Union consisted of Corporate Members, Honorary Members, Associates and Associate Clubs and Institutes. Corporate Members were those clubs which subscribed a halfpenny per club member per month to Union funds. Members were individuals who subscribed not less than 5s annually. Associates were club members who paid 1s per annum for the associate card. Associate Clubs and Institutes were clubs which paid not less than 3s to the Union. Honorary Members were elected by the Council. Each corporate member, or associate club, having between 50 and 200 subscribing members or holders of the associate card was entitled to elect one member of the Council; they could elect two members with over 200 subscribers, and three with over 500. Any provincial club paying not less than 10s a year could elect one member. This arrangement, untidy though it was, gave the Union its first elected Council in 1884:

Name of Club	*Representatives*
Alliance	Charles Temple
Boro' of Finsbury	Edward Morton
Battersea Liberal	Charles B. Finch
Barnes Artisans	C. F. Parker
Bryanston	T. C. Collet and J. W. Rodaway
Carlyle	David Hart and A. N. Hennessey
Camden and Kentish Town	H. A. Elwood
Cobden	J. S. Brown, Emmanuel Hopes and William Mahoney
Commonwealth	Fletcher Pape and William Westall
Cromwell	Edward Fulcher
Devonshire	E. C. Cleaver
East London	E. Woodfield
Enterprise	John Heasman
Hackney Wick	J. Dunton
Hammersmith	J. O'Callaghan
Heddington (Wiltshire)	Rev. F. Du Boulay
Loughborough	Edward H. Smith
London Nelson	James Louis Cain
London Patriotic	Henry A. Fuller
Morley (Yorkshire)	William Wright
North London	W. F. L. Bennett and R. W. Woods
New Clifden Social	C. Maddock
Park Town	J. Kellett and T. Foreman
Primrose	J. Draper
St James and Soho	W. Morgan and W. Fritz
St Mark's, Grosvenor Sq.	A. R. Pyle
St Pancras	H. Baker
St Paul's	J. B. Jones
Tower Hamlets Radical Club	H. Davis and J. C. Mellish
Tower Hamlets Radical Assn	Alfred Foster
United Radical	Edwin Dorrell and W. Thomas
Vauxhall Bridge	J. T. Wadham

In addition to these elected members of the Council, there were also twenty-four members elected from amongst the subscribers. These were:

E. R. Blatchley	W. Minet	A. J. Spencer
W. Digby	T. A. Nash	Stephen S. Tayler
R. Edgcumbe	Hodgson Pratt	Capt. Verney, RN
T. Fishbourne	Alfred Preston	Frederick Verney
A. Heward	E. S. Pearson	H. J. Van Laun
Rev. S. D. Headlam	Mrs Paterson	D. Walker
Mark Judge	T. Pagliardini	George Winch
C. E. Maurice	W. H. Sands	Rev. Thornhill Webber

Initially, that 1884 constitution also included provision for all those distinguished Vice-Presidents – but they were swept away in 1886 when the second Special General Meeting was held (see Appendix 2, which gives details of the 1886 constitution). That year, the Honorary Secretaries disappeared as well. But still there remained within the Union that uneasy combination of clubmen and subscribers; of those who actually helped to run clubs and those who thought that clubs were good for the working classes, a contradiction that had lain at the heart of the Union since its formation nearly a quarter of a century before. That was to be resolved in 1889, but not before the Union was to find itself deeply embroiled in all the turmoils that were going on in the world outside.

As we have already seen, there was a strong movement of radical opinion running through the London clubs. In *From Self-Help to Glamour*, John Taylor put it thus:

> There is no doubt that the new-found independence of the clubs, when working men began to run them, was itself a stimulus to political activity. These were truly workers' clubs – self-governing, self-expressing, and increasingly class-conscious. The institutions of the Victorian establishment were vigorously attacked: the Church of England, the monarchy and the Tory party coming in for a full measure of the clubmen's fire, and in the war of Capital and Labour the most advanced of the clubs were not afraid of taking sides. Nor was the politics stemming from the clubs a mere collection of slogans. Political education was highly sought after, and most clubs regularly engaged lecturers to expound upon the controversial topics of the day . . .

And it was these very same clubs – the Commonwealth Club, the London Patriotic Club, the United Radical Club among them – that were now finding representation on the Union Council. Often they called themselves 'Radical' clubs, but those that linked themselves together through the Federation of Metropolitan Radical Clubs were well to the left of the Liberal Party, and were starting to link up with the Social Democratic Federation and the other socialist societies that were to coalesce in the formation of the Labour movement. Even the Union's own *Journal* started to reflect this spirit as the London working men's clubs of the 1880s began to acquire a reputation for atheism, a 'German element' (no doubt a reference to Karl Marx and other émigrés), republicanism, and attacks upon the orthodoxies of the State.

Queen Victoria celebrated her Golden Jubilee in 1887, and this gave the radicals an opportunity to put forward their views. The

West Kensington Park Radical Club presented a lecture entitled, *The Queen's Jubilee, or Fifty Years of Flunkeyism and What It Has Cost the People*. The Political Secretary of the West Marylebone United Club observed in the *Journal*:

> A schoolfellow of his wrote the name of the Prince of Wales as the Prince of Whales; although laughing at the time, he had since considered that his companion was not, perhaps, so far wrong, after all inasmuch as Royalty is very fishy, and, although princes may not be whales, they certainly are sharks . . .

The John Bright Club in Paddington reported that its Political Committee had passed the following Resolution:

> This Council protests against the expenditure of any sum by the School Board for London for an illuminated address to be presented to the Queen, and would suggest to the members of that body that a more practical and honest method of displaying their loyalty would be to subscribe for the same among themselves, and not to wantonly waste the ratepayers' money, which is collected for a more praiseworthy object than to obtain promotion for flunkeys or aid the spread of flunkeyism . . .

This same club, the John Bright, was proud of its radicalism, and announced in another issue of the *Journal* that:

> There has not been a move on the political chess-board but what we have been in it – the abolition of the House of Lords, opposition to Royal Grants, votes of sympathy and condolences, attendances at Radical Conferences and assistance to Skye Crofters, Affiliation to the Radical Federation, People's League, Municipal Reform League etc . . .

The members of the Star Radical Club in Herne Hill went even further. It was reported in the *Journal* in 1888 that they were committed to:

1. Home Rule for Ireland
2. Manhood suffrage
3. Women's suffrage
4. Abolition of the present House of Lords
5. Dis-establishment of the Church
6. Repeal of the land laws
7. Expenses of contested elections to be thrown on Consolidated Fund or rates
8. Triennial Parliaments
9. Enfranchisement of leaseholds
10. Free and higher education for the masses
11. Railways to be controlled by the State

12. Legislation for the masses and not for the classes
13. Right of meeting in Trafalgar Square

These were not isolated examples. Many working men's clubs of that period were now pushing to the fore of what was being proclaimed as the class struggle. The United Radical Club, which was among those represented on the Council of the Union, had its banner unfurled by Charles Bradlaugh, and the *Journal* commented that the banner

> . . . proved to be in elegance of design and workmanship, one of which the members may be justly proud. The obverse side bears the name of the club and an artistically conceived emblem of its political and social nature, whilst the reverse displays a figure of Liberty trampling upon the prostrate form of Despotism, with his shattered shackles and his minions, Priestcraft and Privilege . . . the colouring is striking, but well-toned and the whole is mounted in rich, appropriate style . . .

Banners like these were held as the clubmen took to the London streets, marching from club to club on a Sunday proclaiming their beliefs, and seeking to influence the communities in which they lived. Here are four more examples, taken from the pages of the Union's *Journal*:

> *West Marylebone Liberal and Radical Club* . . . on Sunday morning great efforts were made in the neighbourhood of Paddington Green to bring together as many people as possible for the purpose of augmenting the demonstration in Trafalgar Square . . . the procession moved away in the direction of the Square, and marched along as orderly and as comfortable as possible, until the Crimean statue in Pall Mall was reached. It was then noticeable that a strong body of foot and mounted police was drawn across the road, who refused to allow us to proceed further. Nothing daunted, the procession pushed forward, only to be driven back by the blows from the batons of the so-called 'guardians of the peace'. After a severe tussle, during which blows were freely exchanged on both sides, the police wantonly charged the inoffensive bystanders who stood about the pavement. . . .

> *West Southwark Liberal and Radical Club* . . . went, preceded by our band, to join the Lambeth Progressive Club, after which we followed the South London clubs on their way to Trafalgar Square; but on reaching Bridge Street, seeing the way blocked by the police, we determined on going to Hyde Park, to avoid a breach of the peace; but we were charged by the police, brutally maltreated and scattered in all directions, maimed and wounded. Our banner was torn from us, and the bearers truncheoned in a most merciless manner. The flag was at length rescued by Mr William Rhodes, of the latter club, and will be returned to the rightful owners in an honourable and orderly manner. . . .

East Finsbury Club . . . came in for a good share of the hard knocks, when we were stopped by the police at the top of St Martin's Lane. I am glad to say that the members stuck to the banner as long as they could, and they did not give way till a great many were wounded. I am very pleased to have to state that half of the banner was recaptured by one of the member's wives and Mrs Besant. . . .

John Bright Club . . . writing as one who accompanied the Western contingent – and now nursing a fractured arm in consequence – words utterly fail to convey a description of the savage and wanton brutality enacted by the police. The scene at Waterloo Place, at the foot of the Crimean Statue – a spot to be long remembered by members of the West-end clubs – baffles description . . .

All these quotations from the *Journal* of the Working Men's Club and Institute Union referred to a major rally held on 13 November 1887, which became known as 'Bloody Sunday', and the North Camberwell Radical Club subsequently passed a resolution declaring that

This meeting . . . denounces the infamous tyranny of the Tory Government, and the cowardly attacks made today by the police and military, acting under orders, on crowds of unarmed Englishmen, peacefully exercising their legal rights of procession, and endeavouring to hold an orderly meeting. . .

All of this was a far cry from the eager preachings of the Rev. Henry Solly, the quiet diplomacy of Hodgson Pratt, and the concerned lectures of the Dean of Westminster or the Earl Rosebery – and there were moments in the 1880s when it seemed quite possible that this wave of political fervour would overwhelm the Union. The first touch-point came in 1885, by which time the Union had its own elected Council, although Lord Brassey continued to be the Union President and all those distinguished Vice-Presidents were still holding office. The Radical clubs were deeply embroiled in two big issues of the day – the demands for Irish Home Rule, and the refusal of the House of Commons to let the atheist Charles Bradlaugh take his seat after he had been elected MP for Northampton. The newly-elected members of the Union Council thought this was a matter in which the Union itself should take a lead, as well it might have done but for the calming influence of Hodgson Pratt. B. T. Hall, who came to know many of those involved in what soon became a major political crisis for the Union, commented thus in *Our Fifty Years*:

Pratt . . . took the chair at most meetings, and, even where difference was most acute, it is certain that the love and affection all bore him assisted in giving peace, if not harmony, to these strenuous times. How strenuous they were: how fiercely men thought, and how rudely they spoke; how intolerance moved all classes, it is difficult in these gentler and more tolerant days to recall. New ideas sprang into the field and battered at old custom. The workers were just enfranchised, and iconoclastic. The Irish Question split every class of society. The refusal of the House of Commons to allow Mr Bradlaugh to take his seat, stirred the workmen of London to fury. There was a new cleavage, violence of thought and speech were normal, and the men who took a middle course were like to be buffeted by both sides. It was for the Union a difficult and a troublesome time. . . .

The Bradlaugh incident was perhaps the most serious of all. At the Council held on 7 April 1885 a proposal was made by Mr Emmanuel Hopes, of the John Bright Club, that the name of Mr Charles Bradlaugh be added to the list of Vice-Presidents, and in spite of the opposition of Hodgson Pratt and such influential speakers as W. H. Sands, T. A. Nash, W. Minet and T. F. Hobson, supported as they were by H. Fuller, the resolution was carried by a majority of one! Disaster was prophesied by the opponents of the proposal, and things swiftly happened.

T. A. Nash resigned his Hon. Secretaryship, Lord Lyttelton (son of the pioneer), the Duke of Westminster, Wyndham Portal and others resigned the Vice-Presidency. Thus led, the Worcestershire Branch or District Union seceded bodily (Lord Lyttelton was its Chairman), and the Hampshire District Union, of which Mr Portal was chairman, did the same – giving as reason their inability to send delegates to meetings of the Council. Worcestershire Union had 47 clubs, Hampshire 16. The gallant Squires of Kent, headed by Lord Harris, were equally vexed, and they and their district (numbering about 30 clubs) also withdrew, although surreptitiously later, in 1888. In 1886 Mr Bradlaugh, becoming aware of all the havoc wrought in his name, wrote to Lord Brassey withdrawing it. 'My only desire is, and has been, to befriend the clubs,' he wrote. 'I shall be as ready to help in my poor way without holding office.'

His 'poor way' was to assist clubs by a Lecture given gratuitously in the largest hall obtainable. To secure attendance at such, tickets at one shilling, sixpence and threepence were eagerly purchased, and £50 easily raised. In such a manner Bradlaugh had assisted very many clubs . . . looking back it can be agreed that the election was unwise, and that they who withdrew because of it were wrong. But it offered an illustration of the difference of attitude of the workmen members, and that of others, and there can be no doubt that the treatment accorded to a man, whom many thousands of workmen believed to be (as many yet believe he was), the greatest and best, did colour and embitter subsequent proceedings, as did the attitude of Mr Hodgson Pratt towards the Trafalgar Square riots and Bloody Sunday . . .

The risk of an incident such as this causing a split in the Union diminished with the decision to broaden the Constitution still further. The removal of any provisions for electing Vice-Presidents also dealt with the immediate problem, that of using such a device to promote 'political' candidates.

And then once the Union had chosen to register as a 'society' under the Industrial and Provident Societies Act in 1889, and to make every club a shareholder, the risk diminished further still – because the Union was at last in the control of its members, and not under the influence of any one group, be they the early aristocrats or the later radicals, who each in turn had seemed anxious to turn the Union this way or that.

Democracy was the prize that so many had been searching for; it was also the guarantee that the Union would endure.

7

The Union was lucky to have J. J. Dent as its General Secretary during that period of political upheaval. It was the one period in the Union's history when it could so easily have gone in any one of many different directions, and a steady pair of hands was needed in charge of day-to-day administration. Dent had those.

Like so many of the pioneers of the Labour and trade union movements, Dent came from a solid working-class background. He was born in Northampton in 1856. His father and grandfather were bricklayers, and this was the trade Dent turned to himself, having had little formal education. He became an assistant labourer, a bricklayer's labourer and then a bricklayer before coming down to London in his teens and plunging into Radical politics. He joined the Eleusis Club, becoming its secretary, and, according to B. T. Hall, 'no Liberal or Radical movement was possible in the old Borough of Chelsea without the assistance of "young Dent"'. In later years, Dent was required to give up politics when he became a senior civil servant; this was in 1893, when he was appointed Labour Correspondent at the Board of Trade, thus ending his period as the Union's paid General Secretary; but this was not the end of his work for the Union.

On giving up the secretaryship, he became a member of the Union Executive and then Vice-President, succeeding Stephen Seaward Tayler as President in 1909. Dent retained other interests that were in similar vein, if not party-political; he supported the housing co-operative movement and the Working Men's College, and later became secretary of the Hodgson Pratt Memorial Ltd, a trust which was set up after Pratt's death in 1907 to commemorate his work through organizing an annual Hodgson Pratt Memorial Lecture, Hodgson Pratt Essay Prizes, travelling scholarships and a memorial scholarship to Ruskin College.

Although himself a natural radical, and, incidentally, a strong personal supporter of Bradlaugh, Dent was also a patient, practical man, who realized that he had to help the Union steer a middle course, and it was this quality that he brought to its counsels during that very difficult period of conflict. He saw that the Union had to work with the Radical clubs without being taken over by them, and equally he understood that it was his role to persuade them to make an effective contribution *from within*. With the support of Hodgson Pratt as President and Stephen Seaward Tayler as Chairman of the Executive, Dent managed to steer the Union through the crisis that followed the Bradlaugh incident; it was as a result of his diplomacy that most of the clubs that seceded eventually came back, and the Radical clubs of the East End – who had formed an East End Radical Union and then the Metropolitan Radical Federation – rejoined the Union.

Dent's other great contribution was the organizational one of giving the Union the basic structure that has survived to the present day: the constitution that was agreed in 1889 and registered under the Industrial and Provident Societies Act was sound and effective in its simplicity, and enabled the Council to link all the member clubs firmly within the Union. The new rules required each club to hold at least one share in the Union. The shares each had a 5s value, and clubs could hold one for each hundred members, with a maximum of four. A similar sum, that is between 5s and £1, also had to be paid annually to the Union. Of itself, this compelled the Union to keep proper membership records, which was something that had not been done before. Estimates of the Union's membership had varied widely, both in Solly's day and later, but now the figures had to match the Union's income – and that meant accuracy! At once the figures changed. A membership of 543 clubs had been claimed in the Annual Report for 1885 – in 1887 the real figure turned out to be 328. Of these, nearly half were in London.

The Union's growth naturally gave it enemies. The most vicious were the Licensed Victuallers. But they were not the only ones. The leaders of our movement frequently found themselves opposed by Temperance supporters, and sometimes even by individual members of the police force. Our relationship with the Law has mostly been friendly, but there have been exceptions. Such a case occurred in 1885, when some policemen tried to enter the Hatcham Liberal Club and to obtain drink – unsuccessfully. The policemen responsible were themselves prosecuted, and subsequently dismissed from the force. This incident prompted the Union to call a conference to discuss the way in which visitors could be recognized, and clubs protected, when associate cards were used; the result was the introduction of Visitors' Books, which are in use to this day. In another case, the Trustees of the Starch Green Radical Club were sued in an attempt to make them personally liable for the sum of £42, which was the value of a delivery of goods to the club. At the request of the Union, T. F. Hobson defended the Trustees and secured a judgment that there was no personal liability, and that any liability lay against the assets of the club when it was registered under the Friendly Societies Act.

By this time, the Union was pledging itself to give legal advice to any member club that found itself in difficulties; this advice was largely given by Hobson, a young barrister who had recently moved to London, and who had been introduced to the Union by Minet. They were close friends, and became joint editors of the *Journal*, and besides giving their legal opinions, also helped many clubmen learn the intricacies of accountancy.

Minet, who was also a barrister, was the first to become involved in the Union's affairs. He had been Treasurer of the Bryanston Club since 1875, and then became its Chairman, although he continued to keep the club's accounts for some forty years.

Of William Minet, B. T. Hall wrote in one of his profiles of the 'Men of the Movement', which first appeared in the *Journal* and were then published as an appendix to *Our Fifty Years*:

> ...many a Club Secretary, blessing the simple yet comprehensive Union system of Club book-keeping, will learn with pleasure that they owe the ease and accuracy of their work to him. He it was who designed the account books which have brought success to Clubs and pride to secretaries. He counts it his greatest glory to have shown Clubs how to keep their accounts regularly, to have been the architect of that edifice of regular and systematic work which enables the Clubs of the Union to compare with any business organisation. He is keen on Co-operation, was once the Secretary of a Co-operative Mineral Water Company (which did not succeed), and has been since its beginning a warm advocate and practical helper of the Co-operative Builders...

Minet, who first became a member of the Union Council in 1881, also helped to draft the Model Rules for Clubs, and such pamphlets as *The Duties of a Club Steward*, and *Clubs and How to Start Them*. Outside his work for the Union he was a philanthropist, giving Myatt's Fields and the Minet Free Library to the people of Camberwell, although always a man of great modesty, reluctant to talk about himself, or to play any part in public affairs. His friend Hobson, however, although equally reticent in many ways, became a skilled orator and local politician.

Hobson had been born in 1858, and educated at King's College, London, and New College, Oxford, before studying in Germany and France. He was called to the bar by the Inner Temple in 1884, and practised on the North-Eastern Circuit. From 1886 to 1908, he served in the Inns of Court Rifle Corps, retiring with the rank of major, but he remained fiercely radical, like so many of the men then active in the Union. Of him, B. T. Hall wrote:

> Time has not withered, nor many disappointments staled, his fidelity in this respect, and he is as 'red hot' now as on the day he left New College to face the world. To him discontent is not only divine, but a primal necessity to the workman . . .

This, then, was the way in which the Union was developing. In the early days, there had been that strong Unitarian influence beneath that aristocratic veil; then the more radical leaders emerged, with a background in the Co-operative movement and in local government, and now the Union was fusing all these influences together and, largely under the guidance of Dent, was becoming a much more solid institution, providing services and advice to its members on all the problems they faced daily in starting and managing clubs, and exercising a much quieter form of leadership. With the growth of its own democracy, the Union started to stabilize, and to develop an identity of its own, as the number of member clubs grew steadily from 328 in 1887 to 627 ten years later, and then, 1,445 by 1911 and 2,207 by 1921. When clubs ran into trouble, the Union would now fight on their behalf – and, even more important than that, would pass on to the other clubs in the Union the lessons learned.

Sometimes, as in the cases concerning the Hatcham Liberal Club and the Starch Green Radical Club, the Union's work would be mentioned in the press. There would be the occasional *cause célèbre*. When the London stipendiary magistrate Mr Curtis Bennett refused to issue a summons against a club steward for 'withholding' the moneys belonging to a club, the Union went to the High Court and secured an order of *mandamus* requiring him to do otherwise. But, mainly, it was the quiet, painstaking work of men like Dent, Minet and Hobson – and then, later, B. T. Hall – which enabled member clubs to cope with difficult clauses in leases, the licensing laws, tax officers, or local magistrates showing little sympathy for clubs.

The growth of democracy throughout the Union meant that there were now clubmen taking office in their clubs without necessarily having had any training in book-keeping, accountancy, bar management, employment law, tax law, or the basic principles underlying the purchase and sale of goods. These new club officers

were working men who may have learnt a trade or skill, but had
rarely been given any kind of managerial responsibility, and, more
often than not, had received only a limited education. Even more
than before, the Union now began to play an important role in the
education of the ordinary working man. But this was not education
of the kind envisaged by the Rev. Henry Solly, with scholarly classes
on philosophy or classical literature; this was much more serious
stuff – the real, practical education of teaching men to understand
a balance sheet, to know how they had to negotiate with architects
and builders, or to deal with brewers, so that they could become
effective clubmen.

One has only to visit the clubs of Britain to see how successful
this has been. Years later, George Orwell wrote of the northern
clubs in his book *The Road to Wigan Pier*:

> The English working class . . . have a wonderful talent for organisa-
> tion. The whole trade union movement testifies to this; so do the ex-
> cellent working men's clubs – really a sort of glorified co-operative pub,
> and splendidly organised – which are so common in Yorkshire.

What Orwell said of those clubs was true of so many elsewhere,
and it was partly the influence of the Union and partly the sheer
challenge of being given the job to do that made so many working
men good clubmen.

With these kinds of change taking place, the Executive soon
started thinking again about the possibility of the Union building
its own offices. This had been one of Solly's dreams, and back in
1867 it had been reported that 'between £600 and £700' had been
donated towards the fund for 'Central Buildings'. Solly had envisaged the opening of something akin to an educational institute,
with himself as Principal, and had suggested that the premises
would cost £12,000. The Prince of Wales, the Duke of Bedford, the
Duke of Devonshire and the Duke of Buccleuch had all sent in
donations, but, as Solly admitted in *These Eighty Years*:

> . . . the scheme did not altogether please some of our Council . . . and
> so we moved on, grumbling, croaking, laughing, and working, hoping
> much one day about the Central Hall, cast down and troubled the
> next, with a canvasser going round and getting in with our personal
> application, altogether about £600 – not much compared with our
> need, but a nest egg. At one time there was a very good chance of our
> getting St Martin's Hall in Long Acre, which would have been well
> adapted for our purpose. But we could not strike while the iron was
> hot, and the chance soon slipped away . . .

In the years that followed, the £600 that had been put aside just dwindled away, largely in the form of 'loans' to various London clubs, who had then regarded them instead as 'gifts' that did not have to be repaid. 'This is the shady episode of the Union's story,' said B. T. Hall.

In 1885 it was suggested that the Union should raise further funds and join the St James and Soho Club in setting up a club house, meeting hall and offices. This proposal was rejected by the Union Council, which considered that it would be more fitting for the Union to own its own premises, and a sub-committee was appointed to look for new premises. Its first reaction was fright. The cost would be far too great, and since the Union only possessed *net* assets at the time of £250, the reaction was understandable. It was therefore agreed to start saving for the future, with all money received in the form of personal subscriptions or donations – which were still bringing in £180 a year – being put aside in a special Central Hall Fund. This time, there were no 'loans' – although there were many requests – and in March 1892 the Annual Report stated:

> ... The most important incident of the year has been the purchase of a freehold site on which to erect the Central Hall and Club, of which we have been dreaming for the last 25 years, but which many of our friends have long ceased to look upon as possible of realisation, and smiled when the subject was alluded to in the Annual Reports, which year after year announced that we were still hoping to shortly reach the goal.
>
> At last, however, the policy of steadily accumulating the Central Hall Fund and refusing to permit it to be frittered away in gifts and loans to clubs which were in financial difficulty has been justified. A site has been secured in a splendid position, easy of access from all parts of London, and large enough to enable us to carry out the whole of the programme which we have discussed for several years past.
>
> The site has cost about £8,000 and it has a frontage to the Clerkenwell Road, adjoining the Holborn Town Hall, of 46 feet and a depth of about 130 feet. A part of the site is covered by two factories, and plans have been prepared for adapting these buildings to our requirements and for utilising the unoccupied portion of the land. The cost of the alterations and new buildings, including furnishing, will be alone £11,000, and for this the Union will secure central premises, of which we are sure all our members will be proud. Mr W. D. Caroe, MA, FRIBA, has been appointed Architect.

This was, said B. T. Hall, 'a most reckless undertaking'. The Union did not possess the financial resources for such a venture, but Lord Brassey, who had always been such a generous friend to the Union, gave a personal guarantee to Lloyds Bank against their loan of £8,500, without any other security, and a mortgage of £5,500 was also raised. In addition, the Women's Trade Union League made a loan of £2,000 from a fund that had been established by Lady Dilke as a memorial to Emma Paterson, widow of the Union pioneer Thomas Paterson, who had herself once been employed as the Union's Assistant Secretary (see page 55). There were also smaller loans from individual clubs and club members totalling £2,500. B. T. Hall noted subsequently that '... the Building began with a burden of Debt of over £18,000; at 5 per cent, a charge of £900 per annum upon the Union's funds. A remarkable, unusual, and not very promising condition. Contemplation of the financial future could only be indulged in when reinforced with a deep draught of optimism ... nevertheless, the work was in hand, and the year 1892 occupied with the erection of the new Building.'

And then came a bolt from the blue.

When the delegates gathered for the Council meeting on 4 February 1893, they found that a slip of paper had been added to the agenda, mentioning that Mr Anthony Mundella, MP, then President of the Board of Trade, who had recently established a Labour Department within his Ministry, had offered the post of Labour Correspondent to J. J. Dent, who had accepted it and resigned his position as Secretary of the Union. 'The meeting was very cordial in its congratulations and in its recognition that in his new post Dent would do the State good service,' recorded B. T. Hall, noting wryly that there were also some who 'thought he [Dent] ought not to have taken the post, although the salary was £300, rising to £400 per annum. These were they who in 1890 had thought his salary should not have been increased from £150!'

Dent himself replied to the delegates, and

> ... acknowledged that it was an unfortunate time for him to leave their service, and it was with mixed feelings that he tendered his resignation at a time when they were building the Central Hall and Offices. He had paused some time before accepting the appointment, for his interest in the work of the Union was dragging one way and his family interests the other. He had sacrificed other positions to continue in the Union service, and when he recollected the difficulty that they had to decide that he was worth £200 a year, he felt that with the claims of a growing family he could not now hesitate – and knowing that his future work was to help on the Labour Movement, he felt it incumbent on him to take the position. When he thought of the growth of the Union and its future responsibilities, he felt that a much stronger

man than ever was required for Secretary to guide them through the troubles arising in the future. He hoped it would be a long time before he severed his connection with the Union, and as a delegate he would always be glad to assist the new Secretary . . .

A testimonial consisting of an address and a cheque were presented on behalf of the clubs to Mr Dent on his retiring from the secretaryship.

Dent spent the rest of his working life at the Board of Trade, although he remained an active clubman and, as we have seen, joined the Executive, became Vice-President, and later President of the Union, a position which he held from 1909 until 1922, working throughout that period with his successor, B. T. Hall, who was Secretary from 1893 to 1929, and whom many believe to have been the key figure in the Union's history.

At the time of Dent's departure, the Union was just on the point of moving into the new headquarters, and had become, in B. T. Hall's words, 'a complete and self-contained organisation, its base well set, its form determined, its life assured'. The new Secretary could see that his role would be different to that of Dent, who had done so much to consolidate the Union after that period of division.

During Dent's ten years as Secretary, the Union head office had started to provide a range of services to member clubs. Apart from the legal and financial advice given to clubs by Hobson and Minet, the Union had also established a Stores department to supply clubs with account books and other stationery. G. Shore was in charge of this. W. G. Stroud became the Union's first auditor, and, in 1891, a full-time member of the Union's staff when the Audit Department was established. The Circulating Library had been built up over the years, latterly under the control of Mr W. C. Waller and then, in 1890, by Vaughan Nash, who was later to become private secretary to two Liberal Prime Ministers, Sir Henry Campbell-Bannerman and H. H. Asquith.

Throughout this period, the Union was served by officers of high calibre who could undoubtedly have risen in other professions had they chosen to; something was keeping them together as a team, and although they were all too genuinely modest to leave memoirs or records of their personal achievements, it seems probable that this extraordinary blending of men to a cause was inspired by the way in which Stephen Seaward Tayler and Hodgson Pratt worked together as close personal friends. Tayler served on the Council for thirty-five years, and for seventeen of them he presided over the

Executive meetings while Hodgson Pratt was the actual President; it was an extraordinary partnership, and one that strengthened Dent's hand and then, later, B. T. Hall's. Both men had the confidence that a secretary feels when he has a strong committee working with him.

In *Our Fifty Years*, B. T. Hall recalled, in a passage that was unusually philosophical, how he saw his role on taking office:

> The task and policy for the future could be faced without fear of internal difference, or distracted by the sheer necessity of prolonging life, which had hampered and distracted [my] predecessors. Firmly upon its feet, there was for the Union now but to progress and to develop – to extend its borders and to deepen, by useful service, its hold upon its parts. The lines of action, and the tasks which lay ahead, were clear. It had to establish its financial security against all possible accidents of the future. It had to secure its clubs against attack. It had to come to some settlement in its relationship with the clubs of the provinces. It had to determine its relations with the State. It had grown too large a part of the community to be able to proceed without consideration of the effect of its progress on others than itself. It was clear that even if it wished this latter, the State would not permit, and would soon come to question the place of the movement within it. So there was both a Colonial and Foreign policy for consideration. Beyond all this, yet in its results affecting it all, was the task of introspection, of diligent searching within, the repair of weaknesses, the excision of malignant growths, the expulsion of impurities, the securing of intrinsic health by the meeting of every legitimate want, the use of every opportunity. The Union had unity in form. It must also have it in sentiment and ideal. It must polish and perfect its parts so that their character should be their greatest security against hostile attack. . . .

B. T. Hall became Secretary in March 1893, and that same month he and the other staff moved into the new Club Union Buildings, which were formally opened by Lord Brassey six months later, on Friday, 15 September 1893.

The original scheme was that the front building, in addition to providing accommodation for the Union, should also provide offices which could be rented by trade unions and other bodies, who would also be able to use the meeting hall. There was also a curious proposal to open a club on the premises. This club would have had no members as such; it would have been under the control of the Union Executive, and used by associates.

'That such a plan should have been thought possible of success is rather curious,' commented B. T. Hall, adding: 'A club without membership is impossible. The government of a club except by members who subscribe to it is also impossible. . . .'

It was in finding a solution to that problem that the famous Central Club was formed. The inaugural meeting was held on 13 August 1894, and the Club rented its premises from the Union, paying initially £200 a year, and then later, after the hall had been extended, £425 a year, with the Union paying for some of the lighting, plus all rates and taxes.

The new headquarters helped many other organizations. The London Trades Council held its meetings in the hall. The Women's Trade Union League rented half a floor, and the Amalgamated Society of Railway Servants a whole floor. Among the other organizations which either rented smaller offices or made occasional use of the rooms provided were:

> The National Association of Operative Plasterers
> The Metropolitan Association of Operative Plasterers
> The Electrical Trades Union
> The Amalgamated Society of House Painters and Decorators
> The National Union of Bakers and Confectioners
> The Silver Trades Council
> The Associated Carpenters and Joiners
> The Amalgamated Society of Coal Porters
> The Goldsmiths and Jewellers' Society
> The United Patriots' Friendly Society
> The Small Silver Workers' Society
> The Amalgamated Society of Chasers and Engravers
> The Silver-Plate Workers
> The National Union of Clerks
> The National Union of Shop Assistants
> The Central London Branch of the Electrical Trades Union

With so many tenants paying rent, the new headquarters should have been a great success financially, but B. T. Hall, who was always prudent when it came to money matters, was far from satisfied, and complained in *Our Fifty Years*:

> ... they have never paid their way. The Buildings account was properly charged with the interest payable upon the money borrowed to erect them. (In later years as the debt was diminished the debit was also – but incorrectly by strict accountancy). The result was that the outgoings for Rates and Taxes (£300 per annum), Caretaker's Wages, Gas, Repairs, Interest, etc., without allowance for Depreciation, came to about £1,400, whilst the total rent received, including that paid by the Union for its own accommodation, never reached more than £1,200 and sometimes only £1,100.

On the whole, disregarding depreciation, and allowing a debit of 4 per cent on cost, the Union Buildings have occasioned a loss in cash since erection of £6,000. If the most modest allowance for depreciation be made the loss will rise to £12,000, to which at least another £1,000 must be added as cost of sundry alterations made to suit tenants.

The experiment of becoming a Land and Property Owner has cost the Union £13,000 to date. . . .

B. T. Hall revised the figures for *Our Sixty Years*, painting an even more gloomy picture, and if at first his pessimism sounds odd, we must remember that in those days property values seldom changed as dramatically as they have in recent years, and it was quite common for buildings to depreciate in value rather than increase. Inflation was almost unknown! The passing years were to prove Hall wrong, but in so many other respects he was to become one of the most dominant characters in the Union's history.

Like so many of the Union's pioneers, Hall was a radical who could easily have gone into politics, and a career in the House of Commons, and very nearly did; but instead, at the age of twenty-eight, he became the Union's General Secretary, holding the position from 1893 to 1929, during which period the Union's membership increased six-fold, and it acquired much of the character that it retains today. This profile of him was written by Jesse Argyle, a former journalist who was Vice-President of the Union for twelve years from 1909 before succeeding Sir Herbert Praed as Treasurer:

Born at Tonbridge, Kent, in 1864, Benjamin Tom Hall came to London when four years old, and has lived here ever since. His school days, like most of the present Labour leaders, were not prolonged, for we find him leaving St Paul's School, Bow Common, and starting working life at the age of twelve. Already, however, he had distinguished himself, for he was top boy at the school and a prodigy in scriptural knowledge – curious circumstances in view of the opinions on matters theological which he afterwards developed. His first situation was that of a printer's reading boy, but at the end of two years he became apprenticed as a carpenter, served the regulation five years, and emerged a full-fledged journeyman at 19. With characteristic enterprise, he at once set up as a builder, but not meeting with much success in this (quite an exceptional circumstance in B.T.'s life), he put in seven years as carpenter with the Val de Travers Asphalte Company.

In the meantime he had become very active in political and Labour movements, and so attracted the attention of Mr J. Havelock Wilson, of the Seamen's and Firemen's Union. Offered by Mr Wilson the charge of the office of that union, Hall did not hesitate to accept the position, although it involved the supervision of a large staff, with the necessarily complicated and extensive accounts of an organisation of 60,000 members.

Here he remained until 1893, when he was elected Secretary to the Club and Institute Union. The following communication, received at that time from the Seamen's Union, shows how he had performed his work for that organisation:

In October, 1891, B. T. Hall was appointed Accountant and Assistant Secretary of the above Union. His work was to control the accounts and administration of 84 Branches, nearly 200 officials, £14,000 worth of house property, and an income of more than £2,000 per month. He has kept these accounts with absolute accuracy and punctuality, and has brought to the administration sound judgement, great firmness, and unequalled tact. He has introduced into every vein of the organisation an order and a system unknown before, and peculiarly invaluable now. He has been entrusted with business negotiations of extremely important and delicate character, and these have been carried out with success and completeness. He has developed great familiarity with the law of Merchant Shipping, and his advice is much valued. He has all the qualifications of a successful businessman, a keen and far-sighted administrator, an accurate accountant, and a skilled and capable organiser. His services will be as great a gain to any other institution as the loss will be irreparable, we fear, to this Union. The Club Movement has, however, our heartiest sympathy, and we certainly wish him success.

From the day on which he assumed his new post until the present, B. T. Hall's business career has been that of the Club Union; in the great prosperity and high status to which it has attained lies the best evidence of the ability and zeal with which its affairs have been directed by its chief executive officer. One other testimony may, however, be fittingly added, coming as it does from the late Mr Hodgson Pratt, whose keen insight into character and wide knowledge of men none who knew him will for a moment question. Writing to Mr J. J. Dent in 1895, he says of B. T. Hall:

It was an immense piece of good fortune to secure the services of such a man when you retired from the post of Secretary. In all England the clubs could not have found a man more qualified for the arduous duties of that position, one becoming more important every day as the clubs grow in number.

He really combines a singular variety of gifts – force of character, firmness, moral courage, insight, common sense, knowledge of men, and great tact. These qualities give him, of course, an influence for good which is all essential to the right development of this great social organisation.

Indeed, I am inclined to think that in some respects the task is more difficult than that of an officer in the Co-operative or Trade Union movements. In the latter the field of action is more definite and understood, and perhaps those movements are less liable to serious dangers. The very success of the clubs numerically may bring into the movement a large influx of men who are not in the least conscious of the ideals which the founders of the Union had in view. It is wonderful to see how often it happens that there seems to be some sort of providence in the appearance at the right moment of such men as Hall.

Giving evidence before the Commission, he gained the reputation for masterly defence of the interests of the clubs which he has since well maintained. Adhering to an accepted motto, 'Eternal vigilence is the price of safety', he is ever alert against attack, his judgement being invariably sound in estimating the importance, or otherwise, of any legislative design upon the clubmen's citadel. Witness the ill-starred attempt at interference with clubs in the abortive licensing measure of the Government in 1908. Hall's famous *Campaign Journal* was a trumpet call which reverberated in every workmen's club, an armoury of powder and shot, rousing to action as 'the red glare on Skiddaw roused the burghers of Carlisle'. Great, indeed, is the debt which clubmen owe to our B. T. for his skilful and triumphant general-ship. . . . Something must be added regarding his position as citizen and man.

As already hinted, he has from his youth up been actively associa-ted with Labour and Progressive politics. Active almost to aggres-siveness (some even whisper 'autocratic' at times), he is, and looks like, a born leader of democracy, though he carries far too much ballast ever to become a demagogue, and does not hesitate to tell friends and supporters 'what he thinks of them' if occasion arises. He long held the position of Chairman of the Labour Party in Deptford; has filled several other offices – all honorary – including those of registration agent and agent to the candidates at both Parliamentary and local elections, for he would never accept payment for such work. He has fought numerous elections himself, and was an Alder-man of his Borough, holding the Chairmanship of its Assessment and General Purposes Committees until, in the interests of the rapidly growing work of the Club Union, he resigned those positions. Fighter, diplomat, and administrator, as he is, this retirement must have been a real sacrifice . . .

When still in his early twenties, before taking up his post with the Union, B. T. Hall was also a keen member of the Fabian Society, working alongside George Bernard Shaw, Annie Besant, Sidney and Beatrice Webb, Ramsay MacDonald, Keir Hardie, Ben Tillett and Walter Crane. Sadly, there is no detailed record of his work within the Society because much of its pre-1939 correspondence and other material was donated to a salvage drive in 1942 as part of the war effort, but from the few scraps of information that remain we can see that Hall could easily have gone on to a Parliamentary career or membership of the London County Council, had he chosen to.

Down in Deptford – where he lived then at 29 Childeric Road, New Cross – Hall was the election agent for Sidney Webb, one of the greatest figures in the early history of the Labour movement, who used to stand as a 'Progressive' candidate in the years before the Labour Party officially put up candidates for the London County Council. Webb was a member of the LCC from 1892 to 1910, and regularly achieved the highest vote of any Progressive candidate in London, which says much for B. T. Hall's skills as his agent. It was Sidney Webb who proposed Hall for membership of the Fabian Society in 1892, and the following year the Fabians published Hall's pamphlet, *Socialism and Sailors*, which was No. 46 in their series of Fabian Tracts. (Of the previous 45, Shaw wrote 8 and Sidney Webb, 23; the forty-seventh was written by John Burns.)

The Fabians were to become the most influential intellectual force within the Labour movement, and by the time Labour was elected to form a government just after the Second World War, there were 229 Fabian Members of Parliament, including ten Cabinet Ministers. In their early days, B. T. Hall was clearly seen as one of their rising young men. The *Fabian News* reported his election as General Secretary of the Union; that Fabian Tract listed his position with the Union on its title page, and in different issues of *Fabian News* it was reported that Hall was standing for election to the Deptford Guardians (April 1893), was inviting Fabians to enter the Union's essay competition (September 1893), had been appointed by the Secretary of State for the Colonies as a member of the Committee of the Emigrants Information Office (March 1894), was lecturing in different parts of London (March and April 1894), had been elected for St Paul's, Deptford, in the London Vestry & Guardians elections (December 1894), and so on.

This is of some importance in the Union's history, because at that time the London clubs formed the bulk of the Union's membership and many of them were party-political. The Fabians regarded the London clubs as an important part of their audience. When the *Fabian Essays* were published in 1889, the preface stated that 'Country readers may accept the book . . . as a sample of the propaganda carried on by volunteer lecturers in the workmen's clubs and political associations of London . . .', and the organization of these lectures was an important feature of the Fabians' work. W. S. De Mattos was employed as Lecture Secretary, and in the year in which B. T. Hall was elected to the Society 600 lectures were arranged in London and a further 300 in the provinces, with members of the Society delivering a total of 3,339 lectures during the year in different parts of the country. Many of the Union's member clubs in London were the venue for these lectures, which ranged from straightforward propaganda – Hall himself regularly lectured on 'The State and the Sailor' or 'Sailors and Politics' – to lectures on the Civil War, or the poetry of Walt Whitman.

In his *History of the Fabian Society* (published in 1918), Edward R. Pease wrote:

> In the early nineties the Liberal and Radical Working Men's Clubs of London had a political importance which has since entirely disappeared. Every Sunday for eight months in the year, and often on weekdays, political lectures were arranged, which were constantly given by Fabians. For instance, in October 1891, I find recorded in advance twelve courses of two to five lectures each, nine of them at Clubs, and fifteen separate lectures at Clubs, all given by members of the Society. In October, 1892, eleven courses and a dozen separate lectures by our members at Clubs are notified. These were all, or nearly all, arranged by the Fabian office, and it is needless to say that a number of others were not so arranged or were not booked four or five weeks in advance. Our list of over a hundred lecturers, with their subjects and private addresses, was circulated in all directions and was constantly used by the Clubs. . . .

It was from this background that B. T. Hall came, encouraged, no doubt, by the similar sympathies of Hodgson Pratt, Stephen Seaward Tayler and other members of the Executive who were then so largely drawn from the Liberal and Radical clubs of London. In their way, they were as remarkable a group of men as Solly's original aristocrats: a cohesive group that worked together, and then gradually prepared the way for further change, expanding the Union into the provinces, and then extending the constitution still further so that the Union soon became a nationwide organization, with an Executive drawn from different parts of the country.

Like most of the major turning-points in the Union's history, this later extension did not come suddenly; there was a gradual change in the balance of opinion within the Union as B. T. Hall started to take a strong grip on its central administration, and the personalities who had exerted such an influence over the past thirty years began to retire.

Hall recorded their passing thus in *Our Fifty Years*:

> Hodgson Pratt, who had sought to retire in 1883 because of his age, and had been elected President in 1885, continued to occupy that post until 1902, when he retired, and Stephen Seaward Tayler was elected

in his place. Mr Pratt resided largely abroad, and his chief Presidential function was in attendance at the Annual Meetings, at which he delivered addresses full of power and eloquence and lofty exhortation. On his retirement it was decided to perpetuate his association with the office, and a portrait of him was purchased from Felix Moscheles for one hundred guineas, so that in presentment as in spirit he dwells ever in the Union's counsels. He died at his home at Le Pecq, near Paris, at the age of 83, on February 26th 1907. His body was brought to England and interred at Highgate Cemetery on March 4th in the presence of all the Union's officers and a great crowd of club members, hastily assembled at the sad news, from Yorkshire and Durham as from the Midlands and the West and South. Thus passed the great man to whose labour, with no injustice to Henry Solly be it said, the movement owes the most. He was one of the greatest men of his day, and but for his self-effacing modesty would have been known to all the earth for his manifold labours on the world's behalf . . . four years before the death of Mr Pratt, Henry Solly had passed away in the peace and quiet of the old-world village of Childrey, near Wantage, in Berkshire, where he had for many years lived amongst his children and grandchildren. He was within a few months of 90 years of age when on February 27th, 1903, he was laid to well-earned rest. His interest in the clubs and the Union which he founded remained keen to the end. He was a regular reader of the *Journal*, and so keen upon the matters therein dealt with that latterly his daughter asked for it not to be sent, as it occasioned excitement, which was to be avoided . . .

During the long years when Mr Pratt held the Presidency, the actual work of the office was performed by Mr Stephen Tayler, who without intermission attended every monthly meeting of the Council and every weekly meeting of the Executive, until, elected President on Mr Pratt's retiral in 1902, he left the meetings of the Executive in the hands of his successor in the Vice-Presidency J. J. Dent. On May 13th, 1909, he presided at the Annual Meeting, and after 42 years' service asked to be allowed to withdraw. Mr J. J. Dent was elected President for the ensuing year, and then Mr Tayler left the meeting, the whole audience rising and singing, 'Should Auld Acquaintance be Forgot?' On Thursday, October 28th, in the same year, he, too, passed away in his 86th year. On Monday, November 1st his body was cremated at Golders Green.

No man since the beginning of the Union has rendered it such length of unbroken service as did Stephen Seward Tayler. Solly founded, Pratt worked and preached, Tayler spent every week in the humble necessary work of administration. If there is unity and cohesion now in the Union none can say how much of it was due to [his] gentle diplomacy and wonderful wisdom . . .

8

Legend has it that B. T. Hall was the toughest leader the Union has ever had. His friends would describe him as a 'genial autocrat'. Touring the clubs he was popular with members, always affable, but behind his desk at Head Office he was a man to be feared, austere in manner and personal habits, commanding respect rather than affection. This reputation lived on long after his death; when I was writing *The First Century* twenty-five years ago there were still active officers in the Union who had either met B. T. Hall, or worked with someone else who had, and the very mention of his name was enough to provoke a wary look and a sharp intake of breath. And yet there can be little doubt that his was just the kind of character the Union needed in control of its day-to-day administration.

In its first thirty years, the Union had grown into a large movement, although still largely London-based; it had gone through a total change of character, and yet only recently had it achieved any real sense of purpose.

In the last chapter we saw how B. T. Hall had found the Union 'a complete and self-contained organisation, its base well set, its form determined, its life assured ... the lines of action, and the tasks which lay ahead, were clear. It had to establish its financial security against all possible accidents of the future. It had to secure its clubs against attack. It had to come to some settlement in its relationship with the clubs of the provinces. It had to determine its relations with the State.'

Therein lay the broad strands of Hall's secretaryship, the years between 1893 and 1929, when the Union broadened out, increasing its membership more than six-fold, becoming totally democratic and truly national, and financially secure with strong local branches. This pattern became clear as the years passed, although, as with all organizations, it was often the problems that occupied Hall's mind; what he called 'noteworthy incidents' in his own account of that period in *Our Fifty Years*.

What was known in the clubs as the Skegness Disaster occurred in 1893, when by the overturning of a yacht, Mr W. S. Hawkins, one of the Auditors of the Union, and six other members of the Clapton Park Club, were drowned. An appeal to the clubs realized £1,000 in relief of their dependants.

A testimonial consisting of address and cheque were presented on behalf of the Clubs to Mr Dent on his retiring from the secretarial post.

In 1893, too, it had been decided by the Council to contribute 25s monthly to the John Burns Wages Fund, which was continued until 1896, when the tightness of the Union's funds, and the inevitable dissatisfaction with Burns, led to its discontinuance.

In 1894 the Union clubs raised by direct collection £3,200 for the then locked-out miners. In this year, the Union was most successful in establishing points in club law.

In the Queen's Bench Mr Hobson also obtained the decision of the Court in the case of *Rankin* v. *Hunt*, that a clause in a lease prohibiting the sale of intoxicants did not apply in the case of a club, and also – in the matter of the United Radical Club – that a Receiver cannot be appointed to carry on a club.

1895 saw more legal victories in the lower courts, one of the most important being that in which it was held that a club is not responsible for the safety of a member's overcoat or other property left in the club.

A small book, the first to deal with working-class club life, *The Club Land of the Toiler* by T. S. Peppin, was published by J. M. Dent and Company. It dealt very sympathetically with the clubs and the Union, and was fortunate to secure a preface by the Rev. Canon Barnett.

In 1897 Mr Justice Grantham decided that terms in a lease limiting the use of certain premises 'to an ordinary dwelling house' do not cover a club. A grant was made by the Council of £25 towards a Testimonial Fund for Mr George Howell, ex-MP, and one of the earliest of the Union workers.

In 1898 the Secretary took 'his tremendous proselytising and propaganda power' to Ireland, but with little ultimate success. (The Union still has very few member clubs in Ireland.)

In 1900 the Report of the Licensing Commission was published. Successful assessment appeals characterize this year. In the King's Bench in 1901 Mr Hobson obtained a decision against the Wolverhampton magistrates, who had held the supply of a bottle of stout to a messenger from a member to be illegal.

In 1902 the salary of the Secretary was raised and placed upon a definite footing. In 1903 an Assistant Secretary, Mr W. H. Berry, was appointed, and an Audit Department constituted with Mr W. G. Stroud in charge, relieved of his other general duties.

In 1904, a visit of 320 clubmen to Paris in support of the Entente Cordiale was organized by the Secretary and Mr Hugh Bryan, Secretary of the Association of Conservative Clubs. The party was received with open arms by the Municipalities of Versailles and Paris, banqueted by the Chamber of Commerce and several other societies. Mimi Pinson contributed to a Sunday evening entertainment in the grounds of the Astronomical Society, the British Ambassador entertained them at a garden party at the Embassy, and a deputation was received by President Loubet.

In 1905, the Council referred to the Executive the consideration of a proposal to obtain a club representative in the House of Commons. The Executive reported against the proposal, which was also opposed by the Secretary and was dropped.

In each year an active propaganda campaign was carried on in the provinces, the Secretary attending as many as fifty meetings a year. In July 1907, the health of the Secretary broke down under the tremendous pressure of his work, following the death of his wife, and he was sent away to the sea for two months – to restore him, fit and ready for the fray which, it was foreseen, would tax all his energies early in 1908.

For several years before that, there had been demands for legislation, either to control or tax clubs. B. T. Hall had noted that 'not a single Session of Parliament assembled but found proposals before it'. A Manchester Licensing Reform Committee in 1892 had propounded a Bill compelling registration with the Licensing Justices, taxation at five per cent on the receipts from the consumption of intoxicants, and providing penalties and refusal of renewal of registration if a club were used for drinking purposes only, or there was drunkenness on the club premises. This Bill was introduced by Sir H. Roscoe, MP, Jacob Bright, MP, C. S. Roundell, MP, and others. In an amended form it was reintroduced in 1894 and 1895, but never secured a second reading. There was, too, the United Temperance Bill of 1894, which modestly proposed a Licensing Fee calculated at 10 per cent on the receipts for intoxicants. Mr Leonard Courtney (later Lord Courtney of Penwith) provided, in a Bill introduced in 1895, for registration on similar lines to Sir Henry Roscoe's Bill. But he added that every member should pay an entrance fee of £1! The licensing fee was to be fixed by a popularly elected board, and there were no penalties for drunkenness . . . Herbert Roberts (son-in-law to the arch-enemy of the period, W. S. Caine, MP) had a Bill for Wales. It proposed that any body of more than ten persons associating themselves only for the supply of intoxicants should be liable to a fine of £5 each, or, in default of payment, imprisonment for three months . . . Other bills were introduced, and then towards the end of 1895 it was announced that there would be appointed a Royal Commission which would enquire into and report upon the Licensing Laws.

The Commission was composed of representatives of every interest. Brewers, distillers, Gilbeys, publicans, teetotal fanatics, moderate tee-totallers, temperance men – all had a representative. These were to be balanced by the addition of seven others of no particular views or interest. And so a fairly competent Commission was got together, with Lord Peel as Chairman and Sir Algernon West as Vice-Chairman. In June 1896 it was decided that the Commission should include clubs in the scope of its enquiries. Immediately the Union claimed representation. Nearly two-thirds of the Commission, it pointed out, were members of the alliance between trade and teetotal-lers, which had been so continuously operative against clubs. Its protest stirred Members of Parliament considerably. It was the begin-ning of an acquaintance with the clubs as an influence in politics. The new Secretary was at work. It was agreed on all hands that the clubs had a substantial grievance. This decision was communicated by Mr Arthur Balfour in the following friendly terms:

September 21st 1896

Mr B. T. Hall
Dear Sir,
    I have been communicating with Mr Sidney Peel, the Secretary of the Licensing Commission, on the subject of your letter of September 1st. It is for this reason that some delay has occurred in sending you a reply.
    I fully understand, and sympathise with, the interest taken by your Executive in the proceedings of the Commission, which will undoub-tedly have to consider questions affecting all places where sales of intoxicating liquor take place. While, however, there are grave objec-tions to adding to the numbers of the Commission after substantial progress has been made with the inquiry, I do not think that the inter-ests, either of the clubs belonging to your association, or of the much larger number of political and other clubs throughout the country, will be in any way injured by leaving the constitution of the Commission unaltered. Many members of the Commission are much interested in the successful management of workmen's clubs, and have taken part in their establishment. Their great value is recognised on all hands, and the most anxious desire to do them justice animates, I have reason to know, both the Chairman of the Commission and all its members.

It would be of the utmost importance, no doubt, that the Commission should have the opportunity of examining such evidence as your Executive can place at their disposal; and I am confident that to this the fullest and fairest consideration will be given. In this way the interest of the clubs will be far more effectually served than by the mere presence on the Commission of a single gentleman, appointed for the sole purpose of representing these institutions.

I remain, yours faithfully,
Arthur James Balfour

The case against the clubs was presented principally by teetotallers and police superintendents. The publicans formed a committee to collect evidence of the clubs' shortcomings and wrongdoings, and this committee made an appeal in the press for assistance, pointing out that it was difficult to find out facts, or even the names and addresses of clubs. The difficulty as to the facts had not prevented in the preceding years a constant flow of criticism and allegations – 'the dreary drip of defamatory declaration' at banquets and in the press. But to speak at a dinner was one thing, to give evidence was another. Hence the Committee's difficulty. Mr B. T. Hall handsomely offered his assistance. 'I enclose,' he wrote, 'a list of names and addresses of over 500 clubs, into whose conduct you may enquire, and I will be glad to assist your inquiry in any way' . . . The principal police evidence against the clubs was given by the Chief Constables of Manchester and of Leeds. The first attributed all drunkenness after hours in Manchester to the clubs. Asked as to night houses and brothels, he replied that there were none to his knowledge in Manchester! Subsequently light was thrown on the attitude of the police in this town by the disclosure that at the time of this remarkable evidence there were not only brothels in Manchester, but the principal of these were owned and run by the leading members of the detective service, whilst all the breweries paid a subsidy on a fixed scale to every police officer from inspector to constable. Swiftly, too, fell the sequel to the evidence of the Chief Constable of Leeds, he retiring in dishonour from his posts, after threats of proceedings by the clubs. . . .

Apart from evidence of this character and of the undoubted existence of what the Commission described as 'abominable dens kept by foreigners' in the West End of London, the evidence against clubs was of a fragmentary character, consisting principally of isolated instances of clubs alleged to have been misconducted. The London police magistrates spoke strongly in favour of workmen's clubs.

The case for the clubs was 'presented by Mr B. T. Hall, the Secretary of the Working Men's Club and Institute Union, who gave his evidence with remarkable lucidity and ability' (to quote the Report), and by Mr Hugh Bryan, of the Association of Conservative Clubs, and Mr John May, of the Yorkshire Federation of Liberal Clubs. Mr Hall was under examination for several hours, and, on his rising at the conclusion, Sir Algernon West (then Chairman) spoke in a very encouraging and kindly way of the good work of the clubs, amidst a chorus of endorsement from the Commissioners present. It was generally felt that the attack had failed, and the defence had been invulnerable. The Report was awaited with easy confidence.

Whilst referring to the evidence given on behalf of the union by its Secretary, the following summary of the suggestions for legislation (if legislation were considered necessary) made by the Union are worthy of being set out:

SUGGESTIONS AS TO CLUB REGISTRATION

Made to the Licensing Commission by Mr B. T. Hall on behalf of the Working Men's Club and Institute Union in 1907

1. That all Clubs should be registered by an authority constituted for the purpose, which shall, if the rules, etc., conform to the regulations it may make, register the Club.

2. That all rules should provide (a) the method of election of Members, and that a minimum of at least seven days shall elapse between nomination and election; (b) Under what circumstances membership lapses; (c) The hours of closing and opening; (d) The keeping at the Club of a list of the Members' names and addresses; (e) The method of election of Committee or governing body; (f) Provision for the complete control of the Club by its Members equally; (g) Provision that rules may only be altered by a general meeting of Members; (h) Provision for the regular meeting of the Committee or governing body.

3. That each application for registration should be accompanied by sufficient sets of such rules as to enable one copy to be kept for the inspection of the public at the offices of the registering authority.

4. That all applications for registry be upon a form supplied by the registering authority, which shall provide for a sworn declaration by the applicants of the names of the responsible officers of the Club, and that no person whatsoever is financially interested, directly or indirectly, in the supply of exciseables.

5. That each Club shall make an annual return of its income and expenditure (from and for all sources) upon a form provided and duly audited and vouched.

6. That no visitors be permitted to enter a Club during hours when Licensed premises are closed.

7. That it be an offence for any visitor to purchase or attempt to purchase any drink in a Club.

8. That evidence of breach of rules should be evidence of mala-fides.

9. That all penalties should, on the second occasion of complaint, be drastic.

10. That an officer of the registering authority should have power (on reasonable suspicion as to the bona-fides of any Club) to attend such Club and inspect all or any of its books.

11. That no police officer be empowered to enter any such registered Club (save as a member) without the warrant of a magistrate.

Many of these recommendations were incorporated in both the Commission's Majority and Minority Reports, and one other interesting feature of the Report was that it attempted, for the first time, to ascertain the total number of clubs then operating in the United Kingdom. A survey was conducted in every police district, and from this it was established that the total number of clubs in which intoxicants were sold was then (in 1896) as high as 3,991. Of these, 660 were in London, with 1,583 in the English counties and a further 1,291 in the English boroughs, 122 in Wales, 157 in Scotland and 178 in Ireland. Among the English and Welsh counties, Yorkshire with 312 and Lancashire with 383 had the most clubs. Cheshire had 89, Hampshire 67, Staffordshire 60, Warwickshire 51 and Glamorganshire 45.

Among the boroughs, there were these figures: Manchester 85; Bradford 81; Oldham 69; Leeds 61; Liverpool 49; Sheffield 41; Huddersfield 39; Stockport 34; Halifax 31; Salford 30; Cardiff 29.

The Report went on to say:

By an arrangement with the Inland Revenue a system of affiliation is permitted, by which a card can be issued to a member of one of the clubs, giving him honorary membership of all the other clubs in the Union. This privilege is carefully guarded, and precautions are taken to insure identification ... the rules of the Union [are] a good indication of the lines on which legislation will be gladly welcomed by the better class of working men's clubs. ...

The clubs felt very strongly the evils of bogus clubs, and desired to put them down. It would be hypocrisy to say that drunkenness did not exist in their clubs, but it was rare and always discouraged. The average expenditure on exciseables per member per week was about 1s., including tobacco and mineral waters; food was seldom supplied, because the men were not there at meal times. The Union would pledge themselves to the statement that where bona-fide working men's clubs existed, drunkenness declined both statistically and really.

We fully agree with all that has been said by Mr Hall and others as to the benefits to be derived from properly constituted and well-conducted clubs. We believe that such clubs can and will do much to meet the needs awakened among the working classes by education and general improvement of conditions for some better means of social intercourse and recreation than those provided by the public-house. Happily the days are passing when the public-house can be complacently described as the poor man's club. . . .

The Report was published in 1899, but nothing was done in Parliament until 1901, when Mr Caine introduced a Bill dealing with clubs. Mr (later Sir) Thomas Whittaker moved an amendment to the Address calling for legislation. Mr Caine offered his Bill to the Government. In reply, it was announced that a Bill dealing with clubs was being prepared by the Home Secretary, Mr C. T. Ritchie. The Bill was introduced early in 1902, after the Home Secretary had discussed its provisions with B. T. Hall, and despite attempts by the Temperance movement and the Licensed Victuallers to have various hostile clauses added to it, the Bill duly became law, with the Home Secretary saying in the Commons that he had the greatest sympathy for workmen's clubs, paying tribute to the Union for the way it 'had refrained from public agitation against this Bill, because they realised the evil it was intended to meet . . . [and that] he wished to acknowledge in the strongest possible manner the attitude of the Union'.

Later, on the Bill being given its third reading in the House of Commons, the Home Secretary went even further in his compliments to the Union:

> I am sure that the House will agree with me that we must enlist on our side in this matter the best opinion of the best clubs, including working men's clubs. I know that that great organisation – the Club and Institute Union – not a political body, but which comprises a large body of the Workmen's Clubs, is as anxious as the House can possibly be that the evils we complain of should be suppressed. If we do not carry the favourable opinion of these clubs with us harm will result . . .

The Executive of the Union duly conveyed its thanks to Ritchie on the Act becoming law, and he replied:

August 27th 1902

Mr B. T. Hall
Dear Sir,
    Please convey to your Executive my great appreciation of their thanks for the attitude I assumed in connection with the club clauses of the Licensing Act. It is a great gratification to me to know that in dealing with a very difficult question I have been able to give satisfaction to so important an organisation as that of the Club and Institute Union. For this result much is owing to the intelligent attitude assumed by them and the advice and assistance rendered by yourself.
                    Yours truly,
                        C. T. Ritchie

The new legislation provided for the registration of clubs, and was designed to curtail the growth of drinking clubs and discourage drunkenness; B. T. Hall made sure its provisions were understood by the Union's membership by writing a booklet, *The Licensing Act and Clubs*, of which 65,000 copies were sold.

Later, there were further Acts introduced to cover Scotland and Ireland, and further attempts by the Temperance supporters to tighten controls on clubs. Then in 1906 the Licensed Victuallers Trade Protection Association went further, and produced a Bill of their own suggesting that the police and licensing magistrates should have the same powers in relation to clubs that they already had in respect of public houses. Having published their Bill, the Victuallers then sought a meeting with the Chancellor of the Exchequer, Mr Asquith, who replied:

> To what was said on the question of Clubs I listened with a great deal of sympathy. I have long been of opinion, and am strongly of opinion now, that the law should be made stronger than it has hitherto been, and that the abuse should become the subject of effective legislation, and more effective administration by the Police, the Magistrates, and the Local Authorities.

It appeared to the Union Executive that these comments contained the threat of more damaging legislation, and so they complained to the Prime Minister, Sir Henry Campbell-Bannerman, who replied that the Chancellor had

> ... understood the remarks of the [Victuallers'] deputation, and certainly intended his own observations to apply to clubs – no doubt forming a small minority of such institutions, which were carried on mainly for the purpose of supplying intoxicating liquors in what is regarded as illegitimate competition with the public-houses. It was very far from his intention to cause any reflection on the objects or management of the great body of genuine workmen's clubs.

When the Victuallers sent another deputation, this time to meet Sir Henry Campbell-Bannerman to discuss the same issue, the Prime Minister replied:

> Then you complain very much of the clubs – of the multiplication of clubs. Clubs were dealt with, as you know better or more vividly than I may remember it, in 1902. There may be some respects in which that legislation may be deficient, and further restrictions may be necessary. I do not pronounce any opinion upon that; if there are, we should be willing to consider it, but I don't think the numbers quoted can be relied upon, because amongst other things that legislation required that every institution of the nature of a club had to be registered. . . . Genuine

workmen's clubs which are real working men's clubs ought not to be harried or interfered with in any excessive degree; at any rate, not beyond what is absolutely necessary. But the whole question deserves full examination and consideration, and I have no doubt that there will be every disposition to interfere with any illegitimate use of the liberties given, or left, under the Act of 1902; but, at the same time, there will be a strong desire to prevent undue interference with perfectly harmless clubs in which no mischief can arise.

For the moment, the clubs seemed safe enough – but the Executive and the Union officers felt fresh anxieties when Asquith succeeded Campbell-Bannerman as Prime Minister, and it became known that another Licensing Bill was being drafted by the civil servants. Asquith had long expressed the view that 'facilities for drinking' should be reduced, and when he did so invariably bracketed clubs together with public houses. B. T. Hall was in no doubt of the dangers that lay ahead, and the January 1908 issue of the *Club and Institute Journal* carried this editorial:

A FATEFUL OR A FATAL NEW YEAR?

At the risk of appearing gloomy at a time when cheer should fill each mind, we venture to hope that Clubs are preparing for what will be undoubtedly the most fateful year which in its 45 years of life the working-class club movement has seen. The Union is non-political, but it would not be far from the fact if we assumed that 75 per cent of the Union clubmen voted for the present Government. These say that it is absurd to suppose that the Liberal Government will, without warrant of fact or national necessity, aim a blow at workmen's clubs at the bidding of a few fanatics who are known to be hopelessly out of touch and antagonistic to the healthier, manlier, liberty-loving character of the people.

Such clubmen are living, we honestly believe, in a fool's paradise, for nothing is more certain than the willingness of the Liberal Party to shipwreck itself at the bidding of these raucous-voiced sirens. It has been done before. It will be done again. It is but imitation of the ostrich not to see the situation clearly. We are glad to see that the Metropolitan Radical Federation has spoken strongly and unitedly. We hope other Liberal organisations will do the same. If, in spite of this, the Government is still disposed to suicide, then it becomes the duty of its supporters, more than of others, to interpose forcibly and save it from itself and from those sad, and bad, men and influences who and which are hateful to nine out of ten Englishmen who harbour a sane mind in a healthy body.

At the end of February 1908, the Government Bill was introduced. The worst fears of the clubs were realized. It contained

practically every objectionable proposal which the Parliamentary
Committee on Mr Ritchie's Bill had rejected. It sacrificed the clubs
to the twin wolves of teetotal fanaticism and trade interest. It was
as bad a Bill as the worst enemy of the clubs could have drafted. It
distinguished betwen rich and poor. It prohibited supply of intoxicants in clubs for consumption off the premises in any smaller
quantities than $4\frac{1}{2}$ gallons of beer or two gallons of whisky. It
subjected clubs to the licensing bench. It gave the police unlimited
right of entry into clubs as into public houses. It closed a club for
five years for a first offence, however small. It gave opportunities to
any person or persons to object to the registration and it gave the
licensing bench, not the courts, the power to hear such objections.
It imposed personal liability and fine upon the club secretary, and
it added to the offences for which a club might be struck off the
register the oft-objected-to and ambiguous phrase, 'that it is used
mainly as a drinking club'.

Then ensued a fight, from which the Union emerged almost
entirely triumphant, and the Government wiser men with a
modified Bill. As the honours are almost all on the Union's side,
there need be no lengthy or detailed description of the campaign.
The Secretary of the Union set the heather aflame with an article,
the chief characteristic of which was invective, entitled 'The Eve of
St Bartholomew', which appeared in a Campaign Edition of the
Club and Institute Journal, of which 100,000 copies were published in
March as 'A Call to Arms Against an Anti-Liberal, Reactionary
Proposal for Class Legislation', and which drew the comment in
the *Morning Leader and Northern Echo*: 'Let me assure Mr Hall that if
he thinks that Bright, Bradlaugh and Gladstone, even if combined,
could be more scarifying than he is, he does himself an injustice.'
Great conferences of clubmen were held in Leeds, Newcastle,
Manchester, Leicester, Southampton, Cardiff and London,
addressed by members of the Executive and by the Officers, where
the objections of the Union were confirmed and opposition organized.

It was not a very restful time for Members of the House of
Commons. Interviews were had with groups of Liberal MPs, with
the Labour Party, the Labour-Liberals (then distinct from the
Labour Party), and finally with Mr Asquith himself. In the end
practically the whole of the Government proposals to which
objection was taken were withdrawn or amended, except the
'mainly a drinking club', to which the Government obstinately
clung. Relief settled on the clubs and on the Liberal and Labour
parties, who agreed that all the trouble was due to the fact that Mr

Asquith did not meet the Union before, instead of after, he had drafted his Bill. In fact, there can be no doubt that the Thomas Whittaker influence obtained the upper hand of the Government, which had not realized how clearly and definitely the clubs were capable of stating their case, and how good that case was. In the effort made, the Association of Conservative Clubs, the Federation of Liberal Clubs, and the small Kent Association rendered valuable aid. In the end, as is known, the House of Lords threw out the Bill, an affront which the Government was powerless to resent, or challenge. But the demonstration, which cost the Union over a thousand pounds, was not lost. Its memory will remain as a chastening influence on those who seek lightly and without due regard to lay violent hands on the clubs. Philip Snowden (later to be Chancellor of the Exchequer) wrote in the *Christian Commonwealth*:

> The oustanding feature of the debate on the club clauses was the obvious state of fear and trembling under the threats of the Club Union, in which most the members were. It is simply amazing that Members of Parliament, from the Government through every party in the House, should stand in such fear of offending the members of drinking clubs. MP's who have been prominent as extreme Temperance men have been paralysed by the fear of the consequences of interfering with the members of these unlicensed drinking dens to carry on as their inclinations led them.

In the years that followed, other Bills were introduced in the House of Commons with similar intent, but all fell through lack of support; the episode had shown that working men's clubs were now recognized as an important social institution in their own right, and it seems likely that one side-effect of this furore was a wider realization in the country as a whole of the work that the Union could do to protect clubs.

Side-by-side with this increasing public profile for the Union's work came steady growth in membership, and then a widening demand for local branches and provincial representation on the Executive; once this process had taken its natural course, all other related problems – particularly that of the Union's finances – were to be solved as well.

Since the Union's foundation, many attempts had been made to bring the clubs outside London into closer contact with the movement. But there were many difficulties, which would seem slight in the modern world of today: the problem of transport and communications, so easy to resolve in these days of trains, buses, cars and telephones, to say nothing of computer terminals, was then a major stumbling-block.

There had been a conference at Wednesbury in Staffordshire as early as January 1865, when, with Lord Lyttelton in the chair, it had been decided to form a Staffordshire District to link the clubs and mechanics' institutes which were flourishing in that part of the Midlands. In the same year, a Kent Union was formed. In the following year, the Rev. Henry Solly was instrumental in forming a Metropolitan District Association of Working Men's Clubs and Institutes, which had a Member of Parliament, A. H. Layard, as chairman. (It had been through this association that Hodgson Pratt and George Howell had first become active supporters of the Union.) In 1866, District Unions were formed in Northumberland and Durham, centred on Newcastle, and in Hampshire, and attempts were made to form others in Yorkshire and Manchester. An annual fee of 5s to the Union was set, but the report for 1866 stated:

> The Council are strongly of the opinion that more can be done by the Local District Unions for the welfare of clubs in their districts than by the Parent Society. With a view to leaving clubs free to give contributions from their too often slender resources to the proposed District Unions the Council have resolved to abolish the fee of 5s a year, retaining only the payment of a registration fee of 2s 6d on the club joining the Union.

Unfortunately, this was misplaced optimism; the provincial clubs were never as prominent within the Union during the last century as they have been in this, and for many years the Union was largely a London phenomenon. The only successful district union seems to have been Worcestershire, and even that eventually became little more than an association of village institutes concentrating on teaching members how to cultivate their allotments. Attempts were made around 1875 to form district unions in Hampshire, Manchester and Kent. These, however, did not integrate themselves fully with the Union. Kent and Hampshire seceded over the Bradlaugh incident, while Manchester became an independent organization, resisting every overture until 1921, when it became a branch of the Union.

Bringing Manchester into the fold, having established and stabilized branches elsewhere in the provinces, was to prove another of the lasting achievements of B. T. Hall's secretaryship, for it was this process of consolidation that gave the Union its sure financial foundation. Encouragement to do this had come from the Rev. Dean

Dickenson, who had been one of the members of that Royal Commission on the Licensing Laws to which Hall had given evidence in 1897. Dickenson has said:

I understand and follow the close enquiry and the drastic requirements which precede the admission of a club to membership of the Union. But with clubs everywhere, how can you or could you guarantee that these all continue to live up to the standard you set up?

This question set B. T. Hall thinking, and his answer was by the establishment of a strong branch organization; the years of his secretaryship were to see him concentrating on its achievement.

As we have already seen, a separate association was already flourishing in Manchester, but the first branch of the Union, as such, was formed in Swindon in 1894. This expanded and eventually enveloped clubs in neighbouring areas, its name being changed to Wiltshire Branch in 1917. This branch produced that fine clubman, Tom Jenks, its first President and for many years a forceful chairman of the Union's Finance Committee. Even today, Swindon has a high proportion of clubs to its population and the branch (now known as Wiltshire and Western Counties) now has over 120 clubs extending through Gloucestershire and Avon down to Devon and Cornwall.

The second branch to be formed during B. T. Hall's secretaryship was Northants (1898), which was extended to include Bedfordshire in 1920, and later amalgamated with the third branch to be formed, Buckinghamshire (1902), which was centred on Wolverton, a strong club town with the bulk of its membership drawn from the Wolverton railway works. (Derek Dormer, currently the Union President, was formerly Secretary of Buckinghamshire Branch and is now Secretary of South East Midlands Branch, which incorporates these former branches.

In 1904, three more branches opened: South Yorkshire, York City and Wakefield District. There had been several previous attempts to start a branch in Yorkshire, but it was not until Councillor J. H. Bagshaw was appointed Secretary in April 1904 that South Yorkshire took root. Bagshaw started with an initial membership of fifty clubs – and, like the present Secretary, R. C. Linstead, served on the National Executive. This branch now has over 180 clubs, and is still one of the most active and progressive.

York City Branch, also inaugurated in 1904, had only nine clubs to begin with, and even though its membership is still restricted to just the city itself, now has nearly 50 clubs in membership. The present Secretary of the branch, which is noted for organizing games, contests and flower shows, is Vincent James, who succeeded the former 'father' of the branch secretaries, Arthur Willis, who distinguished himself in the post between 1921 and 1956.

Wakefield Branch, in common with Durham County, which was formed the following year, has contributed many national leaders to the Union, notably its long-serving Secretary Edward McEnery, who became the Union's President in 1946 and held that office until 1969. Councillor Arthur Bates, who was the national Vice-President during much of Ted McEnery's presidency and succeeded him as President from 1970 to 1981, also came from Wakefield Branch, as did the late Alderman Alf Carr, who was a distinguished Executive member and twice Mayor of Wakefield. In addition, the branch was lucky to have two exceptional predecessors to McEnery in W. F. Adams and H. Hodge, who laid the foundations for what is now a branch of nearly 100 clubs, noted particularly for its educational work. Now, history is repeating itself in Wakefield; the present Branch Secretary, Brian Winters, has also gone on to become Vice-President of the Union.

Durham County has also produced an exceptional number of fine clubmen, including two former national Presidents, Robert Richardson, MP, and John Thompson, a carpenter on the railways, who also became President of the General Railway Workers Union before it became incorporated in the National Union of Railwaymen. But when Northants Branch was formed in 1898 there was not one single Union club in County Durham! By the time the branch was founded only seven years later, it had an initial membership of no less than 58. Since then, it has always been a strong branch – its membership today is well over 300 – setting an example to others with its emphasis on educational work. Like Wakefield, it has been a branch fortunate in its officers, with J. Bland, Joe Bray, Tom Nelson, Stan Hall, Jack Johnson and now J. Amos. Jack Johnson is now the Union's General Secretary.

The year after the formation of Durham County, B. T. Hall was to see the baptism of five more branches – Leeds and District, Huddersfield and District, Heavy Woollen District, Bradford and Halifax, and Northumberland – which are all still active today. Leeds made little progress until Harris Claughton was elected Secretary in 1914; under his leadership, the branch expanded rapidly, opening up its own shop and showrooms, and stock-taking and audit departments. Claughton died in 1932 and was succeeded by

Joe Thornton, who in turn was followed in 1939 by Sam Appleyard, a popular and hard-working executive member, too, who was sadly missed when he retired. Norman Sharp, who succeeded Appleyard in 1956, also succeeded Sam on the Executive. The present Secretary is J. Ellis, who also represents Leeds on the National Executive.

Huddersfield also started in a small way, and, like Leeds, owed much of its success to one man – in this case, W. H. Richardson, a hard-working Executive member who was succeeded in 1947 by W. Booth and in 1954 by W. Hoyle. The present Secretary is T. Holling, who has 54 clubs in his area.

Heavy Woollen, originally known as Spen Valley, came into being because clubmen in that area found it difficult to take an active part in Wakefield Branch affairs for geographical reasons. The Batley and Dewsbury districts were later merged to form the present branch of 48 clubs. The first Secretary was T. Harrison, who was followed by George Lovatt, G. Hepworth and the present Secretary, C. Howroyd. Long before this branch was founded, Hodgson Pratt and J. J. Dent had attempted to found one in Bradford and Halifax. Their efforts in 1886 and 1887 were to no avail, and it was not until B. T. Hall's 'reign' that clubs in the area became organization-conscious – though, even then, it was 1906 before the seeds bore fruit. The first Secretary was Bill Semley, who twenty years later was succeeded by Arthur Wallwork, and in 1938 by H. T. Richardson, who also served on the Executive for many years. The present Secretary, K. Wainwright, also serves on the Executive, and has 110 clubs in his area. Northumberland, however, was severely handicapped in early days by a bad secretary, and several years passed before it really started to flourish, notably under the secretaryship of Joe Wanless, who was followed in 1941 by Bob Hogarth and in 1960 by Joseph Nixon, who joined the Executive the following year. These days the work is divided with E. Moore, the Branch Secretary, and H. Drysdale, representing the 165 clubs in the area.

The next branch to be formed was Colne and Burnley (1908), which very nearly formed itself. The district originally came under Manchester, but as many clubmen thought Colne and Burnley were too far from Manchester to be properly co-ordinated a separate league was formed in 1904. It was from this that the new branch was born. J. H. Turner was the first Secretary, and he was followed by J. H. Lofthouse, Harold Barnes (a distinguished Executive member from 1921 to 1945), J. E. Pugh, T. H. Waterworth and the present Secretary of what is now known as Burnley and Pendle

Branch, Bill Ormerod, who is also a member of the National Executive.

In 1909, B. T. Hall oversaw the formation of North Staffordshire Branch, again a small one of only fourteen clubs, which suffered at first because of its size. Fortunate, however, in its first Secretary, Alderman Harry Leese (later a prominent member of the Executive and the City's first Lord Mayor), and then in his successor, Oscar Snelson, who remained on the Executive until 1961, the branch found just the men to build up the Union's prestige in North Staffordshire. Today the Branch Secretary, S. Robinson, continues the tradition of also serving on the Executive, representing 110 clubs, including many in North and Mid-Wales.

In 1909 the South Wales Branch was also established. This, too, has proved successful, with, like Leeds, its own trading and auditing departments. From the start, South Wales Branch has been noted for its educational activities, and in its early days the branch purchased a site at Langland Bay for £1,200. This was presented to the Union and the convalescent home would have been built there if the Union had not been able to subsequently purchase the Langland Bay Hotel. The first Secretary was J. Kinsman, who was succeeded by Bert Rowe, Tom Knight and C. P. Hughes, the present Branch Secretary, who represents an area of nearly 250 clubs, both in that post and also on the National Executive.

All the branches that B. T. Hall had been able to foster up to 1909 had been in the provinces, where the Union had been slow to take root prior to his secretaryship; its activities, as we have seen, had been concentrated in the Metropolis. But in 1910, the monthly Council meetings were abolished and the London area itself was reorganized to form four separate branches – North-East, North-West, South-East and Kent.

When London North-East Branch was formed, there were 49 clubs within its area and the branch was lucky to have in Councillor W. J. Lewis a hard-working Secretary who distinguished himself outside the Union as Mayor of Bethnal Green. Subsequent Secretaries included W. J. Tyler, G. F. Carter and now J. Ahern, who has 117 clubs 'under his wing', including clubs in Norfolk, Suffolk and Bedfordshire. Mr Ahern is also a member of the National Executive. The first Secretary of the London North-West Branch was J. Tozer, who served on the Executive for many years until his death in 1939, when he was succeeded by H. J. Diston. This Branch now has 135 member clubs, including many in Berkshire, Hertfordshire, Oxfordshire and the old county of Middlesex, and its Secretary, J. C. Tobin, also serves on the National Executive.

London South-East Branch had only 20 member clubs at first, but a succession of good Secretaries (J. J. Woolf, H. Holding, J. B. Adams and now Bernard Guess) consolidated its position within the South-east suburbs and in Surrey and Sussex, and today the branch has 145 member clubs. The doyen of the metropolitan secretaries was, however, Joe Beech, Secretary of one of the smaller branches, Kent, for well over fifty years after its formation. The Kent branch now has 130 member clubs, and its present Secretary, W. H. Jones, also represents the area on the national Executive.

The year after these changes were made in London, the Leicester clubs were enfranchised. There had been many clubs in Leicester since the very early days, but the first branch was not formed until 1911. The first Secretary, H. Fookes, had 25 clubs, but Leicester rapidly expanded to become one of the foremost 'club cities' under the leadership of his successor, Sid Anstee, who held office from 1925 until his death in 1951 and was also a highly respected chairman of the Union's Finance Committee. He was followed by Harry Gilmore, who also served on the Executive, and now T. S. Flanaghan, who similarly combines the two posts, representing nearly 100 clubs, many of them exceptionally well-equipped and financially healthy.

The next year, 1912, Cleveland and District Branch was formed to bring together the clubs in this part of north-east Yorkshire. The first Secretary was J. H. Burlison. Today the membership is 50 clubs and the Secretary, Dennis Brearley. The same year, clubs in the Doncaster area of South Yorkshire grouped together into Doncaster and District Branch, whose Secretary for many years was P. Allot. The clubs in the area expanded rapidly with the growing importance of the Doncaster coalfields, and today the Secretary, C. Bailey, has nearly 120 clubs.

In 1913, Hampshire Branch was formed, and its membership of 94 clubs today includes those on the Isle of Wight. Secretaries have included A. Powell, J. H. Mintram, who served on the Executive from 1944 until his death in 1958, and F. Scammell. The present Secretary, R. J. Etheridge, is also a member of the National Executive.

Many attempts had been made during Henry Solly's secretaryship to form a branch in the Midlands; indeed, one was established at Wolverhampton, though it was unsuccessful, but when one was inaugurated in 1914 with a retired schoolteacher, Oliver Bill, as Secretary, this soon took root. Today the West Midlands Branch has approximately 250 members. Oliver Bill was succeeded as Secretary by W. J. Galpin, Dick Harper, O. E. Cotterell and, lately, Colin Horton, who died so tragically in 1986, having served as Branch Secretary since 1981 and as a member of the Union Executive since 1975. Colin had been Chairman of the Union's Education Committee, and was also a member of the Finance and General Purposes Committee.

Three years after the formation of the West Midlands Branch, another was formed, in neighbouring Warwickshire, which today draws much of its strength – the membership totals 128 clubs – from Coventry. The Secretary is R. S. Owen, and J. F. Cooke represents the area on the National Executive. Derbyshire Branch, which was also formed in 1917, had to battle against the wind for the first few years because many clubs in the area were slow to join the Union. Membership today now totals 80, and the Secretary, D. J. MacMahon, is also a member of the National Executive.

Another three years elapsed before the next branch, Furness, was formed in 1920 and this, like Doncaster and Cleveland, was for the purpose of consolidation. Clubmen in this remote north-west corner of Lancashire were finding it difficult to take an active part in the Union. Its Secretaries included J. Campbell, Alf Brown and J. Thomson. The clubs in that area now form part of the Cumbria and District Branch, which has 64 member clubs. The present Secretary is K. Brown.

The last of the branches to be formed during B. T. Hall's secretaryship was Monmouthshire. Previously its clubs had been included in the South Wales Branch, but 'home rule' was achieved in 1921. The first Secretary was G. Davis, who was succeeded by W. Edgar Roe, who saw the branch grow steadily during his period of office. Membership grew to over 100, although the area has been affected in recent years by the cut-backs in the coalfields of the Welsh Valleys: many of the Valley clubs opted to join the Monmouthshire Branch. The present Secretary, L. R. Parry, also serves on the National Executive.

These branches, which owe much to the support if not the stimulus of B. T. Hall, live on – indeed, the only branch which was not formed during that period was Scotland (see page 195). This expansion of membership, grouping the clubs together and then consolidating their strength, was one of his great achievements, but this was not solely due to him; he happened to be the right man in the right place at the right time to reflect a general mood that was then developing among clubmen, and to act as its catalyst. During the nineteenth century the clubs had been prepared to accept decisions imparted from a head office in London; now, they wanted to take part themselves in the affairs of the Union.

The Reverend Henry Solly

Hodgson Pratt

J. J. Dent, CMG, 1883–1892

B. T. Hall, 1893–1929

GENERAL SECRETARIES:

R. S. Chapman, CBE, 1930–1951

Frank R. Castle, 1951–1964

J. B. Holmes, General Secretary 1965–1973

F. O. Morris, CBE, General Secretary 1973–1982

D. J. Dormer, FSVA, CMD, Vice President 1970–1981
President 1981 to date

B. Winters, CMD, Vice President 1982 to date

J. Johnson, General Secretary 1982 to date

Until 1901, no member of any club outside London had sat upon the Union Executive; in January of that year the Northants Branch nominated its Secretary, C. Underwood, for a seat thereon, and he was elected. When he retired, John Hill took his place, but B. T. Hall noted in *Our Fifty Years* that no other district followed this example, 'the Provinces being apparently content to be ruled from and by the Metropolis. But a feeling was growing in favour of representation. The Council had been to some extent getting more into association with the Provinces by the practice of holding some of its monthly meetings at provincial clubs.'

Beginning with venues in the Home Counties, the Council meetings had gradually extended themselves over a wider area until in June 1908 they found themselves farthest north at the Darlington Working Men's Club. At this meeting, Mr J. H. Bagshaw of the Wath and West Melton club moved:

> That the Rules of the Union be revised, and that the Executive be instructed to communicate with the whole of the Clubs and Branches of the Union requesting suggestions, if any, to this end.

He said that whilst he had no feeling of antagonism to the present Executive, and did not believe that the work of the Union could be better done, he felt the time had come when the Union should be more representative in character. Bagshaw added that 'the provincial clubs had been the youth of the movement, but were growing up to manhood and wanted the rights of citizenship'.

The proposal was accepted on behalf of the Executive by Jesse Argyle, who said that the Executive felt the reasonableness and the necessity of the proposal, and welcomed it. The motion was carried unanimously, but before the Union had communicated with all the clubs another election to the Executive was held, and a Yorkshire candidate was elected to the Executive, with Mr Bagshaw himself only eight votes behind (Bagshaw was elected to the Executive later the same year, and continued to sit thereon until his death in 1921).

Bagshaw's rather tamely worded resolution had merely asked that the rules of the Union should be amended, and the views of the members sought. The suggestions soon came in, and a sub-committee was appointed to examine them, eventually recommending that the Executive should be elected directly from the membership, the clubs being arranged into electoral districts. Meetings were duly held in each area to ensure that the recommendations had a wide acceptance, and at these meetings B. T. Hall produced details of the Union's growth which demonstrated

the need for reform. His researches showed a shift in the distribution
of the Union's membership over the previous two decades. In 1889
nearly half the Union's clubs had been situated in the Metropolis;
now there were more clubs in Lancashire and Cheshire than there
were in London, and more than twice as many in Yorkshire:

District	1889	1899	1909
Metropolis	154	153	159
Home Counties	28	64	89
Wales (including Monmouth)	2	7	42
West Midlands	11	34	84
Ireland	—	3	1
South Western	7	18	18
Southern Counties	6	76	74
Eastern Counties	10	16	14
East Midlands	17	77	112
Lancashire and Cheshire	68	129	211
Yorkshire	26	99	341
Northumberland	—	2	46
Durham	—	2	125
Cumberland, Westmorland, and Scotland	—	3	6
	329	683	1,322

Inevitably, the membership agreed to the suggestion that there
should be wider representation; the new rules provided for seven
electoral districts, with provision for greater representation from
the Metropolis because of the long traditions that the Union had in
London. The districts were rearranged again twelve years later, to
reflect further changes in the distribution of the Union's membership, but this was the initial warding:

Electoral district	Number of members
1. METROPOLIS (the area comprised within a twelve-mile radius of Charing Cross) and the Home Counties – Middlesex, Essex, Herts, Kent, Surrey and Sussex	6
2. WALES (including Monmouth); West Midlands (Derby, Stafford, Shropshire, Hereford, Gloucestershire, Warwick, Worcester); Ireland and South-Western (Cornwall, Devon and Somerset)	2
3. SOUTHERN COUNTIES – Dorset, Hants, Oxford and Wiltshire	1
4. EASTERN AND EAST MIDLANDS – Lincoln, Cambridge, Norfolk, Suffolk, Bedford, Leicester, Rutland, Huntingdon, Notts, Northampton, Berks and Bucks	2

The Union's first 'Members of Parliament' were elected at the first 'General Election', held in June 1910. They were:

Thomas Brown, a Durham accountant who had lived in London for many years, was President of the Central Club and a rate collector with Southwark Council;

Councillor Edward Garrity, President of the Finsbury Radical Club, Chairman of the LCC Schools for Finsbury, Chairman of the Holborn Guardians, a Finsbury councillor and Editor of *Club Life*;

Councillor Arthur Holden, a Labour member of Woolwich Borough Council, President of the Amalgamated Engineers' Club in Plumstead and of North Kent Branch;

George Knowles, for more than thirty years a member of the Hackney Gladstone Club, and for thirty-six years a member of the Cigar Makers' Trade Union, having been a member of its Executive, its Vice-President and President (B. T. Hall noted that he was 'big and burly, fond of a joke, and sings a good song');

James Matthews, Editor of *Club News*, who had been Librarian of the St Albans Holborn Working Men's Club, a founder of the Penge and Beckenham Liberal Club, and Political Secretary of the Hatcham Liberal Club, and had also worked as confidential clerk or private secretary to the financiers Bischoffsheim and Sir Ernest Cassel;

J. Tozer, a carpenter who had been Secretary of the St John's Wood Club in Marylebone for eighteen years, and Secretary of the North-West London Branch of the Union;

Councillor H. T. Richards, Secretary of the Ferndale Band Musical Institute, and Chairman of the Pontypridd Liberal Club; he was also Secretary of the Liberal Association of East Glamorgan, and a leading Welsh Baptist;

F. W. Swinnerton, a Staffordshire man who had lived in Coventry for twelve years, and had been President for three years of the Coventry Working Men's Club, which remains one of the oldest clubs in the Union; he was a schoolmaster;

T. A. Jenks, who had been President of the Swindon Branch for seventeen years and had been 'closely associated with the Adult School movement';

John Hill, who had been a member of the Union Executive since 1902, having been appointed Secretary of the Northampton Branch the previous year; he was also Secretary of the Northants Branch of the Workers' Educational Association, and had been for eight years a Poor Law Guardian; he was a member of the Northampton No. 1 Branch of the Boot and Shoe Operatives' Union;

J. G. Mobbs, who had been President of the Northants Branch, Vice-Chairman of the Kettering Rifle Band Club, Chairman of the United Clubs' Hospital Committee, and of the Joint Clubs' Committee for Organising Ambulance Classes;

K. T. S. Dockray, MA, President of the Manchester Branch and a solicitor practising in the city; he took an active interest in the University Settlement in Manchester, conducting classes on economics, and was also one of the organizers of the Poor Man's Lawyer Department;

James Stevens, for thirty-two years a member of the Mossley Liberal Club; President of the Mossley Workmen's Club for fifteen years, and for eight years a member of the Lancashire Union of Liberal Clubs, and a member of the Board of Management of the Mossley Co-operative. He was by trade a cotton spinner, and a member of the Spinners' Trade Union Committee, and Assistant Registration Agent for the Prestwich Parliamentary Division;

Councillor J. H. Bagshaw, whom we have met before, a former schoolmaster; Secretary of the South Yorkshire Branch, and of the Wath and West Melton Club; he was also a member of the Ardsley District Council, and a Past Provincial Grand Master of the Manchester Unity of Oddfellows;

Councillor Arthur Gledhill, a member of the Dewsbury Town Council, President of the Huddersfield Branch, and described by B. T. Hall as 'pleasant and modest and level-headed';

Tom Shires, President of the Wakefield Branch, who had sat for five years on the Rugby Union County Committee, for three of them as Vice-President; he was a foreman moulder by trade, and during his years on the Union Executive was a great supporter of the convalescent homes;

Allan Wright of Leeds, a compositor, born in Castleford, whose father had been one of the founders of the Workman's Institute and Co-operative Stores; he was a member of the Kingston Unity of Oddfellows, became their Chief Secretary, Editor of their *Miscellany*, and a well-known lecturer on history and music;

Councillor R. Richardson, a check-weighman at Ryhope Colliery, near Sunderland, and a member of the Ryhope Social Club;

he was a member of Durham County Council, Chairman of Ryhope District Council, a local magistrate, and later became a Member of Parliament, and President of the Union;

John Thompson, a carpenter and keen trade unionist, who was also Vice-President of the Durham Branch, and a keen clubman in Darlington; and

Martin Weatherburn, for several years Secretary of the Cramlington Liberal Association and brother-in-law of the MP, Thomas Burt; he was President of the Northumberland Branch, and formerly Chairman of the Hartford Parish Council and also Chairman of the Cramlington School Board.

With their election in 1910, the Union became a truly 'national' organization for the first time and it was this, and the formation of the Union's branches, that was to prove to be B. T. Hall's lasting achievement. Thereafter, there were to be occasional changes in the electoral districts, but the principle remained; the Working Men's Club and Institute Union had become a national institution, linking together working men's clubs throughout the United Kingdom.

9

Another lasting achievement of B. T. Hall's thirty-six years as General Secretary of the Union lay in his pioneering work for the convalescent homes. Hall himself compiled an account of the building of the first two homes at Pegwell Bay and Saltburn for publication in a magazine in 1911, and then adapted this material for inclusion in *Our Sixty Years*:

As far back as 1878 the Council considered the possibility of establishing a Seaside Home for members, their wives and families. A house was rented at £60 per annum, at 2 Royal Place, Margate, and furnished at a cost of £120. Donations of £10 each from Samuel Morley MP, Hodgson Pratt, Lord Brabazon, W. C. Venning, J. Corbett MP, Dr Hardwicke, Hamilton Hoare, the Devonshire Club, £10 from the Union, £15 from sundry Union clubs, and other small items were received towards this. It was formally opened on September 2nd, 1878. Among those present were Mr W. A. Weigall and Lady Rose Weigall, to whom was recorded a special vote of thanks for their cordial interest in the project.

It would appear that no attempt at the provision of food was made, as the charge to a single man for one week was 3s 6d for a bed, and to married people with children 6s 6d for a room.

Complaint was made that the railway companies would make no concessions as to reduced fares, as was usual with convalescent homes, which this was certainly not.

'From April to June, 1879, a considerable number of married persons with their children availed themselves of this advantage,' says the Report for that year. But 'the necessity of making the House self-supporting and the fact that while the expense of maintaining it continues through the year visitors use it only in summer' (which probability does not seem to have been foreseen) 'has obliged the Council to charge more than was originally intended.' The Council is much disappointed. It cannot see how the difficulty is to be overcome, and Brighton is talked about as a change of site. £24 is received in Donations and £23 from Residents. The outgoings are £108.

In the Reports for 1880, not a word is said about the House but the accounts show £15 received and £94 expended, and another item, small and poor, but eloquent, 'Sale of Furniture at Ditto £15'. Thus the Sea

Side House experiment ingloriously ends. It costs £322. It returns but £38, and its Furniture, on which £120 has been spent, is sold for £15. Its principal achievement was to add another heavy burden upon the then slender and embarrassed finances of the Union.

PEGWELL BAY

At a meeting of the Council of the Union at the East St Pancras Reform Club on Saturday, February 6th 1892, the following resolution was moved by N. W. Oviatt (Victory Club) and seconded by Jesse Argyle (North Hackney), and carried –

That this meeting do take into consideration the advisability of establishing a Convalescent Home, and that a committee be appointed for the purpose of drawing up a scheme.

The committee appointed consisted of N. W. Oviatt, F. Campbell, Ben Ellis, J. W. Dorman, J. H. Holmes, T. J. Mason and Jesse Argyle, who had agreed to act as honorary secretary.

The committee met and produced a very modest scheme, estimating an expenditure of only £600 per annum, and subscriptions of but £4 4s per annum from the largest clubs, down to a guinea from the smaller. A large house on the South-East Coast was to be leased and adapted for the residence of 15 'patients', as the term then was.

Circulars were sent out to the clubs, and some few ready responses were made. But on the whole the scheme fell flat. To quote the words of the Union Annual Report 1892–1893, 'the result in definite promises of cash support did not seem to promise the realization of this particularly useful and valuable proposal'.

And so it hung until June, 1893, when one day Hodgson Pratt called on me (I had been appointed Secretary of the Union in the previous March) and said he had had some conversation with Mr Passmore Edwards, who would like to see a deputation on the matter. So Mr Pratt, with Oviatt, Argyle, Dent and myself, went round to the *Echo* office and there saw Mr Edwards. He asked whether we would guarantee to keep such a house going if he gave us one. We gave him this assurance, and we parted on his saying, 'Very well, go and find your site, and I will buy it, and build you a home on it.' This was tidings of comfort and joy indeed. Made known to the clubs, it was received with enthusiasm and gave a necessary stimulus to the proposals before them.

We sought for sites. I went with Mr Pratt to look at a piece of land at Birchington, but Mr Pratt voted it too cold. Then Dent, Oviatt, Argyle and I went to Whitstable and Herne Bay prospecting. Poor old 'Judge Oviatt'. I shall never forget how full he was with joy and pride in his task, and how he made known our quest for 'a little piece of freehold land' to everyone encountered.

For one reason or another we were unable to fix up anything, when in May, 1894, we heard from Mr Passmore Edwards that he himself had hit upon the right sort of place, and had bought a disused hotel and grounds at Pegwell Bay. This spot, so famous now, was unknown to me or to any member of the Committee then, and I was sent down to find the Bay, see the building, note all its salient features and come back and report. On my arrival I found the builders and decorators in possession, and the place nearly ready for occupation. I need hardly say that my report as to its situation was a favourable one. I remember how puzzled I was roaming about inside the building to find myself on the other side of the road, for I had not been conscious of entering the now bright, but then black, subterranean passage which crosses the road. For the home is constituted by two distinct buildings on different levels joined by the under roadway passage referred to.

But the terrace, with the sea rippling at my feet, appealed to me as rendering the situation admirable. It was to be months before I learned the advantages of situation which are possessed by the Home, the gentle fall into the hollow which shelters it from all winds but the south, the thousand and one charms which led a visitor to remark that 'it seemed as if countless centuries had been preparing the place for its purpose, and that some wise light had guided our footsteps there'.

However, the report made, there was one matter in doubt – what about the furniture? 'Did Mr Edwards propose to furnish it?' asked some. It was clearly impossible to ask him, as it was unreasonable to expect him. And so an urgent appeal was made to the clubs. We estimated that £5 would furnish a bedroom (we had not the standard of modern days), and we said that we would put up over a door the name of any club or person who would give us £5, a practice that was later discontinued. We raised £250 in two months, a wondrous feat in those days, and we gave an order for £300 worth of furniture.

The next task was to advertise for a superintendent and matron. Out of 120 applicants we selected Mr and Mrs Boyland, and no better selection was anywhere or ever made. All sorts of folk applied, and the workhouse master and matron, the latter a lady of great width of frame (whatever of judgement) were common types. I remember well that Mrs Boyland's slighter, graceful figure and obvious culture were counted against her by one member of the committee who thought she looked 'er-er-ah-um-well, rather-er-er-frivolous', the last word jerked out in desperation at finding no word to suit. The idea that beauty and grace and culture were to be more powerful influences in the making of democracy than force, punishment, and dictation were then but little understood. We have travelled far since then. There have been variations in the original agreement with Mr and Mrs Boyland, but no committee of the Home has ever had a single moment's cause to regret the choice of the first. And for the residents, is not their judgement written on every club notice board? It was also expressed by two presentations, voluntarily organised by the clubs. Both consisted of illuminated address and silver service, and the second, presented in the Union Hall in July 1918, on the occasion of their Golden Wedding day, added also by personal jewellery, and a cheque for £450. Though Boyland –

serving us and serving humanity – has passed away, Mrs Boyland still remains to endear herself to all residents by her assiduous cultivation of their comfort when in her charge, and by her personal charm of character.

Thus then came the place. Its selection has often been credited to some wondrous sagacity and universal knowledge of mine. Here explodes that idea. I never saw the place till it was nearly ready for occupancy. The furniture installed and the Boylands put in charge, we were now all ready for the formal and actual opening as a Home, performed by Mr Passmore Edwards, under the presidency of the then Mayor of Ramsgate, Alderman Blackburn, on Bank Holiday, August 6th 1894. Hodgson Pratt and Stephen Tayler made speeches in thanks to Mrs Passmore Edwards; the Mayor was thanked on the motion of 'Judge' Oviatt and C. T. Perry, the 600 club folk present cheered the Home and its donor, the artillery of the heavens fired several salvoes, for it was not the kindest of days, and our first Home was launched.

From the day of its opening, on that August Bank Holiday of 1894, the Home was a success. As each resident came back to his club he spread the tale of its charms. Large excursions organised by the Home Committee took tens of thousands of London clubmen to Pegwell. Far and wide spread its fame. A picture fund realized £100 in a few months. The Home then accommodated 32 residents, but before the third year of its life had passed it was clear to the committee that extension would be required.

We had a meeting of the Home Committee at Pegwell one Sunday, and in the little garden in the rear (for the orchard was not then ours) we decided that we could manage to spend £2,500. We had no money. The Union had none, being indeed then much pressed itself for cash. Some of us were, however, confident that the Home had so established itself in the affections of the clubs of London and the Home Counties that we could borrow and beg all such a sum. Borne down (or uplifted rather) by our optimism the doubtful agreed.

We appealed to the clubs, and we engaged, on Mr Passmore Edwards' recommendation, his architect Mr Maurice Adams, to prepare drawings, adding bedrooms with bathrooms, and on each floor large lavatories, where residents could wash without, as then, doing so in bedrooms, an arrangement of great economy and infinitely more satisfactory to residents. We soon found out that our allowance of £2,500 was likely to be considerably over-stepped. Mr Passmore Edwards suggested the formation of the centre Tower, and gave us £500 towards its cost. When the plans were complete and tenders invited the lowest received was that of Messrs Jarman and Son for £4,312. This was accepted, but outlay did not end here. The owner of a small dilapidated shop, on the east side, raised a 'light and air' protest, and was bought out for £120 and his shanty pulled down, thus leaving a strip of garden on that side.

There was a right-of-way between the old building and the garden on the west, leading into an orchard at the rear, and when we started to build the owner of this found our tower projected some inches over the right-of-way and served us with an injunction. We overcame this by buying him, and the orchard, out for £550. All this, of course, was piling up the financial burden. But we secured a little relief, for the aforesaid garden on the west straggled off into the roadway, and for widening purposes the Ramsgate Corporation agreed with us to pay the £120 which we had given for the shanty and to build for us the wall (costing another £153) which now bounds our estate.

Altogether the first extension cost us £6,471, the tower alone accounting for £1,200. To the cost of the building must be added £600 for the furniture. So our heroic estimate of £2,500 had grown to over £7,000! And financially we were in parlous plight indeed. The builder, however, accepted Bills, which we (borrowing all the money we could from clubs and members) somehow managed to meet, but with a debt of £5,000.

The foundation-stone was laid on Saturday, July 10th 1897, by Mrs Passmore Edwards, in the presence of a crowded gathering under the presidency of Stephen Seaward Tayler, the Corporation of Ramsgate, and, amongst others, Miss Phyllis Broughton honouring us with her presence. On July 2nd, 1898, just twelve months after, the new wing was opened by Mr Passmore Edwards, and the accommodation, now raised to 62, was availed to the full.

Trade, happily, was good, and the clubs prosperous. The responses to our appeals for money were liberal indeed. I am not now talking of Subscriptions enabling clubs to send members into residence, but Donations given towards paying off the debt. In 1898 no less than £986 was given us. The *Journal* organized a 'horse race'. A picture of a racecourse appeared, in which several clubs represented as horses and jockeys were shown as competing for the honour of being first in the list of donations to the Special Appeal. The St James' and Soho won with a donation of £105, the Mildmay came next with £100, and then the Kettering Working Men's with £60. In 1899 the gift total was £945. In 1900, £1,072; the St James' and Soho adding another £100 this year! It would be invidious to particularise when all were so good, and £1 from one club is equal to £5 from another. But memory will place grateful tribute to the St James' and Soho and Mildmay as the foremost in giving, the while it remembers the little Regency, which, with but 150 members, gave us £25 to £30 every year. It was all very wonderful and very inspiring to the Committee, and by 1905 we had nearly paid off the whole debt, and come to consider a further extension.

The wing on the terrace was (like the original building entirely) a poor ramshackle affair, and whilst enough to accommodate 32 residents for food and social hours, was not suitable for 62, a very unpleasing crowding ensuing at meal times and on inclement days. So in 1905 it was resolved to pull it down and erect a larger and better equipped building. The task was allotted to Mr W. Wadman (most ingenious, far-seeing and excellent of all architects), the tender of Mr Woodhall (recently Mayor of Ramsgate) for £3,054 was accepted, and on Easter Monday, April 16th, 1906, the second extension, costing in all £4,000 was opened by Mr J. J. Dent, who laid a commemorative tablet with a dexterity at which the audience wondered, not knowing that this was no 'prentice hand', and the Home became complete, and as it now remains.

A further and final extension was made in 1914, when a wing was added to the bedroom block, bringing up the total possible accommodation to 72. At the same time 'The Conyngham' Cafe opposite the main entrance was purchased for £400, and pulled down, a small bowling green and old English garden taking its place. The total cost of this final development was £1,800. The Home was completely renovated then, and subsequently in 1920 and 1921 a Special Appeal realized £2,000, which was spent in improving the furniture and equipment, with a view to bringing this the first of the Homes to the same level and standard of comfort as characterise the later Homes.

On Sunday, January 19th 1919, Herbert Samuel Boyland passed from our service. His end was sudden. He had parted with his wife and children but a few minutes when, walking along the Pegwell Road, his heart stopped beating, and there died at the age of 58 one of the ablest and most faithful officers ever enlisted in the Union's service. His work in the Home had won the affection of thousands. His local work for the public, and especially the victims of the Great War, brought him high honour amongst his neighbours, a notable gathering testifying to this at his funeral . . . .

SALTBURN

Whilst I am compelled to deny myself credit for the discovery of Pegwell, I think I may claim it of the Saltburn Home. It was on April 29th, 1905, that I first found myself in Saltburn. The Durham Branch had been constituted that Saturday afternoon at a meeting in the Shakespeare Hall, Durham, and I reached Saltburn at midnight, as the nearest station (as far as I could trace), from which to reach the Cleveland village of Brotton, wherein a workmen's club had been formed, which I was to visit.

On Sunday morning I walked from Saltburn to Brotton along the path now familiar to thousands of clubmen, saw the club and its officers, and in the afternoon found myself back in Saltburn, with no means of reaching home until Monday morning, for the North-Eastern Railway is scant of Sunday trains. I wandered round the peculiarly clean and orderly little town, and saw the present Saltburn Home building 'To Let'. I managed to get a look round and over it, and then went down to the beautiful sands to dream. How *could* we, *would* we ever, or *how soon* would we establish a second Home? And, under the influence of the inspection of the building, the glorious sun and sands and sea, I thought me that here was the place and there the building. But I never dreamed that the latter would be available in the time, far distant as it seemed to me, when we should want it. I made close inspection of the slopes behind Cat Nab and overlooking the salt burn (Skelton Beck) in search of a prospective site for a distant day's need.

In this year of 1905 two things forced themselves upon attention; one, that Pegwell was availed of to the full, and two, that the counties of York and Durham were manifesting enormous club development. From consideration of these two things the dream of a second Home took more solid shape, and, within a few months of my reveries at Saltburn, a circular was issued by the Executive in which £3,000 was offered from the Union funds if the Northern clubs would support the scheme of a second Home, the basis of which was set out. It was estimated that the building and furniture would cost £12,000.

I had, of course, been busy, as had our Northern Branch secretaries, publishing the idea at every meeting in the Northern area in the interim, and on June 23rd, 1906, the clubs of Colne and Burnley organised a big conference, with the Mayor in the chair, at Blackpool. The meeting was enthusiastic, and the only ripple on the smooth surface of agreement was caused by the endeavour to get the site then and there indicated. Of course, the undoubted charms of the Fylde Coast were dilated upon, with many tributes to its health-restoring power, but, as I listened, my mind went back to that Sunday afternoon at Saltburn, and dwelt again on the building I had seen there. Six months later (January 19th 1907) came a great meeting at Wakefield, which finally raised the second Home out of the region of suggestion, and made it a thing to be set about forthwith. The meeting was held in the hall of the Wakefield Co-operative Society, with that loyal friend of the clubs, Alderman Kingswell JP, Mayor of Wakefield, in the chair. This meeting was addressed by Mr E. A. Brotherton, MP for Wakefield, Sir J. Compton Rickett MP, Alderman Hudson, J. J. Dent, Jesse Argyle and myself. And, whilst speaking of Wakefield, let me say that whilst many were the workers in the North, none, I think, compared with Mr W. F. Adams, the secretary of the Wakefield Branch, in industry, competence and enthusiasm.

The clubs had begun to respond to the circular readily, and there was £1,000 in yearly subscriptions guaranteed by February 1907, and nearly £400 received in donations. The Executive then sent a note to all clubs which had promised subscriptions, asking for nominations of site. Many places on the North-West and North-East were proposed, but on a ballot being taken, Saltburn received 85 votes, against 57 recorded for Blackpool. That the town was one of quiet and rest more desirable by the convalescent than the hurly-burly gaiety of Blackpool, and also that it is admirably placed for railway service doubtless contributed to the result. Then it was discovered that the building I had seen had been taken as temporary premises by the Silcoates School and would be shortly vacated.

In August, 1908, Mr W. Wadman visited the said premises and made a report to the Executive, and on November 21st following a deputation of Northern Branch representatives, accompanied by Mr Wadman and myself, went to Saltburn to inspect. It was a horrible day. We saw Saltburn at its worst, and the Home, empty, barrack-like, and gloomy in its interior, by candle light. Then, at a conference held at 'The Queen', we discussed the situation, the money aspect and what could be done to transform the interior of a building noble in outward aspect, eternal in construction, but cheerless and repulsive in its barren and sombre dormitories inside. That the latter could be accomplished Mr Wadman assured them. They believed him. That the money would be all right I asserted. But, as in the Pegwell extension, there were those who were cautious and doubting. Eventually the conference decided unanimously to recommend the Executive to open negotiations for the purchase of the Home.

This the Executive at once did. The price asked was £7,000 – less than half the original cost. We bluffed boldly and offered £6,000 at outside, in a 'take it or leave it' tone. We waited anxiously enough for the reply, for we should have been foolish not to have paid £10,000, if unable to obtain the place for less. In a week came the answer – £6,000 was accepted, and the second Convalescent Home came into being.

I have not yet said anything to describe this building of which the Union had now become possessed. It is of splendid construction, and will be a building as perfect as ever when the remnants of the original building at Pegwell shall have crumbled to dust. It was erected in 1872 by Sir Joseph Pease, and was supported by him till financial disaster overwhelmed him. It occupies 6,000 yds of freehold land (5,922 to be exact) abutting on Marine Terrace and overlooking the lovely Hazel Grove. The land cost £2,012, or about 7s per square yard. The building cost £12,734. A total of £14,746. To produce such a building to-day would (with land) cost £30,000 at least. Not then, this, a bad bargain for the Union. [B. T. Hall was writing this account in 1922, at which time the Union had just acquired another plot of land between the Home and the sea (thus preserving the view) at a cost of £1,400. This latter acquisition was 3,920 square yards.]

Its internal economy (except its unrelieved bareness, dormitory bed-rooms, and absence of provision for social enjoyment) was admirably arranged, the Home proper in front, the great dining hall built like a church (over 30 ft from floor to ridge) in the centre; and laundry, staff-rooms, and kitchen (lofty and oak-timbered like a baronial hall) in the rear. There is a terrace and fine sweep of garden in front, and a large open space, now converted into bowling green and gardens, in the rear. It is the finest building in Saltburn, and would be a noteworthy and commanding edifice anywhere. The large kitchen garden, which had run wild, was converted into a bowling green and flower garden, and some thousand trees and shrubs planted, securing both privacy and shelter from the Nor'Easter, a fairly regular and boisterous visitor to Saltburn.

The building acquired, Mr Wadman was commissioned to transform the interior, and on this some £2,500 was spent. How well was the work done only a personal inspection could convey. What was sombre, barren and barrack-like, became bright, comfortable and splendid. The *Daily Mail*, after inspection, termed it 'a workmen's Palace'. It has been visited by hundreds of local residents and tens of thousands of clubmen, amazement and admiration characterising the sentiments of all. Of course, many (and, oh! the pity of it, many of these being workmen) thought it 'too good for the working man'.

But, happily, money was coming in well, and there was a prospect of more. For once in a way we were able to do almost all that we could wish, and so it is safe to say that nowhere in the world, then, was there a workmen's institution so magnificently equipped as the Club Union Home at Saltburn. Mr Wadman devoted himself to the work in real enthusiasm. I think the clubman in him worked harder than the architect, but as both he laboured without tiring, and no man more deserved the encomiums heaped upon him and his work at the final opening ceremony. Amongst other features I may mention that each bedroom has a radiator, and each resident may thus have in his bedroom the degree of warmth he pleases. In 1911 the Committee added a Winter Garden, a pleasant lounge within shelter in any season, at a cost of £400.

I say *final* ceremony, for we had two. The taking over of the building as it stood, and its dedication to our use, was performed on Whit Monday, May 31st 1909, by Mr W. G. Urwin JP, chairman of the Saltburn District Council (Mr Jesse Argyle, Vice-President, in the chair), in the presence of some 5,000 clubmen and their wives. Never before had Saltburn seen such an influx of visitors.

The work of alteration and redecoration was not complete until September, and on Saturday, the 11th of that month, the Home was formally opened by the Rt Hon Sir (then Mr) Herbert Samuel, MP for the Cleveland Division. A luncheon (Mr Dent presiding over a distinguished gathering including a representative of every Union Branch) was first given, and Mr Samuel then addressed a crowded gathering of men and women in the south courtyard, to which gathering the suffragettes vainly sought admission, with ladylike intent to smash up the proceedings. The gathering and the Home (as well as the complete outmanoeuvring of the suffragettes) came in for a great deal of notice from the Northern Press, and I think did much to establish the very much improved attitude towards workmen's clubs visible in many quarters.

A small sub-committee, consisting of Councillor J. H. Bagshaw, R. Richardson CC JP and Martin Weatherburn, had charge of the furniture arrangements, after the Executive Committee had approved certain samples. We determined, as I have indicated before, that only the best was good enough. As the Home now stands it is a model which each club should set itself to endeavour to imitate. If it were possible to pass every club member through the Home, as I earnestly wish it were, there would soon be a revolution in the furnishing of clubs, dismal and poor as some are, unambitious, common-place, and unteaching as are many. When will all club committees learn that in the material environment with which they surround their members, no less than in the moral, lies their chief opportunity for usefulness? The furniture, pictures, and equipment at Saltburn are as effective as the climate in the restoration of physical and mental health.

I must devote a paragraph to the pictures, for they are one of the features of the interior, and I think my principal joy. For they represent the result of a personal appeal I made to the Southern clubs. My idea was that no nicer way of demonstrating the fellowship of North and South could be devised than that the South should supply the pictures for the Northern Home. This they did, excepting that Bradford, South Yorkshire and Wakefield Branches insisted on contributing a picture each. When we furnished Pegwell we were not quite happy in the result of our appeal for pictures. We asked for pictures and got photographs – one I remembered of the three waiters of the —— Club, who asked that the photo should be put in the entrance hall!

It is difficult for a committee to decline any gift well meant, however unsuitable. So I asked and obtained the consent of the Executive to have full control of the picture supply, guaranteeing that I would raise £150 in an appeal to the Southern and Midland clubs. The result was amazing. I got my £150 all right – and another £250 worth of pictures as well. The Eleusis (through the generosity of Mr E. Horniman MP, one of its members) sent a famous Academy picture, *Hagar and Ishmael*, by Margetson, which had cost £100; the St James' and Soho an oil painting of a Yorkshire coast scene by George Chambers (whose work may be seen in the Tate, Greenwich and Kensington Galleries), which the club bought for £13; the Hatcham Liberal paid £10 for a delightful water-colour by H. H. Parker, *A Surrey Hayfield*; the Northants clubs £15, *Ledr River*, an oil painting by the same artist; the Central, Mr Wadman, South Yorkshire, Wakefield and Bradford contributing other oil paintings by well-known men, and I purchased for £18 10s a noble oil by Gustave Breanski. But I think the *Two Cronies*, presented by the Mildmay, is the favourite of residents at the Home.

Besides all these are some 300 other pictures, oils, water colours and prints. I wish I could acknowledge here all who helped. In the wide north corridor, used as a lounge and smoke-room, I put up some of the water colours of Cynicus, which, if not 'things of beauty', certainly are 'a joy for ever' in their smile-provoking satire. Although there are over 300 pictures installed, so wide and lofty is each room and corridor, we should be glad of more, and have cordially to thank The Fellowship (of which more anon) for its gift of a large and boldly executed oil, *The Fellowship of the Sea*, which now faces the entrance hall.

In the selection of a superintendent and wife the Homes Committee and Executive felt they had an anxious task. For on the character and temperament of these the success of the Home depends. The good fortune of the Union did not desert it, and in Mr and Mrs Reed it was as lucky (or as happily discriminate) as when the same task presented itself at Pegwell. Both have the exact qualities required, both are devoted wholly and solely to the daily life of the Home, both have earned the praises of the residents in their charge. They are, too, enthusiastic gardeners, and Mr Reed, as a mechanic, finds his early training of considerable use and profit to the Home's administration. (On the completion of the Grange Home in August 1916, Mr and Mrs Reed were appointed to take charge there, and Mr and Mrs Seagrave, who had both a long experience at Benenden and other similar institutions, were appointed at Saltburn. Again the Union found itself fortunate in obtaining faithful and competent officers.)

In the matter of finances we had none of the struggles which distracted us in the first extensions of Pegwell. The appeal for donations towards the building produced £1,500 before the formal opening. To December 31st, 1911, £2,526 had been received. The debt remaining on both Pegwell and Saltburn – £8,000 – was in 1912 merged in a Jubilee special appeal. Then came Grange before the debt had died, and consequently other appeals, resulting eventually in the complete extinction of all debt on the three homes in 1919. In the Donations, there was a generous response, outrunning the estimate. As I said in referring to Pegwell, it is invidious to mention names, as a gift of £5 from one club is equivalent to £50 from another, but I think I must mention the largest donors: The South Kirkby Diamond Jubilee, £100; the Hoyland Common, £82 10s, and (most welcome from the South) the Mildmay Carnival proceeds, £70.

It was thought by many that it would be necessary to close this Home during the winter months. That theory has been entirely upset, for the Home has never for a week been without residents. For nine months of the year the applications for residence outnumber (often double or treble) the accommodation. There is a happy life possible within doors, to which the construction of the winter garden has very materially contributed. The construction of the bowling green and the planting of shrubs in the garden cost another £200.

GRANGE

The celebration of the Jubilee of the Union in 1912 saw it with two Homes established and self-supporting, with a debt of £6,746 (on January 1st of that year) remaining. This encouraged the Executive to seek to meet the demands which came from both South-West and North-West for the establishment of a Home in each. Mr Wadman and I paid visits to South Wales, and afterwards to Rhyl, and then to

Grange-over-Sands. I unhesitatingly decided that before any more scouting be done, the Executive should look at Grange and the site we suggested there. They came, they saw and were conquered. Ideal place, ideal site, unparalleled aspect! Agreed unanimously – *the* place. And so at a cost of £1,430, some 15,370 square yards (3¼ acres) of site was acquired at the end of 1912. Mr W. Wadman was commissioned to prepare plans for a building to accommodate 70 residents at an estimated cost of £12,000. Oh! these modest estimates, so eternally falsified! The original plans had to be reduced to accommodation for 56 – and then the lowest estimate was for £17,357, that of W. Till, a local builder. On Whit Monday, 1914, the foundation stone was laid by Mr Jesse Argyle in the presence of a large gathering representative of North Country folk. The Rev. Vicars Gaskell, Chairman of the Grange Urban Council, occupied the chair, supported by members of the Council. Cash (including £100 from Barrow clubs) and promises (including gift of a billiard table by the St James' and Soho Club, a piano and table for Entrance Hall from the North Kent Branch) were received by the Secretary, and everyone went to spread abroad the glories of Grange.

Wet weather and then the War hampered building. Difficulties may delay, but daunt or deter not the Union Executive Council, and on August Bank Holiday, August 7th 1916, the Home, fully equipped, was formally opened by C. Duncan, MP for Barrow, supported by the Rt Hon. C. W. Bowerman MP, J. Bliss MP and Col. J. W. Weston MP. Mr J. J. Dent presided, and there was a large and enthusiastic crowd. And so Grange began. The building proved disastrous to the contractor, the War having greatly increased all costs of material and labour. The Union gave him an additional £1,000 to help cover this, but it is greatly to be feared that it was inadequate and left him without profit. The fine building is the only tribute paid him. The Lancashire and Cheshire Branch generously met the cost (some £450) of providing a full-sized Bowling Green in the front grounds of the Home. Both as a building and in its equipment the Grange Home challenges comparison with anything of its kind, or with the best hotels of the country. Two rooms were added (giving four beds) in 1921 at a cost of £1,300. The total cost of the building and furniture has exceeded £26,000.

LANGLAND

I have mentioned earlier that in 1912 the Executive was considering both a South-Western and a North-Western Home. The South Wales folk were very keen on having such a Home in their midst. But the demand from the North was greater, as was the constituency from which support would be drawn. The clubs in Glamorgan and Monmouth were far and scattered. And so the North-West had place. But the South Wales and Monmouthshire clubs were not idle. They gave solid manifestation of their enthusiasm by raising some £1,200, and eventually purchasing a site at Langland Bay, where, after visits to many other places which the Branch Committee, Wadman, and I made, we had decided that we had reached *the spot*. Just as at Grange, opinion was unanimous. Langland Bay is the most beautiful spot on the South Wales seaboard. The site secured, the War prevented progress, and costs of building were prohibitive. But the Executive felt and appreciated the keenness of the clubs, and decided to build at whatever cost. Mr Wadman got out plans for a Home to accommodate 40 residents – this, it was estimated, would cost over £40,000. Yet the Executive decided to proceed. The preliminary steps, submission of plans to the local authorities, were taken. Then came a hostile move from the local gentry. The workmen presumed to come between the wind and their nobility. An injunction against building a Home on the site was launched. The Executive proceeded. It was whilst in Swansea on the submission of the plans to the Swansea Corporation that I heard that the palatial Langland Bay Hotel, although not exactly in the market, could be purchased. I need not detail the steps taken.' But within six weeks the Hotel, 'lock, stock and barrel' – furniture, fittings, stock, building and nine acres had passed into the possession of the Union at a cost of £20,000 only! The stock and furniture were valued at £5,000. The property is, however, leasehold for 36 years further only. A sum of £4,000 has been invested by the Union at compound interest to meet the expiration of the lease.

Fine as the hotel was considered as a hotel, it was not in equipment up to our standard, and in bringing it up to this, both as to furniture and fittings, general hygienic and other improvements, a further outlay of some £8,000 has been necessary, plus the sum of £4,000 which has been invested at compound interest to accumulate against the expiry of the lease. The total donations and gifts received up to the day of opening, Easter Monday April 17th 1922, exceeded £10,000. There is thus a debt of £22,000 remaining to be discharged. The money required was raised entirely by loans from clubs and club members – in one month.

The home was formally opened by the Rt Hon. C. W. Bowerman MP, supported by the Mayor, Alderman and Councillors of Swansea and other secular and ecclesiastical dignitaries, Mr J. J. Dent CMG presiding over a good assembly of Welsh clubmen.

The method by which the Homes are maintained is purely voluntary in character. Any club subscribes what sum it pleases. Such sum is placed to its credit, and for every resident sent the account is debited at the rate of 30s per week, any credit balance being carried forward from year to year. Many, perhaps most, clubs which subscribe pay a fixed sum yearly – once in pre-war days calculated at the rate of 1s per member per annum, now 2s is required – and this is found to be normally sufficient to cover all possible residents from the club. The cash outlay on each resident weekly is now about £2. Thirty shillings is thus found by the club, the balance of cost, if any, having to be made up out of the Union funds. In 1912 to 1914 complete self-support was achieved, but since the outbreak of the war a considerable sum has had to be found yearly by the General Fund. This is considered unsatisfactory, and it is the constant hope and endeavour of the Homes Committee that no charge for maintenance should fall upon the Union's funds. As will be seen and is noted in the table no charge is set against residents for interest on capital, or depreciation, which are borne by the General Fund of the Union.

The following table shows the cost of a man's stay at a home for a week. It allows nothing for interest on capital outlay or depreciation. If these were added, calculated upon the total original cost, another 12s would need to be added to the total cost weekly of each Resident. The figures are given for the year 1911 and for the years 1920 and 1921. They will indicate how costs have doubled by reason of the war, and by comparing 1920 with 1921 how slowly the prices fall from their maximum:

	1911			1920			1921		
	£	s	d	£	s	d	£	s	d
Food of resident	0	9	3	0	18	11	0	17	8
Wages and food of staff	0	5	6	0	10	3	0	10	0
Fuel, light and water	0	1	0	0	3	0	0	3	$2\frac{1}{2}$
Repairs, renovations of buildings	0	0	6	0	1	6	0	1	$9\frac{1}{2}$
Household and upkeep	0	1	0	0	1	5	0	1	5
Rates and taxes	0	0	7	0	1	3	0	1	5
Stationery, newspapers, games	0	0	5	0	0	10	0	0	$9\frac{1}{2}$
Carriage of residents to and from stations	0	0	2	0	0	$5\frac{1}{2}$	0	0	$6\frac{1}{2}$
Fares and expenses of Committee	0	0	1	0	0	$5\frac{1}{2}$	0	0	5
Insurance	0	0	1	0	0	4	0	0	4
Medical attendance and medicine	0	0	5	0	0	$3\frac{1}{2}$	0	0	4
Garden seeds and plants	0	0	1	0	0	2	0	0	$2\frac{1}{2}$
Telephones and postage	0	0	2	0	0	$1\frac{1}{2}$	0	0	$1\frac{1}{2}$
Sundry small charges	0	0	0	0	0	1	0	0	3
	£0	19	3	£1	19	1	£1	18	7*

* B. T. Hall was 1d out in this calculation.

The outlay on food will be found in excess or even double that of most other Homes. It should be stated in explanation that there is meat or fish at every breakfast as at midday meal, and that there is no dietary or stint. Every resident may eat what and as much as he pleases. The menu is full and varied, and equals in quality and excels in quantity that of a first-class hotel.

The funds for Capital outlay are raised by Loans, either by overdraft from the Union's bankers or by Loans from clubs and members. These

Loans are gradually repaid from moneys received from clubs as Donations, i.e. gifts, securing no equivalent benefit, but for the purpose only of extinguishing the Debt. These Donations had totalled £10,000 by the end of 1910.

In January, 1911, the Executive, at the instigation of the Homes Committee, launched an appeal for the extinction of the total debt on both Homes. At that time the debt remaining was £8,186. The response in the first year was £1,435. During 1912, £2,448 was received in donations (this was the Jubilee year), and this with sundry other small balances, counter-balanced to some extent by accumulating interest, enabled the reduction of the debt to £4,442. In 1913 donations fell to £857, the incubus fell to £3,762. Donations in 1914 of £1,003 brought it down to £2,746 at the end of that year.

In 1915 – the war. And the beginning of the Grange building added nearly £6,000 to the debt in that year, which ended with a total increased now to £8,423, rising, by reason of the cost of the Grange building – in spite of donations of £1,377 – to £9,123 in 1916 and to £9,757 in 1917 (being kept down somewhat by donations of £1,991 in 1916 and £1,429 in 1917).

Grange Home had been opened in August, 1916, and it charmed every one. Trade was good. High wages were general, and 'Flag Day' had been invented. So in the year 1918 donations totalling £6,173 were received, which paid the remaining building accounts, and reduced the debt to £6,744. In 1919, the increase in the Union's general income (due to increase in price of Associate and Pass Cards, and the renewal of these by the tens of thousands of returning clubmen) enabled (with donations of £3,855) the remainder of the Loan Debt to be wiped out by a payment of some £4,000 from the General Fund of the Union.

This must be added to the £3,000 paid from the same source to begin the Saltburn Home. Thus a sum slightly less than £8,000 is the total contribution from the Union funds proper to the capital outlay of some £70,000 upon the three homes at Pegwell, Saltburn and Grange, which stand in the Union's accounts at date, after depreciation, at £54,000. Apart from that £8,000, the total capital outlay has been met by gifts from clubs and members. A record, indeed, for all to be proud of. A democratic triumph.

These figures are exclusive of Langland. Here has been a total cost of £32,000, with donations of some £10,000 received to date. To summarise – the Capital Outlay on the four Homes has exceeded £100,000. Of this, only £8,000 has been contributed from the Union's funds, £70,000 by Donations from clubs and their members, leaving £22,000 owing at the present time, which, there can be little doubt, will be met by Donations from clubs and members within the next five years. I venture to so predict, although at the time of writing optimism is rather difficult.

It would be improper and ungrateful to leave the subject of the Homes without a word as to The Fellowship and the Flag Day.

THE FELLOWSHIP

The Fellowship (alas the past tense!) was composed of little coteries of clubmen who, under the above title, set themselves the task of adding to the amenities of existence at the Homes. The plan (of which Mr H. Dilkes of the Central Finsbury Club was the author) was for 25 members of a club to band themselves together in a Birthday Fellowship. On each man's birthday he paid 1s and each of the others 2d, making 5s in all, this sum to be devoted to the improvement and embellishment of the Homes. Many and charming were its gifts, especially the stained glass Fellowship windows at Saltburn. Each Home participated. The War broke up and separated the members, and since the Peace the scheme has not been revived. The total raised in all was £880, of which the final balance of £190 is being expended upon pictures for Langland.

FLAG DAY

This idea originated in the mind of Mr. J. Hardy, of Clayton-le-Moors, a member of the Executive of the Lancashire and Cheshire Branch. The idea is to devote a day yearly to the sale of a Flag or Button at one penny each. Its product up to 1921 was as here set out:

	£	s	d
1915	779	16	9
1916	613	16	8
1917	412	13	7
1918	1,055	19	0
1919	1,425	16	0
1920	2,018	2	10
1921	1,799	17	9
	£8,107	1	7

A distribution of half-a-million flags is now reached, and although the sad year 1922 may show a decline, it is confidently hoped to produce a net income of £2,000 yearly by this means, thus meeting interest charges and contributing something to the deficit.

THE CLUB AND INSTITUTE JOURNAL

No reference to the Homes would be complete without a few words of appreciation of the help given by the *Club and Institute Journal*. Without it the success would not have been possible. Its help in securing the splendid total of some £7,000 in donations cannot be measured. But its help was as great in this direction as in a score of other ways. The *Journal* is an indispensable instrument in the success and development of the Homes.

It has been said that more capital has been sunk in unsuccessful efforts to float newspapers than in any other form of monetary dissipation. There is always a number of optimists confident of their ability to succeed if others have failed. They see the need for just such a paper as they have in mind, and are confident that the willingness of the public to purchase what is supplied to meet it exists also.

If this confidence coincides with the fact that a very real necessity for such a paper *does* exist, it is not surprising that the effort is made.

In great democratic organisations, to say nothing of the special political activities of the workman, the need of a paper is patent – obvious and admitted by all. The number of persons to whom such a paper must appeal is known to be large. So that its success appears to be certain. Yet it is workmen's movements which contain the record of more journalistic failures (which so obviously and logically were sure of success) than any other. Political, Trade Union and Friendly Society; in all these divisions of democratic activity has effort after effort been made by capable men, only to be met with disheartening want of appreciation.

There *is* great need for a paper. There *are* tens of thousands who want it, but it is *not*, therefore, to be concluded that there will be an adequate sale. The syllogism is never complete. The premises are perfect. The obvious conclusion is no conclusion at all.

Yet hope persists. Struggling organisations with no money to spare refuse to learn from others. In *their* case it will be different. They must have a paper. And one more is added to the tale. The literary work is generally done gratuitously (which is not always the way to save money), and the honorary editors are cheered in a thankless task by a fire of criticism, often from non-buyers, which, coming from all quarters, is of infinite variety. The *Club and Institute Journal* had something of this story.

In 1864, two years after the founding of the Union, the need for a paper was felt, and *The Working Men's Club and Institute Magazine* was published in October of that year by Messrs Jarrold and Sons. It was doubtless written and edited by Henry Solly. No copy of this paper remains outside the British Museum – if there? Its price was threepence, and the accounts show £30 as having been received in twelve months by sales. The cost is not separately shown. It was discontinued in October, 1865, as the circulation was so small, and use was made of the columns of friendly papers for the publication of matters relating to the Union.

But every year the absence of an organ of its own was felt to handicap the Union and in 1875 the Council determined to make another effort, so on Saturday, May 15th, *The Workmen's Club Journal and Official Gazette of the Workingmen's Club and Institute Union* (the current taste for protraction in titles running here) made its first appearance, Hodgson Pratt being the Editor. It was a large quarto in size, of eight pages, of which four were advertisements, and its price was 1d. The contents were largely Union Notices, or reports of the Council Meeting, articles on

Provident Dispensaries, The Condition of the Peasantry in Germany, and such like, with extracts from Mark Twain, and a column of Poetry. Matter of interest was doubtless found in it. But looking at it now it does not seem of a character likely to *excite* interest, nor to have much of 'club' matter in its contents. Someone writes demurring to the two-page articles, and suggesting that the contents should be more paragraphic. But Hodgson Pratt submits that men's minds are not to be treated, like looking-glasses, to a constant series of fleeting impressions. It will be noted that the habit of the time persists in this Editorial utterance. Pratt even cannot escape it. Readers were not to have what they wanted, but what they *ought* to want. The workman is everlastingly dosed with something the chief recommendation of which is that it is supposed to be 'good for him'.

At the end of the twelve months it was found that the paper was selling less than a thousand copies weekly. The receipts were £40, the expenditure £331. It was plain that this could not go on. The experiment was tried of reducing the price to ½d and increasing the size to twelve pages. By some means not clearly shown this succeeded in so far that the yearly loss was reduced to £200, the circulation apparently rising to about 1,250 copies. But this was impossible to continue. The venture had involved the Union in a heavy debt, and in February, 1878, the *Journal* was suspended. Negotiations were set on foot to secure space in the *Co-operative News*, but without success. The absence of the paper was keenly felt, and in 1881 arrangements were made with *Social Notes*, a penny weekly, which lasted till the end of that year, when it also became defunct.

Financial troubles pressed upon the Union, but in 1883, there being a slight relief in the pressure, and the need of the *Journal* being more acutely felt than ever, it was (on Friday, July 6th, 1883) resuscitated (promises of purchases of 600 copies having been received), Mr Mark Judge, then a member of the Council, undertaking the Editorship of a fortnightly issue of eight pages, to be called *Club and Institute Journal,* price one halfpenny. There seems still to have been curious ideas of what a 'club' paper should contain, for No. 3 (following a three-paged report on the opening of a club at Low Moor, Bradford), proceeds to devote two pages to *Notes on Our Food Resources, a Series of Articles descriptive of the Collection of Food Resources in the Parke's Museum of Hygiene.* Interest in this absorbing topic is kept from flagging by the aid of sub-heads such as –

GROUP 1. MAMMALIA – Sub-Group A: Oxen, Sheep and
Pigs. – The Ox.

And then follow two pages in which all that is known of this useful animal is set forth, how that he belongs to the Natural Order of Ruminants, what his status was in History and is in India; how many there are of him, how you can get beef and tongue and sweetbread and black puddings out of him, etc. 'Cowheel is occasionally used for making jellies, etc., and is frequently eaten by the working classes,' is a recondite fact, the communication of which must have been received with breathless interest by the readers. The fact was that Mr Judge, then, as now, an exceedingly busy man, had little if any time for his gallantly undertaken task.

After a few months, Mr Judge announces that he is unable to continue, and 'arrangements have been made to edit the *Journal* from the Union Office,' which means, it is guessed, that William Minet has undertaken the job. The incurable modesty and self-effacement which has characterised the honorary workers in the Union from the beginning leaves this a guess only. But it is a fairly sure one. The paper now records nothing but club news, and the stir in the clubs which is making for the revolution of 1884. There begin to appear articles and rhymes written with distinct, if rude, vigour and force, signed by Richard Gaston, a member of the Boro' of Hackney Club, of which the following is the first:

'Christmas Time in Youth and Age'

Old Father Christmas seems to me
Quite changed to what he used to be;
I recollect I hailed the time
Of mirth, and joy, and pantomime;
With gifts and toys and Christmas cheer,
I wished he'd stay throughout the year.
His name won praises from my tongue;
The cause must be – that I was young.

On Christmas now I set no store;
In fact, he rather proves a bore,
When for his sake long bills I pay,
And, fleeced by all on Christmas Day,
I feel that if he left this year,
And ne'er returned, I'd shed no tear.
He takes my comfort, ease, and gold;
The cause must be – I'm growing old!

What was the circulation achieved is not anywhere shown, nor, owing to the form in which the accounts are presented, can it be accurately deduced from them. It probably reached 2,000 copies, and there was apparently but a small loss (as journals go) of about £20 on the first twenty issues.

In February, 1884, an experiment is made by increasing the size to twelve pages as a 'special issue' at one penny. Valuable articles on legal matters appertaining to clubs begin to appear, and club balance sheets are criticised in a kindly informing way, which renders the hand of Minet obvious, for T. F. Hobson has not yet appeared, and other legal articles are signed by T. A. Nash. So, too, the series of articles on Account Keeping are certainly Minet's. In July, 1884 (though there is a yearly loss of £90) success has so far met the renewed publication that it is announced that the paper will in future be issued weekly. In April, 1885, the size is increased to twelve pages, and the price to one penny. But the appearance of Acrostics and Bret Harte's *Left Out On Lone Star Mountain* indicates that there is difficulty in finding sufficient 'club' copy. The result of the increased price was that the circulation of 2,000, reached at the time of change, fell off. The Editor complains of the difficulty within the limited range of topics possible to the *Journal* of making the paper interesting. But club members (Fletcher Pape and Gaston) write short stories, and Harry Cocking of the Cobden Club, supplies verse, some of which is good, and some not at all bad, every week. The Cobden appears always to have a Poet on the premises, a practice preserved up to the present date.

It is resolved to continue at one penny through 1885. But the loss grows, and it is too heavy to be borne, and on March 12th, 1886, it is decided to allow the paper to pass for a while into a private venture. An agreement is made with Ernest Parke, now of the *Daily News and Leader* and of the *Star*, a young journalist delegate from the Peckham and Dulwich Club (not now existent), and for six months he undertakes to run the paper, the Union guaranteeing against loss to the extent of £2 weekly. The paper is enlarged in size to 12 in by 9 in and is of eight pages. Full reports of Council meetings appear, and in the general brightening of the publication the hand of the trained journalist is apparent. The paper has now (quite improperly) a very definite Radical tone. But even Mr Parke cannot make it pay, and as he clearly cannot stand loss he gives back his trust. He, however, consented to continue as Editor for a while until new plans could be made; these continue until May, 1887. The loss in 1887 is £143.

On Mr Parke giving up, Mr Rodolfe Cuerel, then most active in all good work for the Union, volunteers to take on the task as Honorary Editor, being allowed 10s weekly for expenses. Reporting is said to cost a further 10s weekly. The paper continues in the form in which it was cast by Mr Parke, and compares well with its model. Cuerel, frail in health, feverishly industrious, clear sighted nevertheless, and practical, would put into the paper the maximum of effort, even if nearly every dinner hour suffers. But it does not 'go'. There is a loss of £100, and a committee is appointed in November, 1887, to consider the future. It need hardly be said that at the meeting which appointed the committee there was, as there had always been, a multitude of counsellors. And wisdom there must have been somewhere, for the opinions expressed ranged from every point in the compass of advice. That it should be a halfpenny only was the most insistent. The Committee reported on December 10th, but consideration was deferred until January, 1888. A vote of thanks to Cuerel was proposed by J. H. (who later became Sir Henry and then Lord) Dalziel, seconded by Ernest Parke, and supported by William Minet, three men who 'knew'. Cuerel, in reply, said he never felt so happy in his life as he had done since he gave up the management of the *Journal*, with all the trouble it involved.

Mr H. E. Boyce, Assistant Legal Adviser to the Local Government Board, was one of those middle-class supporters of workmen's clubs who had remained continuously faithful, and represented the Teddington Working Men's Club on the Council. He believed he could succeed where others had failed. A proposal of the Committee to appoint a reporter-editor at £1 a week (!) was withdrawn. A proposal of Mr Dalziel's, that an editor be engaged at £3 3s per week was defeated, and the offer of Mr Boyce to edit the paper with a subvention of £1 weekly for assistance was accepted for six months' trial. It was gallant, but unsuccessful. A special meeting of the Council was held on July 14th 1888, at which it was resolved to appoint a paid Editor, at £2 weekly, and Richard Gaston was elected, defeating J. H. Dalziel by two votes. Curiously, no report of this meeting appears in the *Journal*. The yearly loss had risen to £230.

Mr Gaston's first step was to enlarge the size of the paper by making it 15 inches by 10 inches, continuing with eight pages. He introduced a style of homely personality, and cultivated the musical and entertainment side. Special sketches, short tales, rhyme and paragraphs with bold heading and plenty of space lightened the appearance of the sheet – a very needed reform. Correspondence was encouraged, especially the personal and satirical. Doubtless the paper had a fairly fixed circle of admirers. Its circulation rose to 4,000 copies weekly, and remained fairly constant at that throughout the six years of Gaston's control. He used it diligently to boom Union events, and within his lights served the Union cause most faithfully. But the financial aspect of the matter was not improved. The item, 'Editor's Salary and Expenses £180 10s 6d' was a new burden, and in 1889 the loss was £312. The rise in circulation brought cash for sales and also advertisements, and in 1890 the loss fell to £158. Then the salary is fixed at £2 10s a week and commission on advertisements. But, largely owing to increase in printing costs, the yearly loss rose steadily until it reached £240 in 1893. The Union was in financial difficulties, due to the daring Central Club and Hall venture. There was no money to stand the drain, and in June 1894, financial necessity compelled the discontinuance entirely of the weekly issue, the Editorship went back again to the Office, Mr Gaston and some friends bringing out a weekly entitled the *Club World* as a private venture.

The first issue of the *Journal* in its present form was in July, 1894. It was a poor thing of four pages, and dear at the halfpenny charged for it. The third issue increased to eight pages. The Convalescent Home at Pegwell, then just established, owed much to its persistent advocacy, the Secretary of the Union acting as Honorary Editor, a post held to this date. Then someone suggested that the Union should bear the small cost of printing, and should give every halfpenny for which the paper sold to the Convalescent Home Funds. It was a brilliant idea. The circulation of the paper rose to 6,000, and rose steadily after – to the great benefit of the Homes whilst the arrangement persisted. The circulation grew, until in 1912 a circulation of an issue of from 20 to 24 pages of 37,000, and self-support, was reached, the paper giving also free advertisement of all the things the Union wished to communicate to its clubs, thus relieving the Union's funds of an expenditure for printing and postage which would even then have exceeded £200 per annum. The circulation increased steadily. But after three years of war the cost of labour and material rose so that continuance at the price of one halfpenny was impossible. Increased to one penny it showed in 1919–20 (as did all newspapers) a yearly loss, if the value of the Union's advertisement is excluded from consideration. In 1921 it resumed solvency, and showed a profit of some £150 on the year, with a guaranteed sale (no returns) circulation of 60,000 copies monthly. To the paper's credit must always be remembered its capacity and successful appeal for funds, as witness the many thousands of pounds which have been raised in Donations to the Homes. The *Journal*, in fact, has become an indispensable, but a self-supporting, part of the Union's equipment and machinery.

10

Those years that B. T. Hall spent as General Secretary of the Union were the ones that brought together the different strands of the movement's history, weaving them together to enable the Working Men's Club and Institute Union to become one of Britain's great institutions. Hall was a human dynamo and also an autocrat; a man who got things done without worrying too much how other people felt. Undoubtedly, he managed to accumulate more personal power as General Secretary than any other holder of that post has attempted to gain, either before or since. The very fact that he did so would go against the grain for many working-class organizations, and yet it proved to be no bad thing. Before his appointment the Union had been going through one of those flabby, indecisive phases that many popular movements tend to suffer after a period of dynamism; it needed a dictator to give it a new sense of purpose. The Union found one. And he did.

His was the character that stamped the Union during nearly thirty years of change; his was the mind behind decisions of the Executive; we can see his hand at work at every important stage in his secretaryship, particularly in the Union's brushes with Government and with Parliament.

In previous pages we have seen how Hall gave evidence to the Licensing Commission in February 1897, and how his contention that drunkenness diminished where clubs were established was respected; we noted that it was a Conservative Home Secretary, C. T. Ritchie, who introduced the valuable 'Clubs Act' of 1902 which introduced the principle of registering clubs, and whose main provisions were later merged into the Licensing (Consolidation) Act of 1910.

The great Liberal statesman David Lloyd George, however, was not so amenable to our movement's charms. As we have already seen, he advocated temperance, and in his 1909 Budget as Chancellor of the Exchequer imposed a special tax on clubs of sixpence in the £ on every £1 worth of alcoholic refreshments purchased by any club. B. T. Hall fought hard against this, and various Members of Parliament made a determined attempt to have the tax reduced in the 1920 Budget debate – their partial success came in 1922, when the tax was reduced to 3d. (This tax remained in force until 1 January 1960, when it was replaced by the Club Licence Duty of £5 per annum, and the beer duty was reduced by £2 3s 7d a barrel.)

In educational fields, too, the Union prospered under B. T. Hall. He forged close links with Ruskin College, Oxford, and the Workers' Educational Association, and these were considerably strengthened in 1921 by the appointment of Mr Andrew Temple as Educational Secretary. In that year, no less than twelve scholarships at Ruskin College were held by members of Union clubs. (Today, however, there is only one, since the growth of the State's role in education has reduced the necessity for this aspect of the Union's work.) In this same year, it is interesting to note that £3,000 was spent on organized educational work and special classes were held for members' children. Happily, this aspect of the Union's work is also no longer a social necessity.

That the work the Union was doing was deeply appreciated was clear from the scores of letters received daily from clubs seeking advice on such questions as the recovery of income tax, their relationship with local authorities or the Registrar of Friendly Societies, aspects of rating, and disputes with staff. All were answered by head office, which rapidly became less and less of an austere patron, and more and more the benevolent uncle. Hall was able to reflect on his secretaryship when he wrote in *Our Sixty Years*: 'The 30 years . . . have witnessed the establishment and steady growth of a personal intimacy between the clubs and their officers and the Union, with the happiest of results to clubs and with added power and dignity to the movement. The thirty years, viewed from this aspect alone, afford ground for the most solid satisfaction.' This had, no doubt, been helped by the fact that the Union was now financially secure, and owned its own administrative headquarters at the Club Union House in Clerkenwell Road.

The thirty years had also seen many changes in the people of the movement. Solly, Pratt and Tayler had all passed away; Dent had become a key voluntary figure, and many other stalwarts had also gone. Passmore Edwards, who had helped to found the first convalescent home, had died in 1911 at the age of 88; Sir Herbert Praed had died in 1920 at the age of 79, having been Treasurer since 1881; the former President Lord Brassey had also lived on to a fine old age before dying in 1918 at 82. Others who died during

Hall's secretaryship included Richard Gaston, the former Editor of the *Journal*, who died in 1901; W. J. Fritz, who succeeded Vaughan Nash as Honorary Librarian in 1892 and died in 1900; Edwin Dorrell, who had tried to form the rival organization of Liberal clubs but later supported the Union, who died in 1908; Rodolfe Cuerel, who had helped assiduously with the teaching of club management, who died in 1900; and in 1919 the first convalescent homes superintendent, H. S. Boyland of Pegwell, died. That so many of the early supporters should now be departing was inevitable; the Union was now a long-established movement, and its membership was bounding ahead; in the twenty years following 1892, the number of affiliated clubs rose from 410 to 1,445. Much of the credit for this lies with B. T. Hall, although he was to have his disappointments; his wife's death shattered him in July 1907, when he had to take two months' rest, and his confidence was shaken again when the Assistant General Secretary, W. H. Berry, whom he had encouraged and trusted, disappeared with some £200 of the Union's cash. But even though incidents such as these aged B. T. Hall, his spirit still shone through, and the years following the celebration of the Union's Golden Jubilee in 1912 saw still more consolidation under his guidance.

In 1913, the South Yorks Branch Secretary, Councillor J. H. Bagshaw, and W. R. Clamp of the Audit Department were appointed Public Auditors, and South Wales Branch established its own separate audit department, which has proved of great benefit to other clubs in that area.

All this was threatened by the outbreak of the First World War in 1914, only three months after the Union's members had contributed £935 to a testimonial to mark Hall's twenty-one years as Secretary. The War semi-paralysed everything. The Union continued to help with advice whenever it could, but nearly all progress was stayed. Union and clubs alike were denuded of staff and officers. All efforts were directed to one end – winning the war. The receipts of the Union from all sources fell. The Audit Department was closed for want of staff. The *Journal* showed a loss of £130.

Death laid a heavy hand on the Executive. H. Baker, the oldest, and T. Brown, one of the newest, died in 1914, followed in 1915 by two of the oldest workers in London and Manchester, J. Matthews and J. Stevens. In 1917 they were followed by two Yorkshire worthies, Arthur Gledhill and George Wilson. In spite of all obstacles, however, the Grange home was successfully opened on Bank Holiday, 7 August.

Immediately on the outbreak of war the Union Executive voted

£1,000 to the Prince of Wales Fund. Some 90,000 clubmen joined the Colours in the first year, and of the clubs' membership, composed as they are mainly of middle-aged and elderly men, over 35 per cent joined the Forces. Every member of the Union staff was taken except G. Shore (64), W. G. Stroud (53) and B. T. Hall (51), who, however, served in many other ways – on the Relief Committee, Military Tribunal, Food Control and in Home Defence. One of the staff, Mr Yuill, was killed and two others returned wounded. (One of them, T. G. Nicoll, who was appointed Assistant General Secretary in 1930 and retired in December 1955, carried a bullet in his lungs until he died in 1974.)

Full wages were paid by the Union to all employees. H. S. Boyland was especially active in musical ministry to wounded men in the many hospitals and camps near Pegwell, and there can be little doubt that this work was responsible for his sudden death from heart weakness. Though the war held up the growth of the clubs it did not stay it entirely; the net result was that while there were 1,613 clubs in the Union when war was declared, there were 53 more when the Armistice was announced in 1918.

Many were surprised to find that the progress of the War had not delayed the progress of the Union; post-war developments were even more unexpected. Munition workers, drafted from rural areas to great industrial centres for the duration, had been learning about club life for the first time, and when they returned home after the Peace had been declared they acted as the Union's missionaries. Soldiers, too, finding comradeship in the trenches of the Western Front, came back determined to salvage this at least from the wreckage of war. British Legion and ex-servicemen's clubs were formed in at least a thousand towns, cities and suburbs; many became affiliated to the Union and are still flourishing today. The figures tell this dramatic story; when the Armistice was announced in November 1918 there were 1,666 clubs with 688,972 members in the Union; when the Union celebrated its 60th anniversary less than four years later, on 14th June, 1922, these figures had dramatically increased to 2,269 clubs with a combined membership of 1,150,000. The senseless savagery of the First World War had produced something worthwhile, even if it had not proved to be the war to end all wars. It made the Union the largest of all the working-class organizations, with the result that the working class as a whole now had something they had never had before: clubs where they could relax when their day was done and find a common meeting ground with their fellows. To this extent, Solly's dream had come true – but the reactionary side of his character might have been surprised by its wider significance. The post-war Union's strength was giving the working class of this country the common bond and feeling of solidarity which was to win many of their battles over the next forty years. Unwittingly, Solly had created a great movement which was linking the working men of Britain socially, and so cementing those other links which were being forged in their trade-union branches.

Had the Union been in the wrong hands, this could have done a great deal of harm; but its leaders were sensible men, and the result was that the Union helped to groom Britain's working men to assume responsibility, to exercise authority, and to become leaders in their own communities; in 1922, there were no less than 178 Union members in the House of Commons; 474 were county councillors; 1,497 were town councillors; 1,242 were district councillors; 1,071 were members of boards of guardians, and 1,030 were magistrates. The Union was achieving what the pioneers had hoped it would; it was giving the working men of Britain a chance to prove themselves.

The Union could hardly have been in a better position to face the challenge of the post-war years, and a decision in October 1918 to increase the price of pass cards from a halfpenny to one penny per month was the key to the next stage in its growth; this decision meant that more money was flowing in just at the time when more was needed to expand the homes in response to demands from clubmen who had returned weary from the war. Men of high calibre were needed, too, to be groomed to take over from B. T. Hall, who had now been at the helm for over thirty years. R. S. Chapman was appointed Assistant General Secretary in June 1921, and Andrew Temple was chosen to administer both the educational and recreational sides of the Union's work.

The rapid growth in membership both of individual clubs and of the Union made these appointments necessary and the financial boom that the post-war years brought to the clubs set the climate; the Union was ripe for expansion. Chapman brought something to the Union which Hall, with all his experience, no longer had – youth. And this was important in the radical post-war atmosphere. Chapman was then thirty-two, but already had wide experience; for nine years before the war he had worked for two well-known London solicitors – McKenna & Co., and Rubinstein, Nash & Co. – acquiring a wide practical knowledge of law, which was a necessary skill in his work for the Union. Chapman specialized in conveyancing, and had studied this for two years at Birkbeck College, and subsequently had supervised a large share-transfer

business for Harrods before being called up. During the war he had
served as an orderly room and pay sergeant with the Royal Army
Medical Corps in Greece. Although Chapman had only joined the
Union in 1919, B. T. Hall had been quick to note his potentialities,
and encouraged him to study the Union's work and history; when
the time came for an Assistant General Secretary to be chosen,
Chapman was the natural choice.

Soon after his appointment, the post-war slump occurred; conditions in the industrial areas in 1922 were appalling; men were out
of work in large numbers, and this had its usual effect on family
relationships and health – and on the Union, too. Although the
membership of the Union's clubs had increased by 70 per cent over
the past ten years, the supply of associate and pass cards (the
financial mainstay of the Union) had increased by only 30 per
cent. This was a bad omen, for increased membership meant increased administrative costs, and unless the money came in, the
administration would be severely affected. The Executive were
worried, and, believing the explanation was partly that many clubs
were becoming slack in observing the law about the use of the
cards, issued instructions to each club to tighten up the procedure;
clubs were warned that it was illegal to supply anyone who claimed
to be an associate unless he produced his associate card, pass card
and current subscription card, and also signed the associates' book.
Each club secretary was also warned that he could only issue pass
cards to members of his own club. All clubs were urged to display
notices detailing these requirements, and were asked to persuade
members to pay subscriptions yearly. And it was through this
persuasion, and the increased subscriptions that followed, that the
Executive was able to maintain the Union's income during this
very difficult period that followed the end of the First World
War.

The Executive also decided to lower the age at which the
associate cards could be supplied to members from twenty-one to
eighteen; this decision was a direct reflection of a feeling within
the clubs at the time – only associates could compete in Union
contests, and it was felt that the exclusion of young clubmen was
unfair.

It was about this time, too, that the 'Club Visitation' was held.
This, too, was a direct result of the First World War. Before 1914,
the Union's clubs, generally speaking, had operated smoothly, the
same officers holding positions from year to year with new officials
being groomed rather than plunged into active committee-work.
But the war had changed all this. Many clubmen had been lost in

battle, and many new, inexperienced men were taking their places. This was inevitable, but it meant that there was no longer the same cohesion and interdependence. The Executive came to the conclusion that it would be a good thing to make a complete assessment of the affairs of each club in the Union. A searching questionnaire was prepared for completion by each club (there were some forty questions to be answered), and each branch was asked to ensure that the clubs in its area completed the forms.

This work brought the members of the Executive and branch officials into contact with many of the new clubmen, and also gave the staff at Head Office an opportunity to check the healthiness of each club's affairs. Each report was examined, and no less than 2,000 clubs were given advice where the answers indicated deficiencies in their management. A few clubs objected to the Visitation, and three left the Union rather than have their affairs examined. Seven clubs in the Wakefield Branch also refused to permit inspection, suggesting that the Union had no right to inspect the books of any of its affiliated clubs. A question of principle was involved, and the Executive felt that it had no alternative but to ask the Council to agree to terminate the membership of the seven clubs; faced with an ultimatum, six of the clubs yielded while the other, the Carlton Haw Hill Club, preferred to leave the Union.

In the same year, 1923, J. J. Dent retired as President, having given forty years' service to our movement; he was held in high esteem throughout the Union, and a total of £650 was collected and presented to him by the new President, Alderman Robert Richardson, who also handed Dent an illuminated address which had been beautifully prepared by F. R. Horsman. The address read:

To J. J. Dent, CMG

This address testifies the regret of the clubs of the Working Men's Club and Institute Union and their members in your retirement from the office of President, and their deep appreciation of the forty years' service to the Union, for ten as Secretary, three as Executive Member, fourteen as Vice-President and thirteen as President.

This long devoted service has been marked by wisdom in counsel, courage in action and the upholding of the loftiest ideals of the movement. Your skill as Secretary placed the Union upon an effective democratic basis, and your advice and guidance in succeeding years actively contributed to the steady progress which has characterised it during the years recalled.

You leave to a well-earned leisure, which it is the wish of all may extend over yet many years, compact of peace and happiness to which your well-filled past has given abundant title.

On behalf of the clubs and their members,

Robert Richardson, President
Edward Garrity, Vice-President
Jesse Argyle, Treasurer
B. T. Hall, Secretary

October 6th 1923

This was indeed an occasion for burying the hatchet. Dent had, in fact, had a dispute with B. T. Hall, who wanted to retain the licence to sell intoxicants which was attached to the Langland Bay Hotel at the time of its purchase by the Union. Dent thought the licence should be surrendered, and thus, in effect, that the Home should become 'dry'. Such was the power of Hall in those days that when the dispute developed between them, it was the President who resigned! But at the ceremony to mark Dent's retirement, all this was forgotten and B. T. Hall rose to the occasion with a tribute, which was reported in the *Journal*:

Mr B. T. Hall said that he was asked by the Executive on their behalf, as he could assure Mr Dent of his own, to say that in the long web of their regard closely woven on the loom of many years there was no single rent or even one tangled thread. The current of their affection ran as smoothly, because as deeply as ever, and on its surface there was no single ripple. In token of this they asked Mr Dent to accept this silver casket.

Continuing, Mr Hall said that the casket was typical of their feelings – it was white all through. Atmospheric influence might at times dim its surface, but the slightest friction and its lustre shone as ever.

There was Shakespearean authority that the holder of the silver casket had all that he desired. If this were so then surely Mr Dent would have all that he desired.

Handing the casket to its recipient, the Secretary added: 'Keep this in memory of old friends and colleagues. Keep it as bright as your memory will live with us.'

Dent's speech was reflective; he recalled that as a boy of fifteen he had spent his evenings working with his father to build the hall of the Eleusis Club, and because of this the club's rules were altered to permit him to become a member. Before that, only men over the age of twenty-one had been admitted – and when he became twenty-one, the rules were altered back again! He recalled that when he was elected Secretary, he was almost unknown to the Council; his first years in that office had been the hardest of his life, but it had been a great pleasure for him to watch and help in the growth of the Union, and to see it grow in strength until its reserves totalled over £100,000. Dent went on to contrast the humble beginnings of the Union with its present-day strength and influence, and this, by coincidence, was tested again soon after his retirement.

Early in 1924, a Bill was submitted to Parliament – the Temperance (Wales) Bill – which proposed local option and Sunday closing for clubs in Wales and Monmouthshire. In Part III of the Bill it was proposed that all new clubs should have the prior consent of the licensing magistrates and that all existing clubs should have annual licences and police supervision. Although this Bill applied only to Wales and Monmouthshire, the Executive realized that it might be the thin end of the wedge and decided to do all they could to defeat it. The Home Secretary was electioneering in Burnley, so the Executive waited upon the Under-Secretary to put their case against the Bill, with the result that the Government declined to support the measure. The Bill failed to secure a Second Reading, with its promoters attributing this to the Union's influence. The Executive did not deny this. As Dent said, 'The Union now, in contrast with the days when I first became connected with it, is a rich and powerful body.'

The Union had always been aware of the importance of maintaining close relations with the Government, whatever its colour, and thus at every election the Executive made a point of asking candidates where they stood on various issues affecting the Union; this they did again in the General Election of 1924, and it is interesting to see the scope of the five questions that were put to candidates:

1. Will you oppose any legislation, having for its object the prohibition of the supply or consumption of alcoholic drinks in clubs on Sundays?
2. Will you oppose any legislation designed to bring clubs within a Local Veto Scheme?
3. Will you oppose any legislation which proposes to place clubs under the control of the Licensing Justices?
4. Will you support the reduction of the present enormous Beer Tax (still exceeding ten times that of 1914)?
5. Will you support a proposal to enable clubs to adjust (within the total permitted by the present law) the hours of supply of intoxicants, to meet local conditions as to working times in various industries and districts? The latest hour to be 11 p.m. in the provinces and 12 p.m. in London.

It would have taken exceptional qualities of political evasion to escape answering questions as direct as that, but the questionnaire had one certain advantage: it made every candidate aware that the Union had powerful support in every constituency and, even if only for the sake of political expediency and a wish for self-preservation, this was not a movement he could ignore.

In this same year the Union had become involved in yet another consitutional case, this time one affecting rating assessments. The Pontllanfraith Constitutional Club, Monmouthshire, had purchased in 1921 a dwelling-house, which was subsequently used as a club. Even though the adjoining house was no different in design (indeed, it was better in some ways), the Newport Assessment Committee decided to give the club a higher assessment than the house, purely because it was being used as a club.

The Committee had assessed the premises as a club and had fixed the gross value at £90 and the rateable value at £67 10s, and the Quarter Sessions Justices agreed with the figures on an assessment as a club. The Quarter Sessions Justices, however, were asked to state a case for the decision to the High Court, and they decided that if the basis was to be that of the former use of the premises, the gross value should be reduced to £50 and the rateable value to £35.

The case came before the High Court in January 1924, and was considered by the Lord Chief Justice, Mr Justice Avory and Mr Justice Greer. The court examined the case thoroughly, and decided that certain alterations had been made to the premises in its conversion to a club (in the lower court the counsel for the Assessment Committee had estimated these at £20, and agreed they were negligible). The Committee's counsel opposed the submission of this evidence to the High Court, and thus possibly gave the impression that the alterations were of considerable magnitude; the Lord Chief Justice said in giving judgment that the premises had been converted from 'a dwelling-house into a commodious club'. This was not in fact the case; the club could have been converted back into its former state in a couple of hours, but the court's decision was nevertheless that the club was no longer a dwelling-house, had been specially converted into a club and was therefore more valuable for letting purposes. B.T. Hall wrote afterwards:

> The result is very disappointing for the Union Executive. For many years the Executive had hoped that a case would be taken by an assessment committee before the High Court, so that the vexed question could be judicially determined and a judgement obtained that would be binding upon all assessment committees. The position after much expense remains as before. The Union has not lost the principle for which it has always contended, namely that a club is liable to be rated as land and

premises upon the basis of what a hypothetical tenant would pay for them as rent if they were to be let. But the hoped for decision was not secured in this case, the Union having failed because the case was imperfectly stated.

A few months later Hall himself was involved in a legal action: he was sued for libel by Davenports, the Birmingham brewers, over an article in the *Journal* which had been headed 'Trickster Brewers'. The case was due for hearing before Judge Parfitt and a jury at Birmingham Assizes on 14 July. Sir Edward Marshall Hall opened the case for the plaintiff and was opposed by Sir Henry Maddocks, on behalf of the Union; their legal arguments lasted the whole day, and when the court adjourned the judge expressed the opinion that the case was one for settlement. When the court re-assembled the next day it was announced that the action had been withdrawn, and that it had been agreed that the Union should pay costs; these amounted to £710.

The next month, August, the Labour Prime Minister, Ramsay MacDonald, who had been a member of the Fabians many years before with B. T. Hall, visited the Langland Bay home, and paid tribute to the work of the Union in providing such a beautiful home for the members. He continued:

> You know perfectly well that there are beautiful things in the world and life which no individual can enjoy as a separate individual unless he has an enormous amount of money. There are beautiful pictures. None of you can possess these great masters. You cannot give £7,000 for a picture, or £25,000 for a still more precious picture, but if we can all lay our heads together and our pennies together we can buy them and enjoy them in comfort.
>
> That is the whole theory of social enjoyment, and I cannot imagine a better example of it than this home. When I came to the gate I came in through the gate of a lordly mansion, up the drive and I am shaded by trees that remind me of the ancient aristocracy, the door suggests to me the hospitable entrance to the home of someone who owns many coalfields, and has been most successful in the exploitation of other people's labour. And when I came in I met you – workmen, men and women, still living off the sweat of their own brows, and not off the sweat of somebody else's, and the secret of your possession, the secret of your desires, is just as I have explained.

The Prime Minister's visit was the highlight of 1924, which was an eventful year, though one that brought sadness to the Union as well. The Union's Treasurer, Jesse Argyle, committed suicide by jumping off Highgate Bridge, and the Vice-President, Edward Garrity, had died peacefully in his sleep at the age of seventy-one just before the end of 1923. They were two men of different mettle, but each in his way had contributed much to the Union's achievements.

B. T. Hall had known Garrity even before his appointment as Secretary of the Union; when Garrity was Assistant Secretary of the Amalgamated Society of Railway Servants in 1891, Hall had held a similar position in the Sailors and Firemen's Union. So Hall wrote this obituary of Garrity, which appeared on the front page of the January 1924 issue of the *Journal*:

> He was a member of two Borough Councils; Finsbury, of which he was an Alderman, and Stoke Newington an elected councillor, member of the Asylums Board, School Manager, trustee of local charities and a JP, as well as being President of the Central Finsbury Radical Club and President of the Stewards' Union.
>
> I recall Garrity as a small, slight figure, immaculately attired, a Labour dandy. Top hat, frocked coat, figured waistcoat even then covered by golden testimonies to his success and worth. He was a magnificent orator of the Victorian times.

Jesse Argyle, who died so tragically in August 1924, was a very different man. He had started life as an apprentice on the *Hampstead and Highgate Express*, and was associated with the Union for thirty-five years, being elected Vice-President in May 1909, a post he held for twelve years until he succeeded Sir Herbert Praed as Treasurer. Argyle, who was a pioneer for the convalescent homes, had an active life outside the Union, too; he was a Fellow of the Royal Statistical Society, represented the Union on the governing bodies of the Workers' Educational Association and Ruskin College, Oxford, and was secretary to Charles Booth for thirty years, helping him to write *Life and Labour in London*. In club life, he helped found the Mildmay Radical Club in 1888, becoming first President and a delegate to the Union Council; he attended its first meeting in February 1889, and was then elected to the Executive in July of that year.

Earlier in the chapter we saw how the Union lost the Pont-llanfraith Constitutional Club rating case; this was the first in a series of post-war lawsuits, many of which were instrumental in establishing important principles of the club law.

Another important case came before the High Court in March 1926, and this time the Union was successful. The case concerned the Amble Club, a member of Northumberland Branch, which was compelled to wind up its affairs because it was unable to meet its financial obligations. The club was registered under the Industrial and Provident Societies Act 1893, and proceedings for winding-up were taken under the Companies (Consolidation) Act 1908.

The club had issued loan stock to certain members in accordance with its rules, which were based on the model rules recommended by the Union. In the liquidation proceedings, these loan stock holders claimed to be entitled to share equally with other unsecured creditors in the remaining assets. The Official Receiver, acting as liquidator, made application to the County Court for directions, and the Registrar decided that the claims of the loan stock holders should be postponed until all other unsecured creditors had been fully paid, a decision which would have meant that all those members who had lent money to the club would have lost it. An appeal was made to the County Court, and the judge confirmed the Registrar's order. The Executive then agreed to support a further appeal to the High Court.

The rule around which the whole case centred read:

> Subject to the payment of or a sufficient provision for all subsisting claims on the club, the committee may in its discretion from time to time apply any moneys which it cannot profitably invest to pay off the loan stock holders.

In the County Court, Judge Greenwell took this to mean that other creditors were to be considered before loan stock holders, but in the High Court, F. B. Fuller, who had been engaged by the Union, successfully argued that the rule was merely a domestic arrangement between club members – the only parties to the rules – and was intended as a safeguard to the committee to prevent claims for repayment of loan stock at times when there was no money available to pay it back. The Bench agreed with Fuller that the rule did not postpone claims of loan stock holders in liquidation, and the point was thus established that when a club failed, the members who held loan stock were entitled to share equally in the assets with the other unsecured creditors. Thus, the County Court's decision was reversed and the Union's appeal allowed with costs.

The following year another very important appeal was won by the Union in the High Court. This concerned the Hockwold Village Club, Norfolk, and the principle it established was that when a club hires premises for a special occasion and takes intoxicants there it may supply members at any hour of the day or night irrespective of the normal 'permitted hours'.

The case arose after the Hockwold Village Club had held a sports fête on 3 August 1925, on grounds about a mile from the club. Prior to the fête, the club had sought the advice of the Union Secretary, who advised that they could supply intoxicants to their members in a cottage adjoining the field, without breaking the law, and furthermore that on this special occasion the club was not bound to observe the 'permitted hours' which attached to the club-house since the cottage was not 'club' premises. The police took a different view and prosecuted the club's chairman and secretary, who were convicted and fined. The Executive agreed to support and finance an appeal to the High Court, which upheld the advice given to the Union and declared that the magistrates had wrongly interpreted the 1921 Licensing Act in its application to the circum-stances of this case. The court quashed the conviction and ordered the police to pay the costs of the appeal.

B. T. Hall himself was involved in another libel suit in January 1927, when he was sued by a Welsh solicitor who had taken ex-ception to some comments in a letter to a club which was applying for membership of the Union. Hall, never a man to mince words, had strongly criticized a document which the solicitor had prepared, with the result that the solicitor thought his professional reputation had been aspersed. On 23 and 24 January 1927, the case came before Judge Horridge, who ruled that the letter was privileged. The jury found no evidence of malice. Had any other verdict been given by the court, the Executive would have had to appeal to an even higher court, for it would have meant that future secretaries would have been limited in the advice that they would have been able to offer to member clubs, if that advice reflected adversely on a third party. But, though Hall won, the cost to the Union was high. Costs had amounted to £507, and though the plaintiff was ordered to pay £315, not a penny of this was recovered as he later went bankrupt.

Another important event in 1927 was the introduction of the Union's superannuation scheme, for which the staff had been press-ing for some time. In this, they were helped by Tom Jenks, the Chairman of the Finance Committee, who had always taken a keen interest in their welfare. They wished for a half-pay retirement pension at sixty, but the Executive could not then agree to more than one-third pay, though B. T. Hall himself was later given a half-pay pension of £500 a year without ever having contributed. (The Superannuation Trust Deed was subsequently amended in 1942 to provide for the long-sought half-pay pensions.)

Thoughts were far away from pensions in Manchester and Dis-trict (Lancashire and Cheshire) Branch, however, for they had become the first branch to celebrate their own Golden Jubilee, though they had not been part of the Union for all fifty years; the clubs in Manchester had had a 'union' of their own long before their affiliation to the Club and Institute Union. Great, however, were the celebrations – the Executive postponed its monthly meeting for a week so that all the officers could attend the special lunch which was held at the Exchange Hotel, Manchester, and presided over by the Branch Chairman, K. T. S. Dockray. Speakers included the Union's President, Bob Richardson, MP, and in the evening the Rt Hon. J. R. Clynes was a guest speaker at a jubilee meeting in the Mitchell Memorial Hall, at which a complete set of thirty-five volumes of Robert Louis Stevenson's works and a smoking cabinet were presented to B. T. Hall, and the gold medal for twenty-one years' honorary service to the Union was presented to Dockray.

While Manchester was looking forward to its next anniversary, another link with the Union was coming to an end; Mrs M. E. Boyland, the much-loved Superintendent at Pegwell, was retiring after thirty-three years' service; she had stayed on for another eight years after the death of her husband in 1920, but this was not enough for the Metropolitan clubmen, who had taken Mrs Boyland to their hearts; they spontaneously organized a testimonial, and later (15 October) met at the Central Finsbury Club to pay tribute to this fine old lady and present her with a cheque for £468, a set of carvers and a handbag, which was a special gift from the club itself.

A few weeks afterwards, William Finnigan, an Executive member since 1913, President of the Wakefield Branch and Secretary of the Wakefield Trades and Labour Club and a town councillor, died. Almost exactly a year later his colleague on the Executive, Alfred Augustus Holden, President and Secretary of Kent Branch, also died. In their places came Alderman John Tennant, also a Wakefield councillor and Secretary of the Yorkshire Council of Branches, and Alfred Eperon, a compositor on the *Kentish Mercury* and President of North Kent Branch, while a new representative elected in Durham was J. R. Nicholson, who had been Secretary of Eldon Lane Club, Durham, for nineteen years.

Frequently in the post-war years there had been requests for a fifth home, arising partly from the popularity of the existing homes and also from the fact that clubmen in some parts of the country found it difficult to reach them. The question cropped up again in 1927, and the Executive were even advised of a suitable site in Rhyl, North Wales. This was visited and recommended by the Executive, but some members wondered whether the clubs in the area would support the home; nearly 300 clubs were circularized, and the replies (or lack of them) were so disappointing that the Executive decided to drop the proposal.

In 1926, the Union's gold medal for twenty-one years' honorary service to the movement had been introduced, and in the September 1927 *Journal* it was reported that the Union had decided to make this award retrospective so to be able to honour Minet, Hobson and Dent. Their replies are indicative of the men themselves.

Dent wrote:

Dear Hall,

Thanks for the medal safely to hand. Please convey my thanks to the Executive for the gift which I shall treasure as a reminder of many happy days spent in the service of the Union, and of many lifelong friendships made in the common work for the Club Movement.

Hobson wrote:

Dear Mr Hall,

The charming little medal arrived this morning and I write at once to express my thanks to you and to beg through you to offer to the authorities of the Union my grateful appreciation of their kindness in remembering and recognising my poor services to the cause of the clubs, rendered now so many years ago.

It is pleasant in life to realise occasionally that one is not quite forgotten and it is a kindly thought of the Union to send its older sympathisers a memento of this kind. I value the more so perhaps as it comes to me in my later years when, like most elderly people, I live to some extent in the recollection of the past. Not that I want to exaggerate my age for I am only well into my seventieth year, which nowadays is comparatively youthful, and I am thankful to say that I am well and fit and am supposed not to look my age. Still I can no longer pretend to be young. Both Dent and Minet are older and so it is perhaps as well that the Union has had this pleasant thought while we are all still in the land of the living.

Minet wrote:

Dear Mr Hall,

The token you send me, on behalf of your Council, touches me more nearly than I can tell. It is now over fifty years since my first connection with the Union, then in a small room in the Strand with one somewhat aged clerk. In those days the Union was young, and every form of organisation connected with organisation, rules, accounts, management in general, needed first to be devised and then taught.

While Mr Hodgson Pratt mainly devoted himself to propaganda work, the former task became my share. It is not for me to say how far I succeeded, but looking at the Union today I may, I think, say that the foundation of good club management was well and truly laid.

There are two sides to every question, and if I taught a little I learned far more in the teaching, and your gift will be treasured by me and

mine as an abiding memory of work done in bygone days which has
thus had its value for me as I know, for the Union as I trust.

It was in the immediate post-war years that the Executive began
to contribute fairly large sums to deserving causes – but not to the
more traditional forms of charity. In 1926, the year of the General
Strike, which was consequently a bad year for the Union financially
(the year's surplus on the General Fund was only £77), the Executive contributed £200 to the Sybil Thorndike Miners Relief
Fund; in 1928, £500 was given to the fund organized by the Lord
Mayors of London, Liverpool and Newcastle to alleviate the
widespread distress in the coalfields; in 1934, £250 was contributed
to the Mayor of Wrexham's fund for the families of men killed in
the Gresford Colliery disaster; in 1935, ten guineas was contributed
to two Yorkshire colliery disaster funds and £250 to the Manor
House Hospital; in 1936, £250 was given to the Ruskin College
Appeal, £250 to the national memorial to George V, and £50 to
the Mayor of Barnsley's fund for the families of men killed in the
Wharncliffe Colliery disaster; in 1937, fifty guineas was contributed
to the Lord Mayor of Stoke's fund for the Brymbo Colliery disaster
and a further £300 to Manor House Hospital; in 1938, a hundred
guineas was sent to the Mayor of Chesterfield's Markham Colliery
disaster fund and another £500 to Manor House Hospital (which
were all considerable sums for those times, when a working man's
wage was seldom more than £3–4 a week).

This all began in 1926, and was firmly established as one of the
Executive's possible functions by that £500 donation in 1928, which
brought this comment from B. T. Hall:

> The Executive quite appreciate that this sum, that the whole, even if
> it reaches £250,000, can but touch the fringe of destitution which
> prevails in an industry in which nearly 250,000 men are permanently
> employed. But an appeal having been made, the Executive felt that,
> even as a gesture of sympathy and friendliness with an all too often
> friendless class, largely fellow members of our own, the Union should
> respond as generously as its funds will allow. Its example does not
> appear to have been widely followed. In doing what it did the Executive
> feels that it expressed a sympathy, however inadequately, which Union
> club members share.

The severe unemployment that lay behind the formation of these
funds was one of the reasons why the four homes were so well supported during the nineteen-twenties; indeed, this decade saw great
strides forward in the standard and standing of the four homes.

The twenties had opened with the purchase of the Langland Bay

Hotel and its conversion into a convalescent home; in 1927, the freehold had been bought for an extra £10,000, and in 1928 some adjacent gardens, which had previously been rented, were purchased for £1,077 2s 2d (they were subsequently used for growing vegetables for the home). Two years later the tennis courts, the bowling green, a kitchen garden and part of the foreshore which was included in the Langland Bay site were sold to Swansea Corporation for £3,000.

At Saltburn, too, the Union had been establishing close relations with the local council, and in 1921 had purchased 3,987 square yards of land on the north side of the home for £1,372 so that the sea view should not be obstructed. This was given to the Council in 1929, and was subsequently landscaped with a tennis court and putting green, but the Union did not object to the Council's plans when they announced in 1959 that they wanted to erect two-storied flats there for aged people.

Another important event affecting the homes was the decision of Mr Justice Rowlatt in 1929 that the properties should be exempt from Schedule A tax, and that the £919 which had been paid over the previous six years should be refunded. This was by no means enough to pay off the debt on the homes, which had been £4,500 at the beginning of the year, but it was a help – and B. T. Hall, who was due to retire as Secretary in the same year, made it his aim to see that the homes were free from debt by the time he retired. He made a personal appeal to the clubs and branches on the strength of his coming retirement – and they responded nobly. The debt was wiped off within the year. This was but one of the ways in which the clubs showed their appreciation of the services that Hall had rendered to the movement.

When the time came for him to retire, at the same time as W. G. Stroud, the Union's Auditor, who had been a full-time worker since 1889 and Assistant Secretary to J. J. Dent in 1891, the clubs paid their own tribute to Hall; the twenty-nine Branch Secretaries presented him with a grandfather clock at the 1930 Annual Meeting, and the Executive a canteen of cutlery at a special dinner held at the Hatcham Liberal Club, which was Hall's own club.

Many were saddened by the retirement of this austere but sincere man, but it was a fitting end to the decade – indeed, it was the end of an era, for Hall had held the office of General Secretary for very nearly forty years.

The thirties opened with new faces occupying the principal desks at head office. Bob Chapman was elected General Secretary on B. T. Hall's retirement, Tom Nicoll was appointed Assistant General Secretary, and W. R. Clamp, who had been Stroud's assistant for twenty-six of his thirty-four years' service to the Union, was promoted Chief of the Audit Department.

Twelve nominations had been received for the post of General Secretary, and 1,896 voting papers were returned – a poll of approximately 72 per cent. Chapman won overwhelmingly, with 3,111 votes cast in his favour, nearly 3,000 more than those achieved by his nearest rival, Joe Bray, Secretary of the Durham Branch. Hall wrote in the next issue of the *Journal*:

> It is a matter of considerable gratification that the newcomer to the highest responsible post should have obtained so remarkable a demonstration of confidence and support, for such gives him also support and confidence in his task.
>
> It is now possible for the Executive to record that it, whilst carefully refraining from any interference in the course of the election, wished for Mr Chapman such a vote as he has achieved, for he has long held their confidence.

There were between thirty and forty applicants for Chapman's former job, which was advertised in the March 1930 issue of the *Journal*. Tom Nicoll was chosen unanimously from the short-list to fill this important post. Tom, who was then aged thirty-five, had joined the Union at the age of fourteen and was familiar with all aspects of its administration; for some years he had been personal clerk to Hall, and was also a practical clubman, having been a committee member and for a time chairman of the Fern Lodge Social Club's finance committee.

No sooner were Chapman and Nicoll confirmed in office than the Secretary had to give evidence on the Union's behalf to the Royal Commission on Licensing; it was a gruelling experience, for

several of its members were opposed to clubs and thus Chapman
had to take part in a game of cut, thrust and parry with the Rev.
Henry Carter, Sir John Pedder and Mr Gerald France; but he
proved able to meet the challenge, and the result was that after he
had given evidence for four and a half hours on 27 May, the stock
of the Union had again risen considerably. (One member of the
Commission was Chapman's former chief, B. T. Hall, who, no
doubt, sat there recalling quietly to himself that he had had to face
a similar barrage when giving evidence to the 1896 Licensing
Commission.) The day after Chapman gave evidence, two branch
secretaries, J. W. Kinsman of South Wales and George Davies of
Monmouthshire, also gave evidence, along with Herbert Broadbent
of the National Liberal Clubs Federation, and Frank Solbe of the
Federation of Conservative Clubs; they all opposed police right of
entry and the control of clubs by licensing magistrates. Later,
Chapman and G. E. Middleton, President of the Northumberland
Branch, met representatives of the seven Scottish clubs at the
Loanhead Ex-Service Men's Club and prepared a statement for
submission to the Scottish Licensing Commission, which was pre-
sented on their behalf by Frank Imrie of the Greenock Torpedo
Factory Club.

That the Union's spokesmen had acquitted themselves well there
can be no doubt, as is shown by this quotation from the *Methodist
Times*, which was a paper with a strong temperance influence, and
so not one that would ordinarily have supported our movement:

> In fairness to the club evidence and especially to the work and in-
> fluence of the Working Men's Club and Institute Union, it should be
> stated that there is obviously a great improvement to be recorded during
> recent years in the character and conduct of clubs, and in their use-
> fulness as social and recreative centres.
>
> Indeed, Mr Chapman presented the Commissioners with a new
> conception of club life, in which continuous and congenial com-
> panionship is provided with many added attractions and amenities. He
> also claimed that the workmen's club is one of the most powerful factors
> in the promotion of temperance and the diminution of drunkenness in
> England and South Wales.
>
> Another feature of his evidence-in-chief was the submission of a
> number of constructive suggestions for club registration and control.
> Although on many points raised by Mr Chapman in his précis, tem-
> perance reformers are necessarily at variance with the expressed opin-
> ions and suggestions, a word of congratulation should be given to this
> witness upon the carefully-prepared and evidently well-studied case
> submitted to the Commission for consideration.

The Union had been hoping that B. T. Hall's presence on the Commission would prove a blessing for the clubs when the time came for the Commission to submit its report to the Government, but while the final report was being prepared, Hall died, on 10 January 1931, only two days after being suddenly taken ill with pneumonia.

Harris Claughton, a popular Executive member and a pillar of the Union in Leeds, who himself died only eighteen months later, wrote this front-page obituary for the *Journal*:

> Clubs for the use and privilege of the well-to-do were long before Mr Hall's time. He brought them to working men in villages and towns throughout the land. His personality inspired confidence. He gave to them that faith in themselves which moveth mountains. Under his guidance, clubs were formed in all directions. Successful as units he taught them to be conscious of their common rights and their potential national power. Many have helped in the building of the Union, but he more than any came in personal touch with those who had laid foundations and carried on the work. His capacity for sound judgement in emergencies appeared intuitional, but it was always governed by his habit of 'proving all things'. Therein lay his power. Clubmen by the hundred thousand looked upon his word as law. Thousands feared but respected him. Some few hated him, but by hundreds whose good fortune brought them near him he was well beloved, if but seldom understood. B. T. did not 'wear his heart upon his sleeve'.

Tributes were paid by many closely connected with the Union's work, who had seen for themselves the contribution that Hall had made. These were some:

> There was just that touch of the autocrat in his demeanour that stamped him as a personality, and one with whom it was unwise to take liberties . . . it was always his belief that nothing was too good for the working man.
>
> > – J. R. Nicholson,
> > National Executive member

> To the Labour movement, as to the Club movement, he gave of his best, and to both proved a veritable tower of strength . . . he was, in the truest sense, a pioneer in the Labour cause.
>
> > – Rt Hon. C. W. Bowerman, MP

> He was a sterling good man and one of the straightest and frankest characters I have ever come across.
>
> > – Herbert J. Marcus,
> > the Union's solicitor

> For many years I was closely associated with him and the Union and enjoyed his friendship, and only on rare occasions were there differences

between us. I know the great value of his life's work and, with you, mourn the loss of one who was a giant not only in stature but in brain power beyond most leaders of working class birth.

– J. J. Dent

The year had started badly for the Union, and it continued so. The Executive soon found itself pitched against the Government, this time the National Government, in which the Chancellor of the Exchequer, Philip Snowden, had increased the beer tax (and thus the club tax); then the Union decided to campaign (unsuccessfully) for brewers to be compelled to publish beer gravities; then attempts to form a Scottish branch were unsuccessful; then the Scottish Licensing Commission's Report was hostile; then a popular Northumberland clubman, G. E. Middleton, and a colleague on the Executive from Manchester, A. Liddall Bridge, died, and finally, just as the New Year (1932) began, the Union found itself faced with another setback – the Royal Commission's report was by no means as favourable as had been hoped. Indeed, some of its recommendations were prohibitive.

Snowden had been made Chancellor (a post he had held before) on the formation of the National Government, which had followed the Wall Street crash and the economic crisis which ensued. In the Budget which he introduced on 10 September 1931, Snowden decided to levy a further tax on beer of 31s per standard barrel, thus raising the tax to £5 14s. The Union Executive met immediately to consider this very large increase, which would clearly affect the finances of all clubs, and Chapman consequently wrote this letter to the Chancellor:

September 21st 1931

Dear Sir,

The Executive of this Union (which consists of 2,680 clubs with 930,000 members) has given very anxious consideration to the increased Beer Tax of 31s per standard barrel which you proposed to the House of Commons on September 10, and direct me to write you and enter a vigorous protest against this impost. They do so on the ground that it grossly offends the principle of equality of sacrifice.

My Executive recall the utterances in your budget statement of April 1930, when you said that 'those who spend these sums, often from very inadequate means, contribute to the national revenue, in the main, out of all proportion to their means, and I do not think it would be fair to tax their misapplied expenditure still more.'

The need to make financial provision to balance the budget is recognised, but to place an additional 31s tax (or an average of 24s) upon each barrel of beer, when the existing tax is admittedly grossly unfair, is in my Executive's opinion outrageous. It is not equality to tax the workers, the principal consumers of beer, out of all proportion to their means and then to impose a heavy additional burden.

Assuming the fairness of the pre-war tax of 7s 9d per standard barrel, how can the present-day tax of nearly fifteen times that amount be justified!

My Executive appreciate your difficulties but resent the gross inequity of this increase. While they are not sanguine that they can induce you to rectify their injustice, they desire to record their deep dissatisfaction, so that it may not be assumed that they accept the increase cheerfully. They desire further to intimate that the very earliest occasion will be seized to press for the tax to be adjusted to a figure which is not harsh and unconscionable.

This was but the first shot in what was to become one of the Union's greatest campaigns. The President, Robert Richardson, who was himself a Member of Parliament, and the Secretary canvassed opinion together in the House of Commons, and gained wide support – but not enough! Richardson opposed the increase in the Commons, describing it as 'vicious' and 'immoral'. The Union was, in fact, the only body that saw the immediate effect of the increase, which was passively accepted by other associations and even by the brewers – though they began to squeal when the increase took effect! The increase in Beer Tax also meant an increase in Club Tax, since this was based on the wholesale cost of the beer plus Excise duty, prompting Chapman to write another letter to the Chancellor:

I am instructed, also, to draw your attention to another matter – that of the Club Tax. This is based upon the price of intoxicants supplied to the club. The tax of 3d in £ is paid not only on the actual cost of the commodity, but on the Excise duty, which is included in the price paid by the club. The effect of the increased Excise duty on beer is that the club must pay additional Club Tax upon that increase – a tax upon a tax. The Club Tax is considered to be bad in principle, and is believed to be the sole instance in British taxation of taxing a tax. It has been a long standing grievance of clubs.

The amount of Club Tax is insignificant in comparison with the national revenue, and as a simple measure of justice, and because the tax is bad in principle, my Executive ask that it may be repealed.

Richardson took the campaign a stage further by tabling an amendment to the Finance Bill urging that the Tax be reduced from 3d to 2d – but he had overlooked a clause in the Bill's pre-amble which was worded to prevent any provision for the reduction of taxation being inserted in the Bill, and his amendment was ruled out of order.

The Executive then decided to take the opinion of Counsel to see whether there was any constitutional ground upon which they could challenge the Club Tax in the courts, and sought the advice of Stuart Bevan, KC, who concluded that there was no way of avoiding paying the tax. (Eventually, the Club Tax was abolished in the 1960 Finance Act and replaced by a £5-a-year licence duty.) And so it had to be paid – and this, together with the heavy Beer Tax, hurt many provincial clubs, particularly in areas suffering from the Depression. Chapman wrote in the January 1932 issue of the *Journal*:

> The increased Beer Tax is hitting some clubs very hard, especially clubs in those districts most affected by the industrial difficulties. Even before the imposition of the extra 1d a pint on September 10, many clubmen were frequently deprived of a glass of beer owing to the prohibitive price. The increased tax is a tyrannical imposition upon the working man.

The campaign against the increased Beer Tax was waged for the next two years. In March 1932, the Executive met the new Chancellor of the Exchequer, Neville Chamberlain; this, too, produced no effect – and in the May issue of the *Journal*, Chapman came out with this broadside against the Government:

HOW LONG, O LORD, HOW LONG?

> Are clubmen going to tolerate this vicious taxation for ever? Can it be piled on and piled on till they are all reduced to teetotalism? Will they take it lying down and never rise and wrathfully protest? Will they be bled white and watch the destruction of their clubs and be beguiled into the belief that they are 'patriots' suffering for the good of their country?
>
> Again, fellow clubmen, be ready for instant action. You have nothing to lose but your taxes. You have a club to save.

In the June *Journal*, Chapman was able to boast that the campaign was gaining momentum; clubmen had decided to 'wrathfully protest'. Letters were sent to 2,800 clubs outside the Union asking them to co-operate; 10,000 letters on the Beer Tax were despatched by Union headquarters in eight days; Chapman himself wrote to every MP; the Executive lobbied constantly at the Commons; individual clubmen were asked to buttonhole their own MPs – and did; Sir William Wayland tabled an amendment asking that the tax increase be abolished (this was never debated); George Hicks, MP for Woolwich, tabled another amendment urging that the Club Duty be reduced from 3d to 2d (this was never reached).

There was a great fuss – but it had no effect. The tax was not reduced. And in succeeding years, similar protests were made, to no avail. Before leaving the subject, clubmen may be interested to hear what one young MP, Alan Lennox-Boyd, later Lord Boyd and a future Cabinet Minister, wrote to the Union:

> The tax, to my mind, is extremely excessive, and unjustly penalising, and I consider it will fail in its object of raising more revenue, but Mr Chamberlain insisted that the Government would regard it as a direct Vote of Confidence and that if beaten they would resign. I cannot believe that it is in the national interest that the Government should resign, and so I could not do what otherwise I should like to have done and support the amendment.

If Chamberlain had not insisted on the subject becoming a matter for a confidence-vote, who knows what might have happened? Undoubtedly, there were other MPs who shared Lennox-Boyd's views, but whether there would have been enough to secure either a reduction in the tax or its abolition, we shall never know.

The question of beer gravities was closely related to the Beer Tax, since the gravity determines the amount of tax that is levied; the brewers thus had to choose between reducing the gravity of their beer, or increasing its price. In either case, their decision would gravely affect clubmen. Many brewers advertised that they would not be reducing their gravity, but Chapman had his doubts. The trouble was that there was no means of knowing the gravity of a club's beer since the brewers seldom displayed this vital information either on their barrels or on their invoices – and usually refused to disclose it even when asked.

Chapman enquired, but found there was no means of compelling the brewers to give their customers this basic information – unlike other traders, they seemed able to sell their product without telling customers what they were buying. This refusal on their part meant that club committees could not compare the quality and value of different beers, not knowing how much the price differential was due to tax, and how much to variations in the cost of the actual product. And thus we find the 1931 Annual Report including an enjoinder to clubmen not to buy beer from brewers who refused to disclose gravities.

Eventually, Chapman began to publish details in the *Journal* of the gravities and prices of different brewers' beers, obtained from untapped barrels which had been delivered to clubs. This was eventually stopped because in one case the analyst made a mistake and a brewer threatened to sue for libel after an incorrect analysis of his beer had been published!

Twice in 1930, Chapman and G. E. Middleton, President of Northumberland Branch, visited Scotland to attend meetings – in Glasgow and Edinburgh – attended by officials from non-Union clubs who realized that with the report from the Scottish Licensing Commission due soon, it would be advantageous to present a combined front in the face of any possible subsequent legislation. Several clubs, in fact, applied to join the Union, only to withdraw their applications on discovering that they would have to bring the management of their clubs up to the standard required by the Union.

The following year, the Scottish Licensing Commission's report was published, and contained several objectionable recommendations, including one that the promoters of a club should be required to pay a deposit of £200, another that clubs should not be permitted to open on Sundays, and a third that members should be prohibited from carrying liquor for consumption off the premises. Naturally, the Executive was against these proposals, but it was to be thirty years before the licensing laws were brought up to date.

Even before the Commission's report was published, Middleton had made a joint attempt with Chapman to combine the Scottish clubs into a branch, but he died three months after the report was published, and without being able to bring this work to fruition. Middleton had started his working life in the pits, before becoming active in local politics and in club life. He had helped to form the Mickley and District Social Club, later joining Northumberland Branch in 1909, becoming Vice-President in 1911 and President ten years later – the year after he was elected to the National Executive. Like Harris Claughton, a fine clubman who died the following year, and A. Liddall Bridge, a colleague on the Executive who had risen from a factory bench to become a barrister (but who was inclined to be rather pompous; even when wearing a cloth cap on a coach outing, he would carry a topper with him to wear when visiting clubs), Middleton was an old-world clubman, the sort who made our movement possible.

The Licensing Commission's report, published early in January 1932, was, to quote Chapman, a 'contemptible document, and was the subject of jest and derision by the newspapers ... practically every paragraph breathes repression and tyranny'.

The Commission recommended that the registration of clubs should be controlled by local or county councils, who could object if they thought the promoters were of bad character; that clubs should have a satisfactory structure (an unfair restriction since most clubs have to start in a very small way); that bona fides should be provided to show that the promoters had some legitimate object 'other than that of obtaining registration with a view to the supply of intoxicants', and that the number of original members should be fifty, not twenty-five. Furthermore, they suggested that any neighbour could object to the opening of a club; that clubs could not have their licences renewed if they were frequented by people of bad character or repute, or if members departed from the premises 'in a state of drunkenness'. But the worst was to come:

> It is the practice in many clubs for members to obtain supplies of intoxicants for home consumption. We were informed by club witnesses that this may be due to the inability of members to obtain supplies of a chosen brand in the neighbouring licensed premises. We think the practice is one which, apart from being unfair to licence holders, opens the door to irregularities. In any case we do not think it falls within the range of activities which should properly be associated with a club. We recommend that it should be made illegal.

Legislative threats like these, and constitutional worries of other kinds, were to worry the Union Executive for several years; only the war persuaded them to accept a Beer Tax which all clubmen regarded as punitive. Thus, in the pages of the *Journal* during the thirties there are constant references to the tax, and steps in the campaign to secure its repeal.

In 1933, the campaign coincided with the introduction of a Clubs Bill jointly by the Union with the Association of Conservative Clubs, the National Union of Liberal Clubs and the Golf Clubs' Association, who between them represented 6,000 clubs with a total membership of 2,000,000. The Bill, although it did not receive sufficient immediate support to be accepted by Parliament, influenced the thinking of the country's politicians, and many of its recommendations have been incorporated in subsequent Acts of Parliament.

The memorandum to the Bill pointed out that its main object was to tighten up the law concerning the registration of clubs by making it compulsory to supply certain minimum particulars to the Clerk to the Justices. As Bob Chapman said of the existing law, 'the simplicity of this procedure . . . has enabled night clubs, one-man clubs and tote clubs to get on the register. Often the law has been flagrantly broken in consequence.' Chapman shared with the Executive the view that the sensible approach was to prevent such clubs being established – a much less expensive procedure than allowing any club to form, and then employing police to catch the owners out!

He and the Executive thought that if sufficient safeguards were incorporated in the Constitution then truly bona fide clubs would be free to run their affairs without being troubled by petty restrictions. This view was shared by the other bodies who co-operated to produce the Bill. Perhaps the crucial recommendation was that club secretaries should periodically provide details of the name, address and occupation of the officials on the governing body so that objections to registration could be made if any of the committee were of 'evil repute'.

The Bill also provided that the registration authority should be the county or county borough council, who would have the power to delegate authority to either a committee or a district council, and that the club would have to satisfy such an authority that:

1. it was established for a lawful purpose;
2. no individual had a direct financial interest in any profits arising from the supply of intoxicants;
3. the committee held periodical meetings, with its proceedings properly recorded;
4. at least a week elapsed between the nomination and election of new members;
5. visitors were not admitted unless the club was devoted to athletic, political or education purposes.

In addition, the Bill provided that the local superintendent of police or the council could object to registration on a number of grounds, one being that a member of the governing body had been convicted under the Licensing Acts and disqualified from taking part in the management of a registered club. Right of appeal to Quarter Sessions was incorporated in the Bill, which also specified that police should continue to have the right to apply for, obtain and execute a search warrant if they felt that a club was breaking the law.

Bob Chapman wrote in the February 1933 issue of the *Journal*:

> The Bill makes a proposal which I submitted to the Royal Commission on Licensing, namely that clubs should be taken out of the scope of the Licensing Acts and that the latter, so far as clubs are concerned, should be repealed. The Licensing Commissioners (who obviously could not agree about the matter amongst themselves) neither accepted not rejected this proposal, but mentioned it as a matter for the consideration of the Legislature.
>
> In repealing the Licensing Act, 1921 (so far as clubs are concerned), the Bill would restore to clubs their pre-war freedom in the matter of

the supply of intoxicants. It will be recalled that Mr Lloyd George in introducing the D.O.R.A. proposals gave a pledge that the restrictions should be for the period of the war only. That pledge has not yet been honoured.

No sooner had the details of the Bill been announced (we shall follow its fluctuating fortunes in subsequent pages) than the Union once again began to sharpen its sword to attack the Beer Tax – and this time was partly successful!

This success was achieved after bold and decisive action by the Executive, who bearded the Chancellor in his den on 16 March 1933, when Bob Chapman presented a detailed and substantiated case for reducing the tax. These were some of the things he said:

We are at present examining the annual accounts of our clubs for the year ended December 31st, 1932 – these being sent to us for general statistical purposes. Up to date, 2,480 statements have been received and these show that no less than 63 per cent of the clubs worked at a loss during the year – this notwithstanding that most stringent and heartbreaking economy was exercised.

It is not denied, and we make no attempt to hide the fact, that a large, in fact, the major part of our clubs' revenue is derived from the supply of beer to members. The clubs supply food and other commodities only to a very small extent. Our members could not, even if they wished, afford to feed at their clubs, and must, of necessity, take their food at home wherever possible. Thus a large decrease in the consumption of beer in a club must inevitably affect its finances seriously.

From every quarter of the country comes the same story – decreased takings, dismissals of staff and reduction of wages of those retained to give the minimum of service which the club needs. The renovation and redecoration of club premises is everywhere postponed whilst schemes for the extension or rebuilding of club premises have had to be abandoned. All this accentuates the industrial depression and increases the tremendous army of unemployed.

We pointed out last year that the Beer Tax was making it impossible for many clubs to carry on. Some 78 clubs of our Union have since been unable to continue the struggle and have had to wind up. But this is not the worst aspect of the matter. Before long, hundreds will collapse unless some relief is forthcoming. Many now continue only because of the indulgence shown them by their landlords and other creditors – an indulgence which we fear may not be continued much longer. Many clubs which have acquired and own their own premises have been forced to place them in pawn – to mortgage them – in order to find the means with which to carry on.

Some of these clubs in danger of closing have taken decades to build up. They are the result of years of work and sacrifice. They meet a real need of the community, providing social intercourse, recreation and cultural advantages for their members. The breaking up of these clubs is a tragedy, a grievous loss to the people of the district who lose thus their opportunities for association and friendship with their fellow men.

Our clubs which have become impoverished (largely owing to the high Beer Tax) have been compelled to cease their subscription to hospitals, convalescent homes, and other charities.

Chapman then itemized the effect of the Beer Tax upon the clubs within the different branches, quoting cases in Wiltshire, North-East Lancashire, Birmingham, Kent, Yorkshire, Durham, South Yorkshire, Manchester, South Wales and Monmouthshire, Northants, Bradford and Leicester. The force of his argument was underlined by this ability to quote these specific instances of the effect of high taxation on individual clubs. And Chapman's efforts were rewarded when the Chancellor delivered his Budget on 25 April and announced a reduction in the Beer Tax of 1d per pint. The tax was still heavy, but the Union had won a major battle.

The sadness was that many of the Union's keenest supporters did not live to see it achieving these wider results; within three years of the death of Harris Claughton, many other leading figures in the Union – Oliver Bill, William Semley, Councillor J. W. Johnson, William Minet, T. M. Thornsby, Jonathan Ward, Harry Hodge, J. J. Dent and W. G. Stroud – had all died.

Dent as President, Stroud as Auditor, and Minet as a key adviser, had all helped greatly nationally, while Johnson, as President of Yorkshire Branch and an Executive member, and the others had been towers of strength within the branches. Bill, a retired schoolmaster, was a life member of the Lozells Working Men's Club in Birmingham, and had been Secretary of the West Midland Branch for twelve years. Semley, who was eighty when he died in September 1933, was Secretary of the Bradford and Halifax Branch for its first seventeen years, and helped form the Huddersfield Friendly and Trades Societies Club. Johnson in his twenty-eight years as President of South Yorkshire missed only four Council meetings, and was one of five men who founded the first affiliated club in South Yorkshire, the Monk Bretton Working Men's Club. Thornsby, a member of the Executive for twelve years, had served his own club, Wombwell Reform, for over forty years. Ward, who died in May 1934, was also an Executive member for twelve years and a director of the Northern Clubs Federation Brewery, and had helped to form the Choppington Station Club in 1900. Hodge, who died in December 1934, had been Secretary of Wakefield Branch since 1914 (on his death the future Union President, Edward

McEnery, was elected Secretary), and Treasurer of the Lower Hopton Working Men's Club for over forty years.

As long-serving members died, so other clubmen were elected to take their places on the Executive; these were times of great change on the Executive, with no less than eight new members being chosen, which inevitably meant an influx of new ideas. Joseph Wanless, elected in 1932, had helped to form the Northern Clubs Brewery, had been Secretary of Northumberland Branch since 1907, and had founded the Waterford Social Club. Henry Phillips, who was also elected in 1932, was President of the Spring Hill Working Men's Club in Accrington and President of the Accrington Federation. Alderman Joseph Thornton, elected in 1933, had been a member of Leeds City Council since 1921, was Secretary of Leeds Branch, and a member of the Armley and Wortley Socialist Club. Arthur Wallwork, another member elected in 1933, was also a Branch Secretary – of Bradford, Halifax and Airedale – and President of West Bowling Labour Club. Charles William Tarrant, elected in Thornsby's place, was President of South Yorkshire Branch, a retired headmaster, a member of Dodsworth Urban District Council, and Secretary of Dodsworth Central Working Men's Club. Joshua Barraclough, elected in Johnson's place, had made four previous attempts to join the Executive, and had served on the committee of Hoyland Common Working Men's Club for twenty-four years. William Ridley Smith, filling Ward's seat, had been the first President of the Thomas Wilson Club in Low Fell, County Durham, which he had founded, and had started work down the pit at the age of twelve, lifting himself up by his bootstraps to become proprietor of a successful insurance business in Newcastle upon Tyne. William Henry Richardson, Secretary of Huddersfield Friendly and Trades Societies Club, joined the Executive in October 1934, having been Secretary and President of Huddersfield Branch, and for twenty-six years Branch Secretary of the National Union of Foundry Workers.

While these changes were taking place among what had become, in effect, the Union's 'board of directors', similar upheavals had also been occuring within the branches, particularly in Manchester, where W. J. Ellam resigned the secretaryship in 1935, having occupied the position for no less than fifty-six years – one of the longest records of service in the history of our movement. Ellam's pioneering work for clubs in the North West had begun long before this branch became part of the Union; even before he had brought the Manchester Branch into membership of the National Union, Ellam had established a personal friendship with B. T. Hall and J.

J. Dent. On his retirement, the Assistant Secretary, G. Turner, succeeded him, bringing to the post experience in the social, educational and recreative sides of club life.

Thus new officers were taking up key posts in the Union at a time when great decisions had to be taken; we have already seen how the Union's campaigning had achieved a reduction in the Beer Tax, and how the Executive had co-operated with other club organizations to present a Bill to Parliament. Much else was happening, too.

One step which was to prove beneficial to many needy clubmen over the years was the liaison established with the Manor House Orthopaedic Hospital at Golders Green. Early in 1932 the hospital's Chief Surgeon, Sir Ambrose Woodall, and its Organizer, Joseph Hewitt, had met the Executive, who decided to establish closer links with this progressive establishment, and thereafter the Union gave many donations to the hospital. Bob Chapman and Tom Nicoll subsequently served on its management committee, and many clubmen were to receive treatment there in the years that followed.

In our convalescent homes, too, the Executive was laying further foundations; an accident insurance scheme was introduced to cover every clubman from the moment he left his own hearthside to visit a home to the time he returned again, a service that has since helped many clubmen unfortunate enough to meet with accidents just when they were hoping to stay at one of the homes. An innovation at Pegwell around this time was the installation of a lift – a notable engineering achievement for the Union's architect, W. J. Wadman, who built a shaft into the cliff itself to connect the two buildings which comprise the Pegwell home, thus removing the need for members to climb the ninety-eight steps. The cost of this improvement was £3,000.

These new clubmen also had major parts to play in other important events of the thirties: the introduction (unsuccessfully) of a private Bill in the House of Commons; the innovation of the Club Management Diploma; the publication of yet another Bill, which arose directly from a case in Sussex; the adoption of a new Certificate of Merit; and a debate in the House of Lords on the issue of bogus clubs.

The Union applauded the backbench MP J. C. Lockwood (Central Hackney) when he announced after winning second place in the ballot of members for Private Members' Bills in November 1933 that he would be publishing a Bill to standardize licensing hours; this was something that the Union Executive had long thought necessary. In the end, however, the Bill proved to be both incomplete and unsuccessful.

The Bill, as is usual for Private Members' Bills, was brief:

LICENSING (STANDARDISATION OF HOURS) BILL

A Bill to enable licensed premises and clubs to be open for the sale or supply of intoxicating liquor on weekdays, during standardised hours in Cities and Boroughs of over 20,000 inhabitants.

BE IT ENACTED THAT –

1. For Section One, Subsections (1) and (2) of the Licensing Act 1921, there shall be substituted the following:

(1) The hours during which intoxicating liquor may be sold or supplied on weekdays in any licensed premises or club for consumption either on or off the premises shall be as follows, that is to say:

(a) For any licensed premises or club situated within the Metropolis or within any borough or urban district which borough or urban district has a population exceeding twenty thousand according to the last published Census for the time being, from eleven o'clock in the morning till three o'clock in the afternoon, and from five o'clock in the afternoon till eleven o'clock in the evening.

(b) For any licensed premises or club situated elsewhere from eleven o'clock in the morning till three o'clock in the afternoon and from five o'clock in the afternoon till half-past ten o'clock in the evening.

2. This Act shall be cited as the Licensing (Standardisation of Hours) Act, 1933.

3. This Act shall not apply to Scotland, Wales or Northern Ireland.

The Executive thought the Bill, as published, was rather like the curate's egg. They could not see why clubmen should not be able to have a drink between the hours of 3 p.m. and 5 p.m., if they were finishing working at such hours that they would like a pint or two then before going home, or if wanting some refreshment while participating in or watching some sporting activity. It was regretted, too, that the Bill did not include Wales, although the fact that this Bill proposed an extra hour's opening time in London and large towns, and an extra half-an-hour elsewhere, was welcomed. The Bill seemed destined for success, at first, passing its crucial Second Reading stage by 101 votes to 67, but the Government did not give the Bill official support and, in the end, it failed to reach the statute book.

Shortly afterwards, another Bill aimed at the 1921 Act did coast through the Commons – because the Government had been embarrassed by a legal decision. The High Court had decided that the licensing magistrates at Steyning, Sussex, had no right to extend permitted hours in licensed premises to 10.30 p.m. on summer weekdays. This decision would not in itself have been startling, but for the fact that 120 other licensing benches had already reached similar decisions to those at Steyning. This was an embarrassment to the Government, and the Home Secretary, Sir John Gilmour, announced soon afterwards that the decision did not overrule the position elsewhere, and introduced the Licensing (Permitted Hours) Bill which enabled licensing magistrates to grant extensions for parts of the year.

The Club Management Diploma was introduced the same year, and has since proved to be one of the most useful and popular of the Union's facilities. For over fifty years this award has now proved an incentive to clubmen wanting to take an active part in managing their clubs; the scheme's courses on law, accountancy and administration have led to increasing recognition within the movement of the need for club officials to have more detailed knowledge than their predecessors.

The Certificate of Merit was also introduced at around the same time as the Diploma, to enable the Union to acknowledge personal contributions by individual clubmen to the Union's work.

Innovations such as these, and the regular work now being done to maintain the highest standards in the management of clubs, and to help individual clubmen through such facilities as the convalescent homes, meant that the Union was now increasingly recognized as a national institution that did much to ensure that working men's clubs were properly run, providing their members with recreational and social facilities so often unavailable elsewhere. That this was now so widely understood became clear when the House of Lords debated the issue of 'bogus clubs', with many of their lordships emphasizing the Union's work in maintaining standards. These were some of the compliments that were paid during this debate in February 1933:

> These organisations certainly exercise a discipline over their members, and if their clubs were the only clubs, probably no amendment of the law would be necessary.
>
> – Lord Amulree

> The Working Men's Club and Institute Union . . . deserve the highest credit for the tone they have successfully maintained in the clubs affiliated to them.
>
> – Archbishop of York

> The club movement brings relaxation and education in a large

number of towns and villages up and down the country. There is not a word to be said against the movement. In fact, it is deserving of the greatest support.

– Viscount Astor

In a sense, the Union was coming full circle. Back in the days of the Rev. Henry Solly, it had been leading members of the House of Lords who had sponsored individual clubs, and encouraged the formation of the Union; now, another generation of peers was acknowledging the contribution that the Union made to the life of the nation. The Executive were grateful to receive such support, for there were frequent attempts by other politicians to restrict the growth of clubs (particularly by those who had relationships with the licensed trade).

In the latter half of the thirties, this agitation for new licensing regulations continued. A succession of new Bills were promoted in the House of Commons – some favourable, some hostile. With the signs of war on the horizon, and Germany re-arming, these were trying times for the Executive, as, indeed, they were for the nation as a whole. Britain had not given much time to thoughts of war; many had believed, hoping if they could not believe, that the 1914–18 conflict really had brought an end to war. Inevitably, clubmen were as confused as everyone else.

In addition to being involved in the support or defeat of various Parliamentary measures, the Union had other important matters to deal with; there were four more legal cases in which the Union supported individual clubs, and, as always, the continuing ebb and flow of internal events, decisions that were important to the Union, if not of wider historical significance in those troubled times. The President, Robert Richardson, resigned; the Union's Rules were revised again (in 1938); a competition was held to choose a National Club Union sign – this was won by George Ainley of the Hipperholme Working Men's Club in Halifax – and a £250 donation was given to the national memorial to King George V.

But first let us look at the various constitutional issues in which the Union was involved. The Union was now regularly co-operating with other club organizations on legislative proposals that affected their respective memberships; they had all worked together to produce the Clubs Bill in 1933, and in 1935, after canvassing the opinions of candidates in that year's General Election, another joint attempt was made to promote legislation. Many candidates had pledged themselves to support the Union's proposals, and after the Election over eight hundred Union clubs wrote to their Members of Parliament, inviting them to participate in the Private Members' Ballot for the right to introduce a private Bill. R. Gledhill, the MP for Halifax, gained a prominent place in this ballot, and he agreed to sponsor our Bill, whose main objects were:

1. To extend permitted hours generally to 10.30 p.m., thus making applications to the Brewster Sessions unnecessary;
2. To provide ten minutes for 'drinking up' after the conclusion of 'permitted hours' (this proposal finally became law in 1961), and
3. A new system of club registration through local authorities which would prevent the growth of one-man clubs.

The Bill was due to receive its Second Reading on 6 March, and on 19 February Bob Chapman wrote to every member club urging them to contact their local Members of Parliament, asking them to attend the House and support the Bill. But all this was to no avail. The Home Secretary, Sir John Simon, agreed that it was a 'grave affront' to working men's clubs to find themselves cast in the legal position as 'bogus clubs', and then made it clear that the Government would not support the Bill, but would introduce legislation of its own in the next session of Parliament. Gledhill had no option but to withdraw his Bill. This was a great disappointment to the Executive, who were beginning to realize just how cautious every Government was in legislating over licensing hours, even if the Members themselves seemed to enjoy the opportunity of paying a judicious tribute to the clubs in their constituencies. Soon after, the Magistrates Association came out in favour of the Royal Commission's proposals, provoking Alderman Harry Leese, a member of the Executive and himself a JP, to write a detailed attack on these suggestions, including some acid comments on the South Wales Licensing Magistrates – particularly those of Pontypridd and Caerphilly – who had continually shown themselves to be hostile to working men's clubs.

Leese, a pillar of the movement and also a past Lord Mayor of his native Stoke-on-Trent, repeated many of the proposals made by the Union over the previous five years. His objections were sound and well received. When the King's Speech in November 1937 included mention of the Government's intention to legislate against abuses of the law by clubs, MPs from both sides of the House showed themselves aware of the social importance of working men's clubs. Moving the Address on the Speech, Captain Harold Balfour, Conservative MP for the Isle of Thanet, said he hoped nothing would be done 'to hamper the admirable activities of those working men's clubs which form the centres of amenities and welfare in our industrial towns'.

Encouraged by the Government's announcement, the Executive, the Association of Conservative Clubs and the Golf Clubs Association submitted a joint memorandum to the Home Secretary defining the principles they would like to see established in the new Bill. But, once again, the Union's attempt at quiet diplomacy did not have its intended effect. This time, the Government announced that they would not be promoting legislation after all – and with the onset of the Second World War, this proposal was conveniently forgotten.

The anti-clubs faction in the House of Commons did not let up; in March 1939 they introduced another Bill of their own, aimed directly at the Union's clubs, and giving police and magistrates so many grounds for objections to a club that any hostile bench could have started closing clubs down. This inspired Bob Chapman, who though slight in build and quietly spoken could rouse himself to passionate energy against attacks on the movement, to address a front-page appeal to fellow-members in the March 1939 issue of the *Journal*:

CLUBMEN TO ARMS!
KILL THE CUNNING BILL
DESIGNED FOR YOUR DESTRUCTION

And they did! Chapman had mobilized his troops. No less than 96 per cent of the Union's clubs protested to their Members of Parliament. Members of the Association of Conservative Clubs and the Golf Clubs Protection Association did likewise. A. M. Lyons, MP for Leicester East, and Harold Nicolson, MP for Leicester West, announced that they would be opposing the Bill in the Commons – and when the Bill came up for Second Reading, it was defeated by the well-known Parliamentary trick of talking-out previous business.

Very different tactics were required in the other area of national life that the Union found itself drawn into, the Law; no one could talk the magistrates out; here, the Union had to display cool persistence, engaging counsel to defend clubs' interests. There were four major cases which concerned the Union during the latter part of the thirties: one involved the extension of hours of clubs on the Isle of Ely; the second, a new rating assessment for the Llynvi Valley Social Club in South Wales; the third, another 'permitted hours' case, this time in Bradford; and fourth, and by far the most important, the case of the Trebanog Working Men's Club, which was successfully prosecuted in the local magistrates' court for 'selling' (yes, 'selling') intoxicants without a licence.

Union Headquarters, 1893–1962
Clerkenwell Road, London EC1

Club Union House, Upper Street, London N1
Opened in 1962

Pegwell Bay. Opened 1894, closed 1969

Saltburn. Opened 1909

Grange. Opened 1916

Broadstairs. Opened 1971

Langland Bay. Opened 1922

National Executive Committee 1987

Officials & Executive of the All-Party Parliamentary Group on Non-Profit-Making Members' Clubs

Left to Right: Lord Brooks of Tremorfa (Secretary), Mick Welsh MP (Joint Vice Chairman and Treasurer), Eric Forth MP (Committee), Greg Knight MP and Gordon Bagier MP (Joint Chairmen), Michael Meadowcroft MP (Committee) and Roland Boyes MP (Committee).

The Isle of Ely case followed the decision of Wisbech licensing magistrates to extend weekday closing hours during June, July and August 1937 to 10.30 p.m. on the grounds that the 'special requirements' of the district made this desirable. A number of local people disputed that there were any such requirements, and objected to the High Court. Christmas Humphreys, KC, appearing for the licensing magistrates, contended that the 'special requirements' were that it was a rural area where farm workers were occupied until late in the summer evenings, and were thus 'very thirsty' by the time the day was done. The Lord Chief Justice and his colleagues agreed, and the objection was dismissed.

The following year the licensing magistrates in Bradford reached a similar decision. Again it was proposed for much the same reason – with a magistrate joining the National Workmen's Total Abstinence Union and local clergy in an appeal to the King's Bench. This also came before the Lord Chief Justice, and was dismissed.

In the meantime a little club in South Wales, the Llynvi Valley Social Club, had been having troubles of its own. The club had acquired the tenancy of premises rated at £22 per annum, only to find after it moved in that the gross value was increased to £90 and the rateable value to £72. The committee appealed to the South Wales Branch, and to the National Executive, who concluded that the conversion might be held to increase the value of the club, and that therefore in the event of an appeal the club would probably lose. The club disagreed, and, without the Executive's financial backing, went ahead on its own, losing its case at Quarter Sessions. There was no reason why the Executive should have paid the club's costs, since it had advised against the appeal, but the Executive felt that the club had been treated harshly, and agreed to pay its costs of £141 0s 4d, a decision that says much for the relationship between the clubs of the Union.

The fourth case, the prosecution of the Trebanog Working Men's Club, was one of the most important in which the Union had participated. The circumstances were these. The club was a member of the South Wales Branch and registered under the Industrial and Provident Societies Act, supplying intoxicants to members just like any other Union club. The local police prosecuted the club on the grounds that the 'supply' to members constituted a 'sale' and that the club therefore needed a justices' licence under Section 65 of the Licensing (Consolidation) Act 1910. The case was argued before the stipendiary magistrate, Stanley Evans, who listened to both sides carefully and patiently (the Union had instructed both a solicitor and a barrister to defend the club), but decided in favour of the police. This decision meant that every club registered under the Industrial and Provident Societies Act could have been held to be breaking the law and was liable to be prosecuted. Clearly, this was a decision of great importance and the Executive promptly decided to appeal to the High Court. Fortunately, this appeal was successful. The case was argued for six days before Lord Chief Justice Humphreys in February the following year (1940) and because of the importance of the case, he delivered a written judgment later – in a 2,500-word summary of the legal arguments, the crux of which was that the status quo had been restored; the principle of 'supply' and not 'sale' in a members' club had been upheld, no matter under what Act the club was registered. Had the decision been otherwise, there would have been wide repercussions.

By this time the Union was becoming accustomed to the penalties of maturity, the Executive taking events like these in their stride, as part of the march of time. The Union had now been established nearly eighty years, and its foundations were so secure that one generation would pass to another with no major changes in policy or direction. The deaths of Dent and Stroud came as a sadness rather than shock. Dent, by the time he died in February 1936, had reached the age of eighty, and to the end had been a man of fine physique, noted, as in his younger days, for a magnificent flowing moustache. As we have seen, he had joined his first club at the age of sixteen and had served both as Secretary and as President. Outside the Union, too, his had been a distinguished career; for fifteen years he was a director of the Co-operative Permanent Building Society, and he became a respected civil servant. Dent had been Secretary at the time Stroud joined the Union as Accountant and Assistant Secretary, and had been aware over the thirty-eight years of Stroud's work of the sterling qualities of this rather severe, almost military man, whose sharp eyes and bristling, curly moustache made him look the stern Victorian father – which, indeed, he was to the movement's treasurers!

Both had long retired when they died, but their deaths were sad news to older clubmen, followed, as they were, by the demise of those fine Executive members, Herbert Thomson, Northants; J. W. Tozer, North West London; Arthur Wallwork, Bradford; Lt-Col. W. J. Lewis, Secretary of the North East London Branch; and W. J. Wadman, who had been the Union's architect for forty years, having effected the renovations of three homes and the design of Grange.

There were again new Executive members: Fred Morton filled Wallwork's place in 1938; Sam Appleyard was elected in Leeds, where he had been the Branch Secretary; H. Holding was chosen for South East London; E. G. Roberts took Thomson's seat; George Penny, the Warwickshire Branch President, was elected in that area; and the clubmen of North West London chose A. T. Parke to succeed Tozer.

These changes coincided with the resignation of Richardson as President. Bob Richardson, who resigned in September 1938, had been President for sixteen of his thirty-one years on the Executive, and during that time had seen the Pegwell home extended and three new homes opened, while in Durham he had become as popular as an MP as he was as Branch President, being an old-style Labour man who had worked his way up, and done much for his fellow men in the process. One of his last major functions as Union President had been the Manchester Branch's diamond jubilee celebrations only a year before – a large meeting attended by delegates from 123 clubs at the Blackpool Winter Gardens – and on this occasion he was accompanied by the clubman who was to succeed him as President, Jack Thompson, who had been his Vice-President since 1923.

Thompson, with the same sturdy build, broad chin and stubby moustache as his great predecessor, Dent, was seventy-six when he succeeded to the highest position in the Union, supported by an overwhelming majority of the country's clubmen, who knew him not only as a long-serving Executive member, but also as a zealous supporter of the movement in his native County Durham and a proud railwayman; Thompson also became President of the General Railway Workers' Union, which was later incorporated into the National Union of Railwaymen.

Thus, the Union had a new President and a new Vice-President, C. W. Tarrant, a retired headmaster, enthusiastic co-operator and South Yorkshire clubman, and also a number of new Executive members just as the Second World War was declared. This was just as well, with so many clubmen joining the Forces and the Union thus unable to hold any more elections until the war was over.

12

New President, new Vice-President, new faces on the Executive – it seemed as though only the full-time staff remained the same, with Bob Chapman and Tom Nicoll still forming a partnership that was based as much upon friendship as necessity. And then came the greatest upheaval of all – Hitler drove the Union away from hearth and home. It did not need a bomb to warn the Executive that with the Union's headquarters just off Gray's Inn Road, right in the heart of London, they were in a dangerously exposed position; within days of war breaking out, it was announced that the Union was moving, lock, stock and barrel, to Crag Hall, Durley Gardens, West Cliff, Bournemouth, where there was less risk of the Luftwaffe wreaking irreparable damage.

Thus, for the first and only time in the Union's history, the administration of its affairs was directed from a headquarters outside the capital city, where so many emergency decisions gravely affecting clubs were being taken.

The Government, of course, had to impose wartime restrictions – and the Temperance movement immediately made this an excuse to pronounce against clubs. The National Temperance Federation urged the severest restrictions, even to the point of suggesting that all public houses should be closed at 8 p.m. And in Monmouthshire, where the authorities had always been ill-disposed towards clubs, the police urged police supervision of clubs and Sunday closing. This annoyed the Union and also the Conservative Clubs, who joined a depution which met the Under Secretary of State at the Home Office on 29 January 1940. Thereafter, nothing more was heard of the proposal – and Bob Chapman was able to cheer in the April issue of the *Journal*: 'Monmouthshire Pussyfoots get K.O.' Chapman added: 'It is clear that the Home Secretary does not intend the War to be made an excuse for the introduction of legislation to place fetters on clubs to gratify the whims of the fanatical teetotallers.'

However, the Union's clubs were quite prepared to accept restrictions where they appreciated their necessity; no objection was raised to the Emergency Powers (Defence) Act, which gave the authorities the right to seize any premises for military or defence purposes, and it was realized that the Societies (Miscellaneous Provisions) Act, which gave the Registrar of Friendly Societies authority to permit clubs to dispense with or vary certain of their rules, was necessary, if not welcome. .

In addition, Bob Chapman announced in the *Journal* that he could supply rules for any club wanting to admit Servicemen who were not strictly clubmen, but who would appreciate recreation and friendship; clubs were advised, too, that members' subscriptions could be waived while they were in the Forces. The Executive also resolved to loan £10,000 to the Government (unlike many people who were given post-war credits, the Union got its money back!), and many other individual clubs also loaned sums of money to the Government. For many years after the war, the Fillongley Working Men's Club in Warwickshire displayed a letter on the walls, acknowledging the Government's gratitude for its assistance. In addition, the Executive also decided to equip two mobile canteens to provide refreshments for the troops, while Langland Bay home became an emergency hospital for air raid victims (the homes at Saltburn and Pegwell had to be vacated because of the risk of bombardment).

As can be seen, the Executive responded to every call to help the war effort. The National Savings Campaign was backed in the *Journal*; no less than £56,000 was raised by member clubs for the Duke of Gloucester's Red Cross and St John's Ambulance Appeal after the Union Executive had themselves donated £1,000 in April, 1941. Another large sum, £20,886, was raised for the Help for Russia fund organized by the National Council of Labour ('The result is worthy of praise,' commented its Secretary, Sir Walter Citrine); another £10,698 was raised for the same Council's Help for China Fund, and financial support was also given to the Yugoslavia Emergency Committee.

Finance was not the only wartime problem; many clubs were damaged in the Blitz – particularly in London and Coventry – and the Executive arranged a special War Damage Assistance Scheme, with an original capital of £5,000 to help clubs that were in desperate straits, though very few took advantage of this, and many clubs were also in some financial difficulties themselves during the war for another reason altogether: there was a shortage of beer, due to a lack of materials, with all available resources being applied to the war effort.

The most restrictive wartime measure that was passed by the Government was Defence Regulation 55c, which was passed as an Order in Council on 6 August 1942. This enactment, which remained in force (though modified by Chuter Ede) until 1952, virtually prohibited the formation of new clubs, and provided for more rigid control of existing ones. The regulation read:

55c – (1) Where application is made under the Licensing Consolidation Act, 1910, for the registration of a club, there shall be included among the particulars, which are required to be registered, the names and addresses of the promoters of the club, the proprietor, if any, the person, if any, who is or will be the manager thereof, the persons who take part or will take part in the management of the club, the persons who have become or agreed to become members of the club and any other persons who (whether because they have provided or are providing capital for the club or any other reason) are financially interested in the success of the application, together with a statement of the nature and extent of their respective interests. Provided that nothing in this paragraph shall be construed as requiring the said particulars to be included in any return required by the said Act to be made after the club has been duly registered.

(2) Where application is made under the said Act for the registration of a club, the clerk to whom the application is made shall send to the chief officer of police a copy of the particulars required to be registered, and if, within fourteen days from the date when the copy is so sent, the chief officer sends to the clerk a notice stating that he objects on any of the grounds mentioned in paragraph (4) of this Regulation to the registration of the club and giving particulars of the objection, the clerk shall serve on the applicant a copy of the notice and shall not register the club.

(3) Where the registration of a club has been objected to under this regulation, the applicant for registration may within four weeks from the service on him of the copy of the notice of objection, appeal to the court for which the clerk to whom the application was made acts, and the court shall, if satisfied that an objection on the grounds stated to the registration is unreasonable, but not otherwise, authorise the registration of the club.

(4) The grounds on which an objection may be made are as follows, that is to say

(a) that having regard to existing facilities for social amenities, recreation and refreshment and to the objects of the club, the club is not required to meet a genuine and substantial need;

(b) that the premises for the club are, or their situation is, unsuitable for the purposes thereof;

(c) that the particulars which have been supplied on the application for registration are inaccurate or incomplete, or that the chief officer of police is not satisfied as to the accuracy and completeness thereof;

(d) that the character or antecedents of any of the promoters, of the proprietor, of the secretary or of any of the persons who are taking or will take part in the management, or who are financially interested in the success of the application for registration, are such that the club ought not to be registered;

Provided that no objection to the registration of a club shall be made on either of the grounds specified in sub-paragraphs (a) and (b) of this paragraph if it is certified by a competent authority that there is a genuine and substantial need for such a club, and that the premises of the club and their situation are suitable for the purposes thereof.

In this paragraph, the expression 'competent authority' includes the Minister of Labour and National Service as well as the competent authorities specified in Regulation 49 of these Regulations.

(5) Any person authorised in that behalf by the chief officer of police may enter and inspect the premises of the club at any time after the application for the registration thereof has been made and before the club has actually been registered.

The police of Monmouthshire and the Temperance kill-joys had very nearly achieved in wartime what they had long sought over previous decades – but the Union made little protest, taking the view that sacrifice was necessary for the duration of the war. The Executive were sufficiently astute, however, to realize that traditional opponents of the movement would do all they could to prolong the operation of this law once an end to hostilities had been declared. In the October 1942 issue of the *Journal* they sounded this warning:

The Executive are of the opinion that the Regulation, confined to the period of the War, will have little or no effect upon clubs belonging to the Union or in which the Union should be interested, though it may prevent the establishment of bogus and proprietory clubs, the existence of which we have always deplored.

They, however, do foresee the possibility of an attempt being made at the conclusion of hostilities to perpetuate the Regulation, or embody it or its provisions in post-war legislation, and to this they would strenuously object.

As soon as the end of the war was in sight, Chapman and his colleagues raised the issue once again, and, as in the years before the war, co-operated with the Conservative and Golf Clubs Associations to present a united front, calling on the Home Secretary, Chuter Ede (who was himself President of a Union club, the Epsom British Legion Club, to which he had belonged for twenty-five years), to repeal the Order; he refused to revoke it completely, but did modify the regulation in the Emergency Powers (Transitional Provisions) Act, curtailing the right of police to prevent the registration of new clubs.

The four years that Defence Regulation 55c was in existence were trying ones for the nation, and exacting for the Union; many keen young clubmen were lost in the war, and six years passed without any Executive elections.

A. T. Parke, North West Metropolitan, resigned in 1942 and was succeeded by Ernest Connelly, the Branch President. Joe Wanless died and was succeeded in 1941 by George Cook, a former professional footballer who had played for Preston North End, Torquay United and Carlisle, before becoming Secretary of the Shankhouse Central Club at Cramlington, Northumberland. Tom Jenks resigned in 1944 and was succeeded by J. H. Mintram, Secretary of Hampshire Branch for the previous seventeen years. Councillor T. Hargrave was elected in Wakefield when Alderman Tennant died in July 1944; F. W. Luckie in place of Gus Dupree, who had represented North East London for thirty years when he died in 1944; Tom Elliott, a member of Wallsend Coronation, joined the Executive in 1944, and W. J. Richardson died in September 1945. These changes were by Executive decision rather than by the usual process of local elections. In 1944, the former President, Bob Richardson, and the Manchester pioneer, W. J. Ellam, both died.

There were numerous changes at the homes, too. Mr and Mrs Reed retired as Superintendent and Matron at Grange and were succeeded by Mr and Mrs W. Hamilton, who had been in charge of the Langland home at the outbreak of the war; Mrs M. E. Boyland, who had retired as Superintendent at Pegwell in 1927, died in 1942, aged seventy-eight; Mrs Seagrave, Superintendent at Saltburn, retired in 1943. At head office, there was another change when W. R. Clamp, head of the Audit Department, who had been in the Union's service since 1896, retired in 1944. He was succeeded by A. S. Taylor.

In the meantime the Executive had other problems on their minds; there was the constant (and successful) effort to raise money for different war funds. In 1942, the Executive decided to assist the Superannuation Fund, by granting £1,000 and an extra £400 to bring it up to the state where half-pay pensions could be paid. The following year, the Catering Wages Commission was established under the Catering Wages Act to enquire into the existing rates of pay and conditions of employment in the catering industry. Clubs came within the purview of the Act and in 1944 the Union was invited by the Commission to submit a memorandum regarding club employees. It was pointed out that a club did not trade and was not a business in the ordinary sense in that it did not exist to make a profit, as did public houses or catering establishments. It was suggested that as clubs were private premises, and that as the Union had always advocated the payment of generous wages and the provision of good working conditions, the Union thought it unnecessary for the Commission to concern themselves with wages and conditions of employment within member clubs.

Following the submission of this memorandum, a deputation met the Commission, which eventually resolved that the wages of club employees should be included and recommended to the Minister of Labour that a board should be established to formulate regulations for the payment of wages and working conditions for all people employed either within clubs or on licensed premises. This board was established in 1945, and Tom Nicoll, the Assistant General Secretary, and Sid Anstee, who represented the Leicester clubs on the Executive, were appointed to represent the Union. Many months were spent examining the question, and it was not until 1947 that the first order was issued defining minimum wages and conditions. This was a revolutionary measure so far as many clubs were concerned and literally hundreds of letters poured into head office *daily*, as club committees sought advice on their new responsibilities. Tom Nicoll, being a member of the board himself, handled this enormous volume of correspondence, working late into the night for several weeks, and also visiting branches and special conferences to explain the new regulations.

Equally controversial was the question of cash grants to club members, which provoked a vigorous debate within the Union – and one that continued for two years, with tempers sometimes running high on both sides. The trouble all began when Chapman, on the instructions of the Executive, wrote to every Union club in November 1943, pointing out that the rules of the Union prohibited the distribution of club funds among members, and that clubs without such a clause in their constitution were in any case forbidden to do so under the Union's own rule no. 6 (e). Chapman continued:

It has come to the notice of the Executive that some clubs – comparatively few – have broken this long-standing rule of the Union, perhaps unwittingly. The rule was framed and adopted many years ago in the interests and for the protection of clubs – to prevent the frittering away of club funds by these petty periodical payments. There are usually many ways in which a club's surplus funds can be beneficially used – to provide a building fund with which to purchase land and erect a fine club-house, to extend the club premises, to build a club hall, to purchase good and substantial furniture and equipment, to re-decorate and beautify the club premises, to establish a library, to provide a bowling green or a tennis court, and many other amenities.

Chapman went on to stress the need for conserving finances, particularly as many clubs might be hard-pressed after the war (as they had been after the First World War), and he warned clubs that if they broke this rule they would face expulsion from the Union.

Chapman knew that many of the offending clubs were situated in the north-east, and the Northumberland clubmen realized that this letter was, in effect, an ultimatum to them to obey the rules. Even so, some northern clubs continued to ignore the rule and eventually twenty-eight clubs were expelled from the Union for breaking it. Those that were later re-admitted (all but three of them) were asked to give a firm assurance that they would adhere to the rules on re-entering the Union. This was all too much for the Durham Branch, and at the October Council meeting in 1944 they tabled this motion:

(a) We protest against the dictatorial and threatening phraseology contained in the circular issued to clubs in the Club and Institute Union by Mr R. S. Chapman in November 1943.
(b) We, 316 delegates representing 185 clubs in the Durham Branch CIU, hereby request the National Executive CIU to forthwith take the necessary action to have Rule 6 (e) deleted from CIU rules, and thus allow clubs to have local autonomy and control over their finances and resources.

The motions were put to the meeting and overwhelmingly defeated, and all offending clubs were then warned that in future they could expect no mercy – a decision which, however, was waived slightly when victory was declared at the end of the Second World War; the Union declared its own amnesty to give offending clubs a chance to reconsider their position and put their house in order. Chapman again wrote to the clubs:

For the past two years the non-observance of this Rule (which forbids the making of grants generally to club members from club funds) by a comparatively few clubs has given the Union Executive much trouble and anxiety . . .
Following the victory over Japan and the end of the World War, the Executive, not without serious discussion and consideration, decided they would, to mark our victory, show clemency, and re-admit clubs

which they had expelled for breach of this Rule, and not proceed to terminate the membership of other clubs which had broken the Rule prior to September 1st, 1945.

In doing this they felt some little doubt whether clubs which were inclined to break the Rule might mistake this act of clemency for weakness on their part, and regard this action as an indication that they would slacken in their determination to secure compliance. This is by no means the case – *it is the intention of the Executive henceforth to uphold the Rule with more determination than ever.*

They therefore give this notice to every Union club, that if the Rule is broken hereafter, *the offending club will be expelled without any hope of being reinstated to the Union thereafter.*

If there now be any club which is not prepared to observe this Rule of the Union, the Executive desire that the club should, here and now, send in its resignation. This would be preferable to suffering the ignominy of being hereafter expelled from this great Union.

Even so, the Executive were at pains to be reasonable and they informed clubs that exceptions to the Rule would be permitted where committees wanted to show seasonal hospitality to members (up to three pints a year), and where a club wanted to celebrate a special event in its history. But this was not the end of the matter. Many clubs resented having to apply for permission before giving drinks to their own members, and Executive members were lobbied to press for the abolition of the controversial rule – and, in the end, the Executive gave way.

On the morning of the 1946 Annual Meeting, the Executive discussed the matter again, and decided to rescind their decision to allow three points of beer per member per year, and not to interfere with clubs over the question of supplying free drinks, provided club funds were not being dissipated, and to allow exceptions in the case of cash grants for old-age pensioners and members returning from the Forces. Thus ended a rather acrimonious episode in the Union's history; it was not an easy decision for the Executive to expel twenty-eight clubs in one branch, and was certainly not a popular one. But it said much for the Executive that, having found their policy was unpopular, they agreed to modify it. Chapman commented that 'the Executive were broad-minded men, and if their policy had not given satisfaction ... were courageous enough to vary it'.

Just as the end of the First World War had heralded a new, fast-expanding stage in the history of the Working Men's Club and Institute Union, so the end of the Second World War introduced an era of boldness and vigour.

The controversy over Rule 6(e) had caused tensions within the Union, at a period when many club officials were in the Forces; this had tended to delay the growth of the Union, but just as the ex-servicemen of the twenties returned home determined to retain the comradeship they had experienced at the Front, so the men demobbed in 1945 were keen to make their clubs the centres of the communities in which they lived. None were keener than the Executive members elected in the New Year of 1946. These were the first elections since 1938, and produced a major change in the leadership of the Union – a new President, a new Vice-President, and seven new members of the Executive. The following year, six more new members were elected to the Executive, and then five more new faces appeared after the elections of 1949.

Of all these elections, the most important were those held in 1946, when Edward McEnery was elected President. He was strongly supported by the clubs of the North, who knew him as the Secretary of the Wakefield Branch, and of the Yorkshire Council of Branches, and went on to become one of the Union's greatest Presidents, holding the office until he died in November 1969. The then General Secretary, John B. Holmes, recalled McEnery's many years' work for the movement in an obituary written for the December 1969 issue of the *Journal*:

> Edward McEnery was a natural clubman. He loved comradeship. When he joined Moorthorpe Empire Club at the age of 21, he found there some of the comradeship he had enjoyed in the Army during the First World War. And what he found he liked. It was recorded of him then that he was a perky volatile youngster, always demanding to know why something could not be done or another thing could not be done better. In the modern idiom he would not take 'No' for an answer. Moorthorpe saw the birth and growth of an enthusiasm that was to last a lifetime. So it was a natural development in Mac's Club life when Moorthorpe elected him Secretary in 1929. This was the first of many Club offices which Edward McEnery was to hold with distinction.
>
> In 1935, on the passing of Harry Hodge, he was elected Secretary of the Wakefield Branch. Seven years later he succeeded Alderman J. Tennant JP as Secretary of the Yorkshire Council of Branches.
>
> The dynamic drive which took Edward McEnery on a persistent pursuit of getting things done carried him into public life. For a period of 22 years he was Clerk of the South Elmsall Parish Council, the North Elmsall Parish Council and the Co-ordination Joint Committee of South Elmsall, South Kirkby, North Elmsall and Upton.
>
> The year 1945 brought the climax of Edward McEnery's Club life. In December of that year, at the age of 51, he was elected President of the Union by an overwhelming majority. So began a period of high

office, with all its burdens and responsibilities. With true Yorkshire grit he surmounted all difficulties during the most challenging and yet glorious period of Union history and triumphed in all he undertook. In every obstacle he saw a fresh challenge to be met and overcome . . . . in his challenge to Ministers of successive Governments on their ideas and suggestions of what might be applicable to our Clubs, he demanded that nothing should be done to interfere with the social life enjoyed by Clubmen.

A lesser man might have accepted the views expressed and intentions in Bills presented to Parliament, which if they became law would have made serious inroads on the way of life enjoyed and desired by our people.

But a man of the calibre of Edward McEnery, with his deep insight and personal experience of the ideals and desires of Clubmen and their families, resisted at all times any attempt by Government or local bureaucracy to infringe the liberties cherished by Clubmen or to usurp privileges that had been so hardly won over a century of struggle.

At the time that he became President of the Union, Edward McEnery was auditor of the South Kirkby Diamond Jubilee Club and Secretary of the Moorthorpe Empire Club, and had a strong reputation for raising money among the Yorkshire clubs; he had encouraged the clubs to give generously to the different war charities. In the election for the Presidency, he defeated Sid Anstee of Leicester.

The new Vice-President was a 60-year-old miner, Noah Bailey, who was Secretary of the Cudworth Village Club, a member of the Cudworth Urban District Council, and had been on the South Yorkshire Branch Executive for twenty-two years. Elected to the Executive with him were Jackson Hewitson, Secretary of Langley Moor and District Social Club, Durham, who was also a miner; Albert Linstead, who had worked down the same pit as Bailey before becoming Secretary of Lundwood Working Men's Club and later Secretary of South Yorkshire Branch; John Edgar Pugh, Secretary of Lamb Working Men's Club and Colne and Burnley Branch; E. Llewellyn Rees, trustee of Trefelin Working Men's Club, a member of the South Wales Branch Executive, and a traveller for the South Wales and Monmouthshire Clubs Brewery; H. T. Richardson, Secretary of Bradford Branch, chairman of Bradford Co-operative Society and President of East Bowling Independent Labour Club; William Savage, a 58-year-old coppersmith who was President of Patricroft Working Men's Club and a member of the Manchester Branch Executive; and Oscar Snelson, a 59-year-old locomotive fitter who had been President of North Staffordshire

Branch since 1936, and who had defeated the sitting member, George Penny, by only three votes to win his seat on the Executive.

One of the first tasks that faced the new Executive was the reinstatement of the convalescent homes. Possession of Saltburn, which was used later in the war to house children whose school had been destroyed by enemy action, was obtained in 1945. Pegwell had been occupied by the War Department, and was returned in 1946. Langland, which was also given back to the Union at the beginning of 1946, had been used as an annexe to Swansea General Hospital since September 1940. Only Grange had been kept open as a home during the war. In 1946, all four homes were redecorated and re-opened at a time when many war-weary clubmen returning from the Front felt in need of convalescence.

The Executive encountered some difficulty in recruiting staff for the homes, but clubmen were pleased to see Mr and Mrs Hamilton, who had spent the later war years at Grange, return to Langland, while Mr and Mrs W. C. Cornwall were welcomed at Pegwell Bay. (Willie Cornwall had been working at the home since he was a boy.)

Such was the volume of work in administering the homes that in 1947 a Convalescent Homes Secretary was appointed for the first time. Clifford Culling, Secretary of the Horton Grange Working Men's Club in Bradford, was appointed to the new post, which had been created at a vital turning-point in the history of this part of the movement. The National Health Services Act 1946 had led the Executive to wonder whether the homes might be acquired by the State, as part of the Health Service. This anxiety overshadowed the Union's activities in 1946 and 1947, for Clause 6 of the Act implied that all convalescent homes would become part of the Service, along with the nation's hospitals. Bob Chapman wrote to the Minister of Health, Aneurin Bevan, and was eventually assured that our homes would be excluded from the scheme – a decision that relieved many clubmen, who regarded the homes as an irreplaceable part of the Union.

At the same time, the increased demand for accommodation was compelling the Executive to consider acquiring a fifth home. This was the issue that confronted the members who joined the Executive in the 1947 elections, when H. Holding and W. H. Richardson resigned, just after the deaths of their colleagues, William Savage and J. E. Pugh. That year, too, there was a shake-up, with six new members returned. J. B. Adams, a 47-year-old electrical engineer who had been a member of Lambeth Borough Council before the war and a delegate to the London South-East Branch since 1940, was elected, along with F. C. Ansell, a 36-year-old commercial traveller and President of the Albany Social Club, Coventry; B. Rowe, a 53-year-old chartered accountant and Secretary of the South Wales Branch; T. Waterworth, Secretary of Colne and Burnley Branch, a member of the Trinity Labour Club, Burnley, and a well-known club artiste; L. L. Wright, an iron moulder who was President of Heavy Woollen Branch and Secretary of Gomersal Working Men's Club for the previous nineteen years; and William Ollerton, Secretary of Preston and District Federation of Clubs.

The question of a women's home was raised by Kent Branch at the Annual Meeting in Manchester in April 1946, when delegates carried this resolution:

> That this Branch of the Club and Institute Union calls upon the Executive Council to give consideration to the foundation of a fund for the purpose of purchasing and maintaining premises suitable for a Women's Convalescent Home to be made available for women members of affiliated clubs, and wives of members, and calls upon the National Executive to present a report thereon at the end of six months.

This was a controversial issue, since the Executive held that one home could not possibly meet the demand likely from the Union's 160,000 women members and from the members' wives, who were now estimated at over a million. This response was not considered good enough by the delegates attending the Council meeting in October 1946, and it was referred back by 116 votes to 51. The ball was back at the Executive's feet again, and after discussing the proposal once more (and being clearly none too keen on it), they finally agreed to ask the branches to vote on the issue, which resulted in an overwhelming defeat for the proposal.

This was one of those periods during the Union's history when so much seemed to be happening in every section of the movement; the atmosphere was similar to the one that had prevailed in the years immediately following the end of the First World War. Andrew Temple, the Educational and Recreational Secretary, had retired in July 1946 after thirty-two years' service, and he was succeeded by G. F. Ding ('Gen' Ding), his pre-war assistant, who had rejoined the Union's service after wartime service as a captain with the Royal Corps of Signals in Burma. Frank Chawner, Manager of the Stores Department, had resigned earlier the same year and he, too, was succeeded by a fellow-member of the staff, H. E. Bevan, who had spent his war years with the Royal Navy. Another innovation was the creation of the new position of Chief Accountant in 1947, to which A. S. Taylor, head of the Audit Department, was appointed.

The promotion of Ding to be Educational and Recreational Secretary signified an unintentional change of emphasis in this department, which had first come to the fore during B. T. Hall's time. Hall had never been very recreation-conscious and did little to stimulate the department's growth, but this mattered little since time was to show that these activities acquired their dynamic not through forceful leadership by national officers, but through enthusiasm at branch level encouraged by the national committee and the General Secretary. Encouragement of this sort did not come from B. T. Hall; in its early years, the recreational and educational work was left to George Shore, manager of the Stores Department. Later Andrew Temple was appointed to the new post of Departmental Secretary, but he preferred to promote education rather than recreation. At one time, the Union provided fourteen residential scholarships to Ruskin College – one person to benefit from this scheme was George Woodcock, who later became General Secretary of the Trades Union Congress. Today, there is no longer the same urgent social need for the Union to fill and thus only one scholarship is provided, though this does now include a domestic allowance where the holder is a married man. Where a clubman makes good progress, the Union will increase the scholarship from one year to two to enable him to sit for the Oxford University Diploma Examination.

Another branch of education in which the Union has been prominent since Temple's early days is the organization, in conjunction with the Workers' Educational Association, of local schools and classes, lectures in clubs and day schools, which were, in fact, a wartime innovation which was intended as a temporary expedient but proved permanent.

The first summer school had been held at Ruskin College in 1922, and was so successful that spring schools were introduced four years later. During the Second World War, clubmen were disinclined to spend the time away from their wives and families, and consequently day schools were started. The effect of this has been to widen the Union's influence. Today, day schools are still popular and the Union still arranges spring schools and summer schools.

Another important innovation was the six-month correspondence course on club law, administration and accountancy, which was fostered by Bob Chapman. The course was (and is) followed by an examination, and successful clubmen were entitled to place the initials CMD (Club Management Diploma) after their names and to wear a silver medal (now a badge). The scheme has proved a most important means of giving clubmen the legal and financial knowledge essential to the smooth running of a club. Also introduced was the Certificate of Merit, which was also handled by the Education Department, under which a certificate and a silver badge were (and are) awarded to clubmen for long service to their clubs. These innovations were the highlights of Temple's tenure of the post, but when Gen Ding took over, the emphasis began to change; this was not so much because Temple had concentrated on education, as that clubmen themselves were beginning to give more support to recreational activities. The National Team Billiards Championship had been started as early as 1907, and the Individual Billiards in 1919, but these pursuits had not gathered the tremendous following that they have today until some twenty-five years later, though snooker was coming into far greater prominence by the mid-twenties. The National Team Snooker Championship was introduced in 1925/26 and the Individual Snooker two years later. Branch contests also began to gain in popularity, and by 1933 there were already some 300–400 Union trophies. To increase interest even more, it was decided to introduce the Contest Grant Scheme under which the Union made annual awards of £3 (now £10) towards each trophy, and to date grants totalling £350,000 have been made under this scheme. This might have been even greater, but for the decision in 1952 to make all future trophies perpetual. That it has grown so much is due to the hard work done at branch level and in individual clubs, for this is where the games have their roots.

The Union was fortunate in having Gen Ding as the new Departmental Secretary at this stage; having been an army captain during the war, he was a good organizer and this was the skill that was needed in the immediate post-war years as other games became popular in the clubs – darts, angling, dominoes, cribbage, whist, bowls, skittles, don, bagatelle, horticulture, shove-halfpenny, pigeon racing, football, cricket, shooting, golf, dancing, quizzes, athletics, first aid, euchre, chess, singing, table tennis, tippet, draughts, walking, beauty contests, table bowls, tug-of-war and cage bird breeding were all attracting support from clubmen – and today there are trophies awarded for all of them. Two of the most popular are the National Team Darts Championship, instituted in 1947, which attracts several thousand entrants a year, and the National Angling Championship, which began in 1948; both events became so popular that Southern, Northern and Midland regional championships were introduced as well. Today, the Union promotes more games contests than any other organization in the country.

Soon after these appointments had been made to the head office staff, the Union brought its staff back to London from Bournemouth, where their stay had been prolonged – until almost two years after the end of the war – because the premises in Clerkenwell Road had been badly damaged by incendiary bombs. The Executive had tried to find other accommodation, but had been restricted by the Government regulation prohibiting premises suitable for housing from being used for other purposes. Eventually, in 1947, permission was obtained following a direct approach to the Ministry of Works to repair part of our original building for the Union's use.

At the first annual meeting after the return to London the Executive proposed an alteration of the Union rules to allow for additional representation on the Executive in respect of the first 200 clubs in any one electoral area, with a further representative for each 100 additional clubs, a suggestion which was given overwhelming support by the branches. This gave South Wales and Monmouthshire and North West Midlands an extra representative each.

Before the elections for the new seats were held, the Union's biennial elections were due – and again, new faces were welcomed. E. Bexon, Secretary of Bedford North End Club, was elected by Northants and Bedfordshire; R. Harper, a member of the West Midland Branch Executive, was chosen in that area; R. W. Batey, Secretary of Harrowgate Club, was elected in Durham; and J. Allison, a Manchester magistrate and Chairman of the North East Lancashire Co-operative Dairies Association, joined the Executive from the Lancashire and Cheshire area.

At these elections, a new Vice-President, W. H. Waterhouse, Secretary of East Dene Social Club, Rotherham, was voted into office, and two new members came on the following year, 1950, when J. G. Evans, Treasurer of the Newport and District Working Men's Club, Middlesbrough, was elected for Durham and Cleveland, and Tom Eccles, President of the Wolverhampton West End Club, for North-West Midlands.

Meanwhile, the Union was again concerned with constitutional issues; a new Licensing Bill was promoted, an important rating case was taken to the High Court, the third party indemnity insurance scheme was improved and a new group personal accident insurance introduced, a fifth convalescent home was opened at Nantwich, the Scottish Branch was formed and, finally, Bob Chapman's achievements as General Secretary were recognized in 1949 when he was awarded the CBE.

The new Licensing Bill was introduced by the Labour Government in November 1948, with the purpose of extending the state management of public houses, which had been operating for the past thirty years in Carlisle, to the new towns which were being built in different parts of the country. The Executive instructed Chapman to write to the Home Secretary, Chuter Ede, seeking assurances that clubs would not be subject to police right of entry, restriction of source when buying intoxicants and the same opening hours as public houses, as was the case in Carlisle.

Chapman later visited the Home Office to discuss the Bill's provisions personally with Chuter Ede, who subsequently confirmed:

1. that clubs would not have to conform to the same 'permitted hours' as those prescribed for other licensed premises in their area;
2. that commission on intoxicating liquor supplied in a club could be paid to, or received by, any officer or servant of the club;
3. that the prices of beer and spirits need not be the same as those in neighbouring licensed premises;
4. that beer and spirits could be bought for consumption off the premises;
5. that persons under eighteen could be supplied with intoxicating liquor; and
6. that clubs should not have to accept police right of entry.

By giving this latitude, Ede was reassuring the Union that any clubs formed in the new towns would be registered under similar conditions to all other clubs in the Union, and not subject to restrictions similar to those imposed in Carlisle.

This was a victory for Chapman's quiet style of diplomacy, as was the High Court appeal over the Aberdare Ex-Servicemen's Club a triumph for the Executive. This appeal had been made after a Quarter Sessions court had allowed Aberdare Urban District Council when it fixed the rating assessment of the club premises to take take into account

(a) that profits were made by the club from trading in alcoholic liquors,
(b) that the club was not likely to find other accommodation, and
(c) that the clubs in the district had a virtual monopoly in the provision of club facilities.

This raised a question which the Executive had wanted established for many years, though this was the first time that they had been able to find a rating authority that would admit that it had taken 'trade' and 'profits' into consideration, but now that the Aberdare

Urban District Council had shown their hand, the Executive agreed to finance an appeal to the High Court where the case was heard by Lord Chief Justice Goddard, Judge Humphreys and Judge Atkinson, who agreed unanimously with the contention of the Union's counsel, H. B. Williams, KC, that a rating authority should *not* consider either 'trade' or 'profits' in deciding rateable value and allowed the appeal, ordering Aberdare UDC to pay costs.

Negotiations with Lloyds Brokers were concluded whereby, as from 1 October 1947, the indemnity given to clubs under the Union's Third Party Insurance was doubled without any increase in premium. This meant that clubs paying an annual premium of 30s for third party insurance through the Union's brokers were covered up to a maximum of £2,000 instead of £1,000, and for 25s up to £1,000 instead of £500. (Two years later Chapman was able to announce in the *Journal* that another insurance scheme, the Group Personal Accident Insurance, had been negotiated, giving individual members the right to compensation in the event of their being accidentally injured or killed in their clubs.) Thus, in their own clubs and while travelling to the Union's homes, clubmen were covered against the risk of personal accident – an investment which has proved advantageous to many members.

Many clubmen had thought long before the Second World War that a fifth convalescent home for men was needed, and the post-war demand for accommodation raised the question again. Advertisements were inserted in various newspapers for suitable premises, and eventually the Executive heard that the Brine Baths Hotel at Nantwich, Cheshire, was on the market, heard good reports, went to see the premises and agreed to buy the property with ten acres of land for £30,000. The building was well equipped (the furniture was valued independently at £16,000), and situated only six minutes by train and twenty minutes by bus from Crewe, a good club town and a centre of the railway system easily reached by convalescent clubmen. The former hotel had every amenity, too – tennis courts, a bowling green, beautifully laid gardens, a ballroom, a billiards room, games room, sun lounge and fine bedrooms, each well carpeted and furnished, with excellent beds and wash-basins in each room.

It was fitting, after his co-operation over the Licensing Bill, that the opening ceremony should have been performed by Chuter Ede, who heard the President, Edward McEnery, pay tribute to Chapman and Ernie Connelly, an Executive member who was a builder by trade and whose professional skill had been invaluable to the Convalescent Homes Committee while they negotiated the purchase of the new home, and the £60,000 works that were undertaken before the first clubmen stayed there.

Attempts had been made several times before to form a Scottish branch (we have seen already how Chapman and G. E. Middleton had tried before the Second World War), but had always come to nothing – until 1950, when the Executive agreed that clubs in Scotland were sufficiently advanced and keen to justify their now being brought together into one branch. This decision followed three years of preparatory work in the area, and the new branch was formally inaugurated on 17 June 1950, at a meeting held at the Leith Dockers' Hall, chaired by Edward McEnery and attended by delegates from eleven clubs, who elected their officials: Chairman, Baillie R. Christie of the Perth Railway Club; Vice-Chairman, W. McCall, Leith Dockers' Club; Treasurer, J. Harrower, Cowdenbeath Labour Club; Secretary, C. Climie of the Fairfield Working Men's Club, Glasgow; and Branch Executive members, J. Green, O. Dowie, J. Dick, C. M. King, A. B. Gilmour and J. M. Parker.

With the new Licensing Bill, the Aberdare Ex-Servicemen's Club case, the agitation for a women's home, and the opening of the fifth home at Nantwich, these post-war years had been busy ones for Bob Chapman. In the controversy over clubs distributing funds among their own members, he had displayed firmness; in his negotiations with the Home Secretary or with the ambitious clubmen of Scotland, he had shown powers of diplomacy; and in his numerous visits to clubs in all parts of the country, individual clubmen had come to know him both as a counsellor and as a friend. And thus clubmen everywhere were proud that such a distinguished figure in their movement should have been appointed a Commander of the Order of the British Empire in the 1949 Birthday Honours List. Chapman had proved himself of very different mettle to B. T. Hall; he had never tried to dominate the Executive in the way that Hall did, and had thus come to acquire over the years a somewhat closer relationship with the Union's Executive members; his thirty years with the movement, twenty of them as General Secretary, had proved him to be a man who combined caution with courage, and pride with conscience. The award was well earned.

13

Within months of Bob Chapman being awarded the CBE, he announced his retirement and thus a long and distinguished career ended. Chapman was then sixty-two, and had been General Secretary for twenty-one years, after ten years as B. T. Hall's assistant. For some time, he had been suffering from hardness of hearing and the strain of his wife's ill-health, so the Executive realized that they had to accept his decision when he notified them in December 1949 that he wished to resign with effect from the following April. At the January Council meeting H. Walker of the Llanelli Working Men's Club proposed that a national testimonial should be arranged in Chapman's honour, and this was seconded by Alderman J. W. Hill, JP, of the Harlesden Working Men's Club and welcomed by the delegates. This testimonial raised about £3,000.

Meanwhile, thoughts had been turning to the choice of Chapman's successor. Many club committees wrote to the Assistant General Secretary, Tom Nicoll, asking if they could nominate him, but Tom's health was deteriorating, and in the interests of the Union he felt compelled, although reluctantly, to decline. Eventually, nine candidates were nominated and Frank R. Castle of the Plumstead Working Men's Radical Club was elected by an overwhelming majority, receiving 3,838 votes, which was 68.4 per cent of the total votes cast.

Castle was already well known to many clubmen. Before joining the Union staff in 1933 as Legal Assistant, he had spent ten years with a London firm of solicitors and had thus acquired the knowledge that enabled him to revise Chapman's *Five Hundred Points of Club Law*, a handbook that was much used in the clubs, and his advice was frequently sought by individual clubmen who knew him as a lecturer on club law and administration at the spring and summer schools. But Frank's experience was not confined solely to law; he had been a member of the Plumstead Radical Club since he was twenty-one and their delegate to the Kent Branch since 1930, and he was to continue his involvement with the Kent clubs long after his election to national office; he retired from the Branch Executive only in 1958, after chairing its Finance Committee for twenty-five years.

As Castle said in his election address, he could claim to be a 'practical clubman' – just how practical had been shown by his work as Secretary (and founder) of the Kent Sub-Clubs Convalescent Homes Federation, which raised large sums of money for the homes.

The result of the ballot was declared at the end of March, and at the annual meeting at Brighton in April tributes were paid both to Chapman and to his successor. McEnery told the delegates:

> His service has been magnificent and beyond reproach. The existence of a great many clubs today is due to the advice and guidance rendered by Mr Chapman. There has been nothing too big and nothing too little for him to do.

Thanking the President and all the delegates for the tribute and their response to the testimonial, Bob Chapman said:

> I want to thank all the clubs which have borne with me over the long years. I have sometimes made mistakes but I have tried to be just to all men even at the expense of sometimes incurring the wrath of club committees and branch executives. I trust that whatever may be said of me hereafter I shall be accorded the attribute of being fair and just.
>
> I have received through the years much kindness from the Presidents under whom I have served and from my Executive Committees. I can now take every man by the hand and call him friend. I think I can do the same with every Branch Secretary . . . I think our Union has very great possibilities yet. It will grow in size under the guidance of our Committee and under the guidance of Mr Frank Castle. I have been blessed with excellent lieutenants in Frank Castle and Tom Nicoll, who in spite of ill health has always done his bit, a large bit, but who felt that in the interests of the Union he could not undertake all the responsibilities which must fall to the General Secretary of our Union. His courage in subordinating himself is to be commended, and I wish him well.
>
> I commend to you Frank Castle. Perhaps his abilities and merits are not yet fully appreciated. He is a man of very sound and extensive knowledge. He has the ability to handle the Union's affairs, he is extremely industrious, qualities which I am sure will earn for him the reputation of a great Union General Secretary.

The meeting ended. Frank Castle took over as General Secretary, with a portrait of Chapman by the celebrated Australian painter, Will Longstaff, on the wall of his office. Another era had ended; a new one was beginning.

And it began well. No sooner had Castle taken office than he put forward a plan to stabilize the finances of the convalescent homes, suggesting that the price of pass cards – which had remained at 1d per month since 1919 – should be increased to 2d, with the increase going to the convalescent homes to fund the £30,000 gap between income and expenditure. This proposal was formally welcomed by the chairman of the Convalescent Homes Committee, Ernie Connelly, by the Executive and by the Council delegates at Leamington Spa in July 1951, and then submitted to a ballot, with the branches agreeing to the increase by 3,115 votes to 762.

This was followed by a suggestion from West Midland Branch that only clubs that agreed to admit associates should be accepted for Union membership. This proposal was approved by the Executive, who nevertheless decided that the change in policy should not be applied to the forty-two clubs that were already members of the Union and did not admit associates. Consequently, it was decided that after 1 July 1952 only clubmen who held associate cards would be admitted to the convalescent homes.

Castle, who, like Chapman, had Tom Nicoll as his assistant, was soon initiated into the wider responsibilities of the general secretaryship. In July 1951, he, Nicoll and McEnery led a deputation to the Minister of Food, Maurice Webb, over the vexed question of beer gravities, brought to the fore again by the brewers deciding to increase the price of beer by a penny a pint. Later that same month, Castle, Nicoll and McEnery joined another deputation with A. Willis, Secretary of the Association of Clubs Breweries, and Sid Lavers and H. V. Barrass, Chairman and Secretary of the Northern Clubs Co-operative Brewery, to meet the Minister of Works, George Brown, urging him to relax restrictions on the granting of building licences for necessary repairs, alterations and extensions to club premises. The Minister promised that consideration would be given to exceptional and outstanding cases – a promise which he kept.

At the elections for the Executive in 1951, four new members were welcomed. J. S. Beech, Kent Branch Secretary since 1921, was elected following the death of Alderman Alfred Eperon, a founder of the Lee Working Men's Club, who had been on the Executive since 1929; G. F. Carter, Dagenham Working Men's Club, was elected in North-East London; G. Thomas, Secretary of the Leicester Variety Artistes Club, followed Sid Anstee, who had died at the end of January after a lifetime in the movement, and J. Saxton, Secretary of the Bentley Working Men's Club, was the choice of Doncaster clubmen.

Soon after their election, a major colliery disaster occurred at the

Easington Colliery in Durham, in which eighty-four miners lost their lives. Over the years, the Executive had always contributed generously to funds after mining tragedies, realizing that so many miners were members of clubs affiliated to the Union, and shared a common tradition. In this case, however, feelings ran even deeper because a large number of members of the Easington Village Club and the Easington Colliery Working Men's Club died in the disaster. Their colleagues in the Durham Branch contributed £5,125 to the fund to help their wives and children, and another £1,000 was contributed by other clubs, making this one of the most widely supported appeals that had ever been organized within a branch of the Union, with much of the work being done by the then Durham Branch Secretary, Stan Hall.

This willingness on the part of clubmen to help their colleagues in times of tragedy has always been one of the finer features of the Union's history; between the wars, seldom a month passed without a fund being organized in support of some humane or charitable cause, and clubmen always gave generously. People unaware of the Union's good work (and there were always many who had not heard of the work of the Union) had a rare opportunity to hear about our history in November 1952, when a programme was broadcast on the work of the Union by the BBC Midland Regional Home Service. The script was written by Maurice Gorham of the Central Club, Holborn, who had then recently been appointed Director of Broadcasting in Eire. But what listeners probably did not appreciate was that the events they heard described were not so unusual for those who knew how the Union had grown to become a national institution, in which there was always something happening, somewhere.

For the new General Secretary, each day brought fresh surprises. In his second full year in office, Frank Castle had to represent the Union's views in respect of two Parliamentary Bills, the Emergency Powers (Miscellaneous Provisions) Bill 1953, which gave those MPs who were opposed to clubs the opportunity to campaign for the re-introduction of the wartime Defence Regulation 55c, which had been revoked the previous year, and then the Licensing Bill 1953, which consolidated all former legislation into one Act, and made only one small change in the law relating to clubs, a clause prohibiting a club from occupying premises which had been struck off or refused a justices' licence.

Then there was the annual agitation against the Beer Duty (which was then 8½d per pint); the question of beer gravities; several court cases, including two that were taken to the High

Court; and elections arising from the amendment of Union Rules to give increased representation on the Executive.

In Derbyshire and Leicestershire, B. W. Holleworth and Harry Gilmore were elected, while A. B. Collins was successful in the County Durham election which followed the death of J. R. Nicholson, and Alderman A. Carr was chosen in Wakefield after the death of Councillor T. Hargrave.

These elections were of special interest in as much as they brought not only new blood but young blood to the Executive. Holleworth, Secretary of Derbyshire Branch and a senior clerk in the Chesterfield Education Office, became the youngest member of the Executive; Collins, chairman of Hebburn Working Men's Club, was also younger than many; while Gilmore, well-known in Leicester as a magistrate, and Carr, a licensing magistrate and twice Mayor of Wakefield, were both men of wide experience.

Outside experience has always been an important quality in Executive members – particularly that of Ernie Connelly, who, being a master builder, prepared specifications and valuations when these were needed for the homes, and now advised with much of the detailed repair work that had to be done to the war-damaged offices in Clerkenwell Road, which were not fully restored until eight years after the war. The scheme, which included an external face-lift and internal alterations, was partly paid for by a sum of £2,800 recovered from the War Damage Commission.

The legal cases referred to earlier all came together. First was the Borough Club, Gillingham, who, on the advice of the General Secretary, prosecuted a stewardess who had been deficient in a stock account for witholding or misapplying club property. The local magistrates dismissed the summons without even calling on the stewardess to answer the charges, and so the Union supported an appeal to the High Court which was successful, the Lord Chief Justice sending the case back to the magistrates, who subsequently reheard the case and found the stewardess guilty.

Secondly came the Crossgates British Legion Club, Cowdenbeath, who were prosecuted for 'trafficking' (a term used in Scottish law) excisable liquor in a tent they had erected on an outing to Aberdour, Fifeshire. The club was fined, took counsel's opinion on the General Secretary's advice, and then appealed to the Scottish High Court – and won, with costs.

Thirdly came Morfa Social and Athletic Club, Llanelli, which was not strictly speaking involved in a legal action, although it found itself in an embarrassing situation. The dilemma arose in September 1953, when the club applied to its local Council for renewal of its lease – only to be opposed on religious grounds by a local minister, who claimed that the club was failing to respect 'the sacred Sabbath day'. This raised serious complications, and the General Secretary asked Alderman C. W. Bridges, a magistrate and former Mayor of Merthyr Tydfil and also a member of the South Wales Branch Executive, to take up the case personally. This he did, and was eminently successful. Bridges learned that the club, which had only 200 members, had raised no less than £300 for national and local charities in the previous year, and so spoke with a sense of indignation when he appeared before the Council to attack those churchmen who condemn a club without going inside it. His appeal was successful, and the Council decided to renew the lease by 12 votes to 5.

The following year, the Union's long campaigning also came close to achieving another famous victory. For many years, as we have seen, the Executive had been doing all they could to compel the brewers to publish the gravity of their beers. There had been several meetings with Government spokesmen before 1939, and with various Ministers both during and after the war, and one Minister had written suggesting that the only solution was legislation. The opportunity came in 1953 when the MP for Hornchurch, Geoffrey Bing, who was also a distinguished QC, was supplied with all the necessary documentation by the General Secretary, and then tabled a motion in the House of Commons seeking leave to introduce a Bill requiring the brewers to publish their gravities. The motion was agreed by 182 votes to 158, but was not reached when the time came for Second Reading, much to the disappointment of the Executive.

Two events dominated the next two years – another law case, this time concerning the Barry Dock Coronation Working Men's Club, and the reluctant decision to close the home at Nantwich, which had proved to be a white elephant. These were the first two major decisions that faced the two new members of the Executive elected in 1954 and 1955. Derek Dormer, Secretary of the Stony Stratford Working Men's Club, was elected when Ernie Bexon died after only four years on the Executive, and this proved to be the beginning of a long and distinguished career for Dormer, who went on to become the current President of the Union. The second new member of the Executive, Pat Ansell, was Secretary of the Stoke Aldermoor Social Club, Coventry, and Chairman of the Coventry Secretaries' Association.

The case involving the Barry Dock Coronation club was another important one for the Union. It began in April 1954, when the police raided the club and removed all its accounts and records books, which were not returned until the following October, and even then only after pressure from Frank Castle. In September, the police asked Barry magistrates to strike the club off the register, claiming that it was not conducted in good faith as a club, that illegal sales of intoxicating liquor had been taking place, and that it was used habitually by non-members. Frank Castle had been in constant consultation with the club since the raid, and had given the committee detailed advice; it was not disputed that there had been some slackness in the management of the club's affairs, but this was attributed to the fact that the doorman had been given too much work to do other than his door-keeping duties and to the fact that the new steward did not know all the members, and the club's solicitors strongly disputed the suggestion that the club was not being conducted in good faith. Indeed, this latter contention was later withdrawn by the police solicitor and the magistrates refused the application to have the club struck off the register – but nevertheless ordered the club to pay fifty guineas towards the costs of the prosecution. The club committee felt that they had been found Not Guilty and fined, all in the same breath, and, on Frank Castle's advice, decided to appeal to the High Court. The Executive agreed to finance the appeal, which eventually came before Lord Chief Justice Goddard, Judge Ormerod and Judge Gorman, who agreed that the Barry magistrates had had no jurisdiction to make the order – but still made the Union pay costs! It was an expensive lesson, but the Union had now established the principle should any other bench take similar action against a Union club.

Cost was also the key in the unhappy story of the Nantwich home. This fifth home had been established after the war to meet the great demand for accommodation in the homes from clubmen who returned home after service in the Forces. It had been an expensive venture. In those pre-inflationary times, when few working men earned more than £400 a year, the home had cost £30,000 to purchase and another £26,000 had been spent on renovations and equipment. The running costs of the home were £12,000 a year. It was beautifully situated with every possible amenity, but the number of clubmen who applied to go there steadily declined from 1,118 residents in 1951 to 620 in 1954. What was wrong? Only one thing – most clubmen wanted to convalesce at the seaside homes, and preferred that to staying in one of the most beautiful parts of Cheshire. This yearning for the sea meant that the Executive eventually had to take the painful decision to close the home, and only managed to obtain £7,500 for the site.

The good intentions of the Executive had cost the Union somewhere in the region of £100,000, although for a few years the home at Nantwich had taken some pressure off the other four homes, accommodating in all some 5,232 residents.

The decision to close the Nantwich home was accepted by clubmen, with hardly any objection, but a proposal to change the name of the movement from The Working Men's Club and Institute Union Ltd to The National Club and Institute Union Ltd caused a storm throughout the country.

This proposal came from the Executive itself, who explained in the June 1955 issue of the *Journal*:

> It was felt that the words 'Working Men's' were now inappropriate having regard to the fact that over one-third of Union clubs admit ladies as members, of which there are now nearly 200,000, and furthermore it was being recommended to clubs that such lady members should be entitled to be issued with Associate and Pass Cards.
>
> Another view was expressed that by retaining the words 'Working Men's' the Union was keeping alive the class consciousness which the Union is trying to eradicate.
>
> It is felt that the inclusion of the word 'National' in substitution for 'Working Men's' would better indicate the extent and scope of our ever-growing organisation, which is composed of all classes of people, including professional and business men, persons engaged in administrative and clerical positions, such as the Civil Service and Local Government, as well as skilled, semi-skilled and unskilled persons engaged in industry and in manual labour.

There may have been a feeling among some members that 'We're all working men now'. It was a widely held sentiment, and the view expressed by Lord Rosebery when he spoke at the Centenary celebrations seven years later. To some extent, it was true – but the Executive had overlooked another opinion that was widespread in the movement, the view that 'We're working men and proud of it', and the pride that many clubmen felt, and still feel, in the history of the Working Men's Club and Institute Union. The reaction *against* the Executive's proposal was so strong, throughout the length and breadth of the country, that no fewer than 1,008 delegates flocked to the July Council meeting, which was held at the City of Leicester Working Men's Club. Clubmen packed the hall and the balcony, stood standing at the back and around the sides, and massed in every doorway – and those who were called to speak strongly attacked the proposed name-change. When the vote was ultimately taken, *only four votes* were cast in favour of the motion.

Executive and members were united, however, when it came to

honouring Tom Nicoll, the long-serving Assistant General Secretary, who retired at the end of 1956. Members felt the same sense of personal loss that they had felt earlier with the departures of B. T. Hall and Bob Chapman, for Nicoll had worked with all the men of that generation; he had been personal clerk to Hall and Assistant General Secretary under both Chapman and now Castle, and his sound common sense had been appreciated outside the Union as well. The Minister of Labour, Ernest Bevin, had appointed Nicoll to the Licensed Non-Residential Establishments Wages Board in 1946.

This personal affection was clearly shown by the unanimous wish of the Executive to organize a testimonial fund, to which 1,050 clubs contributed, raising £1,360, which the President presented to Tom Nicoll when the Executive visited the Central Club, Wolverton, in August 1956.

There were twenty-two applications for Nicoll's post, and this gave the Executive a difficult and unusual task, for this was the most senior position in the Union that they had to fill themselves, most of the other key positions being subject to election. This was the first time in twenty-five years that the Executive had had to choose an Assistant General Secretary, and they had played no part at all in the selection of General Secretaries. (The tradition that General Secretaries should be elected by the member clubs was a cherished one; when the Union Executive proposed in 1955 that in future they should choose the General Secretary, the motion was strongly rejected by the clubs, who cherished the personal contact that democratic election gave them with the Union's chief executive; it was as big a rebuff for the Executive as the one they received on suggesting that the name of the Union should be changed.)

Eventually, they chose John B. Holmes, Legal Assistant at Head Office since December 1952, to succeed Nicoll. Like Frank Castle, he had had ten years' experience with a private firm of solicitors before joining the Union. Holmes, who was then thirty-five and a member of the Central Club and the West Norwood Reform Club, had served as a Warrant Officer in North Africa and Italy during the war with the City of London Yeomanry (Rough Riders) Regiment.

Shortly after Nicoll's retirement, another of the Head Office staff, Oscar Kerslake, who had assisted in editing the *Journal* and in preparing annual and quarterly reports since 1930, also retired, while that great friend of the Head Office staff, Tom Jenks, chairman of the Finance Committee for twenty years, died in February 1956, at the grand old age of ninety-one.

At that same July 1956 Council meeting at which Nicoll received his testimonial cheque, the President, Edward McEnery, was himself presented with an award: a gold medal for twenty-one years' service to the Union. McEnery received the award at the same time as C. H. Greenwood, A. Gee and J. Henderson, Secretaries of Bradford, Halifax and Airedale and Huddersfield and Doncaster Branches respectively – but, not being able to present it to himself, McEnery received his from the General Secretary, commenting, 'I'm not usually on the receiving end.'

Presenting the medal, Castle recalled that 'Mac', as he was known to his friends, had not been well known outside Yorkshire until 1945 when he was elected President.

> One cannot deny that he is an excellent chairman, firm and fair, impartial and tolerant. Delegates who were at the July Council Meetings last year [the one that considered the motion to change the Union's name] would remember how ably he had carried out his duties in very difficult and trying circumstances.
>
> He presided also over the Union Executive and Finance Committee with a bulldog tenacity, never letting go the ideals and purposes in which he believed.

As can be seen, 1956 was an exceptionally eventful year for the Union – and, legally and administratively, it was a busy year for the head office staff as well.

The Executive were able to negotiate a new comprehensive insurance policy with the Union's insurance brokers, Norman Frizzell and Partners Ltd, and the British Law Insurance Company on very favourable terms – one simple proposal form covering all insurances and one annual premium payable on one date each year.

The same year, important points of law were decided in a case concerning the Coed Ely Constitutional Working Men's Club at Tonyrefail, South Wales, where a former steward was found to be deficient in his stock accounts by approximately £490. The Committee decided to prosecute him for withholding or misapplying club property, but the summons for misapplying was dismissed, the magistrate holding that the proceedings were out of time, having not been instituted within six months of the date of the alleged offence. On the summons for 'withholding', however, the magistrate decided that this was a continuing offence and that the proceedings under that summons were therefore in order.

The magistrate decided that after deducting the steward's £50 cash deposit and allowing £25 for wastages, he must repay £376 5s 8d to the club at the rate of £10 per month, with twenty guineas costs. The former steward considered that this was unfair, and so he appealed to the High Court on the following grounds:

1. that no authority had been given by the club committee to institute proceedings under the Friendly Societies Act 1896, and that the summons had therefore been bad in law;
2. that the summons was out of time since it partly related to deficits occurring more than six months before it was issued; and
3. that the sum due from the steward could only be calculated if proper allowance was made for wastages, but there was no evidence on which the calculations could be made.

The General Secretary considered that the steward's appeal could not succeed on any of the three grounds, and was proved right. The case came before Lord Chief Justice Goddard, Judge Hallett and Judge Ashworth, who dismissed the appeal, with the Lord Chief Justice commenting: 'I think [it] is a very ill-advised appeal for him to have brought.'

Another important event that year was the passing of the Small Lotteries and Gaming Act 1956, which allowed clubs, subject to registration with the local authority and compliance with certain other conditions, to sell tickets or 'chances in a lottery' to non-members. The Act also permitted the game of 'house' (sometimes called 'tombola') subject to some conditions – the playing of the game under this Act was in fact subsequently challenged in the High Court and the House of Lords (see page 209).

The following year the Union was very much concerned with another Bill, the Children and Young Persons (Registered Clubs) Bill, which sought to restrict the admission and employment of children and young people, and would have put club committees in the same position as licensees. This Bill would have prevented clubs from organizing children's Christmas or other parties, dancing classes and other entertainments and would have meant children being left either at home or outside the clubs.

The General Secretary issued a 'Clarion Call' to all Union clubs to take action to kill the measure, and the response was emphatic and effective. In addition, the President and Secretary led an intensive personal lobbying campaign at the House of Commons, contacting many MPs personally, urging them to vote against the Bill. This was very successful. The Bill was defeated at its Second Reading by 101 votes to 38.

Two new members joined the Executive during that year: the Leeds Branch Secretary, Norman Albert Sharp, who succeeded Sam Appleyard, who had been an Executive member since 1938 and died soon after his retirement, and Joseph James, Chairman of the Chirton Social Club, who was chosen to represent Northumberland and Scotland, on the retirement of Tom Elliott, the Northumberland Branch President, who had joined the National Executive in 1944.

The following year Horace Mintram, Secretary of Hampshire Branch since 1927 and of the National Executive since 1944, also died, and was replaced by Edward G. Randell, Secretary of Wiltshire and Western Counties Branch, while W. H. Waterhouse, the Vice-President for the previous ten years, announced his resignation, 'to make way for a younger man'. He was succeeded as Vice-President by Councillor Arthur Bates, who, like McEnery, came from Wakefield – indeed, he had been chairman of the Elmsall Burial Committee while McEnery had been its clerk, and they were both members of the same club, the South Kirkby Diamond Jubilee Working Men's Club.

The Executive member in Warwickshire since 1955 had been Pat Ansell, and in 1958 he was able to help the clubs and the Union make a substantial advance in Coventry, his home town, which had been greatly damaged during the war. This gave the local authority the opportunity to re-plan the city, which they seized, recognizing the importance of working men's clubs in the new residential suburbs that were being planned. For the first time, a city council approached the Union and asked their advice on the siting of clubs. The Executive readily agreed to this request, and Edward McEnery and Frank Castle made several visits to Coventry to work with Pat Ansell, the local Branch President, George Radburn, the Branch Secretary, Jack Stringer, and the Branch Treasurer, Harry Sharrod, in their meetings with the Council. After receiving two memoranda from the Union detailing the objects and functions of the Union, and the joint meetings with the Union representatives, Coventry City Council allocated seventeen sites in the city for the future development of working men's clubs.

As the Union's first century neared its close there seemed to be a growing recognition of the part that it played within society; a realization that in its quiet, measured way the Union spoke for many who had few other spokesmen. These were the signs of a full maturity, that the Union was something unique to Britain, with its clubs now being shown to visitors from overseas, and its leaders consulted as a matter of course on all matters that might concern the recreational and social life of working men. By 1960, the Union's strength was such that it managed to kill a Parliamentary Bill presented by the London County Council, which sought to introduce some of the restrictions contained in Defence Regulation 55c (see page 180). Particularly objectionable was the proposal that new clubs should have to apply to the London County Council before registration, and that the police should have much greater authority. As before, the Executive lobbied Members of Parliament, and when the Bill came up for its Second Reading it was widely opposed, and withdrawn on the ruling of the Speaker.

Part of the strength of the Union has lain in its democratic foundation, which has always meant that the Executive has been representative of the clubs as a whole – and, with the growth of the educational system and the wider opportunities facing people today, this has meant that over the years men with wider experience have been offering themselves for election, often men who have already made a contribution in other sections of the Labour movement, although the Union itself remains resolutely non-party-political and non-sectarian.

Thus, the new Executive members elected in 1960 and 1961 included a miner who was chairman of his local Labour Party and a prominent councillor, J. E. Ambler, elected in Wakefield following the death of Alderman Alf Carr; a retired civil servant, Charles Roberts, elected in South Wales and Monmouthshire on the death of Ned Morgan; an engine driver also prominent as a trade unionist, magistrate and chairman of his local council, Sandy Fretwell, who succeeded Lewis Wright in the Huddersfield and Heavy Woollen Branches; a hospital engineer, A. E. Pointon, who succeeded Oscar Snelson as the representative of North Staffordshire and South Cheshire; a foreman fitter, Robert Shepherd, who was President of the Newton Heath Working Men's Club, Manchester; the secretaries of two branches, Stan Hall, who had been Secretary of Durham Branch since 1950, and Joseph Nixon, Secretary of Northumberland; a branch president, Harry Stubbs of Longbridge Social Club, Birmingham; and another chairman of his local Labour Party, Councillor J. J. Clough, Treasurer of the Hetton and District Working Men's Club, County Durham.

These new members of the Executive represented a broad cross-section of the movement, and this was what the Union needed to have within its leadership when speaking out on behalf of its members, and especially when dealing with legislative proposals or legal problems, which it had to do several times in 1960 and 1961, two years that seemed more difficult than usual.

For the fourth time in six years, the Union financed an appeal to the High Court, and succeeded in reversing a decision of the local magistrates in Lewes, Sussex. This concerned the Plumpton and

District Club, which ran a dance when there was a police raid, and intoxicants with the vessels containing them were taken away by the police. A committee member was prosecuted and fined for selling these drinks, and the magistrates held that the drinks and the vessels in which they had been contained should be forfeited on the grounds that the committee member was the 'owner or occupier' of the premises and directed that the drinks should be sold. The Executive were advised that it was the General Secretary's view that the magistrates had exceeded their authority, and having taken further legal advice the club appealed to the High Court, which decided that the magistrates had had no jurisdiction to make the order for forfeiture and sale, and directed that it be quashed with costs against the magistrates.

Then there was the much publicized case of the Huddersfield Friendly and Trade Societies Club, which was prosecuted under Section 4 of the Small Lotteries and Gaming Act 1956, over the playing of tombola. One of the provisions of Section 4 is that the proceeds from a lottery must be applied for purposes other than private gain. The stipendiary magistrate decided that in allocating the proceeds to club funds the club had broken the law. The question arose, what was 'private gain'? And on this point the Executive financed another appeal to the High Court, which upheld the magistrate's decision. The Executive felt that this was such an important point of law (which could have been applied against a great many other clubs) that the case should be taken to the House of Lords. There, the case was argued before five Law Lords, who dismissed the appeal by a majority of three to two.

The outcome of the Lords judgment meant that the club's conviction stood, so the Executive immediately wrote to the Home Secretary, and subsequently a deputation comprising the President, General Secretary and Assistant General Secretary went to the Home Office to put the Union's case for an alteration to the Act, which was later achieved through a Private Member's Bill.

Upsetting as this decision was to clubs that had been depending on tombola to raise funds, it caused nowhere near as much controversy as the Licensing Bill in 1961, which was attacked with all the energy that Chapman had brought to a similar cause before the Second World War; individual clubmen were again urged to protest to their Members of Parliament – which they did, vociferously. The Executive mounted their own attack on the measure, issuing a statement to the Press and lobbying MPs in the hope of defeating Part III of the Bill, which introduced an entirely new system of registration, which was regarded then as an attempt to place clubs in a similar position in law to public houses. Wide support was received from individual Members of Parliament, many of whom agreed with the Executive's view that no change in the law was needed in regard to bona fide clubs, but the Government Whips were put on, and while the Union did succeed in gaining some amendments, the Bill became law.

This, and many other matters, including a case which the Midland Counties Entertainment Secretaries Council took to the Industrial Court after seeking to impose a new form of artistes' contract on the City of Leicester Working Men's Club, which the Union found disagreeable (the Council lost their case), tended to distract attention from the plans which were already being made for the great landmark in the Union's history – the centenary.

The Executive had purchased a freehold site for new head-quarters at Highbury Corner, Islington, North London, for £45,000 during 1960. Plans were drawn up for a modern building, and a contract entered into with the builders, the Laing Development Company, for £165,000. Work started early in 1961, and on 25 August the Union President, Edward McEnery, laid the foundation stone at a ceremony attended by the local Mayor and Mayoress, Alderman and Mrs Lawrence R. Webster, the two local Members of Parliament, Dr Eric Fletcher and Gerry Reynolds, the builders, representatives from the branches, and those two stalwarts of former years, Bob Chapman and Tom Nicoll. In October, the traditional 'topping out' ceremonies were held, and then, just eight months later, the Union celebrated its centenary with the formal opening of the magnificent new headquarters, which had cost in total, with all the various internal fittings, nearly £250,000.

The Union had found its own way of celebrating its birthday, the end of a hundred years which had seen the emancipation of the British working man, and the development of one of his own unique organizations. Nowhere in the world is there another body like the Working Men's Club and Institute Union; no other nation can point to a movement like ours, and say, 'there is the organization that gave the working man somewhere to meet his fellows, some-where to look to his future, somewhere to make his own life'. In those hundred years the Union had progressed from a small office in the Strand to this magnificent building, as well equipped as the national headquarters of many large industrial firms. One man's dream had been turned into an organization of 3,500 clubs with 2,250,000 members, and assets totalling £31,000,000. And, as the President, Edward McEnery, said at the centenary celebrations on 14 June 1962:

This wonderful symbol of progress has been made possible by the great pioneers of the past . . . today we rank as one of the great social forces in the land, and I desire to lay emphasis on that point. There are so many social bodies working in different ways, but none of them have what we have.

We are animated by a spirit of fellowship and service which is something we should be very proud of. We are rich in experience, we are rich in good purpose – with emphasis on the good – we are rich in understanding. Above all we are rich in self-discipline. Our two million members throughout Great Britain have now a great inheritance.

Representatives from all the branches heard the President's words, and it was fitting that the man he should introduce to open the premises was Lord Rosebery, whose father, then a young man of twenty-eight not yet within sight of 10 Downing Street, had urged the Union towards emancipation at that momentous meeting in 1875. Lord Rosebery, who was afterwards presented with a silver salver, said:

This is a great occasion. When I was first asked to open your new headquarters I was reluctant to accept. When you come to my age you will find that you want to do less and less, and personally I am always frightened that a sudden attack of gout – to which I am addicted – may make me chuck at the last moment.

However, Mr Castle wrote me such a charming letter and mentioned what my father, the late Lord Rosebery, had done for the Club Union when he was President in 1875, that I was glad to accept. I would like to point out that in 1875 my father was an unmarried man of twenty-eight, and I congratulate your predecessors on perspicacity in selecting him, for the Union was then in financial difficulties and he gave it £180 on debenture.

Today, the man we should really think of is the Rev. Henry Solly. It was his idea and his energy that started the Union. He was a Unitarian Minister working in Lancashire and threw over his work there to devote himself to this idea of a Working Men's Club and Institute Union.

This idea fructified in the Law Amendment Society's rooms in Waterloo Place. Why it took place in those rooms I do not know, except that the first President was the Lord Chancellor, Lord Brougham.

This idea of the Working Men's Club Union was not only a wonderful one, but unlike so many good ideas and intentions it has survived and prospered, and has done what Mr Solly set out to do, but which I doubt he ever imagined would be such a gigantic success.

From small beginnings you now have 3,535 Clubs in all parts of Great Britain and over 2,300,000 members. That is a wonderful feat! But I need hardly say that your success did not come without a great struggle.

You had donations from all people, including the highest in the land; but the money was not enough, and it was not until 1875 – the year in which the late Lord Rosebery was President – that the turn of the tide really took place.

This started with the agreement with the Chancellor of the Exchequer, Sir Stafford Northcote, which allowed of Associate Membership between members of one club and the members of others in the Union, by the system of Associate and Pass Cards, and these have been the bedrock of your financial progress.

I note that at the beginning of your history you had great names as Presidents and Vice-Presidents, but not much money. Now, as the Union proceeded towards prosperity so did the great names fade away and you were then ruled and governed in a more democratic and practical manner.

If one casts one's eye back a hundred years one can see how welcome the start of this Union must have been. In those days the working man was housed in badly lit uncomfortable rooms, and the only place where he could be warm and meet his fellow-men was in public houses, the majority of which were very different in those days from what they are now.

In the present day we are all working men – we have to be. On the other hand the conditions of living have improved enormously, and the wealth of the country has been largely diffused among the population. Yet in spite of all this your Union is still filling a vital place in the life of the nation – the proof of which we can see around us in this fine building.

Lord Rosebery was right. Solly could never have imagined the success of the movement that he started, so small were its beginnings. His intention in founding the Union was to assist working men in the evolution from an ill-planned and often cruel industrial society, and now here, a hundred years to the day after the movement started, were its representatives, with prominent Members of Parliament and the Earl of Rosebery as their guests, seated in the flower-decked hall of their new headquarters, and afterwards attending a luncheon with the Labour Party's Chief Whip, Herbert Bowden, and the Leader of the London County Council, Sir Isaac Hayward, as their chief guests. The Union had travelled a long journey, and was now wholly complete in itself.

14

The sixties were boom years for the Union: a decade that began with its centenary, which saw clubs up and down the country expanding rapidly as they invested more and more money in new buildings and extensions, and which brought membership of the Working Men's Club and Institute Union close to its all-time peak. Nearly five hundred more clubs joined the Union. In 1972, membership passed the 4,000 mark for the first time, reaching its highest point of 4,033 in 1974, just before the collapse of the stock market and the closure of several secondary banks, which proved to be the beginning of the seventies recession.

Like other similar booms, it was only seen as such afterwards; at the time, the sixties seemed a time of financial crisis, with one form of pay restraint following another, and the devaluation of the pound. Now, in retrospect, this can be seen as one of the Union's great periods; a time when there was a relatively low level of unemployment, when working men had money to spend, and when clubs felt able to turn to the breweries for loans to finance their expansion. Every issue of the *Journal* in those days told of clubs spending as much as £70,000 on extensions, enlarging bars, building concert halls and new lounges, and sometimes, even – especially in the Midlands and the North – embarking on schemes costing up to £250–300,000.

They were good years, and the Union felt confident.

As the year 1962 ended, the *Journal* proclaimed that this had been a 'momentous year for the Union' and reviewed its success in fighting yet another attempt to give police the right to enter clubs (contained in the Licensing (Scotland) Bill, which was seen as a forerunner for legislation in the rest of Britain), and in the breadth of its activities during the Centenary Year.

That year, 4,000 residents had been accommodated at the convalescent homes; local branch dinners had been held to celebrate the centenary, and all those staying in the homes on 17 June were entertained to a special Centenary Dinner, for which souvenir menu cards were printed. Across the country as a whole even the contests for snooker, billiards, darts and angling had a Centenary ring that year – with over 1,600 Union trophies being presented, another all-time record.

There were moments of sadness, too. During the year one member of the Executive, Evan Ll. Rees, who was President of South Wales Branch, died during his term of office. In the by-election that followed he was succeeded by Tom Knight, a founder member of the Sea View Labour Club, Barry Dock, a keen sportsman, who had been Chairman and President of the Cardiff Ward Games League for the previous twenty-eight years, and was also a director of the South Wales and Monmouthshire United Clubs Brewery. W. R. Clamp, the Union's longest-serving em-ployee, also died, aged eighty. He had joined the Union as a lad in 1896 as assistant in the audit department to the late W. G. Stroud, and had then succeeded him as the head of that department in 1929, staying with the Union until his retirement in 1944. Bill Clamp had retained a keen interest in the Union's affairs right to the end of his life, and had been one of those specially invited to attend the opening of the new head office.

There was sadness, too, when another long-serving member of the Union's head office staff announced his retirement. Cliff Culling, the Convalescent Homes Secretary, had been a clubman since the age of twenty-seven, joining first the Bradford Textile Hall Club, and then in 1933 the Horton Grange Working Men's Club, where he was elected Secretary, Treasurer and Vice-President, before deciding to move to London to take up the post at head office. Once settled in London, Cliff became a trustee of the Putney Club, and also a member of the Hatcham Liberal Club – one of the oldest in the Union – and a member of the Upper Stratton Reform and Bedford South End clubs. Cliff 'lives and works for clubmen', reported the *Journal* announcing his retirement, and Ernie Connelly, Chairman of the Convalescent Homes Committee, commented:

> Cliff's travels throughout the Branches and Clubs over the years have taken up a great deal of his time, but the splendid results obtained have more than repaid him for this. The following give some idea of the monies donated during Mr Culling's term of office.
> Donations £157,761
> Flag Days £40,682
> Lighter Fuel Boxes £23,500
> I have worked with Mr Culling, particularly in connection with the building side of the work, during his period of office, and he has given

this his deep and sincere attention ... although our homes are getting old, the standard of decoration in them is higher than ever before. Mr Culling can be justifiably proud of his share in this grand work.

I invite all Clubs of our great Union to associate themselves with the Testimonial, sponsored by the Executive, to Mr Culling, as a token of our sincere thanks and appreciation for the great service he has rendered to so many of our Clubmen throughout his term of office.

And the clubmen did. The sum of £3,232 7s was raised through the testimonial.

Cliff Culling was succeeded as Convalescent Homes Secretary by Bill Daultrey, who was then aged forty-one and had been working at the Union's offices since 1938, spending fourteen of those years in the Homes Department as Culling's assistant, helping him to run the four homes, which then had a staff of seventy. During the war years, Bill Daultrey had served with a field ambulance unit of the Royal Army Medical Corps in Algeria, Tunisia, Sicily, Italy and Austria, reaching the rank of sergeant, but apart from those years he had spent most of his life either working for the Union, within his own club (the Mildmay Club), or helping the Boy Scouts, which he always said he found the most rewarding of his activities outside the Union.

An even greater upheaval in the internal affairs of the Union came in 1964 when the General Secretary, Frank Castle, announced that he, too, was retiring after forty-three years' service to the Union. Announcing his testimonial, the President, Edward McEnery, wrote to every club and branch in the Union saying:

After being on his own Club's Committee Frank was a delegate to the Union's Kent Branch, and a member of the Branch Executive for 28 years. He came to the Union as its Legal Assistant in May, 1933.

Elected as General Secretary in March, 1951, his period of Executive office has seen more changes in the Union itself and also in the Parliamentary sphere of legislation than has happened to any previous General Secretary.

Although Frank could have retired some five years ago he continued in office, and this longer service during difficult years is appreciated by the Union Executive.

We are sorry to lose one who has not only conscientiously and loyally carried out the heavy responsibilities of his office as General Secretary, but who throughout Great Britain is a highly respected Clubman and endeared himself to all who have met him.

Later on, at the Union's half-yearly Council meeting, which was held at Doncaster on 3 November 1964, there were glowing tributes from many delegates, and the President told the meeting:

I have had considerable experience in the Club movement, and
have had experience of three General Secretaries – B. T. Hall, Bob
Chapman and Frank Castle. I know quite well that Frank Castle has
not been everyone's cup of tea. He has had a difficult job to do, but
I can assure you that he has one of the greatest legal brains this
Union has ever had. I have worked with him for nineteen years and
I have no reservation in making that declaration about his legal
mind.

Even in his retirement, Frank Castle planned to continue raising
funds for the Pegwell home through his work for the Kent Sub-
clubs Convalescent Homes Federation, saying that this would keep
him in touch with the many clubs in his area 'and as a lifelong
clubman and an Associate I shall therefore never be lonely'.

Clubmen responded generously to the Frank Castle Testimonial,
but – at his request – the total amount raised was not mentioned
when the cheque was formally presented to him at the 1965 Annual
Meeting. When the officers came to organize the testimonial, they
were astonished if not embarrassed to find that the Union had been
under-paying its General Secretary for years, and, perhaps
through modesty, Frank Castle had not told them. It was a Union
rule in those days that the Secretary's salary had to be agreed at a
full Council meeting, and it is not every man who likes having his
salary discussed in public by a meeting attended by hundreds of
people.

At the Doncaster meeting, the President reported that the General Secretary had been receiving a salary of £1,667 since 1958 and
during that period all the Union's staff, including other officers
and departmental heads and the Assistant General Secretary, had
received increases totalling $27\frac{1}{2}$ per cent. When this was reported
to the meeting, one delegate commented that even tea-boys were
asking for £42 a week – and other delegates expressed amazement
that even now the Finance Committee was only proposing a salary
of £2,000 a year for the Union's General Secretary. There and
then, another delegate moved that the figure ought to be increased
to £2,100 – and this was agreed by 233 votes to 25.

Against this background, it was perhaps not surprising that Frank
Castle preferred to keep the figures secret on the day of the presentation. But it was generally believed that the membership had
made up for the lapse, and when he was shown the cheque Frank
said that the amount was 'really overwhelming'. And the President
added to the general air of mystery by adding: 'Whatever joy you
may have in receiving this cheque from McEnery, it will be no
greater than the joy McEnery has in presenting it to you!' This

drew a round of applause, with delegates realizing that the cheque represented something more than many years' missed pay increases!

Meanwhile, there had been a strongly contested election for the general secretaryship, with two senior members of the head office staff competing against each other. All told, there were twelve candidates for the post, but ten of these were clubmen whose service to the Union had mainly been at club or branch level – and not one of them received more than a hundred votes. The election narrowed down to a choice between Genard Frederick Ding, who had been Education and Recreation Secretary of the Union since 1946 and who was at the age of fifty the longest-serving member of the head office staff, and John B. Holmes, the Assistant General Secretary, who had deputized for Frank Castle during two periods of illness, and then, at the age of forty-three, had eight years' service with the Union.

When the votes were counted on 7 September 1964, it was found that John Holmes had won the election with 3,077 votes against the 2,262 cast for 'Gen' Ding.

That same year there was also a substantial change in the composition of the National Executive. Three new members were elected in the biennial elections. William Hayes, Secretary since 1942 of the Mountain Ash Workmen's Club, and a former Chairman of Mountain Ash Urban District Council and of the Mountain Ash Trades and Labour Council, was elected one of the two South Wales members on the Executive. The Northumberland and Scottish Branches elected Harry Drysdale, then aged forty-two, a keen sportsman and former long-distance runner who had played football for Hirst East End Club, Northumberland, which he joined in 1948, later becoming Vice-Chairman and then Chairman. Tom Regan, Secretary of Colne and Burnley Branch, was elected to represent Colne and Burnley and Furness Branches. Regan had been a member of the Nelson Gasworkers' Club since 1931, and had spent nine years on the Branch Executive.

In May 1964, three members of the National Executive died within a few days of each other. Charles Roberts, President of Monmouthshire Branch, died on 3 May. He had been appointed acting secretary of the Six Bells Club, Abertillery, at the age of nineteen, and then Secretary shortly afterwards, a position which he continued to hold for the rest of his life, nearly fifty years. Albert Linstead, who died on 4 May (after a severe stroke the previous November), had been South Yorkshire Branch Secretary since 1943, and a member of the National Executive since 1945. He had joined the Grimethorpe Working Men's Club in 1916, and when he moved to Lundwood, near Barnsley, became organizing secretary for the Lundwood Working Men's Club. Albert Linstead had served on both the Education and Recreation Committees, and his death came as a great sadness to clubmen in South Yorkshire when they learned that his wife had died the previous day. Their son, Ron Linstead, later succeeded his father as Branch Secretary and on the National Executive. Robert Shepherd, a member of the Manchester Branch Executive since 1950 and the National Executive since January 1962, died on 10 May. Shepherd had been President of the Newton Heath Working Men's Club for thirty-four years, had founded the local club's snooker league, and had been Chairman of the Manchester, Salford and District Federation of Union Clubs for many years.

The results in the three by-elections that followed their deaths were declared on 7 September, the same day as the ballot for the new General Secretary. The Monmouthshire clubs elected Francis Richard Hill, secretary of the Abercarn Working Men's Club for fourteen years and a member of the Branch Executive; South Yorkshire elected Ron Linstead, who had been deputizing for his father during his illness, and Manchester, William Palmer, a founder member of the Wythenshawe Labour Club.

Elsewhere that summer, the Union scored another major victory, financing an appeal in the High Court on behalf of clubs in Darwen, Lancashire, where the local licensing magistrates had decided that clubs and public houses would both have to 'close' at 10.30 p.m. on weekdays instead of 11.00 p.m. as in previous years. In the High Court, the clubs were represented by Geoffrey Howe, who was then a barrister, and who later became a Conservative Member of Parliament, Chancellor of the Exchequer and Foreign Secretary. He successfully persuaded the High Court that the magistrates had exceeded their powers, and the closing time was restored to the original hour of 11 p.m. Reporting this judgment on the front page of the *Journal*, the retiring General Secretary, Frank Castle, commented:

> With the quashing of [this] order . . . the Union has again shown that it is ever vigilant where the interests of Union Clubs are concerned. Moreover, it is always prepared, where a matter of principle affecting Club law is involved, to assist in every way possible . . .

Throughout the country, clubmen were planning new extensions, opening bars, enlarging concert halls, celebrating golden jubilees and diamond jubilees, staging competitions and major occasions in the history of their branches, but in Preston, Lancashire, there was a unique ceremony. The General Secretary of the Trades Union Congress, George Woodcock, returned to the town where he had spent his earlier years to make a special presentation of the TUC Gold Medal to Jack Allison, who had become one of the first trade unionists in the movement's history to complete a period of forty years' membership on the executive committee of a local Trades and Labour Council. It was a happy occasion for both of them; they had been friends for nearly fifty years, since the days when George Woodcock had worked as a weaver in Preston, and their friendship had its links through the Union. George had gone on to his national career within the trades-union movement after studying at Ruskin College, Oxford, on a Club and Institute Union scholarship, and Jack had gone on to become President of the Manchester Branch of the Club and Institute Union, and a member of our National Executive.

As the year ended, the new General Secretary, John Holmes, whose appointment took effect from 1 January 1965, faced his first year in office, with the Executive just about to appoint a new Assistant General Secretary, Leslie Tibbs, a member of the Mildmay Club, who had previously worked in the Legal and Administrative Department before becoming personal assistant to Frank Castle. Tibbs had joined the staff of the Union straight from school in 1951, and had then returned to the head office staff in 1956 after completing his National Service.

During this change-over period, in the last weeks of what had been a traumatic year for the Union, three more members of the National Executive died. Jack Saxton had been the Doncaster Branch President for over twenty years, and a member of the Union Executive for twelve years. Bernard Holleworth had been Derbyshire Branch Secretary and an Executive member for thirteen years, and secretary of the Hasland Working Men's Club for twenty-three years. Joseph Nixon, Northumberland Branch Secretary and National Executive member, was another clubman who had devoted nearly his whole life to the Union, returning to his club, the Coxlodge and Gosforth Social Club, and becoming its Secretary after war service in the Far East, where he was a regimental sergeant-major.

Their successors were Jack Park, Secretary of the Bentley Working Men's Club and a member of Doncaster Branch; Leonard Starkey, President of the Shaftesbury Social Club and also of Derbyshire Branch; and James Lynam, Secretary and former Chairman of the South Benwell Social Club, Newcastle upon Tyne, and the new Secretary of Northumberland Branch.

One of the first duties that the new General Secretary had to perform on behalf of the Union was to compose a letter on behalf of all its members to Lady Churchill, widow of Sir Winston, whose death in January 1985 touched a chord throughout the nation:

> As General Secretary of this Union, which at present numbers 3,675 bona fide clubs, I consider I must write on behalf not only of my fellow Officers and members of the Executive, but also our two and a half million members, to convey to you and your family deepest sympathy in the loss of your dear husband, Sir Winston.
>
> This Union, which is now in its one hundred and third year, has fought over the years for freedom and the right of Clubmen to enjoy the privacy and privileges of their own Club, and again I believe that our members, together with their wives and children, realise that their efforts and those of the Union prior to 1940, would have counted for nothing if they, together with all other people of this nation, had not been inspired, led and guided by Sir Winston during the momentous years of the Second World War.
>
> I trust, and I am sure that it is the earnest wish of our two and half million Clubmen, together with members of their families, that you will be granted courage and health to bear your sad loss with fortitude, and with the same indomitable spirit of Sir Winston and which you have revealed during your years with your well-beloved husband.

For the nation as a whole, the passing of Sir Winston Churchill seemed to be the end of an era; for the Union, with so many older clubmen being succeeded by younger men, it was a time of change, reflecting perhaps a different mood in the country now that a Labour Government had taken office after thirteen years of Conservative rule. Certainly, there was an out-going spirit, a feeling of expansion; a time for new men and new ideas.

This new mood was reflected in every way; over a hundred more clubs joined the Union that year, more than half of them being either British Legion or ex-servicemen's clubs; the scale of building works now being undertaken throughout the country was growing rapidly and in Northumberland the delegates attending the Annual Meeting even chartered a plane to fly across the Pennines to Blackpool (and that became a habit!). When the National Individual Snooker Championship was staged at the Canley Social Club, Coventry, at the end of the summer it was won by a young man named Ray Reardon, who was then playing regularly at his club, the Cheadle Social Club, and has since become one of Britain's best-known professionals and several times World Champion.

As the President, Edward McEnery, completed his twenty years in office, becoming the longest-serving President in the Union's history, the *Journal* reflected:

> At the age of 51, Edward McEnery was elected President of the Union, and took upon himself the burdens and responsibilities of high office, which he has carried for twenty years. To a lesser man, the strain over so long a period would have been unbearable. Yet, Mac with his true indefatigable Yorkshire grit, has surmounted all difficulties during the most challenging and yet glorious period in our history ... always cheery, with a true sense of humour and with a mastery of the English language, President McEnery has become unmistakeably a philosopher, and his endearing charm enables him to carry out his role as leader and adviser successfully.

When the Vice-President, Arthur Bates, referred to McEnery's long service and achievements at the 1966 Annual Meeting, there was an immediate and spontaneous burst of applause from the 1,600 delegates attending the gathering at Blackpool, and they rose as one man in a show of rare affection. In the weeks that followed, the Union's officers agreed that the time had come for the membership as a whole to be given the opportunity to contribute to an Edward McEnery testimonial. This was announced at the Council meeting in Cardiff the following November, again to spontaneous applause – and the response to the testimonial was so great that McEnery was presented with a cheque for £8,492 at the 1967 Annual Meeting.

Over this period when the testimonial had been first suggested, then discussed, formally agreed, and then arranged on behalf of the National Executive by the General Secretary, there had been more changes in the composition of the Executive.

Towards the end of 1965, Bill Hayes, one of the two South Wales members, died suddenly and was replaced in a by-election early in 1966 by William James Hall, a member of Rhymney Workmen's Club, for ten years Chairman of the Pontlottyn Empire Club, and a director of the South Wales and Monmouthshire United Clubs Brewery. In the biennial elections, also held early in 1966, four other new members were elected. As the result of a rule change, the Scottish clubs were allowed their first direct representative, and chose Thomas Ramage, Secretary of the Leith Ex-Servicemen's Club, Edinburgh, and also Secretary of the Billiards Association and Control Council of Scotland for twenty years. (His brother Walter was the Scottish Billiards Champion for fifteen years, and on three occasions represented Scotland in the world championships.) Jack Truby, who was elected as one of three members for

Durham, had been Secretary of the Crowtrees Workmen's Club, and worked in the Treasurer's Department of Durham Rural District Council. William Elston, elected for Manchester, had been a member of the Blackpool Central Working Men's Club for thirty-nine years, a Manchester Branch member for twelve years and Vice-President of the Blackpool and District Federation of Clubs. James Thomson, the new member for Colne and Burnley, North Lancashire, Cumberland and Westmorland Branches, had been Secretary of the Vickerstown Working Men's Club in Barrow-in-Furness for sixteen years, and was also Secretary of the North Lancashire, Cumberland and Westmorland Branch.

Just a few weeks after these elections, Jack Allison, who had resigned as the Manchester member for health reasons, died after fifty-six years' work in the movement; he had first been appointed a club secretary in 1913, and was later Manchester Branch President, and had served on the National Executive for fifteen years.

With the departure of Leslie Tibbs, the National Executive appointed a new Assistant General Secretary in August 1966. They chose Frank Morris, who had joined the head office staff of the Union in 1964 after thirty years' work in the legal profession, and who was later to succeed John Holmes as General Secretary. Morris was promoted at a difficult time for the Union. Holmes was frequently troubled by ill health.

Members were finding that they could not see the General Secretary when they wanted to and other members of staff were having to deputize for him. However, the great mass of the Union's work – the running of the convalescent homes, the staging of competitions through the recreation department, all its educational work – was largely unaffected, and there were still the usual high-points that a national organization has during the course of a year.

In 1966 the Queen Mother officially opened the Hyde Park Development in Sheffield, touring the Park Gardeners' new club, which replaced the old one, which had been demolished to make way for a large block of flats. The Queen Mother said she was most impressed by the decor of their new concert room, and asked about the kind of shows that were presented there. She was told that the club devoted much of its profits to helping the elderly and young children, by giving them annual dinners and outings to the seaside. As she signed the visitors' book, the Queen Mother commented, 'It's a very wonderful job these Clubs do.'

In the late sixties the *Journal* reflected a growing outside interest in the work of the Union, and its history, as it reported the centenaries of different clubs. The Union was now past its 100th birthday, and so were some of its member clubs – although it would take a rare kind of courage for any man to decide which is the oldest club in the Union! The Coventry Working Men's Club, founded after the 1860 weavers' strike, has a strong claim. So do the Walthamstow Working Men's Club and the Northampton St Giles Club, and there are those who say that the first ever working men's club was formed in South Shields in 1850 – a view that may be disputed by the Reddish Working Men's Club in Stockport or the Weymouth Working Men's Club.

Certainly, with the passing of the years, one can sense within the Union a growing pride in its achievements, and a growing sense outside the Union of its place within society. By the late sixties, those threats from Parliament or the licensed victuallers seemed part of history – and you could even buy a pint of Federation bitter in the House of Commons' own bar! When the then Chancellor of the Exchequer, James Callaghan, officially opened the new £50,000 Aneurin Bevan Labour Club in Caerphilly in June 1967, he was offered a membership card – and said that he was already a member of two other affiliated clubs! It was also pointed out that year that the new Assistant Commissioner at Scotland Yard, Robert Mark, who was later to become perhaps the most distinguished policeman in the history of the force, had long been a popular member of the Leicester Railwaymen's Club and Institute.

That year the Durham clubs elected their Branch Secretary Jack Johnson to the Union's National Executive (he is the current General Secretary of the Union), and the year ended on a happy note with the announcement that the President, Edward McEnery, had been appointed by the Queen an Officer of the Most Excellent Order of the British Empire.

In the biennial elections to the National Executive, O. E. Cotterell, former Secretary of the Hednesford and District Ex-Servicemen's Club and West Midlands Branch Secretary, was elected by clubmen in that area; Arthur T. Gilman, for thirty years a member of the Brownroyd Working Men's Club and recently their Treasurer, was elected by Bradford, Halifax and Airedale, and James F. Cooke, Secretary of Canley Social Club, Coventry, and President of the Coventry CIU Secretaries and Presidents' Association, was elected by Warwickshire.

Another election occurred a few weeks later following the death of John Bromly Adams. Aged sixty-seven, he had been an Executive member since 1948 and, for the past eight years, Chairman of the Recreation Committee. Adams had joined the North Lambeth Liberal and Radical Club in 1919, and had served as an officer of the club for twenty-seven years. The South-East Metropolitan Branch chose as his successor Jack Theodore Rudd, also a member of the North Lambeth Liberal and Radical Club, which he had joined in 1945 while serving in the Royal Artillery, and a member, too, of the Hatcham Liberal and York Clubs.

That year, 1968, the executive was much concerned with the need to modernize the facilities available in the four convalescent homes; on 2 March, the President, Edward McEnery, opened new extensions at Grange, costing £45,000 and providing extra rooms, a passenger lift, new washbasins in every room and better furnishings, but in the case of Pegwell, the executive felt that they had no alternative but to build a new home.

A site was acquired in Broadstairs – an open field off Reading Street – and a new home designed with sixty-one bedrooms, providing accommodation for up to a hundred residents. The following March, the President travelled down to Broadstairs to ceremonially cut the first sod of earth, which he did with a vigorous thrust of his shining silver spade, tossing the clod over his shoulder with a chuckle, prompting a photographer to say, 'I hope I can do that when I'm his age!'

By then Edward McEnery was seventy-four, and had been troubled by some ill-health; he had had an operation at Manor House Hospital in October 1967, and although still as energetic as ever, he was visibly ageing, and was to die before the home had been completed.

On 4 July, the President returned to Broadstairs to lay the foundation stone for the new convalescent home, which he proudly told the gathering would now cost £350,000 and would include common rooms, television rooms, billiard halls, bowling greens, staff quarters and landscaped gardens with a putting green, occupying, in all, four and a half acres. He told the Union's guests that it was now fifty-three years since the Union had last built a convalescent home, and continued:

> We are now in a new age. Social habits have changed and so have the customs of people. We must fit in with the changes, which I think are for the good.
>
> This convalescent home will be here for many years to come, if not centuries. It will stand the test of time.
>
> We have left nothing out of our plans for the home. I think we can safely feel and claim, talking of homes in this country and throughout the world, that this will be the Hilton of convalescent homes.
>
> There will be beauty, colour, and everything to brighten the lives of our members who have suffered serious disablement or illness.

The President welcomed the Chairman of Broadstairs Council, Councillor Leonard Rigelsford, and on behalf of the architects Mr Hubbard Ford presented the President with a silver trowel as a souvenir of the occasion. The architects and the builders, Barwicks of Dover, promised that the building would be completed by the following June, but the President was not to live that long, and even before he died the original Pegwell home was to be severely damaged in the thunderstorms that swept the Kent coast that August.

There were two thunderstorms that caused severe flooding at the Pegwell home, although it was the first, on Friday, 15 August, that did most damage. That day forty clubmen were sitting down to breakfast, with a storm raging outside, when water started to pour into their dining-room, which was below ground level. Within a few minutes, the water had reached waist-level as the men started wading to safety, and one man died while they were all being helped out of the building. This account appeared in *The East Kent Times & Broadstairs Mail* on 20 August:

DAY OF THE TERROR FLOOD

FREAK STORMS CLAIMS ITS VICTIMS

Forty men were evacuated and one died when flood water swept through a 70-year-old Ramsgate convalescent home during freak storms at the weekend.

A wave of sludge and filthy water burst open doors and windows as the men, patients at the Working Men's Club and Institute Union convalescent home at Pegwell Bay, were sitting down to breakfast.

Staff battled with rags and blankets to barricade the below ground level dining room as murky torrents from overflowing drains built up.

But they were unable to hold the tide. Within minutes the room was waist deep in water and the men, whose ages ranged from 40 upwards, had to be evacuated.

They waded into monsoon-like rain and climbed or were carried over a 6ft wall. One man, Mr Sydney John Bennett of Burton Latimer, Kettering, Northamptonshire, died during the evacuation.

Nearby pub the Belle Vue Tavern became 'disaster' headquarters during the hour of terror and landlord Robert Gristwood served whiskey to the trembling evacuees.

Superintendent of the home, which was due to close next year, Mr Richard Burrows, estimated the damage at about £10,000.

'Water surged through like a tidal wave,' he said. 'We could do nothing to stop it. It cascaded down stairs into the dining room like a waterfall. All we could do was get the men out.'

At the time of the disaster general hand Melvin Cranfield was helping out in the dining room.

'It was about 8.45 am and about 40 men were half-way through their breakfast,' he said. 'Suddenly water began gushing through the front door. We barricaded it with old rags and blankets.

'I was at the door myself trying to keep the water back but it was no good. It just started pouring through. Finally when it was up to our waists we hadn't any choice. We had to evacuate.

'It wasn't easy because all the patients have been ill. It was a terrible experience.'

What was the cause of the flooding? The home has flooded before, but never to this extent.

Mr J. B. Holmes, general secretary of the Working Men's Club and Institute Union, said: 'The cause has not yet been ascertained.

'We have made representations to Ramsgate Council in the past over drains being inadequate but larger drains were put down in 1967. I don't think any drain could have coped with a downpour of this intensity.'

Ramsgate Council Engineer Mr H. Spenceley Hole said: 'This was a freak storm. I've never seen anything like it in my life. Water had blocked the pipes with all the muck it was carrying and one field had been stripped bare of topsoil.'

Where possible, residents staying at the home were sent back to their own homes; others were found temporary accommodation locally. The home itself was immediately closed.

A year later Mr and Mrs Michael Burrows, who were later appointed superintendent and matron designate for the new home at Broadstairs, were invited back to Ramsgate by the local Council when the Mayor, then Alderman Walter Duddington, presented them both with the Royal Humane Society's bravery award for their part in helping the forty clubmen out of the building. The citation read: 'Michael and his wife Kim went to the rescue of the patients in imminent danger of themselves being drowned.' And the whole Council stood to applaud these two members of the Union staff as they were presented with their testimonials, with the Mayor saying, 'I feel honoured to be in the presence of people who, when the call goes out, have got the courage to do something regardless of the consequences to themselves.'

When this was reported in the *Journal*, it was characteristic of Mr and Mrs Burrows that they also pointed out that one of the residents, Mr Jeffrey of the Old Shildon Working Men's Club, County Durham, had also shown great courage. At the time he was convalescing after an internal operation, but as the floodwater poured through the dining-room he quickly helped Mr and Mrs Burrows to get the other residents to safety, helping the elderly and less active, and refusing to leave until they had all been evacuated.

This sad end to the Pegwell home, and the ambitious plans for the new building at Broadstairs, dominated the Union's affairs that year, but much else was happening, too; the General Secretary made representations to the Chancellor of the Exchequer, Roy Jenkins, over the changes in gaming machine licence duty contained in that year's Budget, on the effect of Selective Employment Tax on clubs, and on the anomaly that existed when charities were allowed SET refunds but clubs were not, and two important cases were taken to the High Court.

In the first, the Lord Chief Justice, Lord Parker, gave a judgement on a case affecting the Severn View Social Club, which had been refused a licence for a special function by the Chepstow licensing magistrates. The club had asked for a special licence for cabaret and social evenings on two specific dates, but the magistrates had turned down the application on the grounds that any guests attending the functions would have been 'members of the public' as they were not members of the club. The Lord Chief Justice made it plain that when people attended a function in a club as guests of members of that club they were *not* 'members of the public', and he ordered that the application should go back to the Chepstow magistrates so that the licence could be issued.

In the second, the Master of the Rolls, Lord Denning, delivered a judgment on a case affecting the Beeches Working Men's Club and Institute, which had sued a former steward of the club after a deficiency of £130 14s 5d had been found in the stock. Originally, the case had come before a magistrates' court, where it had been dismissed. When the club then took County Court action against the steward, he argued that as the complaint had been dismissed in the first court it could not be heard in the second. Lord Denning then ruled:

> I think the plea is bad for a very simple reason. The issues in the civil action are quite different from the issues in the Magistrates' Court. In order to substantiate a complaint in the Magistrates' Court, it must be shown that the steward has 'withheld' or 'misapplied' property in his possession.
>
> If he has done it fraudulently, he can be convicted and fined as upon a criminal matter, see Section 87 of the 1896 Act. If he has not done it fraudulently, an order can be made against him to deliver up the property or repay the money, see Section 9 of the amending Act of 1908.
>
> But in either case, it only applies where he has 'withheld' or 'misapplied' property. If he has not withheld or misapplied any property, he should be acquitted and no order should be made against him.
>
> A typical case is when there is a deficiency which is not due to any 'withholding' or 'misapplying' by him, but is due to the action of third

persons. Someone else without his knowledge may have taken money from the till. Other people may have surreptitiously had drinks without paying for them. Such actions by third persons would give rise to a 'deficiency' on the cash or stocks, but he would not be guilty of 'withholding' or 'misapplying' any property.

He would not be liable in a Magistrates' Court to any order. But he is liable under a contract which makes him liable to pay any 'deficiency' of cash or stock: and he can be sued for it in the County Court.

Lord Justice Edmund Davies and Lord Justice Phillimore both agreed with Lord Denning's argument, and this was a matter of some importance to the Union because the Beeches Working Men's Club had been using the Union's own standard form of Agreement of Service to employ the steward, and this judgment therefore meant, in effect, that where clubs had bound themselves by such an agreement and the steward then left them with a deficiency on the bar account, they could take the steward to court and get their money back.

During this period, there were also three by-elections for seats on the Union's National Executive. In Hampshire, clubmen elected Fred Scammell, formerly Secretary of Hythe and District Club, Branch Secretary and Branch President, and in his working life a group inspector for the Southampton Waterworks. In South Wales, following the death of W. J. Hall, clubmen elected Colin Hughes, a former Rugby player for Pontypridd, former Secretary of his local rugby club, and Secretary of the Trallwn Working Men's Club, Pontypridd, until he became Secretary of the South Wales Branch. In Manchester, clubmen elected Robert Wood, who had been committee-member, trustee, Secretary and President of the Oxford Social and Bowling Club in Ashton-under-Lyne, and also Secretary of the Manchester Branch Clubs Convalescent Homes Federation.

Colin Hughes and Robert Wood were both congratulated on their election at the half-yearly Council meeting, which was held at the Willenhall Social Club in Coventry on 4 October 1969, which was one of the last meetings attended by the President, Edward McEnery. He was in fine form that day, teasing the delegates and the visiting Members of Parliament on the way in which working people were always being urged to work harder, and to achieve higher productivity:

> Every day in the Press and on radio and television we see and hear a great deal about productivity. We are always hearing this word. Where higher productivity is achieved, then you get bigger dividends, you get bigger wages and the finished article is at a lower price. What a wonderful thing it is, this productivity.

I try to apply it in the style it operates. Nearest my heart is beer. Productivity there is more outstanding than anywhere else. In the first half of this year, productivity in the beer trade went up by 144 million pints of lovely beer.

He wondered then why it was that when the brewers sold more beer, they made more profit and the Chancellor of the Exchequer took more tax – and still the price went up!

It was a characteristic farewell, his last major speech, with a lightness of touch, and yet still encompassing many aspects of the Union's work, and in particular their latest achievement, building a new home at Broadstairs out of their own resources, without borrowing a penny. It was the last time that most delegates were to hear him. Edward McEnery died suddenly on Sunday, 9 November 1969, surrounded by friends, at one of his own clubs, the Mill Lane Club in South Kirkby, Yorkshire. He was seventy-four, and the *Journal* said all that could be said in its next issue:

Clubmen, to whom he was friend, counsellor and guide, have everywhere received the news of his passing with a deep sense of shock and personal bereavement. The Executive and Officers of the Union, whom he led for the past 24 years in a determined and never-yielding fight to preserve the ideals and strengthen the great heritage of the Movement, know that his death is to all of us an incalculable loss . . . it was almost symbolic of Our Mac's unrelenting energy that he died in harness.

15

In the election that followed the death of Edward McEnery, his old friend and fellow member of the South Kirkby Diamond Jubilee Club, Yorkshire, Arthur Bates, was chosen as the new President of the Working Men's Club and Institute Union. It was a contested election, with fourteen other candidates. Arthur Bates secured 3,342 votes against 1,245 for the runner-up, Derek Dormer, who was subsequently elected Vice-President.

For Arthur Bates, this was the high point in a long Union career spent almost wholly shoulder-to-shoulder with Edward McEnery; they had been members of the same club, officers of the same branch, had worked together as President and Vice-President, and, outside the Union, in the same local authorities. Arthur Bates had joined the Diamond Jubilee Club at South Kirkby in 1939, and served as its President from 1946 until he became Vice-President of the Union in 1961. He had been Vice-President of the Wakefield Branch in 1953 and its President in 1960.

The election of the new President was announced at the Annual Meeting, held at the Blackpool Winter Gardens on 4 April 1970, when the principal guest was the Speaker of the House of Commons, the Rt Hon. Dr Horace King, which was a rare honour for the Union because, traditionally, Speakers of the House of Commons had seldom participated in public affairs outside Parliament. This has changed in more recent years, partly through the precedent set by Dr King and more particularly through the Rt Hon. George Thomas, now Viscount Tonypandy, who also became a much more public figure. At the time, however, Dr King's appearance was a rare one, although welcome because he had always taken a keen interest in the working men's clubs in his Southampton constituency. A record attendance – 1,316 clubmen from 561 clubs – heard Dr King say:

I would begin by reminding you of some of the great names in the history of the Union – the Rev. Solly, great secretaries like Dent, Hall and Chapman. In our own time we have had Frank Castle and that great servant of the Union, Edward McEnery.

I had many meetings with Frank and Mac in days gone by when Bills of special interest were going through the House of Commons. Mac devoted the whole of his life to public service. He was an inspiration to all who believe in public service.

This Union just did not happen; it had to be worked for. The pioneers created it and it has grown in numbers to well over three million. This has been accomplished by the devoted voluntary efforts of thousands of Clubmen up and down Britain.

This great progress has been made by the efforts of hundreds and thousands of secretaries and officials and the very competent head-quarters staff now led so well by your present General Secretary, Mr John B. Holmes.

The Club and Institute Union grew out of devoted sacrifice and hard work. Our free society had to be won and preserved through the efforts of two world wars. Freedom is precious. Freedom is fragile. We could lose it if we do not work to preserve it. Everything depends on what we do with it. We must have an economically prosperous Britain. That means devotion to duty.

The running of a club is a highly skilled operation. I also believe that it is the duty of free men to build a good society – not merely a prosperous one. It must be a society in which the strong help the weak, where middle-age helps the old and very young.

Britain would collapse overnight if it were not for those who give something as well as take something from it. There is a great need for service in a voluntary capacity. Those who serve on hospital committees, leaders of the youth movement, those who serve in Clubs are all playing their part. Often they receive nothing except complaints when something goes wrong.

That is what Club life is all about – creating a good society. A bad one is where the only object of its members is to have a good time.

Wherever I have gone I have found Clubs doing good for others. In the war years I used to make appeals for war charities and whenever I launched an appeal the first response came from working men's clubs.

At that Annual Meeting, the delegates were worried by two issues. The first was one that came up frequently over the years; a feeling that if the Union modernized too swiftly, amalgamating branches so that better-equipped regional offices could serve larger areas, something might be lost in the process – the closeness that many clubs felt to their own existing branches, small though some of them might be.

The second issue was even more worrying. This was the way in which some police forces seemed to be using the powers given to them under the Gaming Act 1968 to make unwarranted enquiries into the way clubs were managed, and, in particular, into the personal background of committee members. After approaches from many clubs in different parts of the country, the General Secretary, John B. Holmes, made a statement to the meeting:

> We have received a number of enquiries from all parts of the country on this matter. Applications were made for registration of Club premises under Part 3 of the Gaming Act. That enables Clubs to have installed in their premises gaming machines. As long ago as 1967 we were having discussions with the Home Office for gaming by way of machines only.
>
> The memorandum from the Home Office suggested that the form of registration would be simple and straightforward – a simple form of registration and a limited power of objection. To our horror, six or seven weeks ago when applications were coming in we found in a number of parts of the country the police were making enquiries which were unnecessary and unwarranted.
>
> I sought an interview at the Home Office with the Parliamentary Under-Secretary of State. I wrote to the Chief Constables of West Yorkshire and Northumberland. The reply from the Chief Constable of West Yorkshire was unsatisfactory. We are not prepared to accept the terms outlined.
>
> We had an interview with Mr Roy Mason, MP for Barnsley. Mr Mason, apart from being MP for Barnsley, is President of the Board of Trade and a member of the Cabinet. He undertook, as MP for Barnsley, to see the Home Secretary, Mr James Callaghan. I have received a copy of a letter which the Home Secretary has sent to Mr Roy Mason. Again we do not accept the terms of the Home Secretary's letter.
>
> We repeat that the enquiries which the police are making arising from Club applications for gaming by way of machines are unnecessary and unwarranted. We have had a police officer enquiring not only names and addresses and dates of birth of Club members, but also enquiring what their children do. We have had enquiries as to Bingo and whether any lotteries are run. We have had officers measuring premises. We have had some questions which the police might be entitled to ask, but other questions bear no relation to the Club's application. We see no reason why the police should be allowed to make these enquiries.
>
> I would invite conference to adopt a resolution which can be sent to the Home Secretary by telegram. This reads: THE EXECUTIVE COMMITTEE AND DELEGATES AT THE ANNUAL MEETING OF THE CLUB AND INSTITUTE UNION AT BLACKPOOL HAVE TODAY RESOLVED TO PROTEST IN THE STRONGEST POSSIBLE TERMS AT THE UNNECESSARY AND UNWARRANTED ENQUIRIES MADE BY POLICE OFFICERS CONSEQUENT UPON APPLICATIONS MADE BY CLUBS UNDER THE GAMING ACT 1968.

The meeting agreed this resolution unanimously, and heard another delegate say that in his club in Barnsley, the President,

Vice-President and members of the committee had all resigned because of the way the police were behaving. The delegate, R. Skelly of the Pogmoor West End Club, said:

> I have a newspaper cutting on this subject, in which there is a quotation from the Chief Constable. He says it is important to know who the Committee-members are, and something of their background, and to know whether they are fit members to run a Club. If they refuse to answer, and they are entitled to, they are not likely to get their licence.
>
> This is the first step towards a police state. We have been told today of the dedicated work done by our members. If we are a democratic society then we are entitled to freedom. The methods being used, particularly in my area, are against all the principles which we believe in.

Now, nearly twenty years later, it can be said that there was a background to this whole affair that was unknown to most clubmen at the time: the Act that made fruit machines legal also did something else – it encouraged a criminal fringe, particularly in the north-east, to try moving into the working men's clubs in the hope of making quick cash and untaxed profits. It was fraud on a very large scale, and eventually there were criminal proceedings and also several murders.

This was a scandal that had been building up for some years. There were suggestions that leading London criminals had decided, on the toss of a coin, which criminal 'families' or gangs should operate in which parts of the country, and one particular gang had 'won' the right to the north-east, where they operated behind the shield of a legitimate company, offering finance to clubs which wished to install fruit machines on their premises.

The front company had a legitimate profit-sharing agreement with each club, and eventually it was believed that as many as five hundred clubs in the region signed such agreements, all happy to receive an income from a totally new source, these new machines installed on their premises. The clubs never realized that the hire-purchase payments were far too high for the actual cost of the machines, and the fraud could have gone on for years if the crooks had not gone greedy – their mistake was to start creaming-off the cash as they went round each week, emptying the machines, and making any necessary repairs. Eventually, they started feuding between themselves. Two men were murdered, and it was believed that there may have been more. The Michael Caine film *Get Carter* was based on the case.

In a situation like that, the police had no idea how far the fraud went – so many innocent clubmen found their clubs being investigated in the years that followed as the police and the courts cleaned up the fruit-machine industry.

The present General Secretary of the Union, Jack Johnson, was then Secretary of the Durham Branch, and met many of those involved. 'It was a very clever fraud,' he said. 'The clubs had never had fruit machines before, and so we didn't understand the finances at all, and the fraud could have gone on for years if they hadn't gone greedy. After all, the clubs were receiving an income that they had never had before, and they were all happy with that. It was a great help to many clubs, and they never knew how much other money was involved . . .'

After the Annual Meeting, arrangements were set in hand for the election of the new Vice-President. Derek Dormer was elected with 1,014 votes agaist 732 votes for the runner-up, Alan Garnett, President of the Woodlands Comrades Club in Doncaster. There were thirty-three candidates in the election, several of them also polling well. Ron Linstead, Secretary of South Yorkshire Branch and a member of the National Executive, gained 582 votes, and John James Clough, Treasurer of the Hetton and District Working Men's Club, Hetton-le-Hole, County Durham, and also a member of the National Executive, polled 472 votes.

Derek Dormer had long been one of the youngest members of the National Executive, and although then still only forty-four had already been active in the Union for over twenty years. He was then, and still is, a member of the Higham Ferrars Working Men's Club, Northamptonshire; had been elected Secretary of the former Buckinghamshire Branch in 1950, and in 1954, when still only twenty-eight years old, had been elected to the National Executive. He was then Chairman of the education sub-committee.

After his election, in a message to all members published in the *Journal*, Derek Dormer wrote:

I have endeavoured to equip myself for service at all levels in the Union's structure. Naturally, I am very proud to have been elected as Vice-President on a national vote, and will do everything possible to fulfil the responsibilities of this important office.

Although I have served on a number of important national sub-committees, I have always believed that the future of the Union and its clubs is fundamentally dependent upon a good educational programme, and I hope to continue to serve on the education committee, thereby furthering the union's education programme, but also to serve on any other committee where it is felt I can render further service to Union clubs and their members.

That year, 1970, there were several other events of great interest to clubmen, especially in Windsor, where members of the Old Windsor Working Men's Club – known locally as 'The Iron Room', because they had started in a corrugated-iron building – had moved into fine new premises with three bars and a two-table billiard room. The Club is just down the road from Windsor Castle, and the members were all delighted when the Duke of Edinburgh called in, met the committee and their wives, had a drink, and was shown round the Club. (Three years later portraits of the Queen and the Duke were sent to the Club from Windsor Castle, and these now hang proudly on one of the walls.)

In a year of major elections, there was one by-election, in South Yorkshire, when Harold Hirst was elected to the National Executive; he had first joined a Union club in 1924, the Cudworth West End Club, and then after three years in the Coldstream Guards, he joined the Barnsley Radical and Liberal Club, later becoming its Secretary and Branch President.

Among the clubmen who died that year were Pat Ansell, who had represented Warwickshire on the National Executive from 1955 until 1967, when ill-health caused him not to seek re-election, and Alf Collins, also a former member of the National Executive, and founder-chairman of both the CIU games league and the Secretaries and Chairmen's Association in Jarrow, Hebburn and Bolden.

On a happier note, this was the year that Ray Reardon won the World Professional Snooker Championship for the first time, an achievement of great interest to clubmen in many parts of the country because Reardon had started playing snooker as a boy at the Tredegar Workmen's Institute in South Wales, before going on to take part in many inter-club competitions, the Welsh championship, and also the national championship. In the 73-frame final of the World Championship, played at the Victoria Hall, London, Reardon defeated John Pulman by 38 frames to 35. In those days, Reardon still represented the Cheadle Social Club.

As the New Year started, members of the Executive were looking forward to one major moment in the Union's history – the opening of the new convalescent home at Broadstairs. The cost had now risen to over £400,000, but there were no complaints about that; no expense had been spared in making the home the finest ever built by any working-class organization for its members. There were facilities for taking wheel-chair residents, with a lift at each end of the building (something which had not been possible then in the Union's other homes); a billiard room with two tables; a television lounge; and a large lounge on the first floor with fine views of the

North Foreland lighthouse and Joss Bay. Each of the sixty-one bed-rooms was fitted with a wardrobe, dressing-table and washbasin. In the grounds surrounding the home, there was a bowling green, a putting green and an ornamental pool with fountains.

The first thirteen residents stayed at the home in February 1971, and then the official opening was arranged for 5 June. This cere-mony was performed by the then recently retired Speaker of the House of Commons, Dr Horace King, who, by the time he came to attend the opening, had been elevated to the peerage with the title Lord Maybray-King. In his speech, Lord Maybray-King paid tribute to the late President, Edward McEnery, who had been a personal friend, describing him as 'that great and lovable figure, a very dear friend of mine, as of so many of us . . . I remember how utterly happy he was when, with a few choice friends, he was entertained in the Speaker's State dining-room on the occasion of his being awarded by Her Majesty the OBE. I am happy that he lived to lay the foundation stone of this home. I wish that he were here in person, as I am certain that he is in spirit, on this day of triumph and happiness.' Lord Maybray-King then went on to refer to an old friend from Southampton, the late Walter Powell:

> He was a good Clubman, if ever there was one. Walter used to say to me, 'Horace, nothing is too good for the workers.' We are seeing that come true in every club in the country. There is nobody here who has not seen his own club modernised, transformed beyond recognition, during the past twenty years. And all this because of the efficiency, ability – but above all the devotion and self-sacrifice – of voluntary workers on thousands of club committees.

All the Union's thirty branches were represented at the opening ceremony, but Frank Castle, the former General Secretary, who had long advocated the opening of a new home on the Kent coast, could not be there; he was ill in hospital. Lord Maybray-King and the other guests all signed a telegram to him that read: 'VERY BEST WISHES FOR A COMPLETE AND SPEEDY RECOVERY. ALL OF US ARE THINKING OF YOU AND REMEMBERING ALL THAT YOU HAVE DONE FOR OUR HOMES, PARTICULARLY YOUR BELOVED PEGWELL, AND NOW THE HILTON OF CONVALESCENT HOMES AT BROADSTAIRS.'

The other person who had done much to make the Broadstairs project possible was the long-serving Chairman of the Convalescent Homes Committee, Ernest Connelly, but his health was also failing; he was able to attend the ceremony, but could not make a speech. Instead, the General Secretary, John B. Holmes, thanked Lord

Maybray-King and presented him with a gold wrist-watch as a memento of the occasion. Holmes said:

> The Union has travelled a long and, at times, a hard road. In the years that lie ahead there may be times when once again the road is hard . . . but you can be sure of the untiring efforts of branch officials and club officials. You have our assurance that we will continue to preserve the freedom and privileges our predecessors and the present team have achieved for the Clubmen of Great Britain. Clubmen of today show the world that they do not abuse the freedom and privileges enjoyed and what is equally important, they do not neglect their responsibilities. Having established this, there is no reason whatsoever for any section of the public or government department, commission or board to interfere with the private nature of our clubs and associate members of our clubs.

Over the months that followed, John Holmes was often away from head office; he had frequent bouts of ill-health, and it was for this reason that he said he could not attend the Annual Meeting, held the following year, May 1972, at Blackpool. He was absent when his own salary was discussed, and thus did not hear one delegate say:

> The last speaker said that we want the right man at the right salary . . . I do not know if we have the right man. If you take this as a personal insult it is unfortunate. If we are to get the right man for the job then let us advertise the job and get the right man . . . this is not a criticism of John Holmes. He should face the open market and see what candidates there are from the open field to do his job.

Although other delegates spoke out in Holmes's favour, another delegate said pointedly:

> I have heard how wonderful John Holmes is. I have had no help from John Holmes in the last six months. Since he was off, I have had some from Frank Morris. I have no more to say.

His increase in salary was agreed, but there were a substantial number of delegates who voted against, some on principle, and some because they were clearly unhappy, and this was their way of making a protest. With hindsight, the Union officers know what the problem was; but few knew then. Over the year that followed, it was noticed that he was frequently absent from head office and the atmosphere within the Union, at head office and within the Executive was far from happy. Clubmen tend to be kind men; it is fellowship that brings them together in the first place, and this was a problem that few of them had had to face before. Many were sorry for their General Secretary; they wanted to give him a chance to overcome his problem, and to re-establish his authority . . . and the Union had to continue with its day-to-day affairs. Life had to go on.

Three new members were elected to the National Executive during 1971. Colin Wright was elected by the clubmen of Northamptonshire, Bedfordshire and Buckinghamshire, to fill the vacancy caused by the elevation of Derek Dormer. In the other two by-elections, caused by the death of sitting members, there was only one nomination from each branch. Alec Salt was chosen to replace the late G. F. Carter (North-East Metropolitan Branch), having served for many years as trustee and Secretary of the Langham Club, and G. Larkham, Secretary of the West End Working Men's Club, Chippenham, took the place of the late E. G. Randell (Wiltshire and Western Counties).

The other issue that dominated the year was one that roused great passions: a renewed suggestion that the Union should change its name, and drop the words 'Working Men's' from its title. This proposal (which had been defeated once before, in 1955, see p. 203) was debated at a Special Council Meeting held at the Central Hall, Westminster, on Saturday, 26 June 1971. It was hotly debated.

The Vice-President, Derek Dormer, opened the debate, after the motion had been formally moved by the Union President, Arthur Bates. Dormer made it plain from the start that the Executive were expecting some opposition, and went on to say:

In fact, the Executive are still well aware of the reception received when this was brought forward in 1955, and overwhelmingly defeated. Nevertheless, the Executive are men of courage and a great sense of responsibility and duty, and although they expect there will be some emotions aroused they think it would be wrong if the Executive did not test the feeling now some sixteen years have passed.

There have been changes in our Movement, and the Executive Committee have been requested, quite frequently, to test the feeling again regarding the name. I will try to give you some of the reasons why some of our members feel this proposed change ought to be made.

One thing is the fact that fifty per cent of the Clubs seeking to join the Union do not include the name 'Working Men's' in their title. The Executive wonder how many Clubs outside the Union refrain from joining because of the name. We have to decide whether the expansion of our Movement is being held up for this particular reason. We can be certain that this is a factor to consider.

During the last ten or fifteen years, most Clubs have changed their rules in one special way. When I was a young Club committee member twenty years ago our rules contained a clause which said that the committee should be comprised of at least two-thirds bona fide working men. They do not say that today.

What is the reason for this? Is it because working men have changed? There is no doubt that in some ways they have changed in habits and social behaviour. Club life has changed very much in the last ten years. One thing which has not changed is the image which we get as a Movement. I get very annoyed when I see cartoons and skits and references which depict us as we were some seventy years ago.

I would like to think that we can break away from that image, because most Clubs have tried to move with the times. Our objects have not changed. Rule 2 states what they are. If you decide to change the name, the objects will not be changed. The Executive feel the time has come to see what the feeling is.

Most of us when we talk about our Movement say the 'CIU' or the 'Club Union'. Very few of us say the 'Working Men's Club and Institute Union'. It is not a term we use but of course there is nothing shameful in it if we did. Are we going to change the Union's name? (Cries of, 'No!')

May I make two more points. The National Executive Committee, as you are well aware, have a very arduous task to perform, and in carrying out the important job of dealing with Departments of State and Government Ministers we have to exercise influence. This Union has to have an influence on the country as a whole. Therefore we have to decide, if we are to influence the powers that be, whether a change of name would give us more influence (shouts of, 'No!') or will it give us less influence, or will it make no difference.

From the interruptions that Dormer received, it was clear that he had some opposition in the audience, however mildly he had tried to put the argument; this became clearer still as other delegates came forward to speak. T. Hiley (Bradford Branch) spoke of the Union's 'proud history of fighting for the working class'. Councillor B. Davenport (Manchester Branch) said he was 'a plumber and proud to be classed a working man', and suggested that the Executive should try again in fifteen years' time. H. Kilkenny (Wealdstone Social Club) said tartly, 'maybe the National Executive does not like to be referred to as working-class when it goes to the Royal Garden Parties'. And when the motion was put to the vote, only 107 delegates voted for the motion and 501 against. There was also strong opposition to suggestions that women might eventually become full members of Union clubs.

In April the following year, 1972, Frank Castle died, after a long period of ill-health. Lord Maybray-King wrote to Frank's daughter, Mrs Vaughan:

Your father and I were friends for over twenty years and I was able to help him a little in Parliament in his great work for the CIU. He was a magnificent General Secretary, with friends from one end of Britain to the other. We all mourn the passing of one of England's greatest clubmen and a fine gentleman.

At his funeral, which was attended by the President and most of
the Union's officers, the minister, the Rev. Derek Baker, who had
seen Frank often in hospital, spoke for them all when he said:

> It was the wish of Frank Castle that I should say a few words at his
> funeral service ... [his] particular love within the Union was the
> convalescent homes and I would think that there would be no better
> tribute that could be paid to him, and one which he would appreciate
> the most, than the continuance and the extension of this work.
>
> I knew him only a few years, mostly through hospital visits. On these
> occasions I found him a most likeable companion, his wide range of
> knowledge, but above all his character, which was not cast in the
> modern mould, embracing a great love of life ... he was a man's man,
> and that I believe is perhaps the real secret of his undoubted success as
> General Secretary.

In the months that followed, Castle's old colleagues in Kent
Branch organized a memorial fund, and through this raised £2,000
to open a Garden of Remembrance in the grounds surrounding the
convalescent home at Broadstairs. This was officially opened in June
1974 by T. Gilbert, Chairman of the Kent Federation, who had
worked with Frank for over forty years, with the Rev. D. Baker,
who had conducted the funeral service, performing the service of
dedication.

As I have said on an earlier page, throughout much of 1972 the
General Secretary, John Holmes, was unwell. For five months he
was away from the office, and then, when he did return, was advised
by his doctor to take on only light duties. By an unfortunate coincidence, both the Convalescent Homes Secretary, Bill Daultrey, and
the Recreation Secretary, Gen Ding, also had periods of illness that
year, and so did the Union Accountant and the Stores Manager,
which tended to emphasize Holmes's absence. The Assistant General Secretary, Frank Morris, was left to carry an unusually heavy
workload. It was a difficult period, and eventually, just before the
1973 Annual Meeting, John Holmes accepted a suggestion that he
should resign. The Vice-President, Derek Dormer, told the delegates:

> Most of you are aware that John Holmes's health has been de-
> teriorating for three or four years. I am sure that every Club in the land
> has had the benefit of his wisdom and guidance. We have looked to him
> for guidance. When his health began to give way it led to difficulties.
> Eighteen months ago we hoped he would recover.
>
> Because of his devotion to duty, John came back a lot quicker than
> many others would have done. Coming back so quickly thus contributed

to another relapse. Some people have tended to criticise the Executive Committee for not taking action at an earlier date. The Executive Committee would not be prepared to accept that kind of criticism . . . we hoped that John would recover . . . the National Executive Committee does not have the power vested in it to change the General Secretary. He is appointed by you, the Clubs of the Union. You cannot go up to a man who is ill and say, 'We are thinking of replacing you' . . . we have to remember that John Holmes has worked for this Union for almost twenty years as Assistant General Secretary and General Secretary. There is no doubt that the service he has given has contributed to the wrecking of his health.

And so John Holmes was allowed to depart without undue embarrassment. A testimonial was organized for his benefit. A very sad episode was handled with a kindness that says much for the Union's way of doing things, and in the election that followed Frank Morris was elected General Secretary with a truly staggering majority. He received 4,974 votes against 641 for the runner-up, a sure sign that clubmen instinctively realized that this was a moment for closing ranks, and putting the Union's affairs in order.

The President, Arthur Bates, said all that needed to be said at the following year's Annual Meeting:

> I welcome in the place of Mr Holmes our new General Secretary, Mr Frank Morris. I think it would be true to say that although not elected until the end of September 1973, he has in fact been acting as General Secretary for something like the past two years because of Mr Holmes's illness. During this period members of the Executive have been well pleased with the work done by Mr Morris. . . .

Over the long period that it took to resolve this unhappy matter, the Union's day-to-day life continued, although it is generally agreed now, by those who were involved in the Union's affairs at the time, that some things did go wrong. One of them, sadly, was a major issue. The Union made a serious error of judgement in the controversial field of race relations. During the course of researching this book, I have spoken to many who were holding office at the time, and all volunteered the opinion (without any prompting from me) that the Union should never have allowed itself to become involved in the legal actions that followed the refusal of the East Ham South Conservative Club to admit a coloured person, and the other case that involved the Preston Dockers' Club.

In both cases, Section 2 of the Race Relations Act 1968 was at issue. This was the Act that made racial discrimination unlawful. In both cases, the Union felt that it had to become involved since it had always maintained, throughout its history, that members' clubs were private premises and what they decided to do was their private business. (I am paraphrasing a little so as to put the issue clearly.) Eventually, both cases went to the House of Lords and, even though the East Ham South Conservative Club was not a member of the Union, the Union decided to support the club. The appeal was heard in the House of Lords for seven days in November 1972, and eventually, by a majority decision, the Lords agreed with the Union's argument that the Act did not apply to clubs where there was 'a genuine system of personal selection of members'. The issue dragged on for several years because, by the time the Lords had given their judgment on the East Ham South Conservative Club case, the other case concerning the Preston Dockers' Club was already before the courts, and this put the issue in a different context because the members of that club had resolved to operate a colour bar. Judgment on the latter case was not given until October 1974, and again the Lords agreed with the Union's interpretation of the law.

But this was a victory that was not worth winning; the Union's officers were immediately called to the Home Office, where they were told that the Home Secretary, Roy Jenkins, was going to place a Bill before Parliament making any form of racial prejudice within a club illegal. The net effect was that the Union had damaged its own good name by appearing to condone racial prejudice. This happened to be untrue; the Union had become involved in the legal argument to defend the quite separate principle of privacy, but the damage had been done. This was one of the few times in the Union's history when the National Executive felt compelled to issue a statement of policy on what was clearly both a moral and also a political issue. This it did early in 1975, after the two cases had been finally resolved, when the General Secretary, Frank Morris, signed the following statement on the front page of the *Journal*:

RACE RELATIONS
An Important Statement from the
Union's Executive Committee

The Judgement of the House of Lords in the Preston Dockers' Case has caused many people, including Clubmen, to say that the Union should give a clear lead in the matter of race relations.

This subject has, over some years past, been before the Union's National Executive Committee, but as must be clearly understood by all concerned, a lead could not be given whilst the true intention of the Race Relations Act, 1968, was being questioned by the Race Relations Board.

The Judgement of the House of Lords was given in October, 1974, since which time the Executive has given deep consideration to the whole question of race and has studied all that has been said and written on the matter by those who consider it necessary to give advice to the Union and its Clubs.

The following statement is therefore issued to all Clubs:

The Union Executive, being fully aware of the private nature of a bona fide members' club (which it will at all times seek to protect), considers that conduct by a club committee which is based on colour, race or ethnic or national origins, is unacceptable in that the Union is founded on friendship as is clearly shown on the Union Associate Card, namely –

HONOUR ALL MEN, LOVE THE BROTHERHOOD, USE HOSPITALITY ONE TO ANOTHER, BE NOT FORGETFUL TO ENTERTAIN STRANGERS AND HE THAT NEED HAVE FRIENDS MUST SHOW HIMSELF FRIENDLY.

This declaration of purpose, which was first made 100 years ago, is the foundation upon which this great movement has been built and applies today as it did then and must ever be before club committees in their dealings with their fellow men.

If therefore compulsion by Parliament is to be avoided, the spirit of this recommendation must be complied with.

It is the earnest desire of the Executive that all club committees will give this statement deep and careful consideration and will follow the lead of the Executive which can only result in achieving, in the course of time, the full integration of persons of other races within our community.

There were other issues, too, during these two years, but none so great as these, and, looking back now, there is a general feeling of regret within the Union's leadership that action was not taken sooner; but, as I have explained, the problem arose at a difficult time, and it was one that the new General Secretary, Frank Morris, had to tackle throughout the period when he was acting as 'caretaker', facing election, and then taking up office.

During this period, several leading clubmen died. Tom Knight, who had been elected to the South Wales Executive in 1943 and to the National Executive in 1962, died in February 1973. Harry Gilmore, another National Executive member and for twenty-one years Secretary of Leicestershire Branch, died that same year, as did Harry Stubbs of Longbridge Social Club, who represented the West Midlands on the National Executive from 1960 to 1971. Cliff Culling, who had been the Union's first Convalescent Homes Secretary, from 1947 until his retirement in 1963, died suddenly on 5 May 1974. Later that same year, on 24 December, the former Assistant General Secretary, Tom Nicoll, died at the age

of seventy-nine, so ending one of the last links with the Union's
early days.

Tom Nicoll had joined the head office staff in May 1909, becoming personal clerk to B. T. Hall in 1919. In 1930, when Bob
Chapman became General Secretary, Nicoll had been appointed
Assistant General Secretary, a position which he held for twenty-
five years. Thus, through those years when building up the convalescent homes had been one of the Union's great achievements,
he had been working at the very heart of the Union's affairs with
Chapman, Castle, Cliff Culling and, of course, Ernest Connelly,
who chaired the Convalescent Homes Committee for thirty years.
Chapman and Connelly also both lived on to a fine old age;
Chapman died on 4 April 1975, at the age of eighty-five, and
Connelly on 19 June 1976, at the age of eighty-four (although he
never did admit to his age).

In their last years, this generation of clubmen continued to press
for the modernization of the homes; they lived to see Broadstairs
replace Pegwell, and Connelly, who held office to the end of his
days, laid down the foundations for the modernization programme
that continued after his death. 'Con', as he was known to so many
clubmen, had hoped to see the Union build a new convalescent
home in the north-east, and for some years supported the CHINE
(Convalescent Home in the North-East) fund-raising campaign;
but, eventually, it was decided to concentrate instead on modern-
izing the Saltburn home.

The first of the homes to be modernized was Grange over Sands,
where an additional floor was constructed in the mid-sixties, increasing the capacity to seventy residents; at the same time a passenger lift was installed, and the Superintendent's flat and staff quarters
separated from the residents' area. This work was completed in
1967, and then ten years later a further £50,000 was spent on
reconstructing the kitchen area and improving the fittings from a
fire-safety point of view.

An even larger programme of work was undertaken at Langland
Bay, where £220,000 was spent on building new kitchens and store
rooms and a residents' dining-room; converting the former dining-
room into a lounge; replacing the passenger lift; roof repairs; the
replacement or repair of all windows and doors; fitting vanitory
units in every bedroom; providing more toilets, baths and showers;
refurnishing all the common rooms and staff quarters: and providing new fire escape stairways.

Ernest Connelly lived to see the first three transformations
achieved at Broadstairs, Grange and Langland Bay, and, indeed,

presided over the re-opening celebrations at Langland even though he was then in his eighties and often troubled by serious illness; the programme of works at Saltburn by the Sea was completed after his death. At Saltburn, which had only cost £6,000 when it was bought in 1908, £400,000 was spent on modernization in 1980/81, installing central heating, improving all the common rooms, reducing the number that could be accommodated to forty-seven, and making each room warm and comfortable, with some rooms available for married couples. As the *Journal* commented in 1980:

> The expanse of sandy beach that B. T. Hall first gazed upon seventy-five years ago still stretches from Saltburn to Redcar, the exterior of the building still looks much the same (except for the tower, now without its steeple) but what would Mr Hall make of the colour television, stereo equipment, carpets, electric lights, etc., if he could return now?

It was an imaginative modernization, with the lounge re-sited so that it caught the morning sun, and a corridor installed so that there could be bedrooms on both sides of the building.

And thereby Ernest Connelly left the Union with his own memorial; as the *Journal* said, there could be none better:

> It will be a long time, if ever, before any one person will fill the gap on the Union Executive, and the Homes Committee, caused by the death of this wonderful lovable character. No doubt there will be some discussion as to how his work for the Union can be commemorated. There is no need for a special memorial – there are four already, at Broadstairs, Grange, Langland and Saltburn.

16

In 1977 the Queen became the first reigning monarch to visit a working men's club. It was a symbolic moment in the Union's history, and a great honour for members of the Coventry Working Men's Club, one of the oldest and best-equipped clubs in the Union.

Many months earlier, officials at Buckingham Palace had told local-authority officers in many parts of the country that the Queen and the Duke of Edinburgh wished to celebrate her Silver Jubilee by making a tour of Britain, meeting as many people as possible, without too much fuss or ceremony. When this was discussed in the West Midlands, the Deputy Lord Mayor of Coventry, Councillor Harry Richards, himself a keen clubman and President of the Hen Lane Social Club, suggested that the Royal couple might like to visit one of the city's clubs. This was specially pleasing for the Union, because Coventry City Council had been the first local authority in the country to consult the Union on the siting of working men's clubs, making sure that every local community had its own club.

For a visit like this, the Coventry Working Men's Club was the obvious choice: the oldest club in the city, having been founded in 1860 after the great weavers' strike, and yet also one of the most modern. Like so many early clubs, Coventry had originally opened as a reading room where members could read all the newspapers and periodicals of the time for 1d a week or 4s a year. The club then occupied premises in New Street for forty years from 1862, before acquiring its present premises at 54 Cox Street, which it has occupied ever since. It has expanded over the years, providing a new concert hall (1911), a new façade, entrance, bar and games room (1933), and another new games room (1950). From 1962 onwards, the Club engaged on a rebuilding programme, surrendering part of its own site for a road-widening scheme, and also acquiring the freehold of an old printing works and of some dilapidated cottages so that it could erect a new concert hall, games room, lounges, and then in 1973 two more lounges and the most modern games room in the city. (These were formally opened that year by the then President of the Union, Arthur Bates.)

So, clearly, Coventry Working Men's Club illustrated both the history of the movement, and also its modern outlook – and the arrangements were made for the Queen and the Duke to visit the club on 27 July 1977, when she was received by the Club President, Joe Craig, and the Secretary, Bert Miles, with two members of the National Executive, Jim Cooke and Oliver Cotterell. At the Palace's special request, the Queen and the Duke saw the club just as it normally is, every day, with members playing snooker, darts or cards or having a drink in one of the lounges, and there they also met three of the club's oldest members, Harry Lee: aged 88; Bill Owen, 80, and Albert Hatch, 79.

'The Queen thought the Club was marvellous, and said so,' reported Secretary Bert Miles afterwards.

For clubmen elsewhere, the visit had a wider significance: a Royal acknowledgement of the very special place that their clubs have in the lives of working men, and one that was much appreciated.

For some clubmen there was an irony in the fact that the movement was proud to welcome the Queen to one of their clubs, and realized that one of Britain's two major political parties had now chosen another woman as its leader, and yet many of the Union's member clubs were reluctant to give women equal rights. This was an issue that was strongly debated at that year's Annual Meeting, and one that has still to be resolved; there are those who believe that women should have full rights in every club, and others who maintain (with equal passion) that working men's clubs are what their name implies.

The issue was debated at a special rules revision conference in 1975, and then again at the 1977 Annual Meeting, when delegates rejected a motion that would have entitled lady members to hold associate and pass cards. It was an issue that aroused strong speeches on both sides, with the President, Arthur Bates, urging speakers not to get 'hot under the collar'.

For the Executive, George Moss (President of South Yorkshire Branch) said the rule-change could add greatly to the Union's income, possibly bringing in an extra £500,000 a year, and he urged the delegates to 'do away with this prejudice'. Another speaker, Joe Wolfe of the Clifton Labour Club, Blackpool, pointed out that the Treasurer of their club was a woman and they had two women members on their committee. And A. W. Clifford of Silver Hall Club, North East Branch, added that his club had had women members for the past forty years, and went on to tell the delegates bluntly:

> We are not being men if we deny women their rights. You use them to help in your clubs. I would move from our club that women not only get Pass Cards but that they get the same rights as men. You are a little bit late with this and you have not gone far enough.

Other speakers warned the delegates that they would find themselves forced to change their rules by law if they did not do so voluntarily, but the delegates were adamant; they did not want the rules changed, although there were also some members who argued that the Executive were wrong for another reason: they had not gone far enough, and should have brought forward a more substantial rule-change, requiring all clubs to give ladies equal membership rights with men.

Issues such as these, and others that have been discussed previously in this book, seldom end in a swift decision; it is one of the features of the Club and Institute Union, being the largest democratic organization in the country, that any proposal has to command broad support across the country if it is to result in a change of policy. A delegate keen on pressing for a rule-change might argue that this is a disadvantage; but the tradition has great strengths as well. After a history now stretching back one hundred and twenty-five years, the Union remains a broadly balanced institution, preserving its principles of independence and freedom within the law, and yet adapting with each generation. Its strength lies in its democratic structure. When the Union speaks, it represents nearly 4,000 clubs and a total membership of maybe 2,500,000 people, with the officials of every club accountable to members of that club; with branch officials accountable to each club; with National Executive members accountable to branches, and the President, Vice-President and General Secretary all elected by national ballot. Under such a system, policies do change – but slowly. And this is appropriate for an organization that has to speak with authority for nearly 4,000 clubs, and yet believes that each club should be free to manage its own affairs.

Over the past ten years, the question of admitting ladies to full membership has come before the Annual Meetings with some frequency; it is only there that the issue can be resolved, because a change of rule is required. The attitude of delegates is changing, but gradually. Debates are now less heated, and one year the motion may be moved, seconded – and then passed. For that is the way the Working Men's Club and Institute Union advances.

Meanwhile, as I have stressed elsewhere in this narrative, the Union continues to be a strong organization, able to withstand periods of doubts and even division, because it does have a life of its own.

As each year passes, the nature of the Union changes in subtle ways. As will be seen from Appendix 6, which lists all the Executive members serving at the time of writing, there has been a substantial change in the composition of the Executive over the past ten years, and this has been reflected in the branches and at head office. Younger men have been coming forward, and so the emphasis of the Union gradually alters without it losing sight of the fundamental beliefs that brought it into being.

These changes began in mid-1977, when the South Wales Branch elected Trevor Morgan, Secretary of the Ferndale Club in the Rhondda, to succeed Ron Griffiths, who had resigned, and Durham and Cleveland Branches elected Bill Hubery, for thirty-three years Secretary of the Close House Workmen's Club at Bishop Auckland, to succeed Norman Rutherford, who had also resigned.

George Moss, the Executive member for South Yorkshire, died on 1 October 1978, and in the election that followed Charles Edward Richardson was elected to the Executive, and then in 1980, there were no fewer than eight new members elected.

J. C. Tobin was elected to represent the North-West Metropolitan Branch clubs, having been their Branch Secretary for ten years.

D. Thompson was chosen by the Manchester clubs, having long been a member of the Ingol Labour Club and its Treasurer for two years; he was also President of the Preston Federation of Clubs, a member of Manchester Branch Committee, and Secretary/Treasurer of the Manchester Branch Clubs Convalescent Homes Federation.

W. Jones, who had been Vice-President of the Plumstead Common Working Men's Club and Secretary of the North Hean Social Club, was elected by the clubs of Kent Branch.

D. J. MacMahon, Secretary of the Derby Clarion Club for eight years, President for three years, and Derbyshire Branch Secretary for six years, was elected from Derbyshire Branch.

L. Parry, Secretary of the Abergavenny Labour Club from 1962 until 1975 and Secretary of Monmouthshire Branch, was elected to represent the Monmouthshire clubs.

James Thomson Ramshaw, Secretary of the North Biddick Working Men's Club and Durham Branch President, was elected by the clubs of Durham Branch after the death of Jimmy Clough, who had been a member of the National Executive for nineteen years.

Robin Etheridge, Secretary of the Sway Working Men's Club and Secretary of the Hampshire Branch, was elected by the clubs in that electoral district, following the death of Fred Scamell, the first life member of the Hythe & District Club, who had been Hampshire Branch President from 1950 to 1954 and a member of the National Executive since 1968.

William Smith, secretary of the Bonnyrigg & District Ex-Servicemen's Club, and President of the Scottish Branch, was elected by the Scottish clubs following the death of Tom Ramage, who had served on the National Executive since 1965, when he was elected the first Scottish member.

This change in the composition of the National Executive coincided with a wave of retirements and new appointments at head office, and was then followed – within the space of just a year or two – by the retirement of the President and the General Secretary, and then national ballots for all three top posts in the Union.

At head office, the changes began with the retirement of Gen Ding, at the end of 1977, after forty-nine years' service at head office, over forty-five of them spent in the department where he became Education and Recreation Secretary. Gen Ding had been a very popular officer; he had returned to the Union after his war service with the Royal Air Force, and had re-established the Recreation side of the Union's work with great enthusiasm, having been a keen boxer and footballer in his early days. He had travelled all round the country, helping to organize different sports contests, judging and presenting prizes, and on his retirement the nation's clubmen contributed the sum of over £10,000 to his testimonial.

Over those years, the recreational aspect of the department's work had grown so much that the Executive decided, on his retirement, to establish separate Recreation and Education Departments. On the Recreation side, Peter Miller, then aged forty, was the natural appointment; he had been Gen Ding's assistant, and had worked for the Union since 1957, spending his first three years in the Accounts Department before moving across to Recreation. 'A clubman through and through' was how Gen Ding described him.

On the Education side, there was no obvious successor already on the Union's staff and so the post was advertised; Kevin Smyth, a member of the Northampton Friendly Society Club, left a post within the National Health Service to become the Union's Education Secretary.

A much more difficult problem arose with the need to appoint a new Assistant General Secretary to replace Leslie Tibbs. The Executive chose Neil Robinson, but it became apparent that this was not a successful appointment from the Union's point of view. It had always been the Union's policy that its head office staff should belong to the appropriate trade union, but Robinson disagreed with this requirement, and over this and other related matters there were disagreements between him and other officers and members of the Executive. With employment law so complicated, the Executive agreed to a financial solution: Robinson agreed to resign and the Executive agreed to pay him £16,000 – a decision that prompted questions and criticism at the next Annual Meeting. 'We thought the settlement was the best for us. We were not happy about it but it may have been money well spent,' the Vice-President, Derek Dormer, told the Annual Meeting, explaining that the alternative might have been either an industrial tribunal hearing or civil proceedings, both of which might have been more costly to the Union in the long run.

Once Robinson's resignation had been effected, the Executive moved swiftly to appoint a new Assistant General Secretary. They chose Peter Ford, then aged forty, who came to the Union with a strong administrative background, with experience in the Royal Air Force and eight years in the legal profession (he is an Associate of the Institute of Legal Executives) before becoming Assistant Company Secretary to United Gas Industries, a public holding company.

Ford was introduced to the delegates at the same Annual Meeting in 1981, with the Executive thus being able to assure the delegates that the hiatus had been resolved; it was at this same Annual Meeting that the President, Arthur Bates, announced his own retirement, after twelve years in that office and ten years as Vice-President. In his address, Bates said that he had never written his speeches as President; he had preferred it to come from the heart – and then this year, being his last as President, he had decided to write one, and then torn it up. 'I said to myself, "Bates. Tell your comrades how you feel!"' Then he went on to recall that when he first became Vice-President, as a single man without any commitments, he had gone to his boss and asked for time off to attend to his duties, and was told, 'Take all the time you want, lad – but no pay!'

> I had a struggle. At that time no married man could have held the job because his wife would have wanted a pay packet coming in at the

end of the week. I persevered with the job because I felt that nothing on earth could take away the fact that I could go into a club in any town or city in the land and know that I had a number of friends in it.

He then went on to recall with pride that in every election for the presidency he had received more votes than in the previous one – his last majority had been over 5,000 – and he was only retiring now because he had to go into hospital to undergo an operation, and felt this was therefore the right time for the Union to choose a successor. He talked of the years when he had worked with Edward McEnery, the changes that he had seen in the Union's clubs, and their need to be on their guard against new legislation.

I come to you after twenty-two years in office to say that whilst I have been able to sleep, I stand before you as a very privileged person. The years I have spent as your Vice-President or President have been very rewarding and I have enjoyed every minute of it ... it is my dearest wish that we will all weather this recession. We will if we work for our clubs, and recognise the fact that in the Club and Institute Union we have inherited something left to us by our grandfathers.

We ourselves must be conscious of the fact that whilst we have inherited a movement such as this we must ensure that we, in our turn, pass on to those who follow us a movement that is flourishing and that is run for the benefit of the community.

I never tire of telling Chief Constables that we are doing their job, and that we are keeping the members of our clubs in order because, if they step out of line, we deal with them. I never tire of telling the Mayors of communities that we have presented this country with some of the finest citizens that any country could be proud of.

Therefore, in my last words to you as your National President, may I say how very proud I have felt to have been your leader so long. May you, when I have gone, continue to regard this movement in the way it should be regarded, as one of the foremost movements in the social life of this country. May you go from strength to strength and may God bless each and every one of you.

It was an emotional speech, touching a chord in the audience, who rose as one man to applaud their retiring President. After he had left the conference hall, the Vice-President, Derek Dormer, told the delegates that the National Executive had already agreed to open a testimonial fund for Arthur Bates. Dormer continued:

Since its inception, this Union has been blessed with a number of great Presidents. Amongst them have been peers of the realm, members of the aristocracy, Members of Parliament, men of wealth, men of considerable intellect, and men of great powers of oratory. Arthur Bates would make no claim to any of these qualities. His ability is of a special nature which enables him to unravel complicated issues in a simple and logical way. He is not the type of man who avoids taking a decision for fear that he may be misunderstood.

I have long thought that the most endearing and outstanding qualities of Arthur Bates have been his fairness and his honesty. It is not easy for a man in his position who is expected to comment and advise at National, Branch and club-level, and even at times when he is accosted by individual clubmen about their problems, to speak to them with absolute fairness and without bias or prejudice in any way.

He is one of those special people, fair and honest as he is, who, when it becomes necessary – and occasions do arise from time to time – can be ruthless, but even then he has always been able to maintain scrupulous fairness. I have always felt that when a man has been on the carpet before Arthur, he has always had a fair crack of the whip . . . he is quite incapable of being devious, and is completely and utterly trusted by everybody in our great movement and by people outside . . . he never bears malice and it is because of these qualities that he is, without doubt, the most popular President the Union has ever had, or is ever likely to have.

Dormer's speech was supported by other speakers, and the delegates were told that the Executive had already resolved to contribute £10,000 to the testimonial fund to provide Arthur Bates with 'a nice little nest egg' in his retirement. Over the following months, clubs more than matched the Executive contribution, so enabling the Union to make a retiring gift to Arthur Bates of well in excess of £20,000.

With his retirement, an election was announced for the presidency. Eleven candidates were nominated, and Derek Dormer was elected with an overwhelming majority over all other candidates; he received 4,252 votes against 271 for the runner-up.

Dormer, who is still the Union President, came from a family of clubmen, the tenth child in a family of twelve, of which seven were boys. Throughout their childhood, Christmas parties, wedding breakfasts and other family occasions were all centred on their local club in Wolverton, Bucks, a railway town where Derek's father worked in the engineering workshop. Derek passed his CMD examination at the age of twenty-one, was Secretary of the old Bucks Branch for fourteen years, was elected to the National Executive at the age of twenty-four, and then later, on moving home to Higham Ferrars, was elected Secretary of Northants Branch.

On his election to the presidency, there was another election, for the vice-presidency. This time, there was a curious result. The election was held in September 1981, and David Charles Lougher, President of South Wales Branch, was elected Vice-President. He only held the post for three months. In the usual biennial elections that followed, he was defeated by Brian Winters, the current Vice-President, in one of the closest elections in recent Union history. Winters, who is also Secretary of Wakefield Branch, traditionally one of the strongest branches in the Union, and the home branch of both Edward McEnery and Arthur Bates, won the election after a recount by just ten votes. He received 1,121 votes against the 1,111 for Lougher.

In the midst of all these changes, the General Secretary, Frank Morris, who had received a CBE in the Queen's Birthday Honours List in 1980, and had become a well-respected figure within the Union, announced that he, too, was going to retire, after eight years in the post, although he agreed to remain as a consultant until the end of 1982 to help his successor settle into the job. Frank Morris had been the first General Secretary to be elected to the position after a long career spent elsewhere; his connections within the Union had been few, and, but for the unhappy circumstances surrounding John Holmes's retirement, he would not have had the opportunity. However, clubmen appreciated the way he had travelled all over the country, lecturing, visiting clubs, attending special functions, and so helping to hold the Union together during one of its most difficult periods. They responded generously to the Frank Morris testimonial appeal, again raising over £20,000.

On his retirement, there was another strongly contested election for the post of General Secretary. Jack Johnson, a keen bandsman and the Durham Branch Secretary, defeated Ron Linstead, the South Yorkshire Branch Secretary, by 2,169 votes to 1,776. Both were well-known members of the National Executive. There were five other candidates.

When Jack Johnson moved south to take up his post at head office, there was one more election. Jack Amos, formerly Industrial Editor of the *Newcastle Evening Chronicle*, succeeded him both as Durham Branch Secretary and on the National Executive.

In the last three years there have been further changes with the retirement of Sandy Fretwell, after representing the Huddersfield and Heavy Woollen Branches on the executive for twenty-one years, and the election of his successor, Jeff Lindsay of the Thornton Lodge Bowling Club; with the election of Ray Collins, Secretary of the Essington Working Men's Club, for the West Midlands, and then the election of four more new members to the Executive in 1984. These were F. J. Collins, a trustee of the Longbridge Social Club from 1967 to 1974 and Branch President, in the West Midlands; K. Wainwright, a member of ten clubs and Branch Secretary, for the

Bradford, Halifax and Airedale Branch; George Lawson, a member of the Billy Row Working Men's Club since 1957, for the Durham and Cleveland Branch; and Bill Ormerod, Secretary of Burnley and Pendle Branch, who was elected to represent that district after the death of Stan Pickles.

These changes were accompanied by the retirement of Bill Daultrey, the Convalescent Homes Secretary, who had seen through the £1,500,000 programme to build, rebuild, extend, modernize and refurbish the convalescent homes; this was the programme first put forward twenty years ago by Ernest Connelly, and Daultrey earned a very special place in the movement's affection for his work in seeing that all four homes were brought up to their present high standard.

Bill Daultrey was, by the end of 1984, the last officer still working at Club Union House to have worked for the Union in the days before the Second World War; he retired after forty-six years' service, and clubmen throughout the country responded generously to his testimonial, raising well over £20,000.

Thus, in the space of just two or three years, a new generation of younger men was either elected or appointed to nearly every key position in the Union's leadership, on the National Executive and at head office, which may prove in time to have been as dramatic a change in the Union's leadership as the one which occurred a hundred years earlier when the Working Men's Club and Institute Union first became a fully democratic organization. And this change came just as the Union was approaching its 125th anniversary.

There have been other changes, too. That mood of optimism which swept the movement in the sixties and early seventies, with Union membership of over 4,000 clubs in the five years between 1972 and 1976, gave way to feelings of doubt and even pessimism in the eighties. That great programme of sixties building works, when so many clubs had extended their premises, has been followed by years of recession in the Midlands, the North and South Wales in which some clubs have seen their bar takings dwindle, and others, particularly in the mining areas and the steel towns, have had to close.

And yet these same years have also seen a boom in the Union's recreational activities, with some sports growing in popularity, and the Union itself funding over 2,800 trophies for annual contests both at club and branch level, and also in national competitions. These trophies are now worth over £300,000, and make the Union the nation's major organizer of games and contests, with some – notably snooker – attracting tremendous interest.

One young clubman, Steve Davis of the Plumstead Common
Working Men's Club, won the Union's national snooker contest in
1977/78 (and also came runner-up in the individual billiards contest
the same year), and went on to become an international celebrity.
He still keeps in touch with his old club colleagues. The Union has
also produced several other well-known professional players,
notably Doug Mountjoy and Ray Reardon, and there are other
Union stars who have yet to make the decision to turn professional,
such as Terry Parsons (Penygraig Labour Club), Ron Jones
(Abertysswg Working Men's Club) and Steve Webster (Hexthorpe
Working Men's Club).

Likewise in billiards, the Union championships have produced
three outstanding players – Norman Dagley (Hinckley Liberal
Club), Bob Close (Western Social Club) and Alf Nolan (also Western Social Club) – who have dominated all the major contests in
the last ten years.

Besides these major individual contests, which are now important
events in the Club Union sportsmen's calendar, the Union also
stages its annual Team Billiards and Team Snooker championships,
which have become a source of great entertainment for clubmen.
Each individual branch also stages its own local championships,
and there are other national championships in angling, darts and
cribbage. In different parts of the country, there are Union trophies
awarded in the following contests:

Darts	424	All Fours	18
Dominoes	399	Quiz	18
Snooker	270	Cards	16
Cribbage	252	Bagatelle	13
Angling	158	Cage Bird Shows	12
Bowls	132	Whippet Racing	10
Pool	110	Athletics	9
Whist	98	Shove-halfpenny	8
Golf	78	Shooting	6
Skittles	77	Table Bowls	6
Billiards	68	Euchre	6
Horticultural	42	Tug of War	4
Don	40	Dancing	4
Football	37	Phat	4
Racing	32	Cricket	3

There are also nineteen clubs which stage their own Glamorous
Grandmother contests, and fifty that take part in the Queen of
Clubs local contests, which eventually end in the annual Queen of
Clubs beauty contest, which is held every year in Blackpool on the

evening of the Union's Annual Meeting. Within individual clubs, there are often local competitions – for chess, draughts, or singing – and in South Wales and Yorkshire there are clubs with a brass band tradition.

And they all come together through the Union, making the Working Men's Club and Institute Union a totally unique and wholly British institution; there is no other organization like it, anywhere else in the world, although some countries – notably Australia and New Zealand – do have a few working men's clubs. There are others in Malta and Eire.

What makes the British working men's clubs so different is that they share a common national tradition, which is expressed through the Union. In some towns and cities, there are strong local traditions, too. In Ashington, the mining town in Northumberland, there are twenty-six working men's clubs and only three public houses. Sunderland has thirty-nine working men's clubs. In Coventry and Leicester, the two 'club cities', working men's clubs are the main centres of the cities' social life. Areas such as these may have local associations or branches to link the different clubs, but they still come together nationally through the Union. And running through the Union itself, there is a sense of history, born of fellowship, that binds its members together into one movement in a way that is quite unique.

This sense of fellowship has no religious or political boundaries. Members of every faith and persuasion will be found in the Union's clubs, but their beliefs are not a cause of division. Each generation of leaders has kept the Union on a steady course, avoiding controversies of the day, and ensuring that the Union itself speaks for every member club.

As mentioned elsewhere in this narrative, this may mean that changes in national policy are slow to evolve; but it also gives the Union a rare continuity. When a matter is divisive – like race in the sixties or women's rights today – the Union moves forward cautiously; too slowly for some of its critics, perhaps, but not for its members, and that is essential in a movement as broadly based as this.

This sense of continuity is one of the Union's finer qualities, expressing itself in every aspect of the Union's work. Increasingly nowadays it has a family aspect. In many clubs there are now chairmen, secretaries and committee-men holding positions once occupied by their fathers. In some branches, too, there is now a family tradition. And the Union's strictly democratic constitution ensures that branch and national officers are all men steeped in the history and customs of the movement, well-known to their fellow clubmen.

Even in the Union's head office, there has been a longevity that has matched the traditions elsewhere; Gen Ding, with forty-nine years' service, and Bill Daultrey, with forty-six, were not the first and will certainly not be the last members of the Union's staff to devote their working lives to its cause. Even now, after all these changes in the Union's leadership, there are still long-standing employees like Ashley Waker, the Union Accountant, and Fred Cleveland, the Cashier, who have been with the Union for nearly forty years, and there are others like Peter Miller, the Recreation Secretary, and David Macdonald, the Convalescent Homes Secretary, who joined the Union when its offices were still in Clerkenwell Road.

One has to understand these traditions, the loyalty they represent, and the way they complement the contributions made by pioneers like Hodgson Pratt, J. J. Dent and B. T. Hall, or the more recent work of clubmen like Bob Chapman, Tom Nicoll, Frank Castle or Frank Morris, to gain an understanding of the Union as a living entity now going through another period of change, and yet still a body that would be readily recognizable to any of its earliest champions.

Already, the pattern of change is taking shape, if not its final form.

Under its new leadership, the Union has started taking stock of its own position within the State, has effected changes in the Union rules that extend its powers, and has adopted a higher profile in its relationship with Parliament, the Government and other club organizations.

In assessing its own position, the Union National Executive commissioned the leading national firm of estate agents and valuers, John D. Wood, to prepare a valuation of all the Union's properties as at 30 September 1983. This was an exercise that had never been undertaken before in the Union's history, and it was an important one because if the Union ever did need to borrow large sums of money for the purposes of expansion (which, again, is something that it has not done previously in its history), it would need to know what it was worth. The exercise was revealing. John D. Wood advised the executive that Club Union House, built at a cost of approximately £250,000 twenty-five years ago, was now worth approximately £1,000,000. The convalescent home at Broadstairs, built at a cost of approximately £400,000, was now valued at £800,000, and the other three homes were valued thus: Grange

over Sands, £475,000; Saltburn by the Sea, £250,000; and Langland Bay, £487,500. By the time John D. Wood had assessed all
the Union's branch offices, which are nearly all freehold properties,
they were able to advise the executive that the total value of the
Union's property, including those already mentioned, was
£3,293,500.

As part of this same process of assessing its own standing, the
Union also commissioned the first public-opinion poll ever
undertaken within the movement to find out what people thought
of working men's clubs, why some clubs were declining in popularity, and what could be done to reverse that trend. This poll was
conducted in November 1985 by MORI (Market & Opinion Research International Ltd), one of the leading firms in this field, who
regularly undertake polls for the national press. The MORI report,
Public Attitudes Towards Clubs, was delivered to the Union early in
1986, and showed that there are some areas of club management in
which committees need to change if they are to retain the support of
club members.

The poll revealed that two-fifths of all those surveyed thought
that clubs had too many rules and regulations – although active
clubmen tended to disagree. It was also found that 58 per cent of
clubmen who went to their club more than once a week took a
personal interest in the way their club was being run. The report
stated:

> There is a high level of agreement that club committees tend to attract
> 'Little Hitler' types (61% strongly/tend to agree, 15% strongly/tend to
> disagree). Over a quarter of the sample (28%) strongly agree with this
> statement. Despite this, there is still a strong appreciation of the work
> they do. Nearly three-quarters (73%) think they do a good job with
> over two-fifths (45%) thinking they do at least a very good job. Only
> one in ten (11%) think they do a poor job.
> Over four-fifths (83%) of club members have never sat on a com-
> mittee in a social club. This is less true of men, almost a fifth (18%) of
> whom have served on a committee at some time.

On that vexed question of admitting women to full membership
of clubs, the poll found that there was strong agreement that more
clubs should allow women to become full members – with only 8
per cent saying they should not. Among women who used Union
clubs, it was found that over four-fifths (85%) supported full
membership, but among male members the figure was two-thirds
(65%), a clear indication, perhaps, that this change will eventually
come.

Nearly three-quarters of those surveyed (74%) agreed that there was a good community feeling in clubs, and in the case of Union clubs, over a quarter of members (26%) had been members for twenty years or more. When asked what extra facilities they would like to see provided in clubs, nearly a fifth (19%) said they would like a children's room – which was offset by the fact that nearly one in six (17%) did *not* like children's rooms in clubs!

The value of reports like these, from John D. Wood on the Union's properties and from MORI on the opinions of club members, is that the present Executive is endeavouring to make itself better-informed for its dealings with outside organizations, and here, too, the Union is breaking new ground.

In 1983 and 1984, the Union took the initiative in the formation of the first All-Party Parliamentary Committee, representing non-profit-making members' clubs. An inaugural meeting was held at the House of Commons on 14 December 1983, attended by some fifty Members of Parliament and two peers, from all political parties. The Group has now been expanded, and includes fifty-seven Labour MPs, forty Conservative MPs, three Liberal MPs, one Social Democrat and one Plaid Cymru, with four peers and Lord Brooks of Tremorfa as its Secretary.

With the establishment of the Parliamentary Group, the Union also encouraged other club organizations – the Royal British Legion, the National Union of Labour Clubs, the National Union of Liberal Clubs and the Royal Naval Association – to form CORCA, the Committee of Registered Clubs Associations. The Association of Conservative Clubs was also invited, but so far they have not joined. Through CORCA the Union can now make direct representations to the Parliamentary Group, and also to other bodies like the Association of Chief Officers of Police, the Justices' Clerks Society, the Registry of Friendly Societies, or Government Departments to ensure that the Union has a say on all matters affecting clubs.

The way in which all this is being drawn together by the Union's National Executive, with the head office administration modernized by new technology, better communications systems and computers, was explained to the 1986 Annual Meeting by the President, Derek Dormer. First, he dealt with the work of CORCA and their meetings with the Registry of Friendly Societies:

> It was suggested that the Union, through CORCA, should have an ongoing dialogue and from now on we will be meeting at least twice a year to discuss any matter or issue likely to affect clubs with the Registry

to avoid misunderstandings in the future. I was quite interested in this because for some 20 years I have been canvassing an idea to have a Clubs Act in Parliament to bring most of the things which affect the management of clubs under one Act of Parliament to make it easy to understand and study. I was very pleased that the Assistant Chief Registrar made the same proposal and it is the first time I have got anyone to agree.

I have been told in the past it is impossible, but with his support, that gives me hope for the future. It is a very special goal we should set about now and before the turn of the century hope there will be a Clubs Act, and this will come about between Whitehall, the Registry and CORCA. . . .

I feel in all due modesty that your Executive has applied itself diligently to the problems which working people in general and our movement have been obliged to tackle. I feel that the All-Party Parliamentary Group has played a large part in improving the situation of our movement as a whole. I feel there may be a good case for the Union to set up a political and Parliamentary fund on similar lines to trade unions, all of which are, it seems, conscious of the value of Parliamentary involvement. If such a fund were developed by us, it would, of course, be on an all-party basis.

There is absolutely no doubt that your Union has progressed and has gained some remarkable successes. These have been achieved in an honourable way without violence or hysteria. We find that in a democracy most people and authorities will listen to the voice of this Union. It is impossible for anyone to comprehend the vastness of our Union or the benefit for the working population derived from its activities.

Most of the work falls on the 60,000 club volunteers and the 400 who serve on the Executive Committees of our Branches, and without this small army we could not administer our 3,800 clubs; we could not organise and sponsor 2,800 separate sports contests each year; we could not provide convalescence for 5,000 men and women every year; we could not provide technical education for 10,000 every year; we could not take on the work we do for hundreds of charities every year.

The Union is indebted to those men and women who struggle and strive for the future Club Life of Great Britain, and we look forward to the next twelve months, and to June 1987, when we shall celebrate the 125th anniversary of our Union's history with great hope and a great deal of satisfaction.

And there could be little doubt in the minds of those who heard him speak, or who read the report in the next issue of their *Journal*, that the Union was now set on a course that would take it through into the next century and on to its 200th anniversary.

Appendix I

Rules of the Union
First recorded in the Annual Report
for 1875

I. *Membership of the Union*
The Members of the Union shall consist of all such persons as may contribute to its funds not less than £5 in one sum, or who may subscribe not less than 5s annually; of delegates from affiliated Clubs which subscribe not less than 5s annually; and of Honorary Members appointed under Rule II.

II. *Honorary Members of the Union*
The Council may elect as Honorary Members of the Union any persons who have rendered, or may be thought likely to render, special assistance in promotion of the objects of the Union, the reasons for such election being entered in the Minute-book.

III. *Election of Council and Officers*
The Members shall, at their first meeting, and at every subsequent Annual Meeting, elect from their own body a President, Vice-Presidents, Treasurer or Treasurers, together with a Council, not exceeding thirty-six (exclusive of the Representative Members elected under Rule VI), for the management of the business of the Union. The President, Vice-Presidents, and Treasurer or Treasurers shall in addition be ex-officio members of the Council.

IV. *Appointments Made by the Council*
The Council shall annually select from their own body a Chairman and four Vice-Chairmen, and shall have power to appoint all necessary Committees and honorary or paid officers, assigning to the latter power to appoint Vice-Presidents in addition to those appointed at the Annual Meetings.

V. *Executive Committee*
The current business of the Union shall be carried on under the direction

of an Executive Committee, the members of which shall be selected from the Council, and appointed at the first Council meetings held in January, April, July, and October, and at the first Council meeting after the Annual meeting. The Committee shall, at the first meeting after such appointment, select a Chairman for the quarter. Any vacancies in the Executive Committee shall be filled up by the Council at its next ensuing meeting.

VI. *Representative Members of the Council*
The Council shall, immediately after each annual meeting of the Union, elect on their body a number of members, not exceeding nine, belonging to the affiliated Clubs, there being not more than five of these from the Metropolitan Clubs. The affiliated Clubs in the Metropolis, by means of delegates attending at meetings to be held for the purpose at the Union office (or, when unable to send delegates, by means of communications addressed by their respective Committees to such Delegate Meetings), shall suggest names of persons for selection by the Council as Representative Members. Of the names so suggested to the Council the latter shall elect five. No such representative shall be an officer of the Union. Persons appointed under this rule to be Members of the Council shall be, whilst they so continue, Honorary Members of the Council.

VII. *Nomination of Persons as Members of the Council*
It shall be in the power of any member of the Council to nominate persons to fill vacancies in the Council, and such nominations may be made at any regular monthly meeting of the Council. The name of the person so nominated shall be submitted for election at the next ensuing monthly meeting, due notice being given in the circulars convening the meeting. Every such nomination shall be accompanied by the name of the proposer and seconder.

VIII. *Record of Attendance at Council Meetings and Voidance of Office.*
Any member of the Council, not being ex-officio, not having attended meetings of the Council four times during the year, shall thereby cease to be a member.

IX. *Paid Officials*
No paid official of the Union shall be eligible to be a member of the Council with power to vote.

X. *Bye-laws*
The Council shall have power to make Bye-laws for regulating their proceedings.

XI. *Meetings of the Council*
At the meetings of the Council five members shall form a quorum. All questions shall be decided by the vote of the majority. The Chairman

shall only have a vote in case of an equality of votes, and shall have only one vote.

XII. *Special Meetings of the Council*

The President or the Executive Committee may call a special meeting of the Council at any time, and for any purpose, provided they give at least a week's notice, and state the purpose of the meeting to every member of the Council. The Chairman of the Executive Committee or the Honorary Secretaries jointly shall have the power, on the same conditions, of calling such meetings at their discretion, and shall also do so on the requisition of any five members of the Council.

XIII. *Annual Meeting of Members of the Union*

A General Meeting of the members shall be held in each year at such time and place as the Council may deem most suitable. A notice of the time and place of holding the Annual Meeting shall be advertised fourteen days before the day of holding the same, and the members shall be informed seven days previously by circular. In the event of non-members being invited to such meeting, only members shall be entitled to vote.

XIV. *Annual Report and Audit*

The Council shall submit to the Annual Meetings a Report of their proceedings, and a Statement, prepared and certified by a professional or Government Auditor, of all monies received and expended on account of the Union during the year, and also of all its assets and liabilities.

XV. *Special General Meetings of the Society*

A Special General Meeting may be convened by the President, Council or by the Executive Committee; in the latter case, on a requisition signed by not less than twenty members, including at least three of the Council; such requisition to state the object of the proposed meeting. A notice of the meeting to be sent to each member not less than seven days before holding the same. At any General Meetings seven shall constitute a quorum.

XVI. *Alteration of Rules*

These Rules shall not be altered but by a General Meeting, called for the purpose, or by the Annual Meeting, when the intention of any proposed change shall have been stated in the notice calling such meeting.

Bye-laws

1. The meetings of the Council shall be held at the offices of the Union 150 Strand on the last Saturday in every month, at 3 p.m.

2. At least four days' notice shall be given, by the Secretaries, of every meeting of the Council, to every member thereof, with a list of agenda.

3. The Vice-Presidents shall be requested, at the commencement of each year, to signify whether they are desirous of receiving notices of Council meetings, and, in the event of their not answering, it shall be assumed that they are not desirous of notice.

4. No resolution which appears in the Minute-book of the Council shall be altered or rescinded at any subsequent meeting of the Council, unless notice has been given at a previous ordinary meeting of the Council. and inserted in the notice convening the meeting.

5. The Executive Committee shall consist of not more than nine members, and shall meet at least once a week, or oftener if necessary, and three shall form a quorum. No expenditure for objects not authorised previously by the Council, exceeding £10, shall be incurred during the month by the Executive Committee.

6. The minutes of the Executive Committee for the preceding month shall be read at the usual monthly meeting of the Council next following, and the Council shall take such action thereupon as they may see fit.

7. The Organizing Secretary (if such an officer shall have been appointed by the Council) shall have a seat on the Council, and shall· be eligible to the Executive Committee, but without a vote in either case.

8. The duty of the Organizing Secretary shall be principally that of visiting Clubs and of attending meetings held for their establishment or improvement.

9. The Organizing Secretary shall submit a report of his proceedings to the Council at their monthly meetings in such form as may be prescribed from time to time. He shall also submit at each meeting of the Executive Committee next preceding the monthly Council meeting, accounts of his expenditure for the preceding month, and the Committee shall examine such accounts and present them to the Council.

10. The delegates from affiliated Clubs, referred to in Rule VI, shall be formally appointed from time to time by their respective Clubs, and shall be required, whenever attending meetings of delegates summoned by the officers of the Union, to produce credentials of their appointment by their Clubs. Such credentials must bear the signature of the Secretary of the Club which they represent, and must certify that such appointment has been made at a meeting of the members of the Committee of the Club. Such credentials must also be dated, and show for what period the appointment has been made. No Club can appoint more than one delegate for one and the same period.

11. With reference to Rule VIII, a Record-sheet of attendance shall be kept in the Office, and shall be laid before the Executive Committee on the first Friday of each month.

Appendix 2

*Rules of the Working Men's Club and
Institute Union*

Revised and adopted at a Special General Meeting
held at Westminster College Hall on 8 March 1886

Objects

1. To form a centre of communication between the Members of
Working Men's Club and Institutes and others, of all classes, desirous of
improving the condition of the people of the United Kingdom.

2. To help the industrial classes to establish and maintain Clubs and
Institutes where the Members may meet for business, mental improvement, and recreation.

3. To maintain a Circulating Library, with the best works in the English
language, in all departments of Literature, Science, Art, and Politics, for
the use of the Members of Clubs and Institutes affiliated to the Union.

Constitution

4. The Union shall consist of Corporate Members, Members, Honorary
Members, Associates, and Associate Clubs and Institutes.

5. Corporate Members shall be those Clubs and Institutes which shall,
subject to the approval of the Council, be affiliated to the Union, and
shall subscribe to the funds of the Union one half-penny per club-member
per month.

6. Members shall be those who may be elected as such by the Council
of the Union.

7. Honorary Members shall be those who may be elected as such by the
Council of the Union.

8. Associates shall be those Members of Clubs and Institutes which are
Corporate Members; also those Members of Associate Clubs and Institutes
who pay 1s per annum for the Union Associate Card.

9. Associate Clubs and Institutes shall be those Clubs and Institutes
which shall, subject to the approval of the Council, be affiliated to the
Union, and shall subscribe not less than 3s., or such other sum as the
Council may from time to time determine, per year to the funds of the
Union.

Officers

10. The Officers of the Union shall be a President, Vice-President, and a Council; all to be elected annually, and to be eligible for re-election.

11. The President and Vice-Presidents shall be elected annually by the Council previous to the Annual General Meeting, and shall be ex-officio members of the Council.

12. Each Corporate Member paying to the funds of the Union for from fifty to two hundred Associates, and each Associate Club or Institute having a similar number of Associates, may elect one Member of the Council. Two or more Affiliated Clubs or Institutes which do not individually contain fifty Associates may join together to make up that number, for the election of a Member of the Council.

13. Each Corporate Member paying for from two hundred up to five hundred Associates, and each Associate Club or Institute having a similar number of Associates, may elect two Members of the Council.

14. Each Corporate Member paying for any number of Associates above five hundred, and each Associate Club and Institute having a similar number of Associates, may elect three Members of the Council.

15. Any Associate Club or Institute in the Provinces, at a distance of more than twelve miles from Charing Cross, which subscribes not less than 10s annually to the funds of the Union may elect one Member of the Council.

16. The annual Election of Members of Council by Corporate Members, and other Clubs and Institutes entitled to representation, shall take place in April.

17. Twenty-four Members of the Council shall be elected by the Annual General Meeting of the Union. All candidates for these twenty-four seats to be Members or Honorary Members, and to be nominated by a Member or Honorary Member. All nominations to be sent in to the Council at least four weeks before the date of the Annual General Meeting.

18. Any Member of the Council who shall be absent from the Meetings of the Council for six months shall vacate his seat, unless the Council shall determine otherwise.

19. The Council shall appoint a Chairman, a Treasurer, and such other Honorary Officers as they may deem desirable from the Members or ex-officio Members of the Council; also an Auditor, a Secretary, and such other paid officers as may be required, who shall not be ex-officio Members of the Council.

20. Interim vacancies may be filled up by the Council, excepting any vacancy in the representation of Corporate Members or Associate Clubs or Institutes, which shall be filled up by the Club or Institute represented.

Meetings

21. The Annual General Meeting of the Union shall be held during the month of May in each year, for the purpose of confirming minutes, receiving a report from the Council, the balance sheet, and electing twenty-four Members of Council.

22. Special General Meetings shall be held whenever the Council may think it desirable to convene them, or whenever fifty Members of the Union or five hundred Associates make a requisition to the Council for the purpose. Such requisition to state the business for which the meeting is to be called, and the words of the resolution or resolutions, with names of proposers and seconders, to be submitted to the meeting.

23. The date, time and place for holding all General Meetings shall be fixed by the Council, and notice of the same shall be sent to every Member, Honorary Member, and affiliated Club or Institute, at least seven days before the date of the meeting. Corporate Members and Associate Clubs and Institutes to be entitled to send to every General Meeting one Delegate for every hundred or part of one hundred Associates they represent.

24. At all General Meetings, twenty-one Members, Honorary Members, or Delegates from Affiliated Clubs and Institutes, shall form a quorum; but only Members and Honorary Members shall be entitled to vote in the election of Members of the Council. Except at meetings convened by requisition, any business approved by the Council may be taken into consideration, but only when notice of the same has been included in the notice convening the meeting.

25. The Report of the Council shall include the names of Members of Council elected by the Affiliated Clubs and Institutes for the ensuing year, and the notice convening the General Meeting shall give the names of candidates to be submitted to the meeting for election.

26. The Balance-sheet, showing all income and expenditure, shall be made up to the end of March in each year, and, after being certified by the Auditor, shall, with the Annual Report of the Council, be printed and distributed before the Annual General Meeting.

27. Meetings of the Council shall be held on a regular day once in each month. Not less than five shall form a quorum. The Chairman, in addition to his vote as a Member of the Council, shall give a casting vote where the voting is equal.

28. Special Meetings of the Council shall be convened whenever the Council may direct; also when any ten Members of the Council shall make a written request to the officer whose duty it may be to convene the meetings of the Council. Notices convening Special Meetings to state the business for which they are called.

Bye-laws

29. The Council shall have power to make Bye-laws for the regulation of all matters connected with the Union, provided always that such Bye-laws shall not be contrary to the Rules of the Union.

Alteration of Rules

30. The Rules of the Union may be altered only by a majority at a General Meeting; but no proposal for altering any Rule shall be submitted to a General Meeting unless with the approval of the Council, or 500

Associates, or at least 50 Members of the Union, signified in writing. The Union shall only be dissolved upon the recommendation of the Council; and then only after a resolution for that purpose has been carried by a three-fourths majority of those present at two consecutive General Meetings called for the purpose, at least three weeks intervening.

Appendix 3

Rules of the Working Men's Club
and Institute Union Ltd
and
Standing Orders

(*Author's note*. The broad principles by which the Union is governed were agreed in 1889 when the Union was constituted as a Society registered under the Industrial and Provident Societies Act, with each club becoming a member of the Union. There were subsequent amendments in 1910 and 1975, with minor amendments in other years to bring the fees in line with inflation or to incorporate changes made necessary by later legislation. In 1980 a Standing Orders Committee was formed to deal with any matters concerning the Agenda for the annual Council meetings.

To avoid confusion, and to make this appendix useful for reference purposes, these changes have been incorporated below, bringing these Rules up to date as at January 1987.)

1. *Name*

The society shall be called **THE WORKING MEN'S CLUB AND INSTITUTE UNION LIMITED**, hereinafter called the Union. The registered name of the Union shall be kept painted and affixed on the outside of every office or place in which the business of the Union is carried on, in an conspicuous positon, in letters easily legible, and shall be engraven in legible characters on its seal, and shall be mentioned in legible characters in all business letters, notices, advertisements, and other official publications of the Union, and in all bills of exchange, promissory notes, endorsements, cheques, and orders for money or goods, purporting to be signed by or on behalf of the Union, and in all bills, invoices, receipts and letters of credit of the Union.

2. *Objects*

The objects of the Union are: To carry on the business of general advisers, teachers of the doctrine of association for social or ameliorative purposes, publishers, stationers and booksellers, general traders, agents and manufacturers, both wholesale and retail, of any article which may assist the development of clubs or their members. To provide and maintain convalescent homes, or other institutions for the benefit of the members or wives or children or dependents of the members of clubs which are members of the Union. To provide sporting and/or recreational facilities both indoor and outdoor for the benefit of member clubs and members of such clubs; to provide trophies therefore and to make monetary grants in connection therewith. To provide education and/or educational facilities to member clubs and the members of such clubs; to provide lectures and schools at branch and national level and to make monetary grants in connection therewith. The Union shall have full power to do all things necessary, expedient, or considered by it desirable for the welfare and protection or assistance of, or helpful in any manner to its members, and for the accomplishment of all objects specified in its rules.

3. *Registered Office*
The registered office shall be Club Union House, 251–256 Upper Street, London N1 1RY, or such other place as may from time to time be decided by the Executive. In the event of any change in the situation of the registered office, notice of such change shall be sent to the Registrar within 14 days thereafter in the form prescribed by the Treasury regulations.

4. *Members – Clubs*
Members of the Union shall consist of such clubs as shall be admitted to the Union in manner provided by these rules.

5. *Shares*
A club admitted to membership shall hold one share of £4 and from the date of registration of this complete amendment of rules no member shall hold more than one share. Members holding a share or shares of the value of less than £4 at the date of registration of this complete amendment of rules shall forfeit such share or shares to the funds of the Union and be credited with a share of the value of £4 which shall be charged against the balance of unappropriated profits.

Shares shall not be withdrawable or transferable, and no interest or dividend shall be paid or credited thereon. A club shall forfeit its share on ceasing membership from any cause.

6. *Conditions of Membership*
(a) An application for admission to membership shall be in the form prescribed by the Executive, and unless the Executive decide to decline the application it shall be referred to the Branch within which area the club is situate, in order that a visitor or visitors from the Branch may attend the club to investigate and report upon its management; provided always that the Executive may, in its discretion, depute one of its number or one of the Union officers to make such investigation and report. The

name and address of every club applying for admission to the Union shall be published in the *Club and Institute Journal*, and any objection on the part of a club to its admission, and the grounds of such objection shall be stated in writing, and forwarded to the Union General Secretary within 14 days of publication. Subject to the visitors' report being considered satisfactory by the Executive and the club complying with all the Executive's requirements, the Executive shall admit the club to membership and its name shall be entered on the register of clubs which are members of the Union and on the register of shares. A club which is in membership of an organization which embraces licensed proprietary profit making clubs shall not be admitted or continue in membership of the Union.

(b) A club capable of being registered under the Industrial and Provident Societies Acts or under the Friendly Societies Acts shall not be admitted unless it is so registered, or unless the Executive shall for reasons it considers good and sufficient dispense with such registration.

(c) A club which supplies intoxicating liquor shall not be admitted, or, if admitted, shall not continue as a member unless it adopts the following rule, or a rule to similar purpose or effect –

Should any visitor introduced by a member or an Associate pay for intoxicating liquor he shall at once be removed from the club premises. If introduced by an Associate, the Associate shall also be removed. If introduced by a member, the member may be expelled from membership on the fact being duly proved; and it shall be the duty of any officer or member of the club becoming aware of such breach of the rules to report it at once to the secretary or committee.

(d) A club which supplies intoxicating liquor shall not be admitted or if admitted shall not continue as a member which shall have bound or shall bind itself irrevocably to deal with any brewer, distiller or other tradesman.

(e) A club which supplies intoxicating liquor shall not be admitted, or if admitted shall not continue as a member, which distributes any part of the funds of the club in cash payments to members (except in payment for work done or in consideration of bona fide service rendered to the club), or which pays dividends on shares or interest upon loans advanced to the club at a rate of interest exceeding 5 per cent per annum, or 1 per cent per annum above the Co-operative Bank plc base lending rate, whichever is the greater. This limitation shall not however apply when money is borrowed by way of Bank overdraft or by mortgage of the club's premises.

Any club infringing this rule, or evading it by colourable pretence of compliance shall, on the fact being proved, be dealt with in manner provided by rule 8 (c). Provided always that the Executive shall have power in the special circumstances of any particular case to waive this and the preceding section.

(f) Notice of the refusal or acceptance of a club's application for membership shall be sent to the secretary of the club within 28 days after such refusal or acceptance.

7. *Annual Fee*

A club shall subscribe to the funds of the Union an annual fee of £15 or such other sum not exceeding £30 per annum as may be agreed from time to time by a Council meeting. The annual fee shall be due on the first day of October in each year, or in the case of a club being admitted to membership, on the date it is admitted.

8. *Cessation of Membership or Privileges*

(a) A club failing to pay the annual fee provided in Rule 7 before the first day of November shall be suspended from all privileges, and shall have a notice sent to it to that effect, and if the fee is not paid by the first day of December the club shall cease membership of the Union, and its name shall be removed from the register of clubs.

(b) The Executive on being satisfied that a club has ceased to exist shall remove its name from the register of clubs.

(c) A club may be reprimanded suspended from all or some of the privileges of membership or expelled by the vote of two-thirds of the members of the Executive present at an Executive meeting upon a charge of conduct detrimental to the Union, or for refusing admission to an Associate of the Union on grounds of colour, race, nationality or ethnic or national origins. The nature of the charge shall be communicated to the secretary of the club at the club's registered address at least 14 days previous to the date of the said meeting, and the Branch within which area the club is situate may be required to assist by investigation and report. Any club so charged may submit its answer to the charge in writing to the Executive, or representatives of the club may attend the Executive to answer the charge.

(d) A club which shall supply intoxicating liquor to persons other than its own members and Associates shall be given notice by the Executive to discontinue such practice, and, unless it be forthwith discontinued, the club may be expelled from the Union in accordance with the provisions of sub-section (c) of this rule.

9. *Right of Appeal*

A club suspended or expelled shall have the right of appeal to Arbitrators appointed and selected in accordance with Rule 28. No appeal shall be heard unless made within one month of the suspension or expulsion, and in writing addressed to the Union General Secretary accompanied by a deposit of £50 the disposition of which shall be in the direction of the Arbitrators.

The Arbitrators, or a majority of them, shall have power to alter or rescind the suspension or expulsion, and may order either party to bear the cost of the arbitration. There shall be no appeal from the Arbitrators' decision.

10. *Club Statistics and Management*

A club shall furnish by 1st December in each year to the Union Executive a copy of its last accounts and balance sheet, and such statistical and other information regarding the club as may be necessary to enable the Executive to compile its annual report. It shall also from time to time furnish such information concerning its management as the Executive may require, and for this purpose shall receive visitors authorised by the Executive to investigate its management and give them such information and produce such books and documents as may be necessary to enable them to report to the Executive.

Non-compliance with this rule or refusal or neglect on the part of a club to remedy any grave defect of management shall be deemed to be conduct detrimental to the Union within the meaning of Rule 8 (c).

11. *Resgister of Members*

The Executive shall keep, at the registered office, a register of members of the Union, and such register shall be open at all convenient times to inspection, and shall contain the following particulars:

(a) The names and addresses of members
(b) A statement of the number of shares held by each member and of the amount paid or agreed to be considered as paid on the shares of each member
(c) A statement of other property in the Union whether in loans, deposits or otherwise held by each member
(d) The date at which a club was entered in the register as a member and at the date at which any club ceased to be a member
(e) The names and addresses of the officers of the Union with the office held by them respectively and the dates on which they assumed office.

For the purposes of this rule an officer includes every member of the Executive.

The register shall be so constructed that it is possible to open to inspection the particulars entered therein mentioned in paragraphs (a), (d) and (e) hereof without so opening to inspection the other particulars entered therein.

12. *Associates of the Union*

(a) Associate Cards at the price of £1 each and Pass Cards at the price of 20p per quarter shall be supplied to clubs which are members upon condition that holders of such cards (in these rules called 'Associates') conforming to the regulations relating thereto shall be admitted by such clubs to the club premises. After deduction of Value Added Tax at the rate for the time being prevailing 50 per cent of the value of Pass Cards sold each year shall be allocated to the Convalescent Homes. A club which shall accept this condition and supply such Cards to its members and admit Associates, shall incorporate as one of the rules of the club the following:

Admission of Associates

So long as the club shall remain a member of the Union, all Associates of the Union shall subject to the following provisions of this rule be admitted to the club premises, and intoxicating liquor may be sold to them by or on behalf of the club for consumption on the premises. An Associate before being admitted to the club must produce his sub-scription card (showing that his current subscription to his club has been paid), the Associate Card of the Union, and the current Pass Card issued by the Union, and must write his name and that of his club in the Union Associate Book to be kept for that purpose. The doorkeeper or other appointed official shall compare the signature in the book with that on the Associate Card, and on being satisfied that the signatures correspond shall admit the Associate.

Associates shall have the same rights and privileges, and be subject to the same rules and by-laws as ordinary members except that they must not attend at any meeting of the club, or take away intoxicating liquor for consumption off the premises. The committee may refuse admission to Associates or limit their admission to such times and parts of the premises as they think fit in the interests of the club. Notice of such limitations shall be sent to the General Secretary of the Union.

(b) A club shall refuse admission to a person who is under suspension from another Union Club and shall have power to refuse admission to an Associate under the age of 18 or under such age as is the minimum age for membership of the club in question, or a person expelled from a Union Club or in any case where it so thinks fit in the interests of the club.

(c) No club may issue an Associate Card or Pass Card to a member who has been expelled or who is under suspension from any club which is a member of the Union without permission from the Executive of the Branch in which area the club is situate.

(d) A person expelled or who is under suspension from membership of a Union club who holds a valid Associate Card issued by another club must obtain the consent of the Executive of the Branch in which his club membership is retained before he may use such Associate Card. The Branch Executive may cancel or suspend the use of such Associate Card.

(e) Associate and Pass Cards may not be issued to lady members.

(f) Representatives of clubs appointed to attend Union or Branch Council meetings must be holders of Union Associate Cards and current Pass Cards issued by the clubs they represent and Branch representatives to Union Council Meetings must also hold Associate Cards and current Pass Cards.

(g) A person shall not be eligible for nomination as an officer or member of the Executive of the Union or of a Branch, or if elected shall not continue to sit unless he holds a valid Associate Card and current Pass Card issued by a club in the Electoral District which he is seeking to represent.

13. *Council Meetings*

(a) Meetings shall consist of representatives appointed by clubs and by Branches, who shall be termed the Council. A club may appoint one representative for each 200 members or fraction of 200, but no club shall appooint more than three representatives. A Branch may appoint one representative for each 100 clubs or part thereof subject to a maximum of three. Each representative shall have one vote and the meetings of the Council shall be annual and special.

(b) The annual meeting shall be held in March or such other month and at such other place as the Executive may from time to time decide.
The business shall be to:

(i) Receive a printed copy of the report of the Executive for the previous year.
(ii) Receive the account or accounts and balance sheet, as audited, and the report of the auditor on the revenue account or accounts and balance sheet.
(iii) Consider any business as may be submitted by the Executive.
(iv) Consider any motion (other than a motion for amendment of the Union Rules) submitted in writing by the 31st December of the previous year (a) by a Branch; or (b) by a club, provided such motion has been adopted at a Branch Council Meeting. The General Secretary shall by the 1st February in each year send to each club a preliminary agenda of the business to be transacted together with a copy of the annual report and a statement of accounts and balance sheet.

A club with the authority of its Branch Council (or Branch Executive if no Branch Council can be held during February), a Branch or the National Executive may submit in writing an amendment to a motion contained in the preliminary agenda or annual report to the General Secretary not later than the 1st March.

(c) At least 15 days previous to each annual meeting the Union General Secretary shall send by post to each club a notice of the time and place of the meeting, and an agenda of the business to be transacted.

(d) A club or Branch proposing to send representatives to the annual meeting shall notify the Union General Secretary not later than ten days previous to the meeting of the names and addresses of the representatives appointed to attend the meeting, and a copy of the annual report and a statement of accounts and balance sheet shall be sent to each representative.

(e) A special meeting shall be convened by the Union General Secretary by direction of the Executive, or upon a requisition signed on behalf of 75 clubs, by the Secretary of each on the instruction of its committee and lodged with the Union General Secretary at the registered office. The meeting shall be held at the registered office or such other place as the Executive may decide.

(f) A special meeting shall not be competent to transact any business other than that specified in the notice convening it.

(g) Should the Union General Secretary not convene a special meeting within six weeks after receiving a duly signed requisition the requisitionists may convene the meeting and shall have a claim upon the Union for all reasonable expenses properly incurred in convening it.

(h) A notice convening a special meeting shall state the time and place thereof, and the purpose for which it is convened, and a copy of the notice shall be sent by post to each Union club not less than six clear days before the day of meeting, unless the Executive direct a shorter notice be given.

(i) No special meeting shall proceed to business unless at least 75 representatives be present within half an hour after the time of meeting, otherwise the meeting if convened by requisition shall be dissolved, but if convened by direction of the Executive it shall stand adjourned for at least four clear days of which adjournment notice shall be sent by post to each club.

(j) The President of the Union or in his absence the Vice-President, or in his absence a member of the Executive shall preside at every meeting of the Council and shall have a casting vote only.

(k) No representative, except by special leave of the meeting, shall take part in any meeting unless he has produced the official credential form or card issued by the Union for the meeting.

(l) Elections of Scrutineers shall be by ballot of the representatives at the Council meeting. Nominations must be handed to the General Secretary or in his absence the Assistant General Secretary at such time or times as shall be announced before the meeting commences. The names of those nominated will be announced to the representatives during the meeting and each representative will be supplied with a voting card on which he will enter the names of the four scrutineers of his choice. Such card will at the close of the meeting be placed in ballot boxes to be provided.

The votes so recorded will be counted under the supervision of the General Secretary or in his absence the Assistant General Secretary and the result of the ballot will be published in the issue of the *Journal* then next following.

(m) To facilitate the proper conduct of Council there shall be a Standing Orders Committee which shall consist of four members of the Executive and four persons appointed by Branches (one from each of four Branches in rotation with each Branch Appointee serving for two years). The Union President or, in his absence, the Union Vice-President, or in the absence of both such officers, an appointed member of the Committee shall take the chair. The duties of such Committee will be to consider all motions and amendments to motions proposed by Clubs or Branches and where necessary to call together the Movers of such motions or amendments thereto for consultation and consider all such matters as may be referred to them by the Council, the Executive or the Chairman of Council.

14. *Executive*

(a) The Union shall be managed by a committee to be called the Executive which shall be elected every two years. One-third of the members thereof shall form a quorum.

The President and Vice-President shall be members of the Executive.

(b) For the purposes of the election of the Executive, clubs shall be grouped into electoral districts according to the following schedule. Each electoral district shall be entitled to one representative on the Executive where the number of clubs therein when nominations close is less than 200, and to a further representative if the number of clubs is over 200, and another representative if the number of clubs is 300 or more.

1. North-East Metropolitan Branch Clubs
2. North-West Metropolitan Branch Clubs
3. South-East Metropolitan Branch Clubs
4. Kent Branch Clubs
5. South Wales Branch Clubs
6. Monmouthshire Branch Clubs
7. Hampshire Branch Clubs
8. Wiltshire and Western Counties Branch Clubs
9. South-East Midlands Branch Clubs
10. Leicestershire Branch Clubs
11. Derbyshire Branch Clubs
12. West Midland Branch Clubs
13. North Staffs, South Cheshire and North Wales Branch Clubs
14. Warwickshire Branch Clubs
15. South Yorkshire Branch Clubs
16. Bradford, Halifax and Airedale Branch Clubs
17. Huddersfield Branch and Heavy Woollen Branch Clubs
18. Wakefield Branch Clubs
19. Doncaster Branch Clubs
20. Leeds Branch and York City Branch Clubs
21. Northumberland Branch Clubs
22. Durham Branch and Cleveland Branch Clubs
23. Manchester Branch
24. Burnley & Pendle and Cumbria & District Branch Clubs
25. Scottish Branch Clubs

The Executive shall have discretion to create a new Electoral District when the number of clubs within a present Electoral District reaches 200 or more, but this discretion may only be exercised when the number of clubs within a Branch forming part of the present Electoral District is 75 or more.

(c) A person shall not be eligible for nomination or election or, if elected, shall not continue to sit unless he is a financial member of a club within the area of nomination and election, but any club may nominate a member of any other club within the said area.

A person shall not be eligible for election to the Executive or if elected, shall not continue to sit, who is the holder of a Justices' Licence for the sale of intoxicants, or who shall become the representative or agent of any firm supplying intoxicants, or who is in receipt of remuneration, commission or similar payment on account of intoxicants supplied to or by clubs. Provided always that this restriction shall not apply to an officer or representative of a co-operative society, or company, the shares in which are held exclusively by or on behalf of clubs and/or by members of clubs.

A person who is a candidate for the office of President or Vice-President shall not be eligible as a candidate for the Executive.

(d) Elections shall be by ballot, conducted in the following manner:

Not later than the 30th day of September in each alternate year the Union General Secretary shall send to each club a nomination paper, which shall entitle the club to nominate as many candidates as there are members to be elected for the electoral division in which the club is situate. Such nomination paper shall be returned to the Union General Secretary not later than the 23rd day of October.

A person shall not be nominated without his consent, and the Union General Secretary shall obtain such consent in writing before placing upon the ballot paper the name of the person nominated.

Not later than the 14th day of November, the Union General Secretary shall send each club a ballot paper on which the names of the persons nominated shall appear in alphabetical order, and each club may vote for as many candidates as there are vacancies to be filled. Each vote given shall be counted as equal to the number of representatives which the club is entitled to send to a Council meeting under Rule 13, section (a).

Ballot papers must be returned so as to be received at the registered office of the Union not later than the 14th day of December.

The votes shall be counted under the supervision of the Union General Secretary, or in his absence the Union Assistant General Secretary, by four scrutineers elected at the Annual Meeting preceding the election. In the event of two or more candidates receiving an equal number of votes, the names of such candidates shall be written on slips of paper, which shall be so placed that the names are concealed and the scrutineers shall elect one of their number to draw as many slips as there are vacancies to be filled and the candidates whose names are so drawn shall be declared duly elected. Any vacancy arising amongst the scrutineers shall be filled by the Executive.

(e) Each member of the Executive (including the officers) shall be entitled whilst engaged upon any duties properly attaching to his office, to recoupment for expenses at the rate (in addition to the travelling fare) of £6 for each day, with a further allowance of £6 for hotel expenses if necessarily away from home on any night, both of these rates may from time to time be increased by a Council meeting.

(f) A member of the Executive being absent from two consecutive meetings shall vacate his seat unless he sends an explanation which the Executive consider satisfactory.

(g) Any vacancy arising on the Executive may be filled by the Executive from the membership of the clubs in the electoral district in which the vacancy arises, or the Executive may order that the vacancy be filled by ballot of such clubs.

(h) The Executive shall meet once a month, but a special meeting of the Executive may be called by the Union General Secretary on a matter of urgency or on request being made in writing to him by at least one-third of the members of the Executive stating the special object for which the meeting is required. The President or in his absence the Vice-President shall take the chair at all meetings of the Executive, or in the absence of both of them such person as the meeting shall appoint.

(i) The Executive shall control all business carried on by or on account of the Union. It shall from time to time engage, remove, or discharge all employees other than the Union General Secretary, and fix their duties, salaries, or other remuneration, and may require them to give security in such form as it may approve or determine.

(j) The Executive may appoint sub-committees, but no sub-committee shall incur any liability without the consent of the Executive.

15. *Officers*

(a) The Union shall have the following officers: A President, Vice-President and General Secretary.

(b) The President and Vice-President shall be elected at the same time and for the same period as members of the Executive and they shall remain in office until their successors are appointed. Any club may nominate one candidate for each office, and a voting paper shall be sent to each club, containing the names of the persons so nominated. Should a vacancy occur in the office of President, or of Vice-President, the Executive may either order an election to take place by ballot of the clubs, or may themselves fill the vacancy. A person appointed to fill a vacancy shall hold office until the next election.

The President shall receive an honorarium at the rate of £250 and the Vice-President an honorarium at the rate of £150 per annum, payable in December of each year or such earlier month as he or they may cease to hold office in which case the rate shall be assessed in proportion to the annual rate. Both of these rates may from time to time be increased by a Council Meeting.

(c) General Secretary: There shall be a General Secretary of the Union who shall be elected by a ballot of the whole of the clubs of the Union, and arrangements for such election shall be made by the Executive whenever occasion may require. Each vote given shall be counted as equal to the number of representatives which the club is entitled to send to the Council under Rule 13, section (a). The General Secretary's salary shall be fixed by the Executive and he shall be removable by a Special General Meeting called for that purpose. The following shall be his duties.

(i) He shall summon and attend and keep minutes of all meetings of the Council, of the Executive, and if so required by the Executive, of any sub-committee

(ii) He shall make such returns as the Executive require

(iii) He shall have charge of the documents and other papers of the Union, and shall keep the accounts in such manner as the Executive direct.

(iv) He shall keep all the books and accounts required to be kept under these rules or the Industrial and Provident Societies Acts, and shall receive all monies due from clubs and others, and pay them into the bank at such times and in such manner as the Executive shall direct.

(v) He shall prepare and send all returns required to be made to the Registrar of Friendly Societies

(vi) He shall in all things act in the discharge of his duties under the direction and control of the Executive.

16. *Removal of Members of Executive*

A member of the Executive may be removed from office at any time by the vote of not less than two-thirds of the representatives present and entitled to vote at a special meeting of the Council, called for that purpose.

17. *Accounts of and Security by Officers and Employees*

(a) It shall be the duty of every officer or employee of the Union and its Branches having the receipt or charge of money, his executors or administrators, at such time as the Executive may direct, or upon demand made, or notice in writing given or left at his last or usual place of residence, to give in his account, as may be required by the Executive to be examined and allowed or disallowed by them and on the like demand or notice to pay over all moneys and deliver all property for the time being in his hands or custody to such person as they appoint.

(b) Every officer or employee of the Union and its Branches having receipt or charge of money shall be covered by a Fidelity Insurance Policy in such sum as the Executive may determine.

18. *Books of Account and Inspection*

All books of account, securities, documents, and papers of the Union other than such (if any) as are directed by the Executive to be kept elsewhere, shall be kept at the registered office, in such manner and with such provision for their safety as the Executive may from time to time direct.

Any club or person having an interest in the funds may inspect all the books of account and the particulars in the register of members except those mentioned in paragraphs (b) and (c) of Rule 11 at all reasonable times, but no person unless an officer of the Union or specially authorised by the Executive shall have the right to inspect the loan or deposit account of any other club or person without the written consent of such club or person.

19. *Payment by Cheques*

All payments above £200 shall be made by cheques, signed by such persons as may be appointed from time to time by the Executive for that purpose.

20. *Audit of Accounts*

1. The Union shall in each year of account appoint a qualified auditor to audit its accounts and balance sheet for that year. For the purposes of this rule 'qualified auditor' means a person who is a qualified auditor under section 7 of the Friendly and Industrial and Provident Societies Act 1968.

2. Save as provided in paragraph (3) of this rule every appointment of an auditor shall be made by resolution of a general meeting of the Union.

3. The Executive may appoint an auditor to fill any casual vacancy occurring between general meetings of the Union.

4. An auditor appointed to audit the accounts and balance sheet of the Union for the preceding year of account (whether by a general meeting or by the Executive) shall be re-appointed as auditor of the Union for the current year of account (whether or not any resolution expressly re-appointing him has been passed) unless

(a) a resolution has been passed at a general meeting of the Union appointing somebody instead of him or providing expressly that he shall not be re-appointed or

(b) he has given to the Union notice in writing of his unwillingness to be re-appointed or

(c) he is ineligible for appointment as auditor of the Union for the current year of account or

(d) he has ceased to act as auditor of the Union by reason of incapacity.

Provided that a retiring auditor shall not be automatically re-appointed by virtue of this rule if notice of an intended resolution to appoint another person in his place has been given in accordance with paragraph (5) of this rule and the resolution cannot be proceeded with because of the death, incapacity or ineligibility of that person.

5. A resolution at a general meeting of the Union (i) appointing another person as auditor in place of a retiring auditor or (ii) providing expressly that a retiring auditor shall not be re-appointed shall not be effective unless notice of the intention to move it has been given to the Union not less than 28 days before the meeting at which it is moved. On receipt by the Union of notice of the intention to move any such resolution the Union shall give notice of the resolution to member clubs and to the retiring auditor in accordance with section 6 of the Friendly and Industrial and Provident Societies Act 1968, and shall give notice to member clubs in accordance with that section of any representations made or intended to be made by the retiring auditor.

6. None of the following persons shall be appointed as auditor of the Union:

(a) An officer or servant of the Union
(b) A person who is a partner of or in the employment of or who employs an officer or servant of the Union or
(c) A body corporate

7. The auditor shall in accordance with section 9 of the Friendly and Industrial and Provident Societies Act 1968 make a report to the Union on the accounts examined by him and on the revenue account or accounts and the balance sheet of the Union for the year of account in respect of which he is appointed.

8. The auditor shall have a right of access at all times to the books, deeds and accounts of the Union and to all other documents relating to its affairs, and shall be entitled to require from the officers of the Union such information and explanations as he thinks necessary for the performance of the duties of the auditor.

21. *Annual Return to Registrar*
The Union General Secretary shall send to the Registrar of Friendly Societies once in every year, not later than 31st March an annual return relating to the Union's affairs for the period required by the Industrial and Provident Societies Acts, to be included in the return, together with a copy of the report of the auditor on the Union's accounts for the period included in the return and a copy of each balance sheet made during that period and of any report of the auditor on that balance sheet. The annual return shall be made up for the period beginning with the date to which the Union's last annual return was made up, and ending with the date of the last balance sheet published by the Union before 31st March in the following year, or if the date of that balance sheet is earlier than 31st August or later than 31st January, with 31st December. The annual return

must be made in the form prescribed by the Chief Registrar, and contain such particulars as may from time to time be required in the form.

A copy of the last annual return, together with a copy of the report of the auditor on the accounts and balance sheet shall be supplied gratuitously on demand to every member or person interested in the funds of the Union.

In the event of the Union being dissolved in accordance with the provisions of Rule 32 the last annual return shall be made up to the date of the instrument of dissolution.

22. *Seal of the Union*

The seal of the Union shall have the device of a circle, containing the portrait of Edward McEnery and its registered name in the margin. The seal shall be kept in the custody of the Union General Secretary, and shall be used only under the authority of a resolution of the Executive, and in the presence of two members of the Executive and the Union General Secretary, or in his absence the Union Assistant General Secretary, all of whom shall witness the sealing of the document.

23. *Loans*

(a) The Executive may obtain, on such terms as to the time and manner of repayment as it thinks fit, advances of money at interest not exceeding 5 per cent per annum or 1 per cent above the Co-operative Bank plc base lending rate, whichever is the higher (except money borrowed by way of bank overdraft or on mortgage of the Union's premises) for the purposes of the Union from time to time from any person, society, company or other organisation, whether a member of the Union or not, upon the security of agreements, or promissory notes, bills of exchange, or of mortgages (either legal or equitable) of its property.

(b) The total amount so obtained shall not exceed for the time being £2,000,000.

24. *Power to Receive Deposits*

The Executive, within the limit mentioned in Rule 23 (b) may receive any sums of money from clubs or other bodies or persons, on deposit at interest, repayable on such notice being not less than two clear days, as they fix from time to time, provided that such deposits shall be received in instalments of not more than £2 in any one payment, nor more than £50 in all from any one depositor.

25. *Investments*

The Executive may invest the funds of the Union in any investment in which Trustees are, for the time being by law, authorised to invest trust funds and in the shares or on the security of society registered under the Industrial and Provident Societies Acts, or under the Building Societies

Act, or of any company registered under the Companies Acts or incorporated by Act of Parliament or by the charter provided that such society or company has its liability limited.

26. *Branches*

(a) Any number of clubs within prescribed areas as may from time to time be fixed by the Executive may, with the approval of the Executive, form themselves into a Branch for carrying out locally the objects of the Union. Each Branch may elect, by such method it chooses, a committee and such officers as it may deem necessary. An officer or member of a Branch committee may be removed by the Executive on the grounds of dishonesty, gross incompetence, or neglect of duty, or refusal to carry out the instructions of the Executive or by reason of his having been guilty of conduct which in the opinion of the Executive may discredit the Union. The Executive shall have power to allocate such sums as it may deem necessary to assist any Branch to meet the expenses it may properly incur. The funds of each Branch are the property of the Union, and each Branch shall have power of expenditure limited to its funds. A Branch shall not incur liabilities beyond this without the consent of the Executive of the Union.

(b) A person shall not be eligible as an officer or member of a Branch Committee, or if elected shall not continue to hold office who is the holder of a Justices' Licence for the sale of intoxicants, or who shall become the representative or agent of any firm supplying intoxicants, or who is in receipt of remuneration, commission, or similar payment on account of intoxicants supplied to or by clubs. Provided always that this restriction shall not apply to an officer or representative of a co-operative society, or company, the shares in which are held exclusively by, or on behalf of clubs and/or by members of clubs.

(c) Branches may hold general meetings at such time and place as their Committee may determine, at which the President, Vice-President and General Secretary of the Union shall have the right to attend. A copy of the minutes of such meetings shall be sent to the Union General Secretary within 14 days. He shall submit them to the next meeting of the Executive. Branch rules and any proposed amendments thereto and all procedure and acts of the Branches shall be subject to the approval of the Union Executive and no Branch shall in any matter act contrary to the policy of the Union as decided by the Executive.

(d) Each Branch committee may appoint a representative or representatives in accordance with the provisions of Rule 13 (a) to attend the Annual Meeting of the Union, and the travelling expenses of such representative or representatives and an allowance upon the scale fixed by Rule 14 (e) shall be paid out of the general funds of the Union.

27. *Application of Profits*

Any profits which may accrue shall be applied as follows:
1. In reduction of the value of the furniture, fittings, fixed stock and

plant, at the annual rate of not less than 10 per cent, and of not less than $2\frac{1}{2}$ per cent on lands and buildings.

2. To a General Fund to be used as follows –

(a) In promoting mutual intercourse between members and others interested in improving the condition of the people of the British Commonwealth of Nations.

(b) In promoting and defending the interests of clubs; in the Press or the Courts of Law or in Parliament as occasion may demand.

(c) In promoting education by the establishment of classes, examinations, and scholarships, in providing lectures, and in assisting any associations providing educational facilities for working men and women.

(d) In maintaining circulating and reference libraries of the best works in all departments of literature, science, art and politics, for the use of members.

(e) In promoting such social, provident and recreative objects as may from time to time be deemed desirable.

(f) In the provision and maintenance of, or subscription to, convalescent homes or other institutions.

(g) In contributing to any Superannuation, Provident or Pensions Fund, which may be established for or by the Officers and Staff of the Union.

(h) Any other lawful purpose determined upon by the Executive.

28. *Disputes*

All disputes arising between a club which is a member of the Union or a club which has for not more than six months ceased to be a member, or any person claiming through such a club or under the Union rules and the Union or any officer thereof shall be dealt with as follows:

(a) *Appointment of Arbitrators*

There shall be six arbitrators who shall be appointed by a meeting of the Council, none of whom shall be officers or members of the Union Executive or a Branch Committee.

(b) *Mode of Selection*

In any case of dispute the Union General Secretary or such other person as the Executive may direct, shall, in the presence of some person appointed by the complaining club, write the names of the arbitrators for the time being upon separate pieces of paper, and place them so that the names shall be concealed. The representative of the complainant club shall draw out the papers one by one and the persons whose names appear on the first three papers drawn shall be the arbitrators to decide the dispute and the persons whose names appear on the next three papers drawn shall be in reserve in case any one or more of the three arbitrators chosen are unable to act.

(c) Any vacancy arising amongst the arbitrators shall be filled by the next meeting of the Council.

(d) Two arbitrators shall be competent to hear and decide any dispute, but, if they differ, the dispute shall be determined by one of the other arbitrators.

(e) With the consent of the Executive and of the club a dispute may be referred to the Chief Registrar of Friendly Societies for determination, in which case the foregoing provisions of this rule shall not apply.

(f) The costs of an arbitration shall be borne as the arbitrators direct, and each party shall deposit £50 to abide their decision.

(g) The decision of the arbitrators or a majority of them shall be binding and there shall be no appeal from their decision.

29. *Statutory Application to the Registrar*

(a) Any 10 Union clubs which have been members for not less than 12 months immediately preceding the date of the application may apply to the Registrar in the form prescribed by the Treasury Regulations to appoint an accountant or actuary to inspect the books of the Union and to report thereon, pursuant to Section 47 of the Industrial and Provident Societies Act 1965.

(b) It shall be the right of 100 members, by an application in writing to the Chief Registrar, signed by them in the forms respectively prescribed by the Treasury Regulations:

(i) To apply for the appointment of an inspector or inspectors to examine into the affairs of the Union and to report thereon; or

(ii) To apply for the calling of a special meeting of the Union.

30. *Supply of Rules*

It shall be the duty of the Executive to provide the Union General Secretary with a sufficient number of copies of the rules, to enable him to deliver to any person on demand a copy of such rules on payment of a sum not exceeding 10p and the duty of the Union General Secretary to deliver such copies accordingly.

31. *Alteration of Rules*

Any rule of the Union may be rescinded or altered, and any new rule may be made, in the following manner:

(a) A club may, pursuant to a vote of the majority of members present at a General Meeting, give notice to the Secretary of the Branch in which area the club is siuate, not less than 28 days before a Branch Council Meeting, of its intention to move at such Council Meeting an amendment of these rules. Details of the proposed amendment shall be supplied with the notice.

(b) The Branch Secretary shall place such proposed amendment on the agenda for the next Branch Council Meeting, and if the proposed amendment is approved by the votes of at least two-thirds of the Delegates present at such meeting, he shall give notice thereof to the

Union General Secretary at least 60 days before any Union Council Meeting.

(c) The Union General Secretary shall thereupon place the amendment on the agenda for the next Union Council meeting for discussion only but no vote shall be taken thereon. Thereafter the proposed amendment shall be referred to all Union Branches to be voted upon at Branch Council Meetings each club having one vote. Provided that where the next Council Meeting of any Branch is not due to be held within a period of eight weeks following the date of the Union Council Meeting, the Branch Executive shall (i) call a Special Council Meeting, such Meeting to be held within the said period of eight weeks, or (ii) conduct a postal vote within the said period of eight weeks.

(d) An amendment shall require at least two-thirds of the total votes cast to be carried.

(e) Each Branch Secretary shall within 10 days send the result of the voting on the proposed amendment to the Union General Secretary whose report, together with a digest of the voting, shall be published in the following issue of the *Club and Institute Journal*.

(f) Nothing in this rule shall prevent the Union Executive from placing any proposal for amendment of rules on the agenda of a Union Council Meeting for discussion, and thereafter it shall be referred to the Branches and voted upon in accordance with sub-clauses (c) and (d) of this rule.

(g) No proposal for amendment of these rules which has been defeated shall again be proposed (except by consent of the Union Executive) until a period of three years has elapsed since its last previous consideration at a Union Council Meeting.

(h) No amendment of rules shall be valid until registered with the Registrar of Friendly Societies.

32. *Dissolution*

The Union may at any time be dissolved by the consent of three-fourths of the members, testified by the signatures of the duly authorised signatories appointed by each to an instrument of dissolution in the form provided by the Treasury Regulations.

33. *Value Added Tax*

Where under any of the provisions of these rules or any amendment thereto for the time being in force any sum of money is payable to the Union by a member club whether by way of subscription or otherwise and such payment attracts Value Added Tax then, unless any rule specifically provides to the contrary, a member club shall in addition pay to the Union such further sum as shall be equal to the amount of Value Added Tax at the rate for the time being in force attributable to such sum.

STANDING ORDERS
FOR UNION COUNCIL MEETINGS

1. Every meeting shall have a chairman, who, in the absence of the President, shall be the Vice-President, or, in his absence, a member of the Executive.

2. The chairman shall not vote unless the votes are equal, when he shall have a casting vote.

3. The chairman shall be removed only upon a vote of two-thirds of those voting.

4. A decision of the chairman shall be challenged only by a motion, 'That the chairman do leave the chair.' This, if seconded, shall be put to the meeting forthwith.

5. All persons must be seated, and no one shall speak while the chairman is standing.

6. Any person disobeying the ruling of the chairman may be suspended for the remainder of the meeting, upon the motion of the chairman or of two others, put without debate and carried. Should any delegate so suspended refuse to submit to the order of the chairman and decline to leave the meeting, the club for which he is a representative shall be notified and such offender shall not again be admitted as a delegate for a period of two years.

7. Any person who has not spoken to the question before the meeting may, without notice or speech in support, move, 'That the question be now put' or 'That the meeting proceed to next business', or that the debate or the meeting be adjourned. Either of these motions may, at the discretion of the chairman, be forthwith put without seconding, debate or amendment.

8. When an amendment to a motion is submitted no second amendment shall be taken into consideration until the first amendment is disposed of. If that amendment is adopted, it shall then be put as an original motion, upon which a further amendment may be moved. If the first amendment is negatived, then a further amendment may be moved to the original motion, but only one amendment shall be submitted to the meeting for discussion at one time.

9. All amendments must be relevant to the motion, and must be submitted in writing to the chairman before the mover speaks thereon. No person shall be at liberty to move more than one amendment upon any motion.

10. No motion or amendment may be withdrawn except by consent of the meeting.

11. The mover of a motion or amendment shall be limited to ten minutes, and all subsequent speakers to five minutes. The mover of a motion only shall be allowed to reply, and shall confine his reply to ten minutes and to answering objections raised during the debate. The limit of time herein mentioned may be extended by a vote of not less than

two-thirds of those voting. On a vote being taken the chairman may appoint tellers to count the votes.

12. No person (other than the mover of an original motion) shall speak more than once upon any motion or amendment, but any person may rise to a 'point of order' or for personal explanation, or to ask a question; provided he does so as soon as possible, and adheres strictly thereto.

13. Motions adjourned shall have precedence at the next meeting over new motions.

14. No motion of amendment may be submitted which is the same in substance as a motion or amendment which has been voted upon until a period of not less than twelve months has elapsed, except by consent of the Union Executive.

15. If disorder should arise, the chairman, acting on his discretion as a matter of right, can quit the chair and announce the adjournment of the meeting, and by that announcement the meeting is immediately adjourned and no business subsequently transacted will be valid.

Appendix 4

*Presidents of the Working Men's
Club and Institute Union*

1863–1867   Lord Brougham
1868   The Earl of Caernarvon (?)
1869   Hon. G. Brodrick   (?)
1870   no record
1871   no record
1872   Rt Hon. A. J. Mundella, MP
1873   Rt Hon. the Marquis of Lorne, KT, MP
1874   The Duke of Westminster
1875   Earl Rosebery
1876–1881   Very Rev. Arthur Penrhyn Stanley, Dean of Westminster
1882–1885   Sir Thomas Brassey
1885–1902   Hodgson Pratt
1902–1909   Stephen Seaward Tayler
1909–1922   John James Dent
1922–1938   Robert Richardson, MP
1938–1945   John Thompson
1946–1969   Edward McEnery, OBE
1970–1981   Arthur Bates
1981 to date   Derek Dormer

Appendix 5

General Secretaries of the Working
Men's Club and Institute Union

1862–1867	Rev. Henry Solly
1867	Hon. Auberon Herbert, Hodgson Pratt and Thomas Paterson become joint Honorary Secretaries
1883–1893	John James Dent
1893–1929	B. T. Hall
1930–1951	R. S. Chapman, CBE
1951–1964	Frank R. Castle, MBE
1965–1973	John B. Holmes
1973–1982	Frank O. Morris, CBE
1982 to date	Jack Johnson

Appendix 6

*Officers of the Working Men's Club
and Institute Union Ltd*

PRESIDENT
D. J. Dormer, FSVA, CMD
50 Meadow Walk, Higham Ferrars, Wellingborough, Northants

VICE-PRESIDENT
B. Winters, CMD
11 Meadow Court, South Elmsall
West Yorkshire

GENERAL SECRETARY
J. Johnson
Club Union House, 251–256 Upper Street,
London N1 1RY

AUDITOR
Grant Thornton

EXECUTIVE COMMITTEE
Ahern, J. CMD, 146 Clarence Court, Clarence Road, Grays, Essex
Amos, J., 40 The Briary, Shotley Bridge, Consett, County Durham
Barrowcliffe, K., JP, 176 Greenside Lane, Droylsden, Manchester
Collins, F. J., 34 Norman Road, Northfield, Birmingham, B31 2EW
Cooke, J. F., JP, CMD, 12 Papenham Green, Canley, Coventry, West Midlands
Drysdale, H., 7 Eleventh Row, Ashington, Northumberland
Ellis, J., 15A Worrall Street, Morley, Leeds, Yorkshire
Etheridge, R. J., Greensleeves, Westbeams Road, Sway, Lymington, Hampshire
Flanaghan, T. S., 3 Reynolds Place, Leicester
Garnett, A., 40 Windmill Balk Lane, Woodlands, Nr Doncaster, Yorkshire
Hughes, C. P., BA, CMD, 2 Pencoed Avenue, The Common, Pontypridd, Mid-Glamorgan

Jones, W. H., CMD, 42 Gillmans Road, Orpington, Kent, BR5 4LB
Lawrence, N.A ., 130 Churchyard Avenue, Swindon, Wilts, SN2 1NN
Lawson, G., 30 Myrtle Grove, Roddymoor, Crook, County Durham
Lindsay, J. W., 10 Yew Green Avenue, Lockwood, Huddersfield, West
    Yorkshire, HD4 5EW
Linstead, R. C., CMD, 20 Churchfield Avenue, Darton, Barnsley, South
    Yorkshire, S75 5DR
Little, T. W., 8 Laburnum Close, Townville, Castleford, West Yorkshire
MacMahon, D. J., CMD, 41 Richmond Road, Derby
Morgan, T., 3 Miskin Street, Treherbert, Rhondda, Mid-Glamorgan
Ormerod, W., CMD, 9 Mardenhall Road, Nelson, Lancashire, BB9 9PA
Parry, L. R., JP, 3 Stephen Crescent, Govilon, Abergavenny, Gwent
Ramshaw, J. T., JP, 52 Southcroft, Fatfield Village, Washington, Tyne
    and Wear, NE38 8RD
Robinson, S., 4 Powell Street, Hanley, Stoke-on-Trent, ST1 5JR
Ridd, J. T., 83 Cottingham Road, London SW8 4RN
Smith, W., 18 Campview Terrace, Danderhall, Dalkeith, Midlothian
Thompson, D., CMD, 45 New Rough Hay, Ingol, Preston, Lancashire
Tobin, J. C., 1 Walmer Close, Crowthorne, Berkshire, RG11 6RF
Wainwright, K., CMD, 72 Raeburn Drive, Bradford, West Yorkshire
Wood, R., 75 Fitzroy Street, Ashton-under-Lyne, Greater Manchester
Wright, C. J., 119 Lutterworth Road, Northampton, NN1 5JL

BRANCH SECRETARIES
LONDON AND HOME COUNTIES

1. *North-East.* J. Ahern, CMD, 77 London Road, Grays, Essex
2. *North-West.* J. C. Tobin, 1 Walmer Close, Crowthorne, Berkshire
3. *South-East.* Bernard Guess, 56 Oyster Lane, Byfleet, Surrey
4. *Kent.* W. H. Jones, CMD, 42 Gillmans Road, Orpington, Kent

PROVINCIAL

5. *Bradford and Halifax.* K. Wainwright, CMD, Brownroyd WMC,
    Plumpton Street, Bradford, Yorkshire, BD8 9AR
6. *Burnley and Pendle.* W. Ormerod, CMD, 39 Chapel Street, Nelson,
    Lancashire, BB9 9SW
7. *Cleveland and District.* Dennis Brearley, 10 Oldgate, Easton-under-Nab,
    Middlesbrough, Cleveland
8. *Cumbria and District.* K. Brown, CMD, 1 Pennygill, Flimby, Maryport,
    Cumbria
9. *Derbyshire.* D. J. MacMahon, CMD, 32 Loudon Street, Derby
10. *Doncaster and District.* C. Bailey, CMD, c/o Doncaster Trades and
    Labour Club, 7 Northbridge Rd, Doncaster, Yorkshire
11. *Durham County.* J. Amos, Club Union House, Flass Corner, Durham
12. *Hampshire and Isle of Wight.* R. J. Etheridge, Greensleeves, Westbeams
    Road, Sway, Hants, SO4 0AE

13. *Heavy Woollen District.* C. Howroyd, c/o Dewsbury Textile Workers Club, Room 3, Textile Hall, Aldams Road, Dewsbury, West Yorkshire, WF12 8AE

14. *Huddersfield and District.* J. W. Lindsay, CMD, Room 26, Estate Buildings, Railway Street, Huddersfield, Yorkshire

15. *Leeds and District.* J. Ellis, 3 Westminster Buildings, New York Street, Leeds 2

16. *Leicester.* T. S. Flanaghan, 37 New Bond Street, Leicester

17. *Manchester.* D. Thompson, CMD, 534 Hyde Road, Gorton, Manchester

18. *Monmouthshire.* L. R. Parry, JP, 3 Stephen Crescent, Govilon, Abergavenny, Gwent

19. *North Staffordshire.* S. Robinson, 3 Richmond Terrance, Shelton, Stoke-on-Trent, Staffordshire

20. *Northumberland.* E. Moore, 17 Lansdowne Terrance, Gosforth, Newcastle upon Tyne, NE3 1HP

21. *Scottish.* J. Salmond, 28 Hugo Avenue, Coaltown, East Wemyss, Fife

22. *South East Midlands.* D. J. Dormer, FSVA, CMD, 1 Shirley Road, Rushden, Northants, NN10 9BY

23. *South Wales.* C. P. Hughes, BA, CMD, 5 Lionel Terrace, Rhydyfelin, Pontypridd, Mid-Glamorgan, CF7 5HR

24. *South Yorkshire.* R. C. Linstead, CMD, 5 Eastgate, Barnsley, Yorkshire

25. *Wakefield and District.* B. Winters, CMD, 45 Westfield Lane, South Elmsall, West Yorkshire, WF9 2QB

26. *Warwickshire.* Post vacant at time of writing.

27. *West Midlands.* F. Collins, 41 Lichfield Street, Walsall, Staffs.

28. *Wiltshire and Western Counties.* N. A. Lawrence, c/o Swindon Prospect Club, 29 Belle Vue Road, Swindon, Wiltshire

29. *York City.* V. James, CMD, 28 Southolme Drive, Shipton Road, York.

Appendix 7

Number of Clubs in the Union

The figures for the years before 1889 are unreliable; that was the year in which the Union registered under the Industrial and Provident Societies Act, and thereafter precise records were kept.

Year	Number	Year	Number	Year	Number
1863	no record	1905	1,041	1946	2,987
1864	no record	1906	1,105	1947	3,048
1865	no record	1907	1,195	1948	3,128
1866	no record	1908	1,273	1949	3,199
1867	no record	1909	1,322	1950	3,262
1868	72	1910	1,373	1951	3,299
1869	no record	1911	1,445	1952	3,326
1870	68	1912	1,513	1953	3,340
1871	126	1913	1,558	1954	3,364
1872	245	1914	1,613	1955	3,392
1873	287	1915	1,638	1956	3,403
1874	257	1916	1,638	1957	3,440
1875	312	1917	1,645	1958	3,447
1876	382	1918	1,666	1959	3,473
1877	435	1919	1,764	1960	3,501
1878	450	1920	2,007	1961	3,503
1879	483	1921	2,207	1962	3,537
1880	520	1922	2,336	1963	3,575
1881	no record	1923	2,412	1964	3,625
1882	531	1924	2,447	1965	3,706
1883	550	1925	2,470	1966	3,778
1884	557	1926	2,512	1967	3,840
1885	543	1927	2,544	1968	3,900
1886	no record	1928	2,599	1969	3,935
1887	328	1929	2,626	1970	3,955
1888	365	1930	2,660	1971	3,975
1889	328	1931	2,692	1972	4,006
1890	384	1932	2,706	1973	4,031
1891	422	1933	2,692	1974	4,033
1892	410	1934	2,675	1975	4,029

1893	421	1935	2,719	1976	4,004
1894	460	1936	2,744	1977	3,998
1895	518	1937	2,778	1978	3,994
1896	571	1938	2,814	1979	3,996
1897	627	1939	2,863	1980	3,988
1898	649	1940	2,857	1981	3,984
1899	701	1941	2,849	1982	3,946
1900	710	1942	2,851	1983	3,920
1901	751	1943	2,865	1984	3,860
1902	808	1944	2,896	1985	3,795
1903	937	1945	2,944	mid 1986	3,726
1904	1,002				